South to Louisiana

Also by John Broven

Rhythm & Blues in New Orleans (Pelican,
1978; originally published in England as
*Walking to New Orleans: The Story of New
Orleans Rhythm and Blues*)

South to Louisiana

The Music of the Cajun Bayous

John Broven

Pelican Publishing Company
Gretna 1983

Library of Congress Cataloging in Publication Data

Broven, John.
    South to Louisiana.

    Bibliography: p.
    Includes indexes.
    1. Music, Popular (Songs, etc.)—Louisiana—
History and criticism. I. Title.
ML3477.B76 1983   781.7763   82-1247
ISBN 0-88289-300-9

Grateful acknowledgment is made for permission to
reprint material from: Lou'siana Man, copyright 1971,
by Doug Kershaw, reprinted by permission of Macmillan
Publishing Company, Inc.; and Cajun Sketches, copyright 1962, 1974 by Lauren C. Post, reprinted by
permission of Louisiana State University Press.

Manufactured in the United States of America
Published by Pelican Publishing Company
1101 Monroe Street, Gretna, Louisiana 70053

To the late Mike Leadbitter,
a true friend of South Louisiana

Contents

Preface

What a thrilling moment it was when that letter postmarked "Crowley, Louisiana" arrived at home in Polegate, Sussex, in 1962. In those palmy days young English record collectors wrote frequently to record men in the U.S. Some replied, many did not. Which made Jay Miller's detailed response something special.

"I got into the record business about fifteen years ago as a hobby," he wrote. "I started recording French Cajun records, that is the type of music that is quite popular here in Southwest Louisiana. From that I went into hillbilly music; that, I must confess, is my favorite type of music. I have done quite a bit of writing in all types of music, but I feel more at home writing hillbilly songs. Next I went into recording the blues. I believe that hillbilly and blues music are perhaps the most interesting types of music there is, as they both generally tell a story that is more often than not a true story. After blues music, I started to record various other types of music, including the ever popular rock 'n' roll."

My friend and *Blues Unlimited* colleague the late Mike Leadbitter also received encouraging letters from Eddie Shuler in Lake Charles. Together we began delving into the uncharted mysteries of the South Louisiana music scene. And what treasures we found! Until then I had been blissfully unaware of the bayou origins of rock 'n' roll classics in my record collection like "This Should Go On Forever" by Rod Bernard (London-American), "Sea Of Love" by Phil Phillips, and "I'm A Fool To Care" by Joe Barry (both Mercury). Before long "Sugar Bee" by Cleveland Crochet (Gold-band) had arrived, my first Cajun record!

I began concentrating my research on the Excello label's Louisiana bluesmen Lightnin' Slim, Slim Harpo, Lonesome Sundown, and Lazy Lester; I was buying their records by the boxful from Ernie's Record Mart in Nashville, Tennessee. Meanwhile Mike was introducing the readers of *Blues Unlimited* to Cajun music through his trailblazing "Cajun Corner" column. He was not too vain to admit his own uncertainty: "It can apparently be performed by white, Negro or presumably Creole artists [sic] and some reach a remarkably high standard of musical skill. Frankly we do not know an awful amount about it, but we intend to discover more about this fascinating form and our findings will be published from time to time."

Chided gently by famous blues author Paul Oliver in an article entitled "Cajuns Creoles and Confusion!", Mike soon realized that Cajuns were the white descendants of the French Acadians who were exiled from Canada; the Creoles had a mixed heritage and included the offspring of aristocratic Old World French and Spanish colonists, and of African slaves born in the New World. Leadbitter's Cajun column quickly asserted itself, intriguing some and annoying others in what was, after all, a *blues* magazine.

I made my first trip to Louisiana in 1970 (with Mike, and Robin Gosden of Flyright Records), and was overwhelmed by the generous hospitality of the record men in Cajun country and the bluesmen in Baton Rouge. My initial confrontation with live Cajun music came three years later at the New Orleans Jazz and Heritage Festival. I recorded my pleasure in *Blues Unlimited:* "The Cajun stand was a delight. It's funny, but when I saw the Mamou Band it was the first time I had seen a Cajun band live. And what a therapy for soothing nerves shattered by modern, jet-age society! Just lie back under the blue Louisiana sky, sun beating pleasantly down, a can of Schlitz beer in hand, soaking up the wheezy accordion, the sawing fiddle, the jangly rhythm guitar and those weird French vocals which somehow *mean* so much."

It was dawning on me that it was wrong to think of Cajun, zydeco, and the Louisiana brand of hillbilly, blues, and rock 'n' roll as separate, incompatible entities. There was a unifying factor, a special South Louisiana "feel" that won me over completely. I wanted to discover more; the seeds of this book were sown.

But first I embarked on writing a history of New Orleans R&B. *Walking to New Orleans* (Blues Unlimited) was published in England in 1974; in the United States the book was retitled *Rhythm & Blues in New Orleans* (Pelican Publishing Company, 1978). I would like to think that *South to Louisiana: The Music of the Cajun Bayous* is a natural sequel. Geographical considerations apart, there is a fascinating empathy between the music of New Orleans and that of South Louisiana.

This book is divided into three parts—"Early Cajun and Cajun-Country," "Zydeco and Blues," and "Swamp-Pop and the Cajun Revival." Within that broad framework, I have focused my attention on the record men, their artists, and the music they created together. Although I have tried to keep chronological digression to a minimum, there are the inevitable flashbacks and overlaps. I hope the time chart (appendix A) will help to eliminate any confusion these may cause.

As in *Rhythm & Blues in New Orleans (Walking to New Orleans),* I have relied heavily on the local participants for their stories and reminiscences, liberally sprinkling their colorful words and images throughout the text, like a cook seasoning a favorite gumbo. Nevertheless, I realize how easy it is to falter before an unyielding recorder, and all stated facts have therefore been checked where possible, with limited editing whenever necessary. Interviews carried out by other researchers are credited in the text itself, in the appendix, or in the acknowledgments.

Throughout this work the expression "swamp-pop" has been used in preference to the local term "South Louisiana rock 'n' roll," which is loosely and often incorrectly applied. Likewise the term "Cajun" music is preferred to "French," and "zydeco" to "zodico."

Due to the oral nature of the Cajun tradition, the phonetic spelling of song titles (and even artists' names) has led to many glaring inconsistencies, but I have adhered to the actual record label descriptions as far as possible. Where French lyrics have been transcribed with English translations, I have relied mostly on the past work of Irène Thérèse Whitfield Holmes, Catherine Blanchet, and Ann Savoy. Finally, when Louisiana cities and small towns are mentioned, the state name has been omitted for the sake of conciseness.

With the current revival of Cajun music, the time seems right to try to put some order to the prodigious but fragmentarily documented output of recorded music emanating from such a tiny area of the United States. *South to Louisiana* is an unashamed celebration of a people and their regional music, a music that has given me enormous pleasure and enjoyment. I hope this book gives back something in return.

John Broven
Newick, East Sussex
England

Acknowledgments

The inspiration for this book came from the tragically short-lived Mike Leadbitter, whose research work in the sixties was truly innovative and, I believe, not fully appreciated at the time. I am proud to dedicate the book to him. I would also like to express my deep admiration and thanks to researchers Barry Ancelet, Sam Charters, Pierre V. Daigle, Irène Thérèse Whitfield Holmes, Dr. Harry Oster, Lauren C. Post, Revon Reed, Nick Spitzer, Chris Strachwitz, and Paul Tate, whose studies have made my job so much easier.

In Europe, special mention must go to Ray Topping and Bill Millar for resorting to their files so continuously and unselfishly; Bruce Bastin for information on Al Terry, records for copying, and many Jay Miller snippets; Bill Greensmith for his photography; and Cilla and Mick Huggins for their brilliant artwork. The following have been no less helpful: Robin Gosden and Simon Napier of Flyright Records; Martin Hawkins, Norbert Hess, Tony Russell, Anthony Wall; Lesley Stanford, Paul Harris, and Clive Richardson of the New Orleans Honkin' Tonkin' party; Rod Buckle and all at Sonet Records; Graham Ackers, Jonas Bernholm, Kathleen Callaghan, Gérard Dole, Dave Luxton, Charley Nilsson, Bengt Olsson, Robert Sacré, Bez Turner, Paul Vernon, Cliff White, and Dave Williams; and Stella White for retyping unreadable manuscripts.

In South Louisiana, the warm interest in my work expressed by a multitude of friendly people has been a constant encouragement. My humble thanks must go to Johnnie Allan and Harry Simoneaux for their regular correspondence (and to Johnnie's parents for the Joseph Falcon interview by Lauren C. Post); Richard Allen, Fernest Arceneaux, Joe Barry, Shirley Bergeron, Rod and Jo-Ann Bernard, Camille "Lil" Bob, Jimmy Dotson, Stanley "Buckwheat" Dural Jr., John Fred, Paul Gayten, Henry Gray, Oran "Doc" Guidry, Janet Guillot, Silas Hogan, and Earl King; Levence "Lee" Lavergne and the good people of Church Point; LeRoy "Happy Fats" LeBlanc, Leroy Martin, Cosimo Matassa, J. D. Miller, Gabriel "Guitar Gable" Perrodin, Mac "Dr. John" Rebennack, Gene Rodrigue, Aldus Roger, Marc and Ann Savoy, Marshall Sehorn,

Eddie Shuler, Floyd Soileau, Moses "Whispering" Smith, Warren Storm, Ernie "Roy Perkins" Suarez, Al Terry, Charles Thibodeaux, Ernest "Tabby" Thomas, and Katie Webster. Also André Brière (for the "Jole Blon" translation); Robert Crisler and Mathé Allain of the University of Southwestern Louisiana, Lafayette; Janis LeBourgeois of the State of Louisiana Office of Tourism; Bill Daniels, Peter Guralnick, and Frank Scott; and my New Orleans friends Tad Jones, Jon and Caroline Foose, James and Ann La Rocca, and Terry Pattison. Finally, my editor Frumie Selchen for much advice, good sense, and appreciation of the subject in hand.

I can but hope the finished work is worthy of such generous assistance. Merci, mes amis!

Part

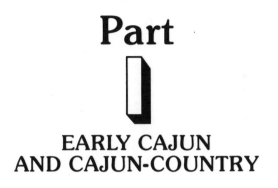

EARLY CAJUN
AND CAJUN-COUNTRY

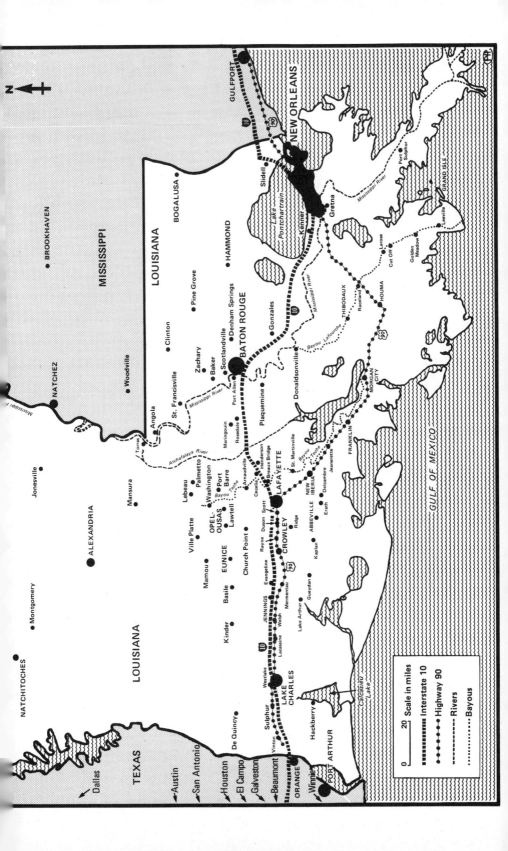

SOUTH LOUISIANA MUSIC TRADITION

EARLY CAJUN BALLADS
Acadian/French/Creole/
Anglo-Saxon Folk Songs

LA MUSIQUE CREOLE
Afro-Caribbean tradition

PRE-WAR RURAL CAJUN
Joseph Falcon
Alphee Bergeron
Angelais Lejeune

PRE-WAR CREOLE
Amadie Ardoin
Adam Fontenot

Nashville Country
American Rock Music
West Indian Ska/Reggae
Tex-Mex Music

PRE-WAR CAJUN-COUNTRY
Leo Soileau
Hackberry Ramblers
Rayne-Bo Ramblers

POST-WAR "CLASSIC" CAJUN
Iry LeJune
Nathan Abshire
Lawrence Walker
Aldus Roger

POST-WAR CAJUN-COUNTRY
Harry Choates
Happy Fats
Vin Bruce
Doug Kershaw

SWAMP-POP
Bobby Charles
Rod Bernard
Johnnie Allan
Warren Storm
Joe Barry
Cookie & the Cupcakes

Influences

ZYDECO
Clifton Chenier
Clarence Garlow
Rockin' Dopsie
Buckwheat
Sam Brothers 5

CAJUN REVIVAL
Balfa Brothers
Jimmy "C" Newman
Belton Richard
Joel Sonnier

SOUTH LOUISIANA COUNTRY
Al Terry
Lou Millet
Larry Brasso

COUNTRY
Hillbilly — Jimmie Rodgers
Jimmie Davis
Western
Swing — Bob Wills
Cowboy — Gene Autry
Honky
Tonk — Ernest Tubb
Hank Williams

SOUTH LOUISIANA ROCKABILLY
Al Ferrier
Johnny Jano

ROCKABILLY
Elvis Presley
Carl Perkins

NEW ORLEANS R&B
Fats Domino
Smiley Lewis
Guitar Slim
Earl King

DIXIELAND JAZZ
Dukes of Dixieland

SOUTH LOUISIANA R&B AND SOUL
Guitar Gable
Carol Fran
Guitar Jr.
Lil Bob

R&B AND SOUL
Ray Charles
Chuck Berry
Little Richard
Otis Redding
Percy Sledge

CROWLEY SWAMP-BLUES
Lightnin' Slim
Slim Harpo
Lonesome Sundown
Lazy Lester

DOWN HOME & CITY BLUES
Sonny Boy 'John Lee'
Williamson
Lightnin' Hopkins
Muddy Waters
Jimmy Reed
T-Bone Walker
B.B. King

1

"The bayous were flowing, the crawfish keep a-growing"

South to Louisiana to the town of Thibodaux,
South to Louisiana to the town of Thibodaux. . . .

Jean Boudreaux left Breaux Bridge in the spring of '44,
With Jean-Pierre his partner and his cousin Robichaux.
They crossed the Atchafalaya as they paddled their pirogue
Through the swamps and the bayous to the town of Thibodaux.

They paddled through the marshlands and the swamps of Louisiane,
With the handles of the handmade oars making blisters in their hands.
But they had to get to Thibodaux, so they went on through the swamps,
'Cause tonight they were taking their Cajun girls to a crawfish sauce
piquante.

The bayous were flowing, the crawfish keep a-growing,
South to Louisiana . . .

Top swamp-pop artist Johnnie Allan sang "South To Louisiana," a modest regional success in 1962 for Viking Records of Crowley, to the tune of Johnny Horton's hit "North To Alaska." The revamped song did nothing to dispel the romantic Louisiana image of blue bayous, steamy cypress-swamps, slow-moving pirogues, and tasty crawfish sauce piquantes. Only the snapping alligators and dripping Spanish moss were missing from the popular conception of the state. Louisianians are willing to tolerate such poetic license because they know that reality, if less exotic, is just as enticing.

"Louisiana is one of the most attractive states in the Union," affirms Eddie Shuler, the veteran Lake Charles record man, "because it has oil, it has water, and it has sea-fishing. As for the environment, we have an all-round, year-around compatible climate. I don't think any other state has that, plus the fishing, hunting, and natural resources, the things that enable you to be proud of a region. And then the companies are all moving down here because of the climate and power, and working conditions and all that are improving tremendously. So that makes this a very attractive region to a potential manufacturer. And the ones that are here are not leaving, so that means they like it too!"

The prominent Louisiana writer Harnett Kane observed that "Louisiana, like France, is divided into three major parts—the South, the North, and the City." This division still prevails. Viewed from South Louisiana, North Louisiana is a world apart, a land of corn bread and hot biscuits, catfish with hush puppies, pecan pie with coffee, beans and greens. The people have a stricter approach to life, different values; it is the Deep South. "There's a big difference between here and North Louisiana, it's almost another country," says Rod Bernard, another leading swamp-pop singer. "There are no French-speaking people up in North Louisiana, all the Cajun French people are down here. Just like New Orleans to here is different, New Orleans is not Cajun French Louisiana, the culture is not the same, but it is closer than the North."

The Cajuns' homeland is shaped like a triangle, its base spreading along the Gulf Coast from the mouth of the Mississippi to the Texas state line, with its peak just below the thriving business city of Alexandria in central Louisiana. Over the years many Cajuns have settled in Texas, especially in the industrial conurbation of Port Arthur/Beaumont/Orange, which has been called Cajun Lapland—"where Louisiana laps over into Texas!"

South Louisiana has not been immune from the general southern postwar shift from an agrarian to an industrial economy, but it remains a basically rural area. The eastern part of the region comprises dreary coastal marsh, drained farmland, eldritch swamps, and idyllic bayous. Further west the coastal marsh continues in a wide belt all the way to Texas; inland the territory opens into the prairies of the western Acadiana parishes. The principal city of Acadiana is Lafayette, with a population of more than 100,000. Dissected by Interstate 10 and Highway 167, it is known as the Hub City, with towns like Crowley, Rayne, Opelousas, Ville Platte, Breaux Bridge, New Iberia, Kaplan, and Gueydan within easy reach. The center of the Louisiana oil business, Lafayette continues to thrive on the black gold.

With a mean temperature of 68° F (20° C), the subtropical South Louisiana climate is ideal for many forms of agriculture. Farming is highly mechanized: The major crops are sugar, rice, soybeans, and yams, with the sugar in the east (they say Cajuns raise a lot of cane on a Saturday night!) and the rice largely in the west. Little cotton is grown, but cattle farming is widespread. Fishing—especially for shrimp—is important, and there is some timber production. But Louisiana's economic prosperity is based primarily on its huge mineral reserves. Petroleum and petroleum-related industries are dominant, and there is also major salt and sulphur production. This natural wealth is enhanced by an abundance of wildlife; many sporting and leisure activities make Louisiana a true "Sportsman's Paradise," as the state license plates proudly proclaim.

The history of Louisiana is as rich as its environment. Ten national flags have flown over the state, and each governing nation has left its mark. France had an especially strong influence: counties are still called "parishes," while the Napoleonic Code (rather than British common law) prevails in Louisiana's courtrooms. It was this French connection that ultimately attracted the Cajuns to Louisiana.

The Cajuns' ancestors were tough, amiable farmers who had sailed from western France in the seventeenth century to settle in the Canadian provinces now known as Nova Scotia and New Brunswick. The colony was originally called "Acadie" after Arcadia, the pastoral region of ancient Greece considered a rural paradise; the word "Cajun" is a corruption of "Acadian." Although Acadia fell to the British in 1710, the French farmers were allowed to remain as neutrals under the Treaty of Utrecht (1713). It was an uneasy truce. In 1755, as war neared again, the British authorities finally demanded that the Acadians swear allegiance to the Crown. Their refusal resulted in the mass expulsion which was one of the blackest episodes in British colonial history. Men and women were separated, children taken from their parents, houses burned, livestock and crops confiscated.

The tragedies of separation and loss following *Le Grand Dérangement* are recorded for all time in Henry Wadsworth Longfellow's classic (if questionably researched) poem *Evangeline.* According to Longfellow, Evangeline, "the fairest of all the maids," lost her lover Gabriel in the Big Upheaval and came to Louisiana, only to find he had moved on. Many years later they were reunited in Philadelphia when he was a dying old man. What some believe to be the true story is just as dramatic: After a long separation, the engaged couple (real names Emmaline LaBiche and Louis Arceneaux) met under the famous oak tree standing alongside Bayou Teche in St. Martinville. But Emmaline's joy was short-lived. Discovering that Louis had married another woman, she had a nervous breakdown and remained insane for the rest of her life.

The migration of the French-Canadian Acadians to Louisiana was neither smooth nor immediate. Many refugees were shipped to the New England colonies, where their language and religion made them unwelcome. Others were sent to the West Indies or back to France; some wandered for twenty years before reaching Louisiana. Initially congregating in the almost empty lands of the Attakapas territory west of New Orleans, the exiles gradually settled in small farming, fishing, and trapping communities throughout South Louisiana.

For almost two centuries the Cajuns remained a race apart, separated from the rest of the South by their language, social structures, and traditions, which underwent only minor changes through the years. Often shunned by outsiders, the people toiled hard during the week, enjoyed themselves on weekends, went to Mass on Sunday, valued family ties, hunted, fished, played card games, raced horses, gambled, and gossiped. They sang and danced at every opportunity and relished their food, which combined the French love of delicacies and a taste for strong, hot seasonings in mouth-watering dishes like jambalaya, gumbo, boudin, *cochon de lait,* and crawfish étouffée.

Even modern America cannot obliterate such a compelling heritage. The Cajuns' strength is in their character. "A Cajun person is, I think, one of the richest people in the world," says Eddie Shuler. "And the reason I think that is because they're some of the happiest people in the world. They love life, they love to have a good time, and they love their friends and family. Money doesn't mean all that much to them. . . . That's a Cajun, a true Cajun."

The Cajuns of South Louisiana are a unique people and their music, which plays an important part in their lives, is a reflection of that uniqueness. From an early age a Cajun child will hear the joyful whoop of a two-step or the melancholy melody of a waltz played on the accordion, fiddle, or guitar to a repetitive beat. If so minded, he will start practicing music at home until he is ready to perform at house parties, *fais-dodos,* country fairs, roadhouses, and clubs. Then, if he is good enough, he may be asked to record and broadcast, but even so he will have to take a regular job to support his wife and family. Sax player Harry Simoneaux is probably right when he says, "Lord knows how many great musicians are holed up in Acadiana country without proper recognition!" Certainly music is the chief artistic expression of the Cajun culture, a culture that has enjoyed a great resurgence of pride in recent years. "We do have our music . . . it has our spirit, our history, our story in it," remarked Pierre V. Daigle trenchantly in his book, *Tears, Love, and Laughter.*

Cajun music, one of America's great down-home musics, has been molded inexorably by the harshness of Acadian history. In an interview for the 1980 BBC radio series "All Across the U.S.A.," Cajun fiddler Dewey Balfa told Anthony Wall of the music's deep emotional qualities: "In Cajun music you can hear the lonesome sound and the hurt [of the poor white man] from the Appalachian coal mines and so on, just like the blues sound of the black man is a sound of deep hurt, deep sorrow. The Acadians had it very tough from Nova Scotia down to Louisiana, and when they did get to Louisiana they had a hard time. And sometimes I feel that the Cajun sounds are of the loneliness and hardship they had back then."

Similar sentiments have been evocatively expressed by author Daigle: "The music bites, burns, and blisters the heart with its cruel loneliness of our Cajun history. Not only the loneliness at the time of our exile, but the later years of poverty, the poor little tenants' shacks in cotton fields and along forests with their mud chimneys, or the big sad old houses with a stairway to the attic and their mournful shutter in the gables."

The root sound of Cajun music is more evident in the waltz numbers than in the livelier two-steps (also known as "specials"). The older Cajuns tend to prefer the waltz songs, appreciating the sad strain of the lyrics and the high-pitched singing in a "heartbreak" key. On the other hand, the two-step tunes with their exhilarating approach have more appeal among younger Cajuns, and are particularly popular outside Louisiana, where the sound is more important than the hard-to-understand, highly individual Cajun-French lyrics.

Cajun music was nurtured on early Acadian, French, Creole, Celtic, and Anglo-Saxon folk songs. The original rambling ballads and lullabyes were sung a cappella, unaccompanied except for the occasional hand-clap or foot-tap, perhaps the beating of a stick or some metallic kitchen implement. The songs were often tinged with sadness, with love and courting the main topics; there were also drinking and humorous poems as well as stories of soldiers, sailors, and children. Generally there was an absence of religious content. Most compositions were intended for home presentation and were passed down orally from generation to generation. During the nineteenth century some French folk songs were transmitted among the literate populace in the form of printed broadsheets, sheet music, and songbooks, and found their way into the Cajun repertoire. But lyrical development in Cajun music was hindered by the audacious instrumental sounds of the fiddle and, later, the accordion.

"Until fifty or sixty years ago," wrote broadcaster Revon Reed, "musicians had very few lyrics or words to their music. Much of the verbal accompaniment was an occasional heartrending cry of a brokenhearted singer, or a boisterous yell of glee, expressed spontaneously or when the mood struck. Connected or discordant, rational or insane, the yells always terminated the mood—classic yells like Jimmy C. Newman's *ee-hee-hee!* or an *aiyee!* or *hey la bas!*

"Later, when words were added, they contained a good bit of the old Acadian earthy philosophy that adhered to the beliefs that it was better to try to live a full life rather than just exist; that it was better to sing loudly and laugh raucously than to curse fate and growl at mankind; and that it was much better to love and trust people than to hate and fear them. These thoughts they express today in their ballads."

"Now the words to French music," adds singer Johnnie Allan, "most of the slow songs are all kinda sad songs, all of them have to do with broken romance and this sort of thing. And if you listen to a lot of the songs, they were very simple, very simply written so the people could understand them. The early Cajuns enjoyed the simple things in life and they associated with this kind of music."

Interestingly, there was a small pocket of wealthy landowners in Acadiana whose musical tastes were far more sophisticated. The contrast between rigid orchestral music and the flexible, irregularly constructed Cajun tunes was explained by Chris Strachwitz in *The American Folk Music Occasional:* "The music of the upper-class Acadians was quite distinct from that of the lower classes. The wealthy landowners preferred brass band music—marches and quadrilles—or salon orchestras that performed polite waltzes and popular compositions. On the other hand the lower classes always had preferred one-steps, two-steps, and rhythmic waltzes played on the accordion. . . . This popular accordion music has survived, but since the 1920s the orchestras have completely disappeared."

The regal accordion is the principal instrument in Cajun music. Invented in 1829 in Vienna, Austria, it became popular in Germany and was introduced in Louisiana by German settlers during the 1870s. The Cajuns gradually made it their own. Initially the accordions, especially the larger Lester and Bruno models, were imported from Germany. But in Acadiana the smaller concertinalike Sterlings and Monarchs—diatonic types preferably in the key of C with ten buttons—became popular. At first the Cajuns were influenced by the regimented German playing style, but they soon adopted their own technique consisting of a series of improvised push-and-pull "puffs." The Cajun accordion therefore became a real "squeeze box," with a loose, emotional sound.

Until the appearance of the accordion, the fiddle had been the favored Cajun instrument, on its own or in duet with the lead fiddle taking the melody and the second carrying the rhythm. The fiddle and accordion combination was a natural evolutionary development, with the triangle (*le petit fer,* "the little iron") providing rhythmic accompaniment; the triangle was held by a string around the left thumb and struck in rhythm to the beat with a metal spike held in the right hand, giving a clear sound of bell-like clarity. During the 1920s the Cajun lineup was altered by the addition of the box guitar, but even more fundamental was the introduction over the next two decades of electric and steel guitars, string bass, and drums. Despite occasional reverses in popularity brought about by changing musical trends, the accordion and fiddle still retain their preeminence, although there are regional variations in the instrumental composition of Cajun bands.

Through the years Cajun music has absorbed many influences, notably from country and western, blues, western swing, and jazz. Yet it has remained a living entity with a distinctive sound, a testament to the strength of the Cajun tradition. The adaptability of Cajun music is hinted at by Joe Barry, the swamp-pop artist from Southeast Louisiana, as he traces—in typically colorful style—developments up to and including the rock 'n' roll era: "Cajun music back then in clubs was fiddle or guitar, usually just one instrument. You used to find with a good fiddle player there was usually no guitar player good enough. And the fiddle is very delicate, if you don't follow him with the right beat you discourage him until he quits playing. But then it blossomed into two, guitar and a fiddle. And the accordion's the thing, you got to have it for that *aiyee!* and that old music that drives you up the wall. So you can say that's a kind of boogie music.

"I watched it through the years and it got stronger to the country thing, but the Cajun thing always stayed. Even right now you can go in little towns in South Louisiana and hit the same old Cajun band they had way back when. With the guitar, the drummer only knows the one beat . . . *doong, doong, doong* . . . the same as loud as he can, boy . . . and *doodoo-doo* . . . just going to town. And man, that floor will shake, I tell you that! That part of Cajun music will never change.

"But the other part developed, it branched to the English thing, it branched to country. And it went strong into South Louisiana [swamp-pop], retaining that Cajun feeling in the music, but it was a whole new style. The horns style, the keyboards style was all different, it was different to rhythm and blues even. Cajun music had come of age. And it stayed there, Jimmy Clanton's 'Just A Dream,' Rod Bernard, Jivin' Gene, Cookie and the Cupcakes. It was something different, it wasn't New Orleans rhythm and blues."

Above all Cajun music is meant for dancing, for having a good time. At the turn of the century, the Cajuns were performing a variety of European dances including the waltz, polka, reel, mazurka, and quadrille (known also as the contredanse), with music to match, but they gradually limited themselves to the ever-popular waltz and two-step. Initially dances were held at home—usually in a front room cleared of furniture—and were known as *bals de maison.* Explained the octogenarian Cajun fiddler Dennis McGee to French field researcher Gérard Dole: "Suppose I had a house, well they came and asked me to lend it for a ball. All right; I gave my consent. They rode around to invite young girls and at night they got together. Women sat down on benches they had made with blocks of wood and planks; they watched their daughters, you know, in these days, a girl couldn't go out alone, no. The boy who had borrowed the house, he was the boss until the ball was through. He decided which couple to put together: he stood at the door and when a guy asked him to dance, he placed him. Sometimes he let him dance, sometimes not. If he didn't like him, he left him backwards, so that he couldn't dance. This one he liked, he placed him each two, three, or four sets.

"Sometimes it was a large house, sometimes it was a small house. When it was big, well, eight, sometimes twelve could dance: your turn came back quick. When it was a small one, there was room for only six maybe. Your turn never came, it took too long and you couldn't have fun. You danced a country dance and a waltz and that was all. Often the houses were packed up and you had better not show up if you hadn't been invited. Now, when a guy borrowed another house, if you had been fair with him, he let you dance, but if you had not been, you had to go back home without dancing at all!"

Eventually this form of home entertainment was superseded by the public dance known as the *fais-dodo*. The first *fais-dodo* halls were built as family gathering places, sometimes in a corner of a farm. Before long they were springing up as large, ungainly wooden edifices in the small Acadian towns. *Fais-dodo* is a term popularly thought to have derived from the time when parents would take their children to dances and put them in a special room, telling them to "fais-dodo" (go to sleep); the adults would then join in the Saturday-night fun. Folklorist Lyle Saxon believed the term was a corruption of "Fête de Dieu."

"A *fais-dodo* could start from nothing," explains Joe Barry, "because you could say, 'Hey, LeBlanc, you and your lady come over, bring your guitar, bring a jug!' And LeBlanc would say, 'All right, why don't we get Bob, Bob Thibodeaux?'

" 'Yeah, sure, he got a new fiddle, too, bring him over.'

"Before you know it, you got a little song on the front porch, *da, da, da, dee.* And somebody go pass down the road and he goes home and gets his axe [guitar]. And soon you've got a yard full.

"Someone could pop up, like some dude would say, 'Hey, I've got a pig' and anything could happen, you know a *boucherie* going in a little while. But all one jerk could start this, it could last two days, it's like a wedding. I mean, when you've got a wedding there, that's serious man, I mean, like you'd better take a couple of days off! These people here can put some away, my man.

"You might have a couple of dances during the week, but your regular *fais-dodo* started probably Saturday afternoon around one o'clock. Then the men would start one by one stopping in, getting a few beers, and somebody would cook a big pot of gumbo. Everybody would sit at the bar, eating gumbo and drinking, drinking, drinking—the bar would start rolling! Come about five o'clock it would empty out, the mood was set.

And they would all go home, take a little nap, and come back again. They wouldn't have too long, believe you me!

"And around 6:30 in the evening the bar would start rolling again. Another pot of gumbo or a stew or a jambalaya, then the families would start coming in. Kids and the wives and all, and they would help call around. And the thing would grow like a giant party, somebody would bring a potato salad and this and that. The musicians would start arriving and very few of them professionals. Usually you'd have one or two that was hired to play and you'd wind up with twenty up there in a jam session. That's how they snowballed where I was from, in Southeast Louisiana, of course different parts of Cajun country got different ways they did it.

"Then it's dancing—the two-step and the waltz. With the two-step the Cajuns like to hit the floor. They're notorious with their left hand, they hug tight with the right, and their left hand is like a swinging ball. And they turn fast and do that two-step and they like to *hit* that floor! I can still remember at the dances I used to play in the early fifties eighty- and ninety-year-old couples that would come dance two or three nights a week till closing time. I mean these people loved to dance and that's part of their life. The dance didn't finish at twelve or one, it finished when the last one couldn't stand up no more, that was it. It looked like a morgue when you walked in, everybody just laying there!

"But the old clubs and all back then—I didn't go through this—was very hard. Back then you had to be a half-fighter, half-wrestler to be a musician. Because most of the clubs back home had chicken wire on the bandstand, surrounded by chicken wire, and people would never understand when they'd walk in. They'd say, 'Why that chicken wire? You don't trust the musicians?' And it was like, 'No, come eleven o'clock you're gonna see what the chicken wire is for, that's to protect 'em!' And old Cajuns, now they get rough. Come eleven o'clock they say, 'Hey, when you gonna play my song?' and another one says, 'No, he's gonna play my song!' and that's why the chicken wire is there because what follows after is like the Watts riots in California!"

Floyd Soileau, the successful record man from Ville Platte, aptly summarizes the importance of music to the Cajuns: "We're a good-timin' bunch. We love to have a good time, love to enjoy life, when we play we play hard, and when we work we work hard. We love our music and we love our food. I guess we're pretty much like a lot of other people in a way, but I don't know what it is, it's just something. . . . I know it myself, I can feel something real bad, have a bad day. And I can grab a Cajun master that I've got in my office, slap it on the recorder, and before the first cut is finished I've changed my mood. And I'm tapping my feet and I just feel like giving the Cajun yell—*aiyee!*"

2

"That first record was 'Allons A Lafayette' "

Acadiana stuttered into the twentieth century, its barriers of splendid isolation broken down by a series of critical events disguised as progress. The relentless advance of the automobile demanded new highway systems, while the burgeoning oil industry brought in an army of outside workers. Just as momentous was the influence of the communications media: radio, phonograph, movie, jukebox, and (later) television. A compulsory educational system with English as the dominant language and the return of World War II veterans who had experienced the outside world for the first time served to hasten the Americanization process. The total effect on a rural people and their traditional life-style was immense.

The Cajuns, immersed in an ever-changing environment, have nevertheless managed to cling to their cultural identity. Their Cajun-French language—which developed independently of the French mother tongue—has survived, and so has their music. Like all folk music the Cajun sound has continued to change and evolve; no musical style remains pure forever. By the early 1920s the gentle Acadian ballads were already an endangered species, but the demands of the new media, particularly the phonograph, ensured that many old songs would be resurrected and fresh songs created. Later these phonograph records would be treasured as prized historical artifacts; for the time being they were intriguing home-entertainment novelties that were secondary in importance to the fleeting pleasures of live dance performances and radio broadcasts.

At the beginning of the recording era northern-based record company executives were uncertain of the merits—or profitability—of any form of southern music. The success of the early blues and hillbilly recordings showed that there were hungry regional markets waiting for more home-spun sounds. Since the recording studios were also based in the North, the companies sent out mobile field units to the major southern cities to record a ragged collection of artists performing old ballads, Mexican border songs, mountain music, Negro blues and spirituals, and polka music—the roots of America's popular music. The opportunity for Cajun artists to record came in 1928, but it was already too late for several legendary musicians, notably accordionists August Breaux of Rayne, Moise Cormier of Bosco, and Armand Thibodeaux of Sunset, whose music has been irretrievably lost in the mists of time.

Happily, the first Cajun-French release, "Lafayette" by Joseph Falcon (Columbia), sold well, and the recording medium became available to other Cajun artists. Falcon's hit record, better known as "Allons A Lafayette," was an irresistible, tuneful two-step sung to the accompaniment of his full-toned accordion and wife Cleoma Breaux's very basic rhythm guitar. Man and woman, accordion and guitar—these were novel combinations in Cajun music at the time, but the song itself, which Falcon had first heard as a child, was reassuringly familiar. It tells the story of a confused lover and his foolish fiancée:

Allons à Lafayette	Let's go to Lafayette
mais pour changer ton nom.	in order to change your name.
On va t'appeler Madame,	They'll call you Mrs.,
Madame Canaille-Comeaux.	Mrs. Canaille-Comeaux.
Petite t'es trop mignonne	Baby you're too cute
pour faire ta criminelle.	to do anything wrong.
Comment tu crois mais moi,	How can you think of anyone but me,
je peux faire moi tout seul.	I can do all right by myself.
Mais toi ma jolie coeur,	But you my little heart,
regarde donc mais quoi t'as fait.	look what you've done.
Si loin que moi je suis de toi,	I am so far from you,
mais ça, ça me fait pitie.	that, that makes me sad.

(The transcription reflects the idiomatic nature of the Cajun French language; translations inevitably miss the color, nuances—and sometimes the point—of the lyrics.)

One of the most impassioned old-time Cajun musicians, Joseph Falcon was singing and playing in the traditional rural Cajun style. He was born in 1900 near Bayou Plaquemine Brulee, just north of the small rice town of Rayne. His father was a poor farmer who grew energy-sapping crops such as rice, cotton, and sugarcane; the cane had to be hauled to the mill after it was cut and boiled out with wood—there was no coal or oil.

When Joe was seven his father agreed to buy him an accordion, but was forced—prophetically—to go to Lafayette since there were none for sale in Rayne. Falcon explained the difficult learning process to author Lauren C. Post: "We couldn't play it in the house, so we went to the barn and started playing it in the barn. We had the biggest trouble over there with the cattle, they wanted to come in with us! I kept banging on the accordion until I struck a tune. It was so many years ago I forgot what tune it was. But I stayed with it and before I turned it loose I kinda started something."

His break came unexpectedly when he attended a dance at Oneziphore Guidry's famed *fais-dodo* hall in Rayne: "Well, I didn't know nothing. I had just took my accordion when I left with my sister with the horse and buggy to go to the dance. And when I got there, his band didn't show up. So he asked me, 'How about you coming in and playing my dance? I'll pay you.' I said 'Oh no! I just play like that, I just play for fun.' He said, 'Come on, I ain't got no music.' So I got up on the bandstand and I started playing. And I played until twelve o'clock, and at twelve o'clock he come there and he paid me four dollars. Boy, I mean, I was glad with them four dollars!"

Joe's historic first recording for Columbia was made in New Orleans in July 1928, courtesy of Rayne jeweler George Burr, who agreed to purchase several boxes of the 78s for sale in his store. Falcon remembered the session clearly when he spoke on separate occasions to Lauren Post and Chris Strachwitz: "Well, the one supposed to sing 'Allons A Lafayette' was a man by the name of Leon Meche from Bosco. He got all ready, and he buttoned up his coat and this and that, and he was getting pale as a sheet. And he looked at me and said, 'You better sing it yourself, I might make a mistake.' So I took over. We went over there, they looked at us—we was but two, just myself and my wife Cleoma Breaux, she played the guitar—but they were used to recording with big orchestras. 'That's not enough to make a record,' they said.

"So George had 250 records paid for before I even went to make them and George started talking. 'We got to run it through because that man there is popular in Rayne,' he said, pointing to me. 'The people are crazy about his music and they want the records.'

"But they said, 'We don't know if it's going to sell.' Then they turned around and asked him, 'How much would you buy?' He told them he wanted five hundred copies as the first order.

" 'Ah! Five hundred. When are you gonna get through selling that?'

" 'That's my worry,' he said, 'I want five hundred!' And he made out a check for five hundred records. They started looking at each other.

" 'Well,' they said, 'you go ahead and play a tune just for us to hear.'

"They was all in those stiff collars with coats on and everything, you know, highfalutin'. So I took out the accordion—and it was a big building, but it was closed—and that thing was sounding like it wanted to take the roof off! So when I got through with the record, 'Allons A Lafayette,' they played it back. In those days them records was about a couple of inches thick and they just could record on one side, you understand. It was some wax, but you couldn't use those records to play on your Victrola. They just used them to stamp the other records. So they played it. And they started going around the machine, all them high bucks listened and listened and listened.

"And they came over to where we recorded and they said, 'Lord but that's more music out of two instruments than we ever heard in our lives. We don't understand nothing, but it's a sweet sound. Pardner, get ready, we're going for good now. We are going to make it!'

"When the record came out, they were right back looking for me. That first record was 'Allons A Lafayette' backed with 'The Waltz That Carried Me To My Grave.' That was the first Cajun-French record that ever was recorded. Among your own people if somebody does something that sounds good and everything, well, that's your people and so, of course, you want to get one. Even some of the poorest country fellows, they buy as high as two records. They ain't had no Victrola, but they buy and go to the neighbor's and play it!"

Popular Lafayette singer Johnnie Allan is related to Joseph Falcon and can recall some of the stories the family has passed down through the years: "Let me think about some of the things Mama talked about him. He came back here with his song 'Allons A Lafayette,' it was an overnight deal. She told me that people would go out and buy like eight or ten records at a time because they'd wear them out so fast, they'd play them over and over and over. The records in those days of course were not the quality of the records that we have nowadays. So they wouldn't last as long, the big heavy needles would just wear a groove in there.

"But she said anywhere that they would perform it was just like a mob scene. He was just that popular. In those days if you're traveling five or six miles on a horse and buggy you're traveling far. She said they'd play around the Lafayette area and people actually left from Lake Charles, Baton Rouge, which would be like eighty miles away, to come listen to him. This gives you some idea as to his popularity. If all of the United States had been French-speaking he would have been an Elvis Presley in his day."

His popularity boosted by "Lafayette," Falcon stopped working on his father's farm and became a full-time musician, playing mainly in the country areas of Southwest Louisiana and East Texas. "The towns have a huge transient population and your rural areas were obviously where your Cajun people grew up," explains Johnnie Allan. "And they associated with that type of music. Mama tells me that Uncle Joe played mostly in nightclubs that were located out in the country, the farmers of the rural areas. When I say nightclubs, they were very old buildings. In fact she said the band would have to get up on a pedestal because the smoke and the heat was so bad, there were no amplifiers or anything in those days so they had to kinda elevate them up there so they could hear the music. The nightclubs in those days resembled an old barn, there were no electric lights, they used gasoline lamps, no tables, just benches all around the hall. [According to Irène Thérèse Whitfield Holmes, the admission charge to one of these dance halls in 1937 was "Gents 25¢, Married men 15¢."] And the people just gathered there and they really didn't sit down, they would stand up dancing all night. She said it was nothing to pack 500 to 600 people in a place like this, packed to the hilt. She said the small little kids would watch up from the windows by the side.

"Joe used to travel to around Port Arthur and Orange, Texas, during the week, he would play out there because in East Texas you've got a lot of Cajun people who moved because of the oil industry, they've got huge refineries out there and the people just moved because of the jobs. Joe would play out there during the week and towards the weekend he would kinda travel back towards Lafayette, this section of the country."

During the thirties Joseph Falcon recorded for Columbia, Decca, Bluebird, and OKeh, with sessions held in New Orleans, New York, Atlanta, and San Antonio. He performed a wide variety of material, including "Fe Fe Ponchaux," "Le Vieux Soulard Et Sa Femme" (The Old Drunkard And His Wife), "Osson Two-Step," "Le Marche De La Noche" (The Wedding March), and "La Valse De Madame Sosten." Falcon's vocals were always emotional, while his accordion remained unyieldingly dominant and Cleoma Breaux's guitar maintained a consistent strumming rhythm. Like the old Cajun—and blues—singers, he wrote his own lyrics but was often unaware of the origins of the tunes. "The number was there but I had to make up the words. Like 'Osson,' it was the name of a little town, but you just have to find a name to put on the record. It's an old two-step," he said.

Falcon was always backed by his wife Cleoma, who, with brothers Amidie and Ophy Breaux made "Ma Blonde Est Partie" for Columbia in late 1928. It was the first recorded version of the timeless favorite "Jole Blonde," better known as "Jole Blon" through Harry Choates's hit recording in 1946. Accordionist Amidie is said to have written the song about his first wife; he is also credited with composing the popular "Hey Mom." Cleoma's other well-known record was "Mon Coeur T'Appelle" (OKeh), a version of the familiar "J'ai Passé Devant Ta Porte," which expressed grief at the unexpected death of a loved one. This much-loved waltz is an essential part of many Cajun musicians' repertoires. The lyrics are always very similar:

J'ai passé devant ta porte,	I passed in front of your door,
J'ai crié, "Bye Bye, à la belle."	I cried, "Bye bye, sweetheart."
Il y a personne que m'a pas	There was no one to answer me,
répondu,	*Oh yé yaie,* that broke my heart . . .
Oh yé yaie, mon coeur fait mal . . .	

Quand j'étais cogné à la porte,	When I knocked upon the door,
Quand ils ont va ouvert la porte,	When they opened it to me,
Oh, j'ai vu les chandelles allumées	Oh, I saw all the bright candles
Tout le tour de ton cerceuil.	All around your coffin.

As the song implied, early death was not uncommon in South Louisiana at the time. Cleoma Breaux herself died suddenly in 1941, just after the great flood in Crowley.

When Joseph Falcon first recorded, the usual Cajun lineup was accordion and fiddle, sometimes with box guitar or triangle. In the thirties radical changes were brought about by the popularity of western music and the introduction of amplified instruments. By 1937 the featured role of the accordion had been usurped by the fiddle, and Falcon's authentic, uninhibited music was suddenly out of date. His pride hurt, Joe refused to record commercially again, although he continued to play dances in the Crowley area, mainly for the older generation. Mercifully, in 1963 he allowed Valerie Post to tape a performance by his Silver Bell Band at a *fais-dodo* at the Triangle Club in Scott. The ensuing Arhoolie album revealed that the dance was a rip-roaring affair with many favorite songs, including "Hip Et Taiaud," "Allons Danse Colinda," "Les Flammes D'Enfer," "Le Tortillage," and of course "Allons A Lafayette." Occasionally the music was rough at the edges—Joe's second wife Theresa Falcon did not help with her overenthusiastic drumming—but the atmosphere was electric.

Joseph Falcon died in Crowley two years later. Johnnie Allan's admiration is easy to understand: "Joe was extremely kindhearted, yet insisted on his musicians keeping strict rules, no cursing or immorality was allowed. Joe Falcon will go down in history. He is *the* guy that's mentioned in any book about Cajun Louisiana, when you talk about French accordion players."

After Joseph Falcon signed with Columbia, fiddler Leo Soileau and accordionist Mayuse Lafleur were snapped up by Victor, Columbia's main rival. Although "Lafayette" was the first Cajun recording, Columbia was somewhat tardy in the manufacturing process and Falcon's song almost failed to be the first Cajun release, as Joe ruefully explained: "Before 'Lafayette' came out, Leo Soileau and Mayuse Lafleur went and recorded. In just a month their record came out, but mine came out eight days before, and I had recorded three months before!"

The impact of Falcon's "Lafayette" in Acadiana was such that by the summer of 1929 Paramount, Brunswick/Vocalion, and OKeh were also recording traditional rural Cajun music. Among the artists being recorded were Amadie Ardoin, the Breaux Brothers, Columbus Fruge, Angela LeJune, Dennis McGee—and Soileau and Lafleur.

Like Joseph Falcon, Leo Soileau was a true Cajun pioneer. He gave the music a new, more sophisticated direction by borrowing freely from outside sources. Soileau told dedicated British musicologist Tony Russell that his career took off when he was introduced to a Victor agent by Frank Deadline, an Opelousas jewelry-store owner who sold records on the side. Soileau and Mayuse Lafleur were sent to Atlanta, Georgia, for a Victor field session in October 1928, and made the first recordings with a Cajun fiddle, including the earthily exciting "Mama Where You At?" Better known as "Hey Mom," this Amidie Breaux song is a model of simplicity:

O mam, et où toi t'es,	O mom, where are you,
Chère mam, comment ça se fait	Dear mom, why is it
Que jamais je te voir encore,	That I never see you anymore,
Chère mam, et où toi t'es?	Dear mom, where are you?

Nine days later the handsome twenty-two-year-old Lafleur was shot dead in a barroom brawl in Basile, an innocent bystander. Soileau promptly teamed up with another accordion player, Moise Robin of Arnaudville. During the summer and fall of 1929 they recorded for three different companies: Paramount in Richmond, Indiana; Victor in Memphis; and Vocalion in New Orleans. Their Paramount version of "Easy Rider Blues" was a remarkable Cajun-blues performance.

From 1930 to 1934 the hard times of the Depression forced the suspension of all Cajun recording sessions. But Leo Soileau continued to play dances throughout Louisiana and East Texas, and on a good night he was drawing over 350 couples. Finding the accordionists too slow for his slick style, he started featuring his fiddle as lead instrument; he also expanded the traditional Cajun repertoire. As western music grew more popular in South Louisiana, other Cajun bands began using stringed instruments, especially the fiddle and guitar, to the exclusion of the accordion.

Formed in 1934, Leo Soileau's Three Aces—there were never less than four musicians—soon shot to the forefront of this embryo "Cajun-country" movement. Apart from the Cajun tradition, their major inspiration came from western swing, a cheerful, spirited amalgam of swing, blues, ragtime, and fiddle music that originated in Texas. After signing for Bluebird, Soileau's string band—without an accordionist, but with the first drummer to play on Cajun sessions—made popular recordings of "La Valse De Gueydan" and "Hackberry Hop" (variants of "Jole Blon" and the traditional "Hip Et Taiaud"), and the familiar "Le Gran Mamou." The smooth, rhythmic music was in sharp contrast to the raw folk sound of Joseph Falcon's performances.

In 1935 Soileau and his band moved to Decca, which had already signaled its entry into the Cajun market by signing Joseph Falcon and

Amadie Ardoin. The group, now called Soileau's Four Aces, cut its first Decca session in Chicago, having made the long journey from Crowley in an old Model-A Ford. Besides Cajun tunes the Four Aces recorded Acadian-styled versions of popular hillbilly songs like "Red River Valley" and "Birmingham Jail." Leo enjoyed the interesting chord changes and melodies of the "foreign" material, priding himself on being able to draw from such diverse traditions as polkas, Mexican music, and square dances. He persisted with an anglicized approach for lengthy Decca sessions in New Orleans (1936) and Dallas (1937). Although some titles were in French, like "Riche Ou Pauvre" and "Embrace Moi Encore," there were only a few genuine Cajun numbers, including "La Blues De Port Arthur" and "Ma Jolie Petite Fille." Mostly the songs were pop or country. Perhaps he had strayed from his Cajun roots, but Soileau was still considered a Cajun musician. After the Four Aces had broken away as a separate unit, records were issued in the name of Leo Soileau's Rhythm Boys until 1940, when falling sales at the onset of war caused Decca to halt all releases by Cajun artists.

During World War II Soileau was resident at the Silver Star club in Lake Charles. At the time the popular Cajun artist Happy Fats was in his band: "Leo was playing for a fellow by the name of Mr. Davies, he had an old club there, the Silver Star, he was a wrestler. Leo had a daily program on radio station KPLC, that's mostly why they hired me, to do the radio announcing. He was a good musician, but I had to take care of him. Leo had quite a few records, he had some good hits like 'Le Gran' Mamou,' and I believe at one time he recorded a version of 'Jole Blonde.' "

After the war Soileau had a long engagement at the Showboat club in Orange, Texas. He also made frequent broadcasts over KVOL Lafayette, KPLC Lake Charles, and KWKH Shreveport, introduced by his theme song "Under The Double Eagle"; the Lafayette and Lake Charles shows were sponsored by Community Coffee. Leo did not record again, apparently content with performing and broadcasting. His musical fortunes were not improved when the accordion gained renewed acceptance in the late forties.

In 1953 this much-respected artist dropped out of music after twenty-five eventful years to work in an oil refinery in Lake Charles and as a janitor in Ville Platte. He retired in the late 1960s. In his prime he had an innate ability to move with the times; he was the first Cajun fiddler to record, and as a bandleader he was a pivotal figure in the careers of other musicians. An Old Timey album of his original recordings was a welcome reminder of his former glories, but sadly he died on August 2, 1980, before its release.

At the end of the Depression there was a flurry of Cajun recordings, coinciding with the general upturn in the record industry. Sales of individual Cajun 78s ranged from 500 to 10,000 in South Louisiana and

East Texas. Jukebox operators, a new breed, were becoming influential customers; it was the popularity of the jukebox, combatting the din of the juke joint, that hastened the development of instrument amplification. The juke joints, prospering in the post-Prohibition era, were ready symbols of music's commercial potential—to draw crowds and to sell liquor. Every speakeasy had to have music, but not every joint could afford a band.

By now groups were beginning to understand that records were an excellent medium to enhance crowd-pulling power wherever they played. Sponsored radio broadcasts, still in their infancy, also helped if the band had a reasonable sound. Certainly inquisitive young musicians were being subjected to—and influenced by—an unprecedented plethora of new sounds.

In this changing climate the Hackberry Ramblers were quick to seize their chance. With an exuberant up-to-date sound (Bob Wills, Jimmie Rodgers, and Bessie Smith were enormous influences), they became the most popular Cajun group of the mid-thirties. The Ramblers' leader, Luderin Darbone from Evangeline in Acadia Parish, told Chris Strachwitz how the band started: "Across the street in Hackberry lived Ed Duhon, who was just learning to play accordion and guitar, and we immediately began playing together. He knew Cajun songs and I knew hillbilly tunes, and plus the fact that the local dance hall featured a colored orchestra every other Saturday night where we learned such tunes as 'Tiger Rag,' 'High Society,' and 'Eh La Bas.' We soon had a large repertoire and after months of hard practice we developed our own individual style and decided it was time to start playing for local parties after we were joined by Lennis Sonnier, another guitarist.

"Prior to this time [in the early thirties] all dance bands in the Cajun country, other than orchestras, featured an accordion with assistance from a fiddler who would bass or second with the fiddle, a guitar, and most of the time the triangle or the 'little iron' as it's called in southern Louisiana. We didn't know how the people would react to our first dance—we were there to play their dance with only a fiddle and two guitars, but to our amazement we were a smashing success."

In 1933 the Hackberry Ramblers began broadcasting over radio KFDM Beaumont, Texas, which had a linkup with Lake Charles every morning. The group moved to Crowley in 1935 to be more centrally situated, and played dances throughout the small towns of South Louisiana and East Texas. Their most requested song was "Corinne Corinna," a real folk favorite. "They played it so good,"Joe Falcon once said, "it was like you could see Corinne. They was real musicians!" During this period they recorded for Bluebird under the direction of Eli Oberstein, scoring their biggest success with a string-band version of "Jole Blonde" sung by Lennis Sonnier. Other gems were "You've Got To

Hi De Hi," a delectable western novelty; and "Te Petite Et Te Meon," a beautiful traditional Cajun song. As the Riverside Ramblers, Sonnier and Darbone accompanied the prolific Joe Werner in 1936 on his tremendous hit "Wondering," a haunting song that became a country-music classic through Webb Pierce's 1952 Decca recording:

Wondering, wondering, who's kissing you,
Wondering, wondering, if you're wondering too.
Every hour through the day that you went away
I've been wondering if you are still wondering too.

Whether they were called the Hackberry or Riverside Ramblers, their records had a full, accomplished sound and were bought throughout the white South, unlike most Cajun releases, which remained strictly local. But the sharp decline in record sales at the end of the thirties led to the termination of their Bluebird contract.

Following a short disbandment, Luderin Darbone resurrected the Hackberry Ramblers in Lake Charles. Along with multi-instrumentalist Crawford Vincent from Gueydan, Eddie Shuler was invited to join the new group: "In the latter part of 1942 I met some fellows who were re-forming a band to play in the local dance halls. They called themselves the Hackberry Ramblers after a small town near Lake Charles. It so happened that I liked music enough to have composed several songs and I got with the band with the idea that they should learn these songs and make a home-demo record, for souvenir's sake and as a memento to my songwriting efforts. The result of all this was that I got hired as a vocalist and had to learn to play the guitar. In those days the vocalist with any down-home band had to be able to also play rhythm guitar, and thus I became a serious musician! I stayed with the Ramblers until 1945, when I formed my own band."

In 1946 the Hackberry Ramblers started playing every weekend at the Silver Star club in Lake Charles, taking the place of Leo Soileau, who had moved on to the Showboat club in Orange, Texas. Every group member had a steady daytime job; there was no chance of earning a living from music. In 1948 the Ramblers were recorded by De Luxe in New Orleans. Although their Cajun fiddle sound was improbably boosted by a trumpet and a tenor sax, the accordion was making a comeback and the records were poor sellers. Five years later the band enjoyed the excitement of recording for Columbia (who had just signed Cajun artist Vin Bruce), paying homage to their favorite club with a tune called "Silver Star Stomp" first recorded for De Luxe.

When the Silver Star engagement ended in 1956 the Ramblers played mainly in the East Texas area, where their popularity lingered on. In 1963 they recorded a tasteful album for Arhoolie at the Goldband studio; the LP featured Darbone's masterful fiddle in a wide range of material including traditional French songs, dances, blues, and rags. "Turtle Tail" was released as a single and sold well in the Lake Charles area. Then the group had a short spell with Goldband and scored a minor local hit with "Cajun Pogo," a bright novelty number. The *Louisiana Enterprise* ran a brief story on the record: "Available on Goldband 1143 by the Hackberry Ramblers, the dance is sweeping Lake Charles, Westlake, Ville Platte, Big Mamou, Opelousas and district. Leading the Ramblers was Edwin Duhon and Luderin Darbone. Promoter of the dance is Edwin's son, Harlon Duhon!"

Shortly after, with Luderin Darbone, Lennis Sonnier, and Edwin Duhon approaching senior citizenship, the Hackberry Ramblers disbanded once more. It was a quiet demise for such a pioneering and progressive group, a group that in its heyday in the thirties had made Cajun music a listenable commodity beyond the confines of rural Louisiana.

In 1936, with record sales holding up after the end of the Depression slump, the Victor mobile recording unit under the direction of Eli Oberstein visited New Orleans to record local hillbilly, blues, and Cajun artists. In what was one of the last major field trips, mammoth sessions were held at the St. Charles Hotel, with more than twenty-five titles recorded each day. The ensuing 78s were eventually released on Bluebird, Victor's subsidiary budget label, at a cost of thirty-five cents per copy, the same price as the Deccas and Vocalions (the Victors and Brunswicks still retailed at the usual seventy-five cents; the lower prices, made possible by reduced recording costs, showed the competitive nature of the market). A "2000" series had already been set aside by Bluebird for its Cajun artists, who generally adopted the popular westernized approach. Among the musicians recorded were Nathan Abshire (as Nason Absher), Amadie Ardoin and Dennis McGee, the Dixie Ramblers with Hector Duhon, Happy Fats and the Rayne-Bo Ramblers, Miller's Merrymakers with J. B. Fusilier, and Lawrence Walker, as well as the redoubtable Joseph Falcon and Leo Soileau. Next to the Hackberry Ramblers, the most successful Bluebird act was that of newcomers Happy Fats and the Rayne-Bo Ramblers.

LeRoy "Happy Fats" LeBlanc is a remarkable, larger-than-life figure who has been playing and supporting Cajun music through all its changes over the past fifty years. In celebration of this achievement, then-Louisiana governor Edwin Edwards, himself a Cajun, granted a successful "Happy Fats Day" in Happy's hometown of Rayne on November 9, 1979. Still living a simple life with his family, Happy has keen memories of the early days, including his first recording session:

"We were contacted by Victor through a fellow here in Rayne by the name of Hillman Bailey who now has a radio station in Natchitoches. This fellow Hillman Bailey, he had a radio shop here and a music store, and he had contact with the Werleins of New Orleans. And we were brought to New Orleans for the first time, and we recorded there in the old St. Charles Hotel. That was in 1936. Victor would come in and they'd hire probably a floor of the hotel and put all their equipment in it. It was very bulky. In those days they recorded on wax and it was very interesting for a Cajun that had never seen anything like that.

"Eli Oberstein was in charge, he was a very jolly man, I'd call him a jolly giant. I'd say he was a man about six feet, five inches tall, a Jewish man. He could be a stormy type of fellow, though, if you didn't get things done right he'd get awful mad for a few seconds. Then he'd come back and say, 'Let's cut a good one!'

"We recorded for Eli most of the time, the latter few we had Steve Sholes in command. Now they've become more centralized since then, most people are sent to Nashville or possibly Camden, New Jersey, to record. In those days they were traveling units. The first ones weren't on the RCA label, they were on their subsidiary Bluebird. Towards the end they put us on the regular RCA Victor black label. We got twenty-five dollars a song for the whole band. That wasn't much if you look at it nowadays, but in them days twenty-five dollars was a good bit of money. We'd make three hundred to four hundred dollars a session, they'd pay our expenses too. We were drinking whiskey, all we needed!"

Eli Oberstein, who took over at Victor from the pioneering Ralph Peer, made frequent field trips to the South during the thirties, recording the full spectrum of regional music for the local markets. Later he became an influential A&R man (an "artists and repertoire" man was the person who directed recording sessions) in the swing-band era. Steve Sholes, who had joined Victor in 1936, worked under Oberstein for three years, eventually going on to head Victor's country music division from 1945 until 1957. One of the founding fathers of the Nashville country scene, Sholes was responsible for signing the young Elvis Presley to RCA Victor from the small Sun label of Memphis, Tennessee.

The Rayne-Bo Ramblers' early Bluebird sides were a delight. A highlight was "Oublies Mois Jamais Petite," on which Happy Fats handled the vocal adroitly and Joe Werner of "Wondering" fame blew a chillingly plaintive harmonica, while the rest of the Ramblers chipped in with a guitar-led rhythmic backing. The group's virtuosity also shone through on "Vain Toi Don A Ma Mort," a sentimental deathbed song:

Viens-toi donc à mon côté,	Come here, now, to my side,
Je suis après m'en aller.	I'm about to go away.
Regardez donc dans le ciel,	Look up into heaven,
Et demandons aujourd'hui	And let us ask today
Que Dieu me pardonne	That God will pardon me
Pour toutes les misères j'ai faites.	For all the misery I've caused.

"Then we had several other sessions," says Happy Fats, "about four or five more, we had Dallas one session, and to Atlanta, Georgia, on another, and Chicago on one. We had one good record, in those days there was no Top Ten or anything like that, but they did have 'Hits of the Week' and in the 1942 edition of some big radio book they put out, we had an ad in there. Our picture came out along with people like the Sons of the Pioneers. We had the 'Hit of the Week,' which was a number we recorded called 'Les Veuve A Kita La Coulee' that I had cut in Dallas for RCA [this very melodic song, better known as 'Les Veuves De La Coulee,' tells how, in the old days, 'the widows of the coulee' used to go to town to buy yellow cotton material to make their own bloomers]. The 'Hit of the Week' I understand was a record that had sold 10,000 in the first week. We had no way of knowing the amount of records sold. As a matter of fact, we were doing them for cash, there were no royalty deals at all."

This success was very satisfying to a man who had a humble start in life: "I was born right here in Rayne in 1915, January 30. In my young days I always wanted to buy a guitar, I loved music. We were always poor people, my daddy was a rice farmer, and one rice season my mother gave me a sack of rice and I traded it to a druggist for a guitar. My guitar style was based on Jimmie Rodgers. I taught myself, and if I'd see a hobo or something with a guitar, I'd go pick him up and bring him home, give him dinner, maybe learn a few chords with him. Then there was a colored boy here in town that I learned a lot from, a fellow by the name of Clarence Locksey, he's still living, I saw him the other day. He knew some chords, he'd play this black blues stuff, I didn't like it too much, I liked Jimmie Rodgers's stuff.

"Just before I started my band I was working at a rice mill here for fifteen cents an hour, ten hours a day. Stacking rice, it was hard work, sure. When I started it was still the Depression. I won't say the Depression hurt me, in fact I think music helped me. It gave me something to do because a fellow of my age at the time it was hard to find a job, there was nothing to do. So playing music gave us an outlet, but back in them days we'd play dances for ten dollars for the whole band—two dollars apiece and two dollars for traveling expenses. We were poor, you see. But you could get a plate lunch for fifteen cents then, meat was about fifteen, twenty cents a pound, and playing three or four dances a week you could make eight or ten dollars a week. That was good money in them days.

"Back then, there was no television, very little radio, the dances were the opportunity to blow off steam. And here in the Cajun country, in Rayne, during this time there was five or six thousand people and there were three big dance halls. On weekends, Friday, Saturday, and Sunday, they'd have dancing, they'd all be full. People would come in, they'd bring them in school buses from out of the country, every one of them would be full of people. They'd dance all night long! We'd just start playing and they'd start dancing. Then about ten o'clock they'd have what they call a 'Treat Your Lady' intermission and then they'd get back and get out till twelve or one o'clock. And play 'Home Sweet Home' and they all went home.

"Now they were different when there was a wedding dance, a *bal de noce.* They had a wedding dance, the wedding couple and their attendants would come in, and they had possession of the floor for the march. They'd make a march around the hall a couple of times, the music they'd play would be the wedding march, and the first two dances were theirs, just them and their attendants. And they'd dance a waltz and a two-step, then their mothers would come in.

"The club I played longest at was the old O.S.T. club here in Rayne. There was also the Club Rendezvous in Ville Platte and the Colonial club in Mermentau, but I'd say Tee Maurice was the club that had the biggest attendance of any for eight or ten years during the thirties. It was at Vatican, north of the Bosco oil field about twelve miles north of Rayne; one of the Rayne-Bo Ramblers' records is called 'Aux Bal Se Te Maurice,' I also had 'La Valse De Te Maurice.' Now they're trying to revive the club, the old place is down but the fellow that owned it has built another smaller place. But this old one, the dance floor was about 100 feet by 100 feet, so it was a pretty big dance floor. The bandstand was at one end with the bar at the other end. They had chicken wire on the windows so they wouldn't come in, in some places they had chicken wire in front of the band. In fact they had chicken wire at a dance hall in the country here, they had a shooting in the middle of the floor and the chicken wire didn't stop them from getting out of that place! You can imagine it, about six hundred people there and somebody starts shooting, got a pile of bodies right in the middle of them, and you think 'I'm gonna get out of here!' "

In 1939, in recognition of their growing popularity, the Rayne-Bo Ramblers were invited by the CBS radio network to represent their home state on the "Louisiana Progress Program"—the first time a South Louisiana band was heard over the national radio network system. On another memorable occasion Happy Fats, a staunch southern patriot (he was fond of titles like "If I Ever Leave The South"), played with his group on the streets of Port Arthur, Texas, from six o'clock in the morning until late evening to promote the sale of war bonds. "At midnight," recalls Happy, "we went to the radio station and played requests for people if they would buy a war bond. One of the officials of a large oil company requested that I do a song called 'My Brown-Eyed Texas Rose.' We did the song and the oil company official pledged his company to buy a $250,000 war bond."

After the Rayne-Bo Ramblers split in 1941 Happy Fats set off to join Leo Soileau's Rhythm Boys in Lake Charles. Cajun music was no longer the simple, introverted music that was still being played in the remoter rural areas of Acadiana; it also embraced a sleeker, westernized sound popular in many parts of South Louisiana and East Texas. The rapid evolutionary process was halted during World War II, when fewer bands were performing and there was no recording activity at all. But this musical hiatus was to last only as long as hostilities continued.

3

"And Harry Choates recorded 'Jole Blon,' that was another thing"

The record industry operated at a low level during World War II, frustrated by a prolonged recording ban by the American Federation of Musicians; internecine battles between the American Society of Composers, Authors and Publishers and the new music publishing organization, Broadcast Music, Incorporated; labor shortages; and a lack of shellac material—diverted from "ballads to bullets." Cajun recordings were an early casualty, but ethnic Southern music was kept alive by a succession of hillbilly hits from Roy Acuff, Ernest Tubb, Bob Wills, and Louisiana's Ted Daffan and Jimmie Davis. *Billboard* spotted this strong trend, observing that "hillbilly music has shown by its work against adverse conditions that when the war is over and normalcy returns it will be the field to watch."

But the major companies did not see the future that way, and by continuing to ignore hillbilly, blues, and other regional forms they missed out on a large slice of the postwar record boom. The new independent operations, armed with the hitherto closely guarded secrets of recording technology, slipped in to satisfy a public eager for its *own* music. As part of the trend towards regional music, there was a welcome revival in the fortunes of Cajun music, as Happy Fats explains: "Cajun music became popular in the forties, I think it was because Cajun musicians came out of the cracks. It was hard to find [young] musicians during the war because everybody was in the army, fighting overseas, and the older people were the Cajun music players. So they came out and started playing, and it was Cajun music. And Harry Choates recorded 'Jole Blon,' that was another thing."

From 1946 on newly formed recording companies in South Louisiana and East Texas started taking an interest in Cajun music. They prospered where others feared to tread. Along with Harry Choates's hillbilly-based "Jole Blon" (Gold Star), other seminal Cajun releases from this exciting postwar period were the authentic "Love Bridge Waltz" by Iry LeJune (Opera) and the almost negroid "Pine Grove Blues" by Nathan Abshire (O.T.). These songs were showing Cajun music at its varied best; performed live, they were perfect entertainment for the crowds flocking to the sweaty, jam-packed dance halls. The music was progressing again: in addition to the familiar fiddle and box guitar, the steel and electric guitars, string bass, and drums were regular accouterments in Cajun bands, and the accordion was making a comeback as well. The hillbilly element was becoming more intrusive, but the basic Cajun emotional qualities were retained, and the songs were being sung in Cajun French.

Harry Choates's legendary "Jole Blon" was based on the much-loved "Jole Blonde" previously recorded by the Breaux family, Leo Soileau, and the Hackberry Ramblers. Harry's big-selling version not only engendered a feeling of cultural pride among the Cajuns; it also introduced their music to a new audience. The tune was promptly picked up by Texas country pianist Moon Mullican, who had an even bigger hit with "New Jole Blon" (King).

By projecting his distinctive fiddle over a jaunty western-swing rhythm, Choates was able to stress the song's perfect melody. Though the Cajun-French lyrics were incomprehensible to many, the sad message came through with clarity:

Jole Blon, jolie fille,	Jole Blon, pretty girl,
Chère petite, joli coeur,	Dear little one, pretty heart,
Tu m'as laissé pour t'en aller	You left me to go away
avec un autre, chère petite,	with another, dear little one,
Dans le pays de la Louisiane,	In the country of Louisiana,
mais malheureuse.	you poor one.

"Jole Blon" was recorded in 1946 for Bill Quinn's Houston-based Gold Star label with its self-styled slogan, "King of the Hillbillies." The reaction was such that the tiny Gold Star pressing plant could not keep pace with demand and work was farmed out in all directions, leading to widespread bootlegging. Eventually Quinn was forced to lease his hot record for national distribution to Modern of Los Angeles, who advertised the song as "Nation's sensational hillbilly . . ."

Born in Rayne in 1922, Harry Choates learned to play guitar and steel guitar as well as fiddle. During the Depression Harry moved with his mother Tave Manard Choates to Port Arthur, Texas, and spent much of his boyhood wandering around local bars and listening to the jukebox music. With a guitar-playing friend he began visiting barber shops to play for customers on a borrowed fiddle. Octogenarian Port Arthur barber Milton Bellot told researcher Tim Knight that the twelve-year-old Harry would rise to his toes when he hit the high notes, much to the delight of the onlookers, who would pitch nickels, dimes, and quarters to the budding genius. During the late thirties Harry joined Leo Soileau's group in Ville

Platte, adopting the *Eh . . . ha, ha!* vocal cry that later became his trademark. Crowley record man Jay Miller played with Harry around this time and remembers that Choates would never stay long with any one band, "but he was a great musician. Never had a good instrument in his life, I often wondered what he could do with an instrument that you could purchase today. Harry couldn't speak French, but he could sing it."

Choates had first performed "Jole Blon" in Leo Soileau's band, but on his Gold Star recording he stepped up the key from G to A. The story behind the hit is recalled by Happy Fats: "Harry played with me in 1938–39, I've got some records on RCA that he cut with me. In fact 'Les Veuve A Kita La Coulee,' Harry played the fiddle on that. He was a very good fiddle player. 'Jole Blon' had become a hit through Leo Soileau, myself, and Harry Choates who recorded it. We were at this club in Lake Charles, they had a lot of soldiers that had come there from the local camp, from the Lake Charles air base and other places on a Saturday night. And they loved this 'Jole Blon.' So I wrote to Steve Sholes at RCA and told him we ought to record this. And he wrote back and said, 'Well, there's a shortage of shellac during the war' and he give me all that. In the meantime Harry Choates went off to Houston, he left the band and got in with a fellow by the name of Bill Quinn. And he made 'Jole Blon' and it was a million seller."

Although he was extremely popular at clubs and dance halls throughout Southwest Louisiana and East Texas, Choates was unable to find a follow-up hit to "Jole Blon." Still with Gold Star, he recorded many charming songs with traditional Cajun origins, including "Allons A Lafayette," "Bayou Pon Pon," and "Poor Hobo." The historically valuable album "Jole Blon," drawn from these sessions, was issued by H. W. "Pappy" Daily's D label. In 1982 Arhoolie released another excellent album of Gold Star masters entitled "The Fiddle King Of Cajun Swing."

After Gold Star, Harry recorded for De Luxe, D, O.T., Allied, Cajun Classics, Macy's, and Humming Bird. Often the recordings were unworthy of his talents as he searched desperately for another hit. His life had become a mess, a wild orgy of wine, women, and song. Then, failing to meet his wife Helen's nonsupport claim of twenty dollars per week for their children's maintenance, he was thrown into an Austin, Texas, jail pending trial in Beaumont. By now a chronic alcoholic, Choates suffered an epileptic fit; after keeping the guards and prisoners awake, he fell into a coma and died. He was buried in Port Arthur, Texas, in July 1951, still only twenty-eight years old.

"In a way he just lost his mind," says Happy Fats, "he was a very bad alcoholic, when he wanted whiskey or a drink, he had to have it. I've seen him break glass with his elbow, right on Main Street in Lake Charles, and crack it open and reach in and get a fifth, a liquor store on Main Street. He just had to have it, that's all he took, one little bottle of whiskey. But they put him in a jail there in Austin, he just killed himself hitting the bars with his head. At least that's the story I heard, there is a possibility that the police killed him, I don't know. There was a big question about that when it happened." (No record of the inquest verdict has been found.)

Harry Choates was indeed a tragic figure, but his spirit lives on, as Johnnie Allan confirms: " 'Jole Blon' is the Louisiana national anthem! I think every section of every country has one song that has been recorded through the years that kind of sticks out, it never fades away. And 'Jole Blon' has been that song in South Louisiana. Harry Choates's is the version that's still remembered. He came in with the fiddle and he was very, very popular back then. Of course I was young in those days, I don't remember him that well, but his records are still being played extensively, especially on Saturday afternoons. You have stations in Jennings, Crowley, in Ville Platte, that have strictly French music, and his records are still being played on there. And you don't play a Harry Choates record unless you play 'Jole Blon'!"

In 1948 Bennie Hess and James Bryant, Bill Quinn's former partners at Gold Star, set up Opera Records in Houston. At the time Hess was playing with Virgil Bozeman in the Oklahoma Tornadoes, the hillbilly band used as backup on most Opera releases. Initially the label slogan (a quaint quirk of the era) was "Hits of the Hillbillies," but it was later changed to the more refined "Hits of Western Music." To capitalize on the demand for Cajun music, Opera issued occasional 78 rpm records by Floyd LeBlanc, Iry LeJune, and Charlie Broussard and the Sulphur Playboys.

Mermentau-born Cajun fiddler Floyd LeBlanc, a member of the Oklahoma Tornadoes, had a minor hit with the popular waltz "Over The Waves." He also introduced the highly promising accordionist Iry LeJune to Opera. Iry's first record, the superb "Love Bridge Waltz"/"Evangeline Special," was a hit in East Texas and Acadiana in 1948; for the first time in more than ten years a Cajun accordion was wailing from the jukeboxes. But Opera did not last much longer. Bennie Hess went on to make his name as a hustling hillbilly singer and record producer, while co-owner Bryant became a successful car salesman. As for Virgil Bozeman, he proceeded to form the O.T. label out of Westlake, with financial help from Lake Charles record-store owner George Khoury.

"Virgil Bozeman came here with his cowhorn operation out of San Antonio," says Eddie Shuler, "and things were so good he just wound up staying here. He evidently discovered the method I was using to make records from somebody else, anyway he was doing the same thing I was doing. He'd go into the radio station and give the engineer a bottle of booze to cut a disc for him and then he'd take the disc and send it off and have the records pressed. George Khoury was his sponsor, so to speak, because he didn't have that much money. He was a good salesman, he had a lot of gab because being a cowhorn salesman he *had* to have a lot of gab!"

Bozeman made a dream start in 1949 when he recorded "Pine Grove Blues" by Nathan Abshire, the best-known Cajun accordionist of modern times, at KPLC radio station, Lake Charles. The O.T. slogan, "Hits of Louisiana," seemed to be no idle boast. "Pine Grove Blues" was a record of considerable importance; it kept the Cajun bandwagon rolling in the wake of "Jole Blon," and it also helped to reestablish the accordion following Iry LeJune's breakthrough with "Love Bridge Waltz." "Pine Grove Blues," based on Columbus Fruge's "Tite Negresse," will always be associated with Nathan. Over a wonderfully hypnotic blues beat pushed along by his own accordion, Wilson Granger's fiddle, and Earl Demary's guitar, Abshire sang rousingly of his wrongdoing woman:

Hey, Nègresse,	Hey "nègresse,"
Où toi t'as été hier soir, ma	Where were you last night, my
nègresse?	"nègresse"?
Tu es arrivés ce matin,	You came home this morning,
Le soleil était après se lever, ma	The sun was already up, my
nègresse . . .	"nègresse" . . .

("Ma nègresse" is a common expression of endearment.)

On the flip Nathan gave "Kaplan Waltz" a delicate, spine-chilling performance in the crying style of Amadie Ardoin. But the song was unfairly eclipsed by the surging power of the top side.

When "Pine Grove Blues" was recorded, Nathan was approaching middle age. Born in Gueydan in 1913, he was the first of Mr. and Mrs. Lanas Abshire's six children. Both his parents were accordionists. The chubby youngster learned to play on a cheap squeeze-box, making his first public appearance at the age of eight at La Salle de Tee-Gar Guidry dance hall in Mermentau Cove. In 1936 he recorded for Bluebird, backed by the Rayne-Bo Ramblers, but a decade of obscurity followed the disastrous decline in the popularity of the accordion. For a while he took up the fiddle, as did many other aspiring accordionists, including Iry LeJune and Austin Pitre. After a spell in the services, Nathan began to build up his career through a one-day-a-week booking at Quincy Davis's famous Avalon club in Basile. "Pine Grove Blues" came next.

Virgil Bozeman sold boxfuls of "Pine Grove Blues" from the back of a large hearse, but he had more difficulty moving Nathan's follow-ups.

"French Blues," originally recorded for Bluebird, was not in the same class, although "Pine Grove Boogie" was as exhilarating as the hit— Nathan's accordion, full of "blue" notes of tonal purity, was outstanding behind Roy Broussard's vocals. Bozeman also recorded the exemplary Floyd LeBlanc "and his Magic Fiddle" doing "Louisiana Stomp," and Harry Choates with the prophetic "Jole Blon's Gone." There were hillbilly releases by Jerry Barlow and by Bozeman himself, and a rare country blues excursion by Cleo Harves, a disciple of the great Texas bluesman Lightnin' Hopkins. But the "Hits of Louisiana" on O.T. suddenly dried up. Bozeman returned to San Antonio, Texas, where he set up the Hot Rod label with local record man Bob Tanner. Later Tanner ran a short-lived Cajun series on his own T.N.T. label, releasing material by Iry LeJune and Aldus Roger recorded by Eddie Shuler in Lake Charles.

Meanwhile George Khoury felt the time was right to launch his own Khoury's and Lyric labels. One of his first moves was to entice Nathan Abshire away from Virgil Bozeman. But the star accordionist was hindered by the "low-fi" sound of the Lake Charles radio stations, and he was unable to duplicate his triumph with "Pine Grove Blues"—"La Valse De Holly Beach" and "Shamrock Waltz" came closest. Although Nathan continued to play local dances, his recording fortunes remained at a low ebb for the rest of the fifties. He was to make a marvelous comeback during the next decade.

Two of the busy national independent labels, De Luxe from New Jersey and Modern from Los Angeles, dabbled briefly with Cajun music in the late forties. The emphasis was on the commercial Cajun-country sound. De Luxe recorded Harry Choates, the Hackberry Ramblers, Happy Fats, and Joe Manuel without success. But Modern, which had leased Harry Choates's "Jole Blon" from Gold Star (and credited it to Harry Coates), scored again with Chuck Guillory and his Rhythm Boys' "Tolan Waltz" on Colonial, a subsidiary label.

Chuck Guillory of Mamou was a good singer and fluent fiddle player who recorded later for Feature and Folk-Lyric. On the Modern recordings his popular westernized Cajun string band included the young Jimmy Newman (vocalist on "Chere Petite") and Papa Cairo, who sang on "Big Texas," another hit for the group in 1949. "Big Texas" was a catchy song about a rejected Cajun lover starting a new life in the distant land of adventure and the great unknown (traveling to Texas is a recurrent escapist theme in Cajun songs). Cairo claims that Hank Williams stole the tune in 1952 and turned it into the world-famous "Jambalaya (On The Bayou)"; some say that writing credits should go to Moon Mullican of "New Jole Blon" fame. In spite of the controversy, Hank Williams's immaculate recording made "Jambalaya" the best-known Cajun-based country song ever.

Papa Cairo, a colorful character born Julius Lamperez in New Orleans, had been a Cajun and hillbilly music performer in Louisiana and East Texas since the mid-thirties. He started out playing the guitar flat across his knees with a metal finger attachment, and when the first regular steel guitars appeared he was quick to buy one. A powerful player, he loved to tell how he used to mystify his audiences by taking his hands off the instrument and magically holding the notes with his feet on the pedals. Shortly after forming his first band, the Daylight Creepers, he was dubbed Papa Cairo by Happy Fats (*karo* is Cajun French for diamond; he always wore the gem in his tie and on his fingers). During World War II he was imprisoned by the Germans. Resuming his musical career after the war, he toured with Ernest Tubb and played with Leo Soileau and Harry Choates before teaming up with Chuck Guillory. The Modern recordings came about after the band was spotted in Eunice, and such was the impact of "Big Texas" that a "Big Texas No. 2" was recorded by Colonial and credited to Papa Cairo and the Boys. In 1951 Cairo rerecorded "Big Texas" in French and English for Jay Miller's Feature label, but after the "Jambalaya" episode he turned his back on recording in disgust.

The Modern Records Cajun sessions had been held in New Orleans in 1948 by label owners Joe and Jules Bihari as part of an extensive southern field trip. Despite the popularity of "Tolan Waltz," "Big Texas"—and "Jole Blon"—the market was too localized for this ambitious concern or its fellow independents, who were discovering the lucrative national attractions of rhythm and blues and hillbilly music. With few exceptions, commercial Cajun music was henceforth the exclusive province of the South Louisiana record men, a remarkable group of entrepreneurs who were equal to the challenge of preserving their unique musical heritage through the medium of phonograph records.

4

"At that time I had numerous people who wanted French records"

Crowley, the seat of Acadia Parish, is a neat, typically southern town founded in 1887 and known as the Rice Capital of the U.S.A. Its growth was inspired by the development of the Southern Pacific Railroad linking New Orleans with San Francisco and by the construction of Highway 90 along the Old Spanish Trail. In summer the town often suffers from overwhelming humidity and drifting dust clouds; the winters are cold enough, they say, for Cajuns to make gumbo on Monday, Wednesday, Friday, and Saturday, and eat the leftovers during the rest of the week. . . .

Although the town itself has little musical tradition, Crowley has been placed firmly on the recording map through the redoubtable efforts of J. D. (Jay) Miller. Miller became the first record man in South Louisiana when he started the Fais Do Do label in 1946, recording humble Cajun music with a distinct western bias. Promotional and distributional facilities were inevitably flimsy, and sales were modest. But as Jay became more involved in the record business he realized there was an outside chance that a major company would lease a potential hit record for national distribution, or, just as beneficial, that a "name" artist would rerecord a local song (a procedure known as "covering" that could mean substantial royalties for the publishing company—although the original artist was only rewarded if he was the actual songwriter). Over the years J. D. was to record—with the greatest sympathy—the full spectrum of South Louisiana music, from Cajun and hillbilly to zydeco, blues, and rock 'n' roll. He gave local artists countless opportunities to make records, and his live productions were of the highest quality.

Generous towards friends and suspicious of strangers, the pioneering Jay Miller has the natural swagger of any successful businessman. His career as a record man began to take shape when he set up the M & S Electric Co. at 218 North Parkerson Avenue in Crowley: "When I came out of the service I went into business, I think it was '46, I went into electrical contracting. And my wife [Georgia, daughter of popular accordionist Lee Sonnier] and I cashed $500 worth of savings bonds, at that time they were known as war bonds. And the building I leased in Crowley was $150 a month. By the time I had bought me a little store I didn't have much money left, I had a big building with not much in it.

"Of course I was always interested in music anyhow, so I figured we would set us up in this field with a music department. And at that time I had numerous people who wanted French records. And French records, apart from 'Jole Blon' and a couple of other Harry Choates records, just were not available. You had the older records that had been made by Joe Falcon, they may have been discontinued. So I just said, 'Well, I'm gonna see maybe if we can make some records,' I didn't know what would be the first step to do it.

"As a boy I listened to what we consider as country now, we used to think of it as cowboy music. That was the days of Gene Autry. The fact is the first guitar my parents gave me cost about eight dollars, it was a great thing for me. Anyway I learned to play what little I know initially from the Gene Autry songbook, I can remember it was twenty-nine cents from Sears-Roebuck.

"My family moved to the Lake Charles area around 1933. I was on radio there as a youngster, I remember my parents got me entered for a contest sponsored by an ice-cream company. The prize was a fifteen-minute radio broadcast each Saturday for a year. So I was on KPLC way back then, just me and my guitar. I was just a youngster, I was singing mostly cowboy songs. We moved to Crowley in '37 and I was fascinated by the local bands. In Lake Charles at that time either they didn't have, or I didn't know they had, any of what we call string bands. When I moved here, well, we had Happy Fats and his Rayne-Bo Ramblers, we had the Four Aces. And we had the Hackberry Ramblers, Luderin Darbone. They worked under two names, the Hackberry Ramblers, then they started playing a broadcast for Montgomery Ward and if I'm not mistaken the name of the tires of Montgomery Ward at that time was 'Riverside,' and they changed their name to the Riverside Ramblers. I was really fascinated by these people. I lived three houses from the drummer of Leo Soileau's Four Aces, Tony Gonzales, so I got really involved."

Jay played his first dance with the popular Breaux Brothers at a dance hall at Cow Island, near Kaplan, which was so remote that there was no electricity for the loudspeakers. His strongest memory is of the Breaux Brothers arguing among themselves throughout the dance and fighting like dogs at the end. He considers Amidie Breaux one of the great Cajun musicians, although Breaux did have a tendency, when drunk, to pull accordions apart in exuberant acts of showmanship.

J. D. continues: "Another youngster, Hank Redlich, lived about three blocks away, today he's my brother-in-law, but he was a guitar player. We'd get together and the first thing we know we had brought ourselves in a harmonica player, we had us a three-piece band. That's how I really got started. We called ourselves the Musical Aces, very closely related to the Four Aces.

"Then I joined a band called the Daylight Creepers, isn't that a name! That name was brought about originally because they had an old Model-T Ford and every time we'd go to a dance we'd get back home at the daylight. We didn't make much money, but we had a lot of fun. Later on I played with the Four Aces, and Harry Choates and I played together. I made records in 1937 with the Four Aces, we didn't have Leo Soileau, he had quit at that time. A fellow by the name of Boyce Jones was playing fiddle then. That was for Bluebird, if I recall correctly, that's when they recorded us on a wax disc. It was made in New Orleans and Eli Oberstein produced the session. We were all nervous because they told us each one of these wax discs cost twenty-five dollars if you messed them up. I just knew we were going to have us a big old bill for messing up a bunch of those, but we made it! I played electric mandolin, it was an all-string band, our manager was Wal Shreve. Recording was such a big thing, it was a thing of grandeur to us!

"Of course the Four Aces got to where we had eight pieces, we changed the name to the Original Aces. At the time Cliff Bruner and the Texas Wanderers were stationed and working out of Lake Charles, playing KPLC every day, half-hour program on KPLC every day at eleven o'clock. When they left and went back to Beaumont we moved from Crowley to Lake Charles and took their place on the air for quite some time. Cliff Bruner I would say was probably the greatest influence.... We were greatly influenced because we got to know them personally. Bob Wills didn't come here very often, I met Bob several years after I had gotten into the country field of music. But Cliff, I met him back in '37, they were a great band. During the war Ernest Tubb and 'Walking The Floor Over You' meant a lot to me."

In 1946 Jay supervised the first recording session for his Fais Do Do label: "I got checking around and found out that Cosimo Matassa had a studio in New Orleans, so I called him, made arrangements, and picked up Happy Fats and Doc Guidry. There were about seven of us in a convertible, we went over there and then we cut the first records. It couldn't have cost much because we didn't have much money. But at that time it was all 78s, 45s were not out then. There weren't many pressing plants, so Cosimo sent these masters for me to the West Coast and it took ages for them to come. But finally they started coming in. The first record was 'Allons Danse Colinda'—we called it 'Colinda'—and 'Chere Cherie.' And I believe it was Fais Do Do 1000, that was by Happy, Doc and the Boys. On the same session we cut 'Don't Hang Around,' that was a thing I wrote, and 'My Sweetheart's My Buddy's Wife.' And a boy by the name of Louis Noel recorded that, he also did 'La Cravat.' Then I decided to set up my own studio here in Crowley; it was the second in the state after Cosimo's."

The first Fais Do Do release, "Colinda" by Happy, Doc and the Boys, sold only moderately, but Happy Fats remembers the record (derived from the Calinda voodoo dance brought to Louisiana by Negro slaves from the West Indies) with affection: "We took the name from a song called 'Danse Colinda,' we got it from a book in a library at Southwestern University, Lafayette. Actually it was a Haitian song, so we just took the name, the tune is not the same, or the lyric. Doc Guidry and I just sat down and we wrote a French song, a two- or three-chord song that is pretty easy to write. Our recording never did make much of an impression, but I've been collecting royalties on it ever since Jimmie Davis recorded it in 1949."

Overall, Happy, Doc and the Boys had a fascinating selection of releases for Fais Do Do, with titles like "Fais Do Do Breakdown," "New Jolie Blond," "La Valse De Hadacol," and "Crowley Two-Step." The 78s are now very rare (in the late sixties Jay Miller offered his entire stock to a local fair for use as sideshow targets). During the forties Happy also recorded for RCA Victor and De Luxe.

Miller's biggest Cajun success in this period was "The War Widow Waltz" by father-in-law Lee Sonnier and his Acadian Stars on Jay's second label, Feature. " 'The War Widow Waltz' had a woman singing on it, Laura Broussard," Jay recalls, "I don't know what she had but I've seen women crying listening to it on a jukebox, so it must have been pretty strong. And I'd give anything if I had the master. The masters we had, the stampers were lost when a pressing plant burned in Los Angeles." Besides Laura Broussard's vocal, the record's highlights were Sonnier's classically perfect accordion playing and the "cowboy" steel-guitar accompaniment.

Miller's other early Cajun artists included Amidie Breaux, Jimmie Choates, Chuck Guillory, and Austin Pete (Pitre). But his star act was Happy, Doc and the Boys.

After the wartime sojourn with Leo Soileau and Harry Choates in Lake Charles, Happy Fats had been invited to tour with top singing cowboy star Tex Ritter, playing Mississippi, Arkansas, Florida, Georgia, and Hollywood. When he returned home, jobs were hard to find—until he teamed up with fiddler Doc Guidry for broadcasting and recording. "It got kinda tough playing dances and things like that, so I booked a couple of sponsors that I was just singing and playing the guitar for. Doc Guidry was a very good violin player, very good fiddle player, I thought he would add a little to it so I got Doc," he says.

Considered one of the greatest Acadian violinists, Oran "Doc" Guidry was born in Lafayette in 1918. After recording with Happy Fats and the Rayne-Bo Ramblers for Bluebird in 1936, he broke away to form the Sons of the Acadians with brother Nason and cousin Ray Guidry. In 1938 this family string band recorded for Decca under Dave Kapp at the Ritz Hotel in Houston. Doc recalls he was sent a list of hillbilly songs that had to be translated into French, a common Decca practice; the session fee was fifty dollars.

In time he built up a strong local reputation based on musical excellence. "Doc's popularity stemmed mainly from his ability on fiddle and mandolin," says Lafayette country singer Al Terry. "He exhibited a mastery of these instruments in a manner which set the standard for many musicians who came later. He was featured instrumentalist with Governor Jimmie Davis during both of Jimmie's successful campaigns for governor, as well as his last unsuccessful attempt for a third term. Doc also recorded as a vocalist [he had a favorite local record, 'Chere Cherie'/'The Little Fat Man' for Decca in 1953], and is still today one of the most respected musicians in the business."

Doc's one-time benefactor, Governor Jimmie Davis, a much-respected figure in Acadiana, rose to political fame after a childhood as a sharecrop farm boy in Beech Springs, near Shreveport. He also had a fascinating career in music. Starting out as a Jimmie Rodgers–influenced hillbilly singer, he recorded for Victor in 1928 and was already a territorial favorite when he signed for Decca in 1936. His subsequent fame as a singer and songwriter rests easily on numbers like "Nobody's Darling But Mine," "Sweethearts Or Strangers," and especially the all-time favorite "You Are My Sunshine"—co-written with bandleader Charlie Mitchell—which has been described as the "most popular and most valuable" song in the history of country music. Davis's entertainment success brought him wealth and prestige, then the governorship of Louisiana. He was elected in 1944 and 1960, twice triumphing over the vagaries of the Louisiana political scene, a hotbed of dissension between Protestants and Catholics, English and French, rich and poor, black and white. In Cajun country his secret for winning votes was adding songs like "Jole Blon" and "Big Mamou" to his campaign program.

Happy Fats also sided with Davis, whom he first met in the late thirties. "As far as my career is concerned I guess he helped me to get started in both recording and songwriting, for this and other favors I owe him a lot, so each time he called I had to go, in all three races." More recently the ex–Rayne-Bo Rambler lined up behind Edwin Edwards of Crowley. Happy is a man of strong right-wing political views: he calls this approach "plain horse sense!"

As the fifties drew near, the Happy Fats and Doc Guidry radio shows were required listening throughout Acadiana. A key factor in the duo's success was Fats's ability to recruit sponsors at will. "Happy would sell his show to used car lots and beer distributors and he's always done that," says swamp-pop singer Rod Bernard. "In fact, if you see his truck around town he's got 'Happy Fats, Great Storyteller with compliments of Budweiser Beer, Evangeline Maid Bread' and all kind of things like that. He's a real, real supersalesman."

"We had a lot of sponsors," agrees Happy Fats. "At one time we were on seven radio stations, most of it was live. We did a lot of traveling, like on a Saturday we would play Opelousas, Lafayette, and Abbeville, three stations. Two of them were live from the stage of theaters they had linked with the radio stations. We appeared on 'Louisiana Hayride' a few times."

Destined to play a vital part in popularizing country music, the "Louisiana Hayride" show was first broadcast on April 3, 1948, from the Municipal Auditorium in Shreveport by radio KWKH, a powerful 50,000-watt station that was beamed over much of the middle South. Occasionally the Hayride threatened the more famous Grand Ole Opry in Nashville, but as soon as its performers gained recognition the Opry spirited them away, giving rise to the show's unenviable sobriquet, the "Cradle of the Stars." The list of artists who got their breaks at the Hayride includes Johnny and Jack, Webb Pierce, Jim Reeves, Kitty Wells, Slim Whitman, Hank Williams, Faron Young, and many more.

The Hayride was widely heard in South Louisiana, and contributed to the further infiltration of country music into the Cajun music idiom. Happy Fats and Doc Guidry were the only regular Cajun guests. "With the Hayride," says Happy, "I was on for Johnny Faire's Syrup, fellow by the name of Murphy, Mr. Murphy owned the Shreveport Syrup Company. I worked down here for him, and Jay Miller had a boy by the name of Bill Hutto who he was pushing. So Jay got him on the Louisiana Hayride and he got us to go back him up in a group. When we got there to put on Bill Hutto, Mr. Murphy told the station manager, he says, 'I wanna hear Happy and Doc.' He bought a lot of time with that station so his word was pretty strong. So OK, Mr. Murphy fixed it up on the network program, which was a half-hour, but they wasn't supposed to take any repeats on it. Mr. Murphy kinda sniggered so we played 'Jole Blon,' there was a tremendous crowd that night—Hank Williams was there playing—we got on and we played 'Jole Blon.' And we got through playing it, they started clapping. Horace Logan, the station manager, was there so I thought he wanted us to quit. 'No,' he said, 'play it again!' 'Well, you said no repeats.' We had to repeat on that network program three times!

"And after that we stayed on for the whole show. We stayed on the whole show in place of poor Bill Hutto which I wasn't glad of, 'cause he was a nice boy, and Jay too. But they invited us back and we went back several times. It was good, we had had some pretty lean times, and this gave me the feeling that Cajun music was graduating up, up to North Louisiana, and all we'd play was Cajun songs. Hank Williams had a lot of influence down here, he was on the Louisiana Hayride. It covered about a quarter of the nation. And Hank, you've got to give him that, he was good, he was really good. He was on like I was, for Johnny Faire's Syrup, he left to go to the Grand Ole Opry. He gave me the job, the Old Syrupsopper, you would sop up the syrup. . . ."

By the mid-fifties Happy and Doc's partnership had been rendered redundant by the newfangled rock 'n' roll music; their simple blend of Cajun and country acoustical sounds seemed to belong to another era. But Al Terry has not forgotten their importance: "Although both attained success, they have never, in my opinion, been accorded the credit they were due. They were the style setters and forerunners of—and had the greatest influence upon—most of the singers and musicians to emerge from the South in later years."

In 1956 Happy Fats was forced to seek employment outside music. With the help of Governor Jimmie Davis he acquired a job as an agent with the Wildlife and Fisheries Department, but after a transfer to the Bond and Building Commission he was fired. "I made a mistake, I actually worked, in two and a half years I missed three days' work. Now this was unheard of in Louisiana politics. We can't have one of our deadheads working, so I lost the job," he says with feeling.

After the initial impact of rock 'n' roll had subsided Happy Fats discovered that the older audiences still wanted Cajun and country music, and he formed the Bayou Buckeroos with Alex Broussard, a successful rice farmer from Judice. Known as the Barefoot Cajun, Alex sang an unusual blend of Cajun and bluegrass in an appealing high voice and had minor hits with "The Year 57" and "Le Sud De La Louisianne" for La Louisianne. Happy and Alex played the clubs and dance halls of Southwest Louisiana, boosting their popularity with a regular radio program on KSIG Crowley sponsored by Albert LeBlanc, then the self-styled King of Mobile Homes and now in real estate. They also performed at many South Louisiana festivals, including the Abbeville Dairy Festival, Breaux Bridge Crawfish Festival, Crowley Rice Festival, Delcambre Shrimp Festival, Duson Round-Up, and New Iberia Sugarcane Festival.

But their main outlet was the "Mariné Show," which they hosted every Sunday morning from 9:30 to 11 on Channel 10, KLFY-TV Lafayette. The title came from the French word *amariné*, meaning well seasoned, and the program was certainly that, featuring as it did a spicy mix of Cajun, country, folk, and spiritual songs; the theme tune was Cliff Bruner's "Jessie Polka." Swallow Records issued a charming companion album, "Cajun And Country Songs And Music From Mariné," featuring a collection of mostly original tunes—including the popular "Bayou Lafourche"—with jaunty string-band accompaniment.

During the mid-sixties the deep-voiced Happy Fats aired his political feelings in a series of controversial releases for Jay Miller's Rebel Records and had a big underground hit with "Dear Mr. President." "It was a civil rights thing," he says, "when they were pushing us down here. It sold over 250,000 copies and Jay Miller gave me a gold record. We didn't have any problems with that, not at all. There wasn't anything violent about it, it was just a joke. I had a car of black people run me down on the highway one time coming in Lafayette and they said, 'Are you the fellow that made "Dear Mr. President"?' I said I was and they said, 'We'd like to buy some records,' they bought about fifteen records. There was a big van full of black people and they loved it. Actually when all this was happening we always got along with the black people down here, that's the Cajun people. And either side at that time they didn't want integration very much, they wanted to go each their own way. And if you notice nowadays it's getting back to where they want to go their own way."

Opening with the refrain *The United States of America, land of the brave and the free,* "Dear Mr. President" was a spoken address by a "confused American" to President Johnson, its message relished by many conservatives and hated by the liberal-minded:

Dear Mr. President,
Pardon me for taking some of your valuable time but before I start my next year's crop I'd appreciate it if you'd get a few things straight for me. The Supreme Court and some of our legislators have changed so many things that our constitution and our forefathers stood for, I'm all confused.

First, I'd like to know if I'll be permitted to plant white and black peas in separate rows of equal length or will I have to mix them together? . . .

My white coon dog won't hunt with my black bird dog. Could I get an injunction to make them hunt together? The black dog won't hunt coons and the white dog won't hunt birds. Do you suppose the judge could use legal persuasion on them or will you send troops to make them hunt together?

Happy Fats felt he had a message to deliver as he ploughed headlong into other provocative political titles like "Birthday Thank You Tommy From Viet Nam," "A Victim Of The Big Mess (Called The Great Society)," "The Story Of The Po' Folks And The New Dealers," and "Vote Wallace

In 72." Usually he was backed by a hillbilly quartet. In 1973 he poured his thoughts into a self-published little blue book called *(What Has Made South Louisiana) God's Special Country;* in it he also recalled the many personalities he had met during a lifetime in music and politics. Typically, he did not mince words: "If anyone is glorified in this book they deserve it," he wrote, "and if anyone is belittled they deserve it too!"

Prior to a serious illness in 1980 (from which he was still recovering two years later) Happy brought his story up to date: "I can't stand up there every night and play, I've got to sit down some. My old fiddler 'Uncle' Ambrose Thibodeaux and his invalid son Merton, he plays electric piano, are in my band. It shows you the Cajun influence, they all insist on Cajun music. The Cajun music and the crawfish go together, one has helped the other! I'd like to add this too, I say Cajun, I don't say French, I don't like to be called a Frenchman, I'm a Cajun. . . . But God's with me, in the music business there's no retiring. You don't have no social security or nothing like that. If you don't save none you're in bad shape. I had a television show for about twelve years, then I went back to radio. Went on KXKW at Lafayette, I stayed there about eight or nine years, then I went to KSIG Crowley. It goes out six to seven on Saturday morning and twelve o'clock on Sunday afternoons for two hours. I record it here at my house and I just bring in the tapes. I've always had a little studio back there that I do my recording."

A major Cajun personality since his days with the Rayne-Bo Ramblers in the thirties, Happy Fats has been a great popularizer of Cajun music. He has remained loyal to his sentimental form of Cajun-country music—and to the Cajun heritage—through many different trends. Jay Miller expresses local admiration when he says: "I've got so much respect for Happy Fats and others like him, they just went on as if nothing happened, kept at it. Fats kept on playing his country music, and making real country and Cajun records."

5

"Well, I don't know what it was, the man said it was Cajun music"

Lake Charles, some thirty miles from the Texas border, is a clean, prosperous town surrounded by lakes and bayous. Trees line the streets, providing welcome shade during the languid, steamy-hot summers, and a delightful white sand beach adds to the scenic beauty. Lake Charles is the seat of the parish of Calcasieu—an unusual word meaning "crying eagle," said to have been the name of an Attakapas Indian chief. The town's main wealth is derived from the nearby oil fields, sulphur mines, and timber forests, whose products are channeled through the busy port, third in size in Louisiana after New Orleans and Baton Rouge. With its large Cajun French population, Lake Charles is also a music town—and the home of record men George Khoury and Eddie Shuler.

Both Khoury and Shuler started out recording a more rural form of Cajun music than Jay Miller. Between them the Lake Charles producers can take credit for boosting the careers of such legendary Cajun musicians as Nathan Abshire, Lawrence Walker, and Iry LeJune; the two record men later had considerable success with other South Louisiana artists.

Like Jay Miller, George Khoury became aware of the postwar demand for Cajun music when he opened a record store during the late forties. The shop is still located at 328 Railroad Avenue, a sad-looking single-story building next to the austere railroad station. The new Interstate 10 freeway has cut off the neighborhood from downtown Lake Charles, leaving an air of gentle decay over what once must have been a thriving black section of town. Certainly the store is now on the wrong side of the tracks. "George had the record shop all the time," says friendly rival Eddie Shuler, "it's still in the same place ... At that point in time that was the only record shop in Lake Charles, that was it. They had to go there to buy their records, and he had the total business. I think he did pretty good in the record shop, and then he was a lucky rascal. Everything he did get hold of would be a hit!"

A slight man of Turkish extraction, George Khoury started in the recording business when he financed Virgil Bozeman's O.T. Records in 1949. After the success of Nathan Abshire's "Pine Grove Blues," George

45

set up his own Khoury's and Lyric labels in 1950. "He recorded quite a bit
of Cajun music," says record man Floyd Soileau of Ville Platte, "quite a bit
of all types of music from the area, from Beaumont to Lake Charles and
the Jennings area. He had some early Nathan Abshire hits, he had some
early Lawrence Walker. . . . Yes, he did have some of the hits."

Lawrence Walker played classic mainstream Cajun music. His biggest
hits for George Khoury were "Evangeline Waltz" and "Reno Waltz," both
released on Lyric in the early fifties. "Reno Waltz," named after the Reno
Dance Hall between Kaplan and Gueydan, was adapted from the favorite
Cajun tune variously called "T'Es Petite Mais T'Es Mignonne" and "La
Valse De Grand Chenier." Walker's performance was full of Cajun soul.
Backed by his accomplished accordion and exquisite twin fiddles, he sang
in a high tenor voice:

C'est la place que moi je voudrais mourir,	That's the place that I want to die,
C'est dans les bras de mon tite bébé.	In the arms of my loved one.
Je te demande pardon pour ça j'ai fait,	I ask your forgiveness for what I've done,
Moi je serais d'accord pour m'en aller dans grand Gueydan. . . .	I'd even agree to go to big Gueydan. . . .
T'es petite, t'es mignonne,	You are little, you are cute,
T'es jalouse, chère bébé, mais je t'aime quand même . . .	You are jealous, dear one, but I love you anyway . . .

With Nathan Abshire and Iry LeJune, Lawrence was a leader in the
accordion revival. By spotlighting the most identifiable instrumental sound
in Cajun music these men helped to halt the lemminglike rush of local
musicians into the arms of country music. Walker was known as the "King
of the Accordion Players"; during the comparatively lean fifties he and
Aldus Roger were the most popular accordionists in Acadiana.

Lawrence was not a full-bred Cajun, but he spoke Cajun French
perfectly. A rice farmer by trade, he was born near Scott in 1908 and
moved with his parents to Orange, Texas, in 1915. As a teen-ager he
formed the Walker Brothers group with brother Elton. Featuring accordion, fiddle, and guitar, the band played both Cajun and hillbilly music. Its
professional sound has been preserved on Bluebird recordings like "La
Breakdown La Louisianne" and "La Vie Malheureuse." In 1936 Lawrence
recorded "What's The Matter Now" and "Alberta" for Bluebird. His
bluesy approach gave the traditional Cajun sound an added dimension. In

the same year he appeared at the National Folk Festival in Dallas. Wrote Lauren C. Post in *Cajun Sketches:* "I was chairman of the Louisiana section of the National Folk Festival held in Dallas, Texas, in 1936. Members of the little Acadian band which played there were Lawrence Walker, accordion player; Aldus "Pop Eye" Broussard [from Rayne], fiddler; Sidney Broussard, fiddler; Junior Broussard, guitar player; Norris Mire, guitar player; and Evelyn Broussard, triangle player and singer. Walker and Aldus Broussard were also the singers, and Elmore Sonnier, an educated and trained Cajun singer from Scott, was a special soloist. The little band was so different and proficient in its folk playing that it was popular wherever it played at the festival."

After World War II Lawrence Walker played for many years at the famous O.S.T. dance hall in Rayne (this venue was not too popular with young red-blooded Cajun males because the lights were bright and the girls were always escorted by their mothers). He was also booked regularly at Landry's Palladium, near Lafayette. During much of the fifties, Johnnie Allan was in his band: "I was playing music with a steel guitar with Lawrence Walker and the Wandering Aces from 1953 to 1958. Lawrence was a big factor in French music, he and Uncle Joe [Falcon] were playing music along about the same time. His songs were all the sad melodic type songs, he was a very good accordion player, very well known in this area. I remember I played steel guitar with him for six years and the crowds were just tremendous almost everywhere we played.

"We performed at clubs like the O.S.T. in Rayne, the Welcome Club in Crowley, the Jolly Rogers in Forked Island, the River Club in Mermentau, the Bon Ton Rouley in Lafayette, and the Blue Moon in Lake Charles. None of the clubs was air conditioned and the cost was usually fifty cents per person. The audience varied in age from about fifteen years old to some in their seventies. Many times the whole family would be present, and liquor was not sold to those under eighteen. Generally we played from nine to one o'clock with no intermission. The band members pitched in to set up and tear down musical equipment, there were no roadies in those days! Lawrence's program consisted mostly of his recorded repertoire, songs like 'Reno Waltz,' 'Bosco Stomp,' 'Evangeline Waltz,' 'Chere Alice,' 'Unlucky Waltz,' 'Yeaux Noir,' and 'Hicks Wagon Special.' He played about four or five country and western songs, but the majority of the job was strictly Cajun-French songs, some recorded by other artists. He did allow other members of the band, including me, to sing a few songs. He was real good, very popular.

"Lawrence was a very proud man, he took pride in his music and always strove to get a good sound. I spent many days and nights at his house, it was easier to get back and forth to school. I have great admiration for the man, he went out of his way to help me get to school; his wife would have my clothes ready and my meals cooked. The last couple of years I played with Lawrence we traveled in style—he purchased a Cadillac limousine which I used on occasion to go to school. I felt like 'Mr. King' driving up to the high school in style!"

After leaving Khoury's, Lawrence went on to record for La Louisianne, Vee-Pee, and Swallow. In 1968 Flyright released the "Jambalaya On The Bayou" compilation, which included two zestful Walker tracks recorded live at a *fais-dodo*, his accordion gloriously dominant. That same year Lawrence died of a heart attack. La Louisianne issued a thoughtful tribute album that featured "Allons Rock And Roll" and "Lena Mae" (1959), two of the first Cajun rock 'n' roll numbers sung in English, and the wonderful old Khoury's hits.

Lawrence Walker and Nathan Abshire headed a powerful lineup of Khoury's/Lyric Cajun artists that included Elise Deshotel and his Louisiana Rhythmaires, Amar Devillier and the Louisiana Jambaleers, Will Kegley, Shuk Richard and his Louisiana Aces with Marie Falcon, the Texas Melody Boys, and Crawford Vincent. The hillbilly faction was primarily represented by Jerry Barlow, Jimmy Newman, and Eddie Shuler, while the blues contingent comprised Clarence "Bon Ton" Garlow, Richard King, and Emma Dell Lee. Without doubt the catalog was an illuminating overview of South Louisiana music in the early fifties. Although George Khoury's recording activities went into limbo with the advent of rock 'n' roll, he was to make a strong comeback at the end of the decade, not with Cajun music but with a new South Louisiana sound—swamp-pop.

In 1949 Eddie Shuler—the other Lake Charles record man—formed Folk-Star Records; a little later he set up the Goldband label, a name chosen for its "commercial appeal." At first Eddie released only a handful of charmingly primitive 78s, mostly by the great Cajun artist Iry LeJune and by Eddie's own hillbilly band, the popular All Star Reveliers. But over the years his Lake Charles studio was to become a favorite destination for many starry-eyed artists, perhaps the most famous among them the thirteen-year-old Dolly Parton.

A lively, aware man now approaching seventy, Eddie Shuler is truly down-home, with an irresistible folksy aura, right down to his distinct southern drawl and twinkling country humor. His business operations are based in a white-painted wooden building at 1468 Church Street, just around the corner from George Khoury's shop. Inside the scene is a real throwback in time, with rows of old television sets, scattered record racks, and an original 1933 Symphonic jukebox obscuring the entrance to the tiny, musty recording studio, itself constructed in 1952. Through the gloom, battered instruments and antiquated microphones filter into view, creating the impression that the technological revolution has yet to assert itself in this part of Louisiana; even the eight-track console machine does nothing to dispel this sense. Still, this is where many influential records— and a few big hits—were created.

Eddie Shuler was born of German-Irish descent in Wrightsboro, a small town in Gonzales County, Texas, and he will gladly tell you the year— "1913, I'm not Jack Benny now!" Music came naturally: "All of my life I had this attraction with music, but I was not hooked as much as I am today. It was just one of those things that evolved into what it is now. But I could hear a song on an old hand-cranked record player back in those days— didn't have radios—well, I could sing this song, the tune and everything. I was hearing songs like 'Valencia,' 'The White Dove,' and Al Jolson's 'My Mammy,' whatever Al Jolson did. And when I was grown, I still wasn't a musician now, mind, and I had no intention of becoming a musician. I just liked music. But somewhere along the process I wrote some songs."

In 1942 Eddie moved to Lake Charles to operate heavy machinery at the new City Services oil refinery. In his leisure time he started playing with the renowned Hackberry Ramblers, although his inability to speak Cajun French presented problems: "Sometimes the French singer wouldn't be there and I'd have to fill in for him. I could sing the words, but I didn't know what they meant. Then the dancers would try to converse in French. The bandleader would tell them I couldn't understand and that's when it got rough. They thought we were just putting them on—that I could speak French and just didn't want to talk to them. They would have been drinking beer and be pretty looped up. It got pretty squalid sometimes!

"Then I went out with my own band after that, Eddie Shuler and his All Star Reveliers. That was from 1945 until 1955, as long as that. Anyway I got quite well known and was given a four-days-a-week radio show on KPLC Radio in Lake Charles. We were a hillbilly band, we called it western swing—Bob Wills type of music, Bob Wills was my main influence . . . but of course I was always interested in a good song, and I'd sing any kind of song."

Just after he began singing professionally, Eddie had breathing trouble that necessitated voice lessons. He remembers, with a smile, the time his music teacher remarked, "you have a beautiful voice and you gonna waste it on that old trash heap, hillbilly music!" With the All Star Reveliers Eddie sang mostly hillbilly songs, but he always slipped in the occasional Cajun tune (as he did later on the band's recordings). He had more competition from nationally known hillbilly record stars than from Louisiana western artists, as he explains: "The popular hillbilly singers in

Louisiana in those days were Bob Wills, Ernest Tubb, Roy Acuff, and Cliff Bruner. Also there was the Spade Cooley thing that came along later, these were some of the memorable bands that we were influenced musically by. And then later Hank Williams came into the picture. Basically the music was western swing until the era of Hank Williams.

"There was one Louisiana fiddler, he played country and Cajun, which was named Will Kegley, and of course another group that wasn't from Louisiana was Moon Mullican, and Cliff Bruner who was right across the border there, fifty-five miles over in Texas. But in this area I was one of the few local country artists they had that could bring in any people in the clubs because at that time it was strictly Cajun territory. I wasn't all that interested in the honky-tonks, but I was like any musician, I wanted to perform and I wanted to expose myself to the public. And that was the only medium we had, we didn't have a choice, we had to go into the honky-tonks, the dives. And of course they had a few good clubs, but they had more dives than they had good clubs. I've seen people killed right on the front door, knocked their head against my car bumper and all kind of things like that.

"There was one time when I had a record that was a No. 1 country record in Southwest Louisiana, 'Ace Of Love,' which was a song I had written. It was my first monster, it was a regional monster, somewhere about 1951. We were playing in a place up in the woods west of DeQuincy, between DeQuincy and Maryville, Texas. And it was a bad road, they'd been working on the road, then there was rain a lot and you had to stay in the ruts to get to the place. So it was still raining and when we went it was like on a weekend and they had a fight there, which was a typical situation, but it was a little more extreme than usual. . . . And we got there and played, people didn't have any other place to go that night, so they all came there. So we had the place full, about five hundred people. And the fellows were all right till they get to drinking, like always they decided to tear up the place and throw it out in the yard or whatever, or beat up everybody in it because all of them are Hercules or whoever.

"So they all got into a fight and they had three deputy sheriffs there and the constable. Well, guess what, the deputy sheriff got up to try to stop it and he wound up on the bottom, then the next deputy sheriff got up to stop 'em and he wound up on the bottom. So they finally wound up, they had all these lawmen on the bottom of the heap and the thing was about twenty-five feet high!

"And of course the thing with a musician that you learned back in those days is that when they start fighting don't stop playing, you never stop playing. If you do, man, they're gonna fight *you*. 'Cause always you play to them, they'll never touch you. So boy I said 'Hey, don't y'all slow down,' 'cause this bunch was right in front of the bandstand. Usually they're in the middle of the floor, but the strangest part is if they're plumb on the other end they'll wind up at the bandstand. But you keep on playing and there they were, about twenty-five people out the front of the bandstand, and I guess they got tired and they finally stopped. And you could take and wring the blood out of those shirts. You know, they didn't have any more clothes on, the shirts were all laying on the floor. It was a horrible thing but there wasn't anybody killed, it was just a typical barroom brawl.

"We played from 8 until 2, it was a long stint. There wasn't any intermissions apart from one intermission of thirty minutes, about 11:30. We'd get all the way from thirty-five dollars to seventy-five dollars a night for a five-piece band. That was pretty good money for the time. The bandleader was a bookkeeper and, funny thing, he'd figure up each man's share on a pad of Bull Durham cigarette papers. Just zip, zip, zip right there on the papers."

Eddie was keeping extremely busy: "I'd play my music, book my band, and in the interim I'd sell my records to the jukebox operators. Travel around, we'd sell quite a few records at personal appearances." His own recordings appeared regularly on Folk-Star and Goldband, and some were even leased to T.N.T. and Khoury's. Besides "Ace Of Love," Eddie had good sellers with "Broken Love," "La Valse De Meche," and "Way Down Under Blues." In 1955 he decided to concentrate on the record labels and start a radio and TV shop. "I gave up the band because my wife didn't like me to play, too many girls, you know!" he quips.

Since 1949 Eddie had been releasing recordings by Iry LeJune, who played the purest traditional Cajun music. There was a certain innocent bravado about Shuler's business approach; Iry's primitive sounds belonged to another age. The two had first met on Eddie's KPLC Lake Charles radio show: "When Iry LeJune came to me he wanted to play his accordion, of course prior to that it was the fiddle that was in, with Harry Choates and this stuff. So I let him play on my radio show. Well the radio manager, Mr. Wilson, almost threw me out of the station for letting this guy play this ungodly music, as he called it. So I said, 'Well, I don't know what it was, the man said it was Cajun music.' Of course I wasn't new to the Cajun music of the fiddle, but I was new to this type. I had never seen this type of thing. And he said, 'Well, if I ever hear you do anything like that on my radio station again, I'm not going to just fire you, I'm going to personally throw you out the front door!'

"Shortly after, I left the station for other reasons, and eight months from that time he had eight hours a day of Cajun music on his show. Of course it was fiddle and accordion, a mixture. Because what was going on was the Cajun people then got together, and they'd go out and buy time, the Cajun business people would sponsor a given show. And the bands then got the publicity for playing and the advertiser got the benefit of the advertisement of this band that he got free. All he had to pay was the radio station. But they wound up having eight hours a day of Cajun music, so that created an interest in Cajun music.

"Then Iry LeJune said he would like for me to put out a record, but of course Cajun artists didn't have any money. But I was a salesman at that point in time and I had a little money—playing all the time, see, I was going on the roads day and night. So he said he had the address of where you make the records and the price was fantastic. Like nine cents apiece for the records, they were the 78s. I said, 'My gosh, they sell those things for fifty cents and they only cost them nine cents!' I thought it was really something. So I told him, 'Well, let me think about it.' He said, 'All I want is to have records out so I can play my dances and make money.' About two weeks later he came back and I said I'll try. I made seventy dollars off that first record. Well, I thought it was fantastic, I think we sold about six hundred copies. That was pressed on the West Coast, there weren't any pressing plants in this region at that time. And so we just continued from there. In that manner I was in a sense in the record business but I didn't realize it. So I kept on pressing his records because he kept on pressing me!

"Every time his dances would fall off, he'd say 'Well, I need another record.' So I said, 'Well, let's see what have we got, what do you want me to put out next?' because I always had a basketful of them hid back there somewhere. In the beginning we'd just go into the radio station and use their disc cutter, and we'd cut an acetate disc and I'd send that off to the pressing plant. It was simple, we didn't have anything invested to speak of in the monetary standpoint, except a few dollars tied up in the record. But the strangest part about it, I wasn't even interested in the lifeline as a record manufacturer. I was just trying to help him out and make a few bucks, that's all I was doing."

Iry LeJune came from the Point Noir area near Church Point, a remote farming region linked by dusty dirt roads that was a haven for the old-time Cajun sound. He was born in 1928, the son of poor tenant farmer Agness Lejeune, and was christened Ira. His musical mentor was his uncle Angelais Lejeune, one of the most popular musicians at *fais-dodos* and house dances in Acadiana during the twenties; as Angela LeJune, Angelais recorded for Brunswick in 1929 after winning an accordion contest in Opelousas against thirty-two other contestants. Because Iry's parents had no money to buy an accordion, he used to visit Angelais's house almost every day to practice on his uncle's accordion while Angelais worked in the fields. Iry was also influenced by Amadie Ardoin and Amidie Breaux.

Since he was nearly blind, Iry was forced to make a living from music. After moving to Lacassine, a small town near Lake Charles, he met Floyd LeBlanc, who took him to Houston in 1948 to record for Opera. Iry's first release, "Love Bridge Waltz"/"Evangeline Special," with its bright accordion sound, was a good seller and a jukebox favorite. Iry boosted his growing reputation by recording "Calcasieu Waltz" and "Teche Special" for Folk-Star, but most of his releases were on Goldband. Everything he did had a poignant beauty, whether he was singing "Duraldo Waltz," "Grande Bosco," "La Valse De Grande Chemin," "Convict Waltz," or "Lacassine Special," a favorite two-step among accordionists, joyful in tune but sad in lyric:

Hé, comment mais toi tu crois	Hey, how do you think
Que mon je va, mon je va faire,	That I'm gonna make it,
Tout le temps dans les misères,	All the time in misery,
Tout le temps après souffert,	All the time suffering,
Jusqu'à la porte à tes paroles,	All because of your words,
À tes paroles que toi, que toi	Of your words that you said to me.
tu m'avais dit.	
Oh, t'as chère vilaine manière	Oh, your dear ugly way
Que toi t'as tout le temps eu,	That you always had,
Faudra que j'oublie tout ça.	I must forget all that.
Si toi tu veux rester	If you want to stay
Avec ton cher nègre,	With your dear nègre,
Mais regard, mais tu peux voir	Well, look, you can just take
Le chemin et t'en aller.	To the road and go.

On record Iry sang as if two centuries of Acadian hardship were gushing out of him, and him alone. His wonderfully full and melodic accordion was usually backed by a simple guitar and fiddle. But his promising career—and his life—was wiped out while he was traveling home from a dance with J. B. Fusilier, formerly with Miller's Merrymakers. The car had a blowout on the highway near Eunice. While trying to replace the flat tire, the two musicians were flung into a nearby field by a passing vehicle. Iry was killed instantly and J. B. was hospitalized for many months.

Iry's records continued to sell after his death. Many of his rare singles are now available in album form, making it easy to appreciate his exceptional talents. "He could squeeze in more notes and still sound smooth and easy," says Eddie Shuler. "He could take a verse and stick in triplets and finger executions that no other Cajun artist ever managed. Even his songs were different, his songs told a story with reasonable situations."

Iry LeJune has to be ranked as one of the greatest Cajun artists.

Impervious to corrupt influences, his high-pitched hurting vocals and spine-chilling accordion work are the *classic* sounds of Cajun music. It is no wonder that he is the idol of so many young Cajun musicians today.

Inspired by the response to Iry LeJune's records, Eddie Shuler became more involved in recording Cajun music in the fifties: "Apart from the late Iry LeJune, who was about the biggest-selling artist in the field, I had some other popular songs, especially 'Lemonade Song,' by Leroy Broussard, and 'Sha Ba Ba' and 'Pestauche Ah Tante Nana' [The Peanut Song] by Sidney Brown," he says. Brown, who first recorded in the mid-fifties with the Traveler Playboys, had his old-timey accordion sound showcased in the Goldband album "Sidney Brown." An interesting and gifted man, he was a famed accordion maker and repairer in the Lake Charles area.

The late J. B. Fusilier, who witnessed the death of Iry LeJune, was another respected Cajun artist recorded by Goldband. Wrote Eddie Shuler in *Blues Unlimited* in 1968: "Jean Baptiste Fusilier was born in Oberlin in 1901, and is one of the few old-timers still playing. His interest in music dates back to his early childhood. At five he would play the violin providing someone would place the chin rest on his neck; his arms were so short that it was only with difficulty that he could reach the strings. He also tried his hand at the accordion and at the age of nine played his first dance. Throughout his teens he played both instruments and was considered very talented by his neighbors. While his friends played their games, J. B. was off by himself playing accordion somewhere. In fact, his whole life seemed to revolve around music.

"In the old days, dance hall operators would invite numerous musicians to play on one night, and the one receiving the greatest applause would then be hired. In this manner J. B. got his first breaks, for invariably he won, though often competing against far older people. In the mid-thirties he was extensively recorded by Victor, first with Miller's Merrymakers and later under his own name. Many sides appeared on the Bluebird label from these sessions, and firmly established J. B.'s reputation. After the war he continued to lead his own band, which included guitarist Preston Manuel and steel guitarist Atlas Fruge, but recorded only intermittently for Goldband. He is best remembered as the man who cut 'Ma Chere Basett' [Bluebird], one of the big-selling Cajun records."

Other early Folk-Star/Goldband artists included Lionel Cormier and the Sundown Playboys, Gene Rodrigue, and Aldus Roger. In the hillbilly field, Shuler released his own records with the All Star Reveliers, and recordings by such artists as Bill and Carroll with the Neches Valley Boys, Red Le Blance and his Crescent Boys, and Pee Wee Lyons (a steel guitarist formerly with Harry Choates). But before long Eddie was shifting his attention to rhythm and blues music and the short-lived rockabilly craze.

6

"I was tickled to death, we were just a country outfit"

Cajuns have traditionally drawn inspiration from the marvelously varied permutations of southern folk music, especially country and western music. It was only a matter of time before country influences, both lyrical and instrumental, became embedded in the Cajun sound. The result of this natural union is evidenced by the "Cajun-country" idiom.

The Cajun-country trend first emerged during the 1930s when Leo Soileau, the Hackberry Ramblers, and the Rayne-Bo Ramblers borrowed from the western-swing bands of Texas, as did Harry Choates a few years later. Other aspects of "hillbilly" music also had a significant effect in South Louisiana: cowboy songs from the movies, and the honky-tonk sound—a hard-hitting, folksy mix of fiddle, steel, and rhythm guitars from the tough southern beer taverns. Nationally hillbilly music suddenly found itself chartbound in the late forties when top artists like Eddy Arnold and the great Hank Williams began poaching more and more radio and jukebox time, quickly leaping into the coveted Cadillac bracket. The increasing popularity of this rural-based music could be attributed not only to the impact of records, jukeboxes, and radio, but also to the continued attraction of cowboy movies and to the steady northward migration of poor southern whites who still clung to their lyrically strong music from "down home."

The growing enthusiasm for hillbilly music is encapsulated in a 1947 *Billboard* advertisement: "The happy-go-lucky singing style is a natural for the jukebox trade. The songs are straight from the hills, and are sung straight from the shoulder. Be sure you have enough of these popular hillbilly tunes . . . the many radio fans will keep the calls coming in."

After the irritation of another musicians' union strike in 1948, big business was poised to take over in the country music capital of Nashville. The term "hillbilly," with all its backwoods implications, was immediately dropped in favor of the more civilized "country and western." Then the recording industry assured itself of an exciting future by introducing three new concepts: magnetic tape, making the recording process easier; Columbia's microgroove record, paving the way for the long-playing

55

album; and Victor's unbreakable 45 rpm seven-inch disc, replacing the cumbersome, fragile 78.

In 1947 Jay Miller showed his awareness of musical developments by forming the Feature label primarily for hillbilly recordings, and by phasing out the original Fais Do Do Cajun series. As hillbilly had always been his favorite music it was not a difficult decision to make. An early country signing, Bill Hutto of Orange, Texas, soon scored with "Some Of These Days," a typical honky-tonk weeper with backing by Doc Guidry and his Sons of the South. Miller began recording the promising hillbilly singer Al Terry and was later responsible for introducing two future Cajun-country superstars, Jimmy C. Newman and Doug Kershaw. Although the Feature catalog was growing steadily, Miller was still operating at grass-roots level, as he explains: "At that time the biggest problem was distribution. I'd get into my car and just load up with records and visit all the jukebox operators and music stores. When we'd get some new releases I'd wait for two or three of them, I'd just load up the car and get cracking!

"The recording process was quite primitive, first they came out with wire recorders and the quality was just no good, of course I didn't know what I'd do after I put it on wire. Anyway I got to reading up on recording quite a lot, then they came out with the tape recorder. I bought a Magnecord GT6, that was when we started making our own recordings, making our own master tapes. We first cut those records at my house, then we fitted up a small studio at my place of business. And it just grew from a one-microphone, one-speaker, one tiny recording deal, it's quite complicated now, we didn't have all this multirecording, multitrack."

In 1951 J. D. had some success with Papa Cairo's rerecording of "Big Texas," followed just over a year later by an Al Terry hillbilly hit "God Was So Good (Cause He Let Me Keep You)." The song had been written as a poem by Jay's wife following their son Jack's recovery from a serious car accident. Miller found the scribbled lines some time later. "I questioned her about it, it was in her handwriting. I realized why she had written it, so I got her to sing it for me. I got Al Terry to record it, a great song. That was his first big-selling record, it was on the strength of that record that I twisted Fred Rose's arm and got him a contract with Hickory Records."

Al Terry was destined to record country music prolifically for many years, enjoying particularly loyal support in South Louisiana. Born Allison Theriot, he was raised in the Acadiana of the twenties on a farm a few miles from Kaplan. He has fond memories of his childhood and of his introduction to music: "My maternal grandfather, Simeon Breaux, had been a leader of the only 'Old Folks Band' in Vermilion Parish, a brass band whose members consisted mainly of my aunts, uncles, and great-uncles, besides grandfather. He played several instruments including cornet, trombone, and clarinet, which was his favorite instrument. There is a good possibility that the only nonwind instrument was drums, as he used a tuba as opposed to string bass.

"My grandfather's band played mostly waltzes, polkas, two-steps, and probably marches. These songs were not the Cajun variety, but probably imported from France, England, and Germany . . . they may have played songs like 'Under The Double Eagle,' 'The Westphalia Waltz,' as well as some of the more popular songs of that day, such as 'After The Ball,' 'Bird In A Gilded Cage,' 'Shine On Harvest Moon,' 'Put On Your Old Gray Bonnet,' and others. The band played for dances in Vermilion and surrounding parishes which were attended by young people as well as their parents and grandparents. My grandfather also operated his own dance hall and continued playing until his death in 1911. This type of music continued to be popular with other similar bands through the twenties, until the small Cajun groups, with accordion, fiddle, guitar, and triangle, became popular in dance halls and on early recordings.

"My first interest was the clarinet, but since I enjoyed singing I became more interested in an instrument on which I could accompany myself. My father was a tenant farmer on my uncle's farm and I first learned chords on my cousin's guitar. Later my father bought me a $4.95 guitar from Sears-Roebuck. Another cousin gave me an old phonograph, the type you had to wind and used steel needles which had to be changed after playing one or two records. He also gave me a stack of old records, many of them chipped and broken. Among them were recordings of Jimmie Rodgers, Vernon Dalhart, Django Reinhart, Riley Puckett, Bradley Kincaid, the Carter Family, and many of the pioneers of country music and jazz; Gene Autry was becoming popular as a recording artist and movie cowboy. I was also tremendously interested in the recordings of Jimmie Davis, then public service commissioner in Shreveport. I met Jimmie during his first campaign for governor and we have remained close friends since then. In the early days, I managed to save enough money from time to time to buy some of these artists' newer recordings, especially the Gene Autry records, ordered from Sears-Roebuck catalogs.

"My brothers and I attended a two-room country school in Cossinade, a community consisting of four houses, a grocery store, a cemetery across the road from the schoolhouse where there once stood a church, and a crossroads. The school was staffed by two teachers, the principal Mr. Dallas Hayes who taught third and fourth grades in one room, and Mrs. Miriam Foote who taught first and second grades in the other room. The schoolmaster and his family lived in rooms adjoining the back of the schoolhouse. After my brothers and I had learned a few chords on guitar, we would gather along with the schoolmaster's son, D. G. Hayes, and play music in the schoolhouse at night. Some of the songs I remember we played back then were 'The Wednesday Night Waltz,' 'The Green Valley Waltz,' and 'Corinne Corinna.'

"Due to a childhood illness I was left with a lame leg, and remained in frail health for most of my early years. After I completed fourth grade our family doctor advised my parents to take me out of school to spend as much time out of doors as possible. Going on to the fifth grade would have meant taking a school bus every day to be transported to Kaplan, three miles away, where higher grades were taught. I spent the next several years doing what I wish I could do again—roaming the bayou country, hunting and fishing. I became a crack shot with a .22 rifle which my parents had given me, and could go out and bring in a dozen or so doves or quail faster than most could with a shotgun. During this time I spent much time playing guitar and singing. On Saturday nights on the farm we listened to the WLS 'National Barn Dance' out of Chicago."

Eventually Al was fit enough to attend Kaplan High School, where he received the American Legion Award at graduation. Then, with brothers Floyd and Charles ("Bobby") and another farm boy, he formed his first hillbilly band, "and believe it or not, the band was named the Drifting Cowboys, about fifteen years before the world heard of Hank Williams and his Drifting Cowboys. With the band we played mostly house parties and occasionally in a regular dance hall. When the first radio station went on the air in Lafayette, about thirty miles from Kaplan, we asked for and were granted an audition. We were given a fifteen-minute program on KVOL every Saturday morning at 10 A.M. On this program I would announce the song titles as well as any engagements we had. A. B. Craft, the announcer on duty (now manager of KPLC-TV in Lake Charles), told me one day that I had a good announcing voice, and would I be interested in coming in early each Saturday to do a five-minute newscast before our program went on the air. This was the beginning of my interest in radio."

During the war years Al continued in radio while Floyd joined the Air Force and Bobby went into the Navy, taking part in the Pacific landings, including the retaking of the Philippines. When war ended the brothers formed another hillbilly group, the Southerners. "I started a daily radio show on KVOL Lafayette with my band, sponsored by the Squirt Bottling Company of Sunset," Al recalls, "as well as a weekly show on KSIG Crowley and a three-times-weekly show on KSLO Opelousas for Red Chain Feeds. This led to a greater demand for personal appearances for the band, and for a long period of time I was booked for eight dates per week—every night plus a Sunday afternoon matinee."

Al Terry made his first record, "I'll Be Glad When I'm Free," for Gold

Star of Houston in 1946. A year later he joined Feature. Singing in a clean-cut manner reminiscent of the cowboy stars, he was accompanied by the Southerners, who provided a standard hillbilly backing of barroom piano, funereal steel guitar, whining fiddle, and jogging rhythm. Between Feature sessions he had auditions for the major RCA Victor, Decca, and Four-Star labels, but was rejected as "too pop, my delivery was too polished and smooth for country music." In late 1953 Al's contract was taken up as an unusual Christmas present to Jay Miller by Nashville music publisher Fred Rose, who was in the process of setting up the Hickory label. Al extended the season of goodwill by having a country hit with the memorably tuneful "Good Deal Lucille," produced by Miller in Nashville. Like Hank Williams's "Jambalaya," the song was written in an intriguing mixture of English and French:

> Goodbye Lou, cherchez vous another man,
> Say 'L'amour pour toujours' if you can.
> You're high class, you've got a past,
> Now you're a wheel,
> Ho ho, good deal Lucille.

Three years later he made a worthy rockabilly version of the song, which has been covered by other country artists including Werly Fairburn (from Folsom in East Louisiana), Moon Mullican, Jack Scott, and Carl Smith.

"Al came up with this song 'Good Deal Lucille'," recalls Johnnie Allan, "we were still living in the country back then, my daddy was a share-cropper—there was no TVs in those days—and I can remember the radio stations playing it quite a bit. That was his big hit, he also had 'Roughneck Blues,' something about oil, and 'Watch Dog' [for Hickory]."

"Good Deal Lucille" opened up a whole new world for Al. He was invited to tour with Red Foley and proceeded to work from coast to coast with many of the Grand Ole Opry packages. One of his proudest moments was being voted No. 1 new singer in a 1955 poll conducted by *Country & Western Jamboree* magazine. In the No. 2 spot was Sonny James, with Elvis Presley at No. 3. . . .

Al Terry has continued recording for many labels without ever duplicating his Hickory successes. His most representative recent release is "This Is Al Terry," an Index album containing remakes of his old numbers. Like Happy Fats, Al has remained faithful to his music, country music. Despite his French upbringing he has seldom recorded Cajun songs: "Although I grew up with Cajun music, speak the language, and am of French Acadian ancestry, I was drawn to country music through my exposure to early hillbilly recordings. On a number of occasions when I ran across Cajun material I felt would be strong, I considered recording Cajun music, but never seemed to get around to it."

In South Louisiana Al is still much respected as an artist and a person. "He lives here in Lafayette," says Rod Bernard, "he was a disc jockey for many, many years, I worked with him at KSLO Opelousas. Al is now with the Louisiana State Employment Department and he still plays some around here. But he's really dedicated to a career now, helping handicapped people. Al is handicapped, he is permanently confined to a wheelchair. He used to walk with a cane, but now he can't walk at all. And Al is helping handicapped people to find jobs and things like that. He's doing real fine, a remarkable man."

Lou Millet, another Feature artist, had built up a strong reputation in the Baton Rouge area, playing dances and making radio broadcasts with his Melody Ramblers prior to waxing the popular "That's Me Without You" for Jay Miller in 1951. Influenced by Hank Williams, Lou sang in the classic honky-tonk style for both Feature and Dot before progressing to country boogies for Ace and out-and-out rockabilly for Republic. He continued recording in the country-music field until the late sixties without ever matching his original Feature hit. " 'That's Me Without You' by Louis Millet," says Jay Miller, "well, that turned out to be a big song. That was a No. 1 song by Webb Pierce, Sonny James did it, and Warren Storm just cut it recently. My intention was to release the records and hope the songs and records would be picked up by the major companies."

Miller's strategy behind his shoestring Feature operation paid off handsomely after he wrote an answer to Hank Thompson's huge "Wild Side Of Life" hit called "It Wasn't God Who Made Honky Tonk Angels" and recorded the song with Al Montgomery, a young girl from Washington, Louisiana. "A friend of mine came in from Nashville, heard our Feature recording and took it back with him. And the second night after he got back Kitty Wells recorded it, 'course that got to be No. 1 for eighteen weeks. So that knocked us out, I was tickled to death, we were just a country outfit," reflects J. D. with pride.

As a song, "It Wasn't God Who Made Honky Tonk Angels" is of interest because of its early presentation of a woman's point of view. Its mood of hurt despair was plaintively conveyed by Kitty Wells as she sat in a bar, listening to "the jukebox playing the tune about 'the wild side of life'," a tune that reminded her how she had been a "trustful wife":

It's a shame that all the blame is on us women,
It's not true that only you men feel the same.
From the start 'most every heart that's ever broken
Was because there always was a man to blame.

It wasn't God who made Honky Tonk Angels,
As you said in the words of your song.
Too many times married men think they're still single,
That has caused many a good girl to go wrong.

The record was bought by women in droves. Although Kitty Wells, the modest Queen of Country Music, never adopted the woman's liberation cause, her success made the way easier for other female singers in the country-music field. (Cajun music continued to offer few opportunities for women, whose place was considered to be in the home; as artists, Cleoma Breaux, Marie Falcon, and Dottie Vincent were notable exceptions.)

"It Wasn't God Who Made Honky Tonk Angels" improved Jay Miller's status with the Nashville country music hierarchy. The hit song led to a songwriting contract with influential music publishers Acuff-Rose—and a firm friendship with co-owner Fred Rose. Like Al Terry, Jimmy Newman was an early beneficiary of this harmonious relationship.

As he surveys his 670-acre Singing Hill Ranch near Nashville, admiring his herd of Appaloosa horses and a few head of cattle, Jimmy Newman knows *he* is one of a rare breed—a Cajun artist who has made it. He has established himself among the higher echelons of the Nashville country set, yet he takes every opportunity to remind fans of his Cajun background. The Louisiana legislature expressed its appreciation of his crusading spirit by honoring him as "One of Louisiana's Foremost Goodwill Ambassadors." According to the citation, Jimmy was "endowed with a natural talent, and chose to serenade his listeners with a unique type of music, peculiar only to Louisiana, and one of Louisiana's richest heritages."

Like many Cajuns of his generation, he was born the son of a humble farmer: "I was brought up in the late twenties as a country boy, on a farm in High Point about ten miles from the town of Big Mamou. My mother is related to Dennis McGee, the Cajun fiddler. I was born of German, Irish, Spanish, French, and Indian descent! I was influenced by Jimmie Rodgers and the Carter Family records, also Bob Wills. As I was growing up we had the privilege of being able to come to town on Saturday night and seeing the western movies of Gene Autry and Roy Rogers. This played a big part in my singing influence later on. When I started in music in 1946 I had very little Cajun influences. I worked with a guy that was a Cajun fiddle player, Chuck Guillory, and I just learned to play Cajun music because it was typical for Cajuns to sing Cajun music. Later on in my career, a couple or three years later, I became familiar with the late Iry LeJune and thought he was a fantastic Cajun singer and accordion player. I also thought the late

Harry Choates was great, but I didn't become as influenced in Cajun music as I was in country music."

As a member of Chuck Guillory's Rhythm Boys, Jimmy specialized in singing hillbilly songs in English and a few Cajun songs in French. During a spell at a Lake Charles club in the early days of local television, the group appeared on a weekly KPLC-TV program. In 1951 Jimmy started recording for Feature, cutting Cajun-country songs like "Wondering" and "I Made A Big Mistake" without much success. Two years later, with Jay Miller's blessing, he financed his own Crowley recording of "Darling," which became a minor local hit when leased to Khoury's (this tear-filled honky-tonk song is better known as "Cry Cry Darling").

"J. D. Miller was in the recording business and I wanted to record," Jimmy remembers. "He was the first person to record me in English, I had done Cajun French before then with Chuck Guillory. We became friends and wrote songs together—'Cry Cry Darling' we co-wrote together. He was the nearest contact at the time, just a few miles away from where I lived. I recorded several sides for him and Feature Records in my early career."

Feeling that Newman needed to be in Nashville to expose his talent, Jay Miller convinced Fred Rose to accept the Mamou singer as part of the same "Christmas-present" deal that sent Al Terry to the country-music capital. After recording Jimmy at his garage studio, Rose changed his mind and transferred Newman's contract with the tapes to Randy Wood's fledgling Dot label in Gallatin, Tennessee, for the cost of the Hickory session—$492. At the session, Jimmy had rerecorded his Khoury's hit as "Cry Cry Darling" (the original recording could not be used since it was nonunion), and now his song shot into the *Billboard* country top-twenty chart in May 1954. Then he had hits with "Daydreamin'," which he admits was inferior to Bud Deckelman's soul-drenched original version on Meteor, and with "Blue Darlin'." The Cajun hero who sang country went from strength to strength as he joined the Louisiana Hayride, appeared on the "Saturday Night Shindig" and "Cowtown Jamboree" shows out of Dallas, and became a member of the Grand Ole Opry in Nashville.

In 1957 Jimmy had his biggest hit yet when "A Fallen Star"—"a ballad-rock song of the fifties, not strictly country"—touched No. 4 in the *Billboard* country chart before crossing over to No. 42 in the *Hot 100* pop chart. It seemed his attractive voice was suited to almost any kind of material; he even recorded rockabilly. During this pleasantly hectic period manager Slick Norris from Houston set up a battle of DJs to find a middle name for Jimmy. T. Tommy Cutrer of WSM Nashville snatched the prize by calling him Jimmy "Cajun" Newman. The "C." has stuck.

Leaving Dot, Jimmy continued to record mainstream country for MGM with only "A Lovely Work Of Art" making any lasting impression. In 1961 he went to Decca, scoring sizable country hits with "Alligator Man" and "Bayou Talk." Two years later he introduced his country fans more formally to his Cajun heritage when he cut the delightful "Folk Songs Of The Bayou Country" album with "Sugar Bee" accordionist Vorris "Shorty" LeBlanc and longtime buddy Rufus Thibodeaux.

Rufus Thibodeaux had been with Jimmy since the early fifties, touring, recording, and playing with him on the Grand Ole Opry. As Jimmy once said, "He's absolutely the greatest, there are a lot of other fiddlers, but none with his touch." Rufus was born in Ridge just outside Lafayette in 1934, and learned the basics of the fiddle when he was twelve. After a stint as a humble sideman in Papa Cairo's band, he started accompanying Jimmy in 1951; he also toured with leading country artists like George Jones and Bob Wills. In 1957 he recorded two haunting fiddle instrumentals for Starday, "Cameron Memorial Waltz" and "Mean Audrey," both named after a hurricane tragedy (Cameron is a small Gulf Coast town that was badly damaged by hurricane Audrey).

For more than a decade Rufus was also a session man at Jay Miller's Crowley studio; he was in great demand during the period from Feature hillbilly and Cajun to Excello blues, playing fiddle, guitar, fender bass, even electric mandolin. In the mid-sixties Thibodeaux moved up front to record a well-received Cajun album, "A Tribute to Harry Choates" (Tribute), with Abe Manuel handling the vocals. During the seventies he cut two worthy instrumental albums for La Louisianne, "The Country Cajun Fiddle" and "Cajun Fiddle." In 1980 Rufus left Jimmy Newman's band and was replaced by the enthusiastic young Wade Benson Landry, a former Louisiana State Junior Champion Fiddler from Abbeville.

Throughout the sixties Jimmy Newman was a consistent country chart-maker for Decca. Most of the time he recorded in the bland Nashville style, wooing choruses and all; his more memorable hits were "DJ For A Day" and "Louisiana Saturday Night." But then trends changed, with the synthetic country-pop productions taking second place to the earthy outlaw sound. In 1974, with nothing to lose, Jimmy turned to his Cajun roots and recorded the "Jimmy C. Newman Sings Cajun" album for little La Louisianne of Lafayette. "Well, I was never happy with the rhinestone image," he confides. Using the once-popular Cajun string-band lineup of fiddle, steel guitar, guitar, bass, and drums, he cut an engaging selection of favorite Cajun songs like "Jole Blon," "Grand Texas," "La Valse De Grand Basile," and "Cher Tout-Toute." The tuneful "Lache Pas La Patate" (a Cajun expression meaning "Don't drop the potato!"—in other words, "Hang in there!") was lifted from the LP and became a surprise hit along the Gulf Coast. In Canada, where Cajun music was finding a receptive market among the French-speaking populace, the single sold

more than 200,000 copies and qualified for a gold record—the first in
Cajun music history and, curiously, the first for Jimmy himself.

He followed this unexpected success with a storming version of Bill
Nettles's "Hadacol Boogie" for the Cajun Country label before rejoining a
Nashville company, Shelby Singleton's Plantation Records. Of the two
Plantation albums that followed, "Progressive C. C." was marred by an
odious fuzz guitar, but "The Happy Cajun" was an inspired collection of
traditional and modern Cajun songs with ebullient backing from his band
Cajun Country, featuring Rufus Thibodeaux, son Gary Newman (formerly
with progressive Cajun group Coteau) on bass guitar, and accomplished
accordionist Bessyl Duhon. Bessyl has impeccable credentials: he is the
son of Dixie Rambler Hector Duhon; played guitar with the Riff Raffs and
the Swing Kings, two popular Lafayette rock 'n' roll bands; and was a
member of the promising Cajun act Beausoleil before joining Jimmy C.

Jimmy Newman's welcome resurgence has done much for Cajun music.
He has the confidence to project the music of the bayous, and his country
fans are loving their introduction to the Cajun culture. His revitalized
popularity was proven by his outstanding successes at the prestigious
annual country music festivals in Wembley, England, in the early eighties.
And he has also reestablished himself with his own people. Happy Fats's
comments are typical: "Jimmy Newman is playing Cajun music on the
'Grand Ole Opry' now. Jimmy is very well thought of down here . . . people
think of him well because Jimmy has been pretty much help and he
hasn't forgotten his Cajun traditions. He's a good artist, he's a good
singer."

Jimmy himself revels in his present role: "I consider myself a Cajun, of
course, but as an entertainer I consider myself a country-Cajun. A Cajun
identifies very strongly with tradition, even today. Although we now live in
Nashville, none of my family can stay away from Louisiana for long. To be
Cajun, the music has to be about Louisiana, so that makes it unique.
Cajuns are pretty hot-blooded people, you don't play too many slow songs
down there. They have two speeds: off and full blast!"

Like Jimmy Newman, Doug Kershaw has made his mark in country
music by way of Nashville, and, like Jimmy, he recorded early on for
Feature. But parallels end there, for Kershaw's popularity with his fellow
Cajuns is not universal despite his deep Acadian roots. He was born in
1936 in Tiel Ridge, a tiny island off the Gulf Coast, and moved to Lake
Arthur with his mother and brothers Edward, Nelson (Pee Wee), and
Rusty after his father shot himself: "he was 41 but he was so weather-
beaten he looked 80," Doug recalled in his autobiography *Lou'siana Man.*
In Lake Arthur Kershaw learned English at school and accumulated
pocket money by shining shoes and playing fiddle on street corners. At the

age of eight he accompanied his guitar-playing mother at a local club, the Bucket of Blood—"and that is exactly what it was!"

In 1947 Doug moved to Jennings (now known as the "Cradle of Louisiana Oil"), and five years later formed his first band, the Continental Playboys, with Pee Wee and Rusty "in his Captain Marvel T-shirt": "When I was about 15 myself and my brothers had this Cajun French band with an accordion, guitar, and a fiddle, while we was going to school. . . . I didn't get blue ribbons or achieve any scholastic awards but I did pass. It was pretty rough, it gets pretty sleepy when you have to play nightclubs and stuff like that. . . . In 1953, we broadcast over radio KPLC Lake Charles but the furthest we was traveling from Jennings was 30 miles. Within that radius we were real popular, but beyond that, people don't speak French."

The next step was to cut a record, in English: "In a little town called Crowley, that was about 19 miles from Jennings, there was this gentleman by the name of J. D. Miller. He had a little recording studio, a record company called Feature Records. I had written a song and I wanted him to record it. And he did make the record ["When Will I Learn," as Douglas Kershaw with the Bewley Gang] and released it over the counter. But I think I got the majority of them. And then this went on for another year, and I was writing a song called 'No No It's Not So' and when I was about finished writing it, I was singing it, and Rusty walks in and starts harmonizing with me, and it was pretty. So we decided to go to J. D. Miller and put it down on tape for him to bring it into Nashville to get it released. And due to that, he calls me back the next day and said he'd decided to release the record on us so we rushed back in and put some more songs down. And this led us to Acuff-Rose and Hickory Records in Nashville. I was 18, Rusty 16. They called us Rusty and Doug. The first record we had out was called 'So Lovely Baby,' another song I'd written. And that really started my writing career as well as my singing career."

Rusty and Doug cut an enterprising selection of country songs for Feature before making the trek to Nashville in 1955 to record for Hickory. Unlike Al Terry and Jimmy Newman, the brothers did not enjoy immediate success. Their country-music career was hampered by the emergence of rock 'n' roll, and the duo took three years to break into the country charts (with "Hey Sheriff"). During that time the Kershaws were making progress with their personal appearances. Starting out at the Louisiana Hayride in 1955, they had a spell with WWVA's "World's Original Jamboree" in Wheeling, West Virginia, before receiving the ultimate accolade, an invitation to join the Grand Ole Opry, in November 1957. At the time they were singing in the close harmony style of the popular Everly Brothers, but their rising careers were halted when they were drafted in 1958. On their return from military service, the *real* Rusty and Doug stood up at an October 1960 Hickory session, recording three spirited Cajun-flavored offerings, "Louisiana Man," "(Our Own) Jole Blon," and "Diggy Liggy Lo." The Kershaws' bold projection of the bright, melodic music of their Cajun heritage, with energetic vocal harmonizing and Doug's exuberant Cajun fiddling well to the fore, paid off when they lit up the country charts with "Louisiana Man," a No. 10 hit, and "Diggy Liggy Lo," a No. 14 success. After waxing the popular "Cajun Stripper" for RCA Victor in 1963 the brothers called it a day as a duo. Rusty became an electrician with a national pipeline outfit while Doug graduated into Nashville's high society as a solo artist and writer.

By 1970 Doug was known as the Cajun Hippie, his jutting jaw protruding through his shoulder-length hair. Supremely confident, he was the darling of most rock critics, who were extravagantly describing his Warner Brothers albums as "a vivid example of contemporary Cajun music, a fusion of traditional backwoods country-folk and rock." *Rolling Stone* was nearer the mark when it noted that "though Kershaw is a Louisiana Cajun he is immersed in the universal solution of Nashville, star-studded Music City." The velvet-suited star even appeared in movies, and gloried in the publicity when "Louisiana Man" was played during the Apollo 12 moonshot. Rusty was not as lucky. He drifted into a dark world of alcohol and pills, but had some respite in 1970, when he cut a gutsy album for Cotillion, "Rusty... Cajun In The Blues Country," produced by brother Doug. Bluesman Lightnin' Slim, for one, would have been proud of Rusty's doomy version of "Bad Luck Blues."

Doug Kershaw is still entrenched in Nashville, making disappointing country-rock albums with little Cajun content. But he continues to make his large audience aware of the Cajun heritage through his dynamic live performances. In South Louisiana he is highly respected by artists and musicians for his musical ability and showmanship, but the Cajun audience still has divided attitudes toward him and his music.

Nevertheless, no country artist from South Louisiana—except Jimmy Newman, and, to a lesser extent, Al Terry—has come close to matching the accomplishments of Doug Kershaw. The lack of successors to this triumvirate of former Jay Miller artists underlines the impoverished condition of the homegrown country market since the beginning of the rock 'n' roll era. Nashville has been calling the country music tune in Louisiana, just as it has done elsewhere.

Back in 1953 and 1954, Jay Miller's Feature catalog was dominated by country music, particularly the classic honky-tonk sounds of Hank Williams and Lefty Frizzell. The label's aspiring Nashville stars and other South Louisiana singers like Wiley Barkdull, Joey Gills, and Dottie

Vincent were joined by a slew of Texas artists including Mack Hamilton and Smokey Stover, even disc jockey "Tater" Pete Hunter—all attracted by the accessibility of Miller's studio just off Highway 90. (Tracks by several of these country artists are being reissued by the English-based Flyright Records in its admirable series "The Legendary Jay Miller Sessions.") During this period Cajun music was just holding its own on Feature with occasional releases from Pee Wee Broussard and his Melody Boys, Lionel Cormier, Abe Manuel, Cleveland Mire, Aldus Roger and the Lafayette Playboys, and Louis Spell; Terry Clement recorded an early version of "Diggy Liggy Lo."

Recording was not Jay Miller's only musical interest. At one time he owned the El Toro club on Highway 90, where many of his country and Cajun artists appeared; had a radio show, "Stairway To The Stars," broadcast by KSIG Crowley; and was involved in "Louisiana Jamboree," a program networked by four radio stations from the Chief Theater in Crowley. But in 1955, with the country and Cajun markets suddenly in ruins due to the unexpected arrival of rock 'n' roll, Jay Miller decided to wind down his Feature operations. If he wished to survive as a record man he had to compromise with the new music; this he did. But, as alert as ever, he realized that there was still a considerable demand for blues records among the southern Negro audience. Yet another chapter in his life story was about to be written.

7

"The music got more primitive as you came to the Southeast"

Cajun music did not evolve uniformly throughout the Gulf Coast; there were—and still are—regional differences in the basic instrumental sound. In the rural prairie parishes of Acadiana (Lafayette, Vermilion, Acadia, St. Landry, Evangeline, Jefferson Davis, and Calcasieu) the accordion generally had the edge over the fiddle. But in the Southeast bayou parishes of Terrebonne and Lafourche the fiddle was dominant until the advent of the guitar and steel guitar. In East Texas, stringed instruments were favored, especially the fiddle and guitar, although the accordion was not uncommon. Singer Joe Barry, a native of the Southeastern region, gives his view of the intriguing local variations:

"As you move from Beaumont and Port Arthur, which is still solid coonass because of the oil boom back then, the music got more primitive as you came to the Southeast. Because these people are like rocks, you can go back and they can tell you who lived here 150 years ago, where their house was at. The music was different because when you got to my part of the country, it was more with fiddles than accordions. If you played the fiddle you were a lot more popular than if you played the accordion, whereas in Opelousas and Lafayette, in that section, the fiddle wasn't so much but the accordion was more the lead thing and as you got towards Texas it was the guitar, and it changes. That's how some places produced more guitar players, more fiddle players."

During the thirties the Southeast Louisiana music scene was influenced by New Orleans jazz and by the western swing of Bob Wills. After the war years, hillbilly music asserted itself at the expense of traditional Cajun music. With Ernest Tubb as their hero, artists like Blackie Dartez and Blue Melancon abandoned fiddles and began using steel and rhythm guitars, performing the popular honky-tonk songs of the day throughout the length and breadth of the breathtakingly beautiful Bayou Lafourche. "Jole Blon" and "Big Texas" were still an essential part of any repertoire, but traditional Cajun songs like "J'ai Passé Devant Ta Porte" were heard less and less frequently.

Vin Bruce, crooning his tuneful, sunny brand of Cajun and hillbilly music, adapted smoothly to this changing environment and quickly established himself as the most popular local artist in the area—a position he still retains. "Vin Bruce, he is the King," says Joe Barry. "He made it to Columbia Records back then, which was a miracle, for a Cajun to be on Columbia. They recorded him in English [and French] and he had a beautiful voice. He's still good, his voice is even better than it was then. If somebody would sign him up and cut him, he's got a Jim Reeves–type voice, real mellow and warm, just as smooth as velvet."

Ervin Bruce was born in Cut Off in 1932, the son of Levy Bruce, a trapper, fisherman, and fiddle player. As a child Vin listened to his father, but heard only one Cajun accordionist—"not like the people out west." Vin started his own music career playing guitar with Dudley Bernard's Southern Serenaders, a popular local hillbilly group which featured drummer Gatewood "Pott" Folse (Dudley is now a disc jockey with radio KLEB Golden Meadow and Pott owns a music store and a small recording studio in Raceland). In 1951, after a spell with Gene Rodrigue's Hillbilly Swing Kings, Bruce was discovered by Columbia Records' New Orleans distributor Henry Hildebrand while the young Cajun singer was broadcasting over a New Orleans radio station. Sent to Nashville, Vin recorded some delightful hillbilly and Cajun sides at the old studio in the Andrew Jackson Hotel, with a backing group that included top guitarist Grady Martin. The biggest seller of all was the haunting Cajun ballad "Dans La Louisianne," coupled with the jolly "Fille De La Ville." The success of this record led to appearances on the "Grand Ole Opry" and even the formation of a fan club. But his contract was dropped during the rock 'n' roll era and he was forced to retreat, without rancor, to a saner life raising cattle in South Louisiana.

In 1961 Vin resumed his recording career with Floyd Soileau's Swallow label, at the behest of producer Leroy Martin. Vin's first Swallow release was "Le Delaysay" (The Divorcee), a very old and sentimental love song brought to Louisiana directly from France. Recorded at the KLFT radio station (now KLEB) in Golden Meadow, Bruce's extremely relaxed version sold well enough to encourage Floyd to commission an album. After an extensive session only two songs were in the "can," but when the superb fiddler Doc Guidry was called in thirteen sides were put to bed in one night. The result was the LP "Vin Bruce Sings Jole Blon & Cajun Classics." Some fifteen years after Harry Choates, Vin made "Jole Blon" a hit all over again when the track was released as a single.

At this time producer Leroy Martin started playing bass guitar with Vin's group the Acadians, and "got him out of the honky-tonks and touring again." Another integral member of the band was lead and steel guitarist Harry Anselmi (who recorded for Jin as Harry Selma). Since 1968 the pivotal figure has been Doc Guidry, who now lives in Houma, where he works as a deputy sheriff of Terrebonne Parish. Vin, a naturally shy person, still did not capitalize fully on his considerable talent. He received several offers to return to the big time, but rejected them all. One particular instance is recalled by Joe Barry:

"When I was in Nashville in 1969 I talked Chet Atkins into signing him up, got him a free jet ticket and a hotel and everything. Really impressed Chet.

"Vin said, 'Well that's good, but not interested.'

"I said, '*Chet Atkins* wants to see you, man!'

" 'Well, he can see me in Cut Off,' and he laughed.

" 'Chet Atkins ain't gonna come to Cut Off. . . .'

"And he said, 'Well, I know that!'

"And that was it, the extent of the conversation. In other words, 'I'm not interested!' But he's eager to sing, I could call him right now in Cut Off, if you'd get a jug here we'll sit down and party, I tell you! But then about 80 percent of the musicians are like that."

Vin Bruce still goes his own sweet way, much preferring to be at home with his family to seeking the false values of the road, and he is quite happy to play house parties for free in the time-honored Cajun tradition. But his popularity is spreading again outside of Southeast Louisiana. He enjoys steady sales of his Swallow and La Louisianne albums, especially strong in Canada, and his festival bookings are increasing—in July 1980 he was proud to appear at the forty-second Annual National Folk Festival at Vienna, Virginia. Meanwhile his local status remains extremely high, as Johnnie Allan confirms: "Vin Bruce is a big personal friend of mine from down in the bayous. He and Joe Barry grew up together. Vin is still recording, he was just recently voted the Citizen of the Year in Lafourche Parish, which is quite an honor in that section of the country. You have to be an outstanding citizen and have contributed to the parish in some kind of way. And they figured his music and what he's done in other things to promote that section of the country merited him the award. The last time I saw him was for the Cajun Festival in Lafayette, and he was performing. Still doing it."

Gene Rodrigue, who had given Vin Bruce an early break, was another popular Southeast Louisiana Cajun-country artist. From Larose near Cut Off, Rodrigue started playing jobs in 1946 as a guitarist with his father, an old-time fiddler. He made his first record in 1953 for Folk-Star in a session that is remembered by Harry Simoneaux, then a member of Gene's Hillbilly Swing Kings: "The song was titled 'Dans Le Coeur De La Ville' (In The Heart Of The Town) and recorded by Eddie Shuler in Lake Charles. The solo part of this side was performed by me on alto sax along with a fiddle player, Leroy LeBleu from Jennings, who harmonized. In those days, this harmony combination was rather unique. We had no French accordion in our band, there were no accordions in our part of Southeast Louisiana."

After signing for Meladee, owned by New Orleans Capitol distributor Mel Mallory, Gene recorded an English version of "In The Heart Of The Town" with Sam Butera on sax. He had greater success with "Jolie Fille," a seminal Southeast Louisiana Cajun song, catchy and flowing, with a backing comprised of strong rhythmic guitar, soaring fiddle, and steel guitar, even a barroom piano. By this time Gene had already built up a strong reputation broadcasting live shows over radio stations WWEZ, WBOK, and WJMR in New Orleans and KTIB in Thibodaux and appearing with major country artists like Hank Williams, Jim Reeves, and Carl Smith.

Like many Cajuns, Gene was forced out of music by rock 'n' roll, but he picked up his guitar again after opening a lounge in Lockport. In 1960 he generated some action with the steaming rocker "Little Cajun Girl," which was recorded by Leroy Martin at Cosimo's Studio in New Orleans with Tommy Ridgley's rhythm and blues band and "a couple of Fats Domino musicians." The record appeared on no less than three labels—Richland, Jin, and Rod (the last two owned by Floyd Soileau). Gene also had a small Cajun hit with the attractive "Le Jour Est La" on Rod. Harry Simoneaux brings the story up to date: "Then Gene swore off music again, closed his lounge, and worked as an oil-field roughneck for three years, in time being promoted to driller. While working offshore he still managed to record a few songs on the Houma label and from there went to work as a salesman in a furniture store. He's still kicking and is a very successful life-insurance agent for National Life and Accident Insurance Company, Nashville, Tennessee. He was their No. 1 nationwide salesman for several years in a row and won trips around the world."

The tall, droll Harry Simoneaux played with Gene Rodrigue and with other top Southeast Louisiana artists like Vin Bruce and Leroy Martin during those prolific post–World War II years. Besides Cajun and country music, his story also embraces the "alternative" scene, including pop, jazz, and classical music.

"My dad Harry Sr. was born in Morgan City in St. Mary Parish. He moved to Lafourche Parish in the early thirties," Simoneaux says. "His family did not speak French, and he forbade me to utter a word of French, in his presence or not. He seemed to think that all of the other residents in his area who spoke French were not as literate as those who didn't. I was probably the only kid from Grand Isle to Thibodaux who was not allowed to speak French. Naturally I understood everything I heard in French because I was immersed in it daily.

"My dad would have loved to have been a musician, but his family couldn't afford to buy him an instrument. So he was determined that as his first-born child I would play something, whether I wanted to or not! He loved classical and pop music, so the first instrument he bought me was a violin, about 1943. But because there were no violin teachers for miles around I lost interest and sold the violin after only a few months. However, because Dad was a postmaster his job required him to make regular trips to New Orleans. When he returned from one of these trips he presented me with a used alto saxophone. This thrilled me to death!

"I soon joined the band at Golden Meadow Elementary School. At this same time my dad arranged for a music teacher to come to our house once weekly to give me an hourly private lesson. He taught me the rudiments of reading [music]. Two years later Father would drive me to a professor in Houma, about forty miles from home, to give me tone lessons and to teach me how to get a nice vibrato—he would make me sit for an hour at a time saying *ya ya ya!*

"Around 1945 Dad organized a band, the Blue Heaven Boys. He did love the song 'My Blue Heaven'! Everyone in the group was between eleven and thirteen years old, and the lineup was myself on saxophone, a trumpet, guitar, and drums. Dad would find jobs for us, bring us to all of these jobs, wait for us to finish our gig, and then bring all of us back home. He was determined to get something going . . . he also got us a weekly live spot on KCIL radio in Houma. Another thing Dad did was to travel to New Orleans to have this black saxman arrange all our tunes. Dad met him because the sax player's group, the Black Devils, used to play once a week at the Jitney Jungle club in Cut Off, my hometown. The Black Devils did only pop tunes. So, you see, we did have a little culture in our backwoods community! Needless to say our young group, the Blue Heaven Boys, was quite a hit in our hometown. We were the only [local] white group playing pop tunes. All of the other groups for miles around were doing country, but *without* fiddles or accordions. Another thing worth noting is that there was only *one* black family in our area. And this covered a stretch from Grand Isle to Raceland, about seventy miles. Because of that I did not have any black musician friends to influence me directly. After this group broke up I played sporadically with Gene Rodrigue and Leroy Martin, among others. One of the big clubs we used to play was the Bellevue Hall in Thibodaux. Later, the Bellevue was split in half and was moved to Galliano via barge! A few years ago, the club, measuring about 175 feet by 85 feet, was burned to a crisp.

"Then I joined up with Blaise Pasqual and the Imperial Aces. We played four or five nights in Grand Isle near Golden Meadow, and one or two nights in Franklin and Morgan City. This was during my summer school vacation in the late forties. It was about this time that bebop was coming in strong. Our group played mainly pop tunes, but we occasionally tried bebop—shades of Ornette Coleman! Then, after the Imperial Aces, I hooked on with Gene Rodrigue and then Vin Bruce."

Later Harry played saxophone in a Lee Allen–honking New Orleans R&B style with some of the best names in South Louisiana, including Bobby Charles, the Dukes of Rhythm (with Joe Barry and Joe Carl), the Swing Kings, and Johnnie Allan. Harry was also a regular session man with Jay Miller. Today he works as an industrial chemical salesman in Lafayette. "When I moved to Acadiana," he says, "it was quite a shock to my ears to hear fiddles and accordions. However, I learned to mix in with this particular side of our musical culture!"

The genial Leroy Martin deserves much of the credit for stimulating the Cajun music scene in isolated Southeast Louisiana. Besides promoting the career of Vin Bruce, he has achieved much as a musician, recording artist, producer, disc jockey, and songwriter over a thirty-year period. Born in Golden Meadow in 1929, Leroy was mesmerized at an early age by the hillbilly recordings of Jimmie Rodgers. Many years later he repaid this inspirational debt when he presented his rare Jimmie Rodgers picture record, given to him originally by Jimmie's widow, to the Country Music Hall of Fame in Nashville.

Leroy started playing music seriously in 1947, as a guitarist with Dudley Bernard's combo the Southern Serenaders, waking up to his native Cajun music only when Vin Bruce began recording for Columbia in the early fifties. In 1954 Martin left the Southern Serenaders to get married, and spent his honeymoon in Memphis, where he saw the last Barnum and Bailey vaudeville show and met the young Elvis Presley. Music was at the crossroads, and Leroy was there. Quickly displaying his musical vision, he formed the Rebels in 1955 to play "semicountry and rock"—in other words, rockabilly. Two years later he made his first record, "Keen Teen Baby"/"Upon This Day," which he released on his own Delta label. "It was meant to sound like 'Decca,' " he says of the name, "only major labels were selling then. I pressed 500 copies and was left with 400!" After this he played with the local Dominoes group before joining the Vikings, who were backing his cousin Joe Barry.

Leroy made his name as a record producer in the early sixties, first with Vin Bruce ("Jole Blon" for Swallow) and then with Joe Barry ("I'm A Fool To Care" for Jin). Often using Cosimo's Studio in New Orleans, he also supervised several sessions for Cajun record man Huey Meaux, notably with Jimmy Donley, Mickey Gilley, and Barbara Lynn. He had not forsaken his own recording career; as Lee Martin he had a handful of worthwhile swamp-pop singles for Jin, including Jimmy Donley's "Born

To Be A Loser" and Rollee McGill's gorgeous "There Goes That Train."
Later he recorded for the Houma label owned by Eldridge Robichaux and
Rod Rodrigue. More recently he has been content to act as manager for
Vin Bruce, and to play bass guitar in Vin's group. Through the years Leroy
has maintained an active interest in radio. Making his debut in 1948, he
became a well-known disc jockey over KTIB Thibodaux, hosting the
"Leroy Martin Show" and playing country and Cajun records. As the
"Cajun Cousin" he still broadcasts weekly over KTIB. He has also
composed over eighty songs, written columns for several Louisiana weekly
papers, and even compiled a Vin Bruce discography. Incredibly, his
involvement in music has always been secondary to his vocation as chief
deputy assessor of Lafourche Parish.

Despite the proximity of Southeast Louisiana to New Orleans, rural
Cajun music was effectively shut out of the Crescent City itself by the
combined might of dixieland jazz and rhythm and blues. Although many
prewar Cajun recordings had been cut in New Orleans, Cajun sessions
there began to diminish in number as studios started springing up in
South Louisiana. Not surprisingly the music was almost totally ignored by
New Orleans record-company owners and producers, although in the mid-
fifties there were two exceptions, Mel Mallory of Meladee with Gene
Rodrigue and Art Petivan of Arcadia with humorist Marion Marcotte,
who was singing at the time with Gilroy Jesselin and his Arcadians.

Over in oil-rich East Texas, on Cajun music's sophisticated western
front, the local scene was kept bubbling in the buoyant, optimistic years
following World War II by the personal appearances of such artists as
Harry Choates, the Hackberry Ramblers, Floyd LeBlanc, Iry LeJune,
Papa Cairo, and Leo Soileau, assisted by the presence of record
companies like Gold Star, Opera, Hot Rod, and T.N.T. In 1952 Cajun
music received a direct boost from Texas when Link Davis had a big hit
throughout the South with the traditional Cajun classic "Big Mamou"
(OKeh). His recording, with alternate verses in French and English,
inspired cover versions from such contrasting stylists as Rusty Draper,
Jimmie Davis, Smiley Lewis, and Ella Mae Morse. The sleepy Acadiana
prairie town reveled in the unsolicited publicity:

> Why did you go away and leave me in Big Mamou?
> Left me for another, left me alone and so blue.
> Please come back, oh chère, come on back,
> Make me happy, live with me in Big Mamou.

Interviewed in 1955 on a farm five miles out of town, retired old-time
fiddler Doxie Manuel remarked in French, "I can remember 'Grand

Mamou' as far back as 1895. When I used to play for a *fais-dodo* it was just a sad, very sad waltz with no words. Suddenly, it would stop being sad and people would holler *Ah, ha, ha!* and would stamp their feet till the kerosene lamps would flicker and nearly fall off the table!"

Link Davis was born near Dallas, Texas, in 1914, and started as a fiddler with the western-swing group the Crystal Spring Ramblers in 1937. He was influenced by Harry Choates and eventually became adept at playing most forms of southern music. Besides "Big Mamou" he recorded such popular Cajun titles as "Jole Blon," "Allons A Lafayette," and a variant of "Hip Et Taiaud" called "Come Dance With Me." In the late fifties Davis became known as "The Man with the Buzzing Sax" after he backed the hit records of the Big Bopper and Johnny Preston. He died in 1972. "He was a great entertainer," says Jimmy Newman. "He took an old traditional song, 'Grand Mamou,' and turned it into an international hit and a standard."

8

"Rock 'n' roll had taken over completely, I was shocked!"

Elvis Presley's famous 1954 Sun sessions in Memphis, Tennessee, ushered in a new breed of country artist. He was young, confident, with slicked-back hair and disrespectful good looks. His music was loud, deafeningly loud, with relentless rhythms generated by eccentric electric guitars and strident string basses. Country music had been given a shot of rhythm and blues; rockabilly was making its dramatic entrance, and the rock 'n' roll age was dawning.

Scotty Moore, the guitar player who changed Elvis Presley's world, gave a beautiful definition of "rockabilly" to writer Peter Guralnick: "It had been there for quite a while, really. You see, from the honky-tonks you got such a mixture of all different types of music, and I think what happened is that when Elvis busted through it enabled all these other groups that had been going along more or less the same avenue—I'm sure there were hundreds of them—to tighten up and focus on what was going to be popular. If they had a steel guitar they dropped it, the weepers and slow country ballads pretty much went out of their repertoire. And what you had left was country-oriented boogie music."

Helped by Elvis Presley's barnstorming appearances on the Louisiana Hayride, the revolutionary rocking sound spread with frightening rapidity to South Louisiana. Country music, which had innocently provided rock 'n' roll with its initial platform, was almost wiped out in the process. Cajun music, like other regional forms, also teetered on the brink in the face of this frontal attack. Several South Louisiana artists added "country rock 'n' roll" to their repertoires, but Al Ferrier and Johnny Jano were the only notable local rockabilly performers.

Al Ferrier was a young country singer from Montgomery in central Louisiana whose first two singles, "No No Baby" and "My Baby Done Gone Away," were pleasant country boogies recorded for Goldband in Lake Charles in 1955. If this was the birth of rockabilly, as Eddie Shuler impishly claims, it was a very quiet beginning. There was no doubt, though, that Ferrier could whip up a good Carl Perkins–type sound with his accomplished group the Boppin' Billies; the exceptional lead guitarist was his brother Brian Ferrier, who had played with Hank Thompson and the Alcan Playboys and accompanied Elvis Presley on the Louisiana Hayride. Playing much of the time in the Acadiana area, Al tried his luck with Jay Miller in 1957. His first Crowley single, "Hey Baby" (Excello), was classic rockabilly; the grease simply oozed from the grooves. Ferrier exuded all the brashness the rock 'n' roll idiom demanded:

Well, hey baby, come on over here,
And let's go boppin' tonight.   (repeat)
Well, with all this lovin' I'll always treat her right.

Well, I got the car, got a lot of mon',
Come on little baby, let's have some fun . . .

But "Hey Baby" did not sell, and Al did not repeat this artistic triumph. After recording much lethargic material for Miller's own labels he hung up his guitar. A decade later, inspired by the astonishing European rockabilly revival, he came out of retirement and recorded again for both Eddie Shuler and Jay Miller, with variable results. But commercial success has continued to elude Ferrier, as drummer Warren Storm affirms: "Al never had a real big hit. At the moment he is working and playing on the weekends in Natchitoches, just around his hometown. He's doing country and western and some of the old fifties things. I am surprised he was never a superstar, all the talent that he has."

Johnny Jano's enthusiastic "Havin' A Whole Lot Of Fun" was another excellent slab of Louisiana rockabilly with echo-laden vocals, primeval guitar, and slapped upright bass. Made in late 1956, it was the first Jay Miller rockabilly recording leased to Excello. But the Nashville label's promotional facilities were geared strictly to the *blues* markets of the South, and Jano's single, like Ferrier's, was ignored. Twenty years later the session warm-up tapes were released in album form by Flyright, to belated acclaim.

Johnny Janot (he dropped the *t* early in his performing career) was born in the small town of Eunice in the heart of Acadiana. He played Cajun and country music before switching to rockabilly with his group the Jumpin' Jacks. After the Excello single he recorded the rock 'n' rolling "Mabel's Gone" for Goldband in 1957; he later made sporadic recording forays into the country-music field, primarily on the Jador label. He has recently cut two Cajun albums, "Sings Cajun Pure" (Goldband) and "I'm Proud To Be A Cajun" (Delta, of Texas), the latter release with support from the excellent Phil Menard and the Louisiana Travelers. Johnny's lifeblood is his original love, the radio. While living in Eunice he became a disc jockey at the local KEUN station; later he moved to KLOU Lake Charles. He now hosts the very popular "Cajun Bandstand" show beamed by KLVI Beaumont every Sunday morning. Heard from Corpus Christi, Texas, to New Orleans, the broadcast is so successful that there is a waiting list of advertisers. Johnny also has a regular newspaper column, "Johnny's Jambalaya," and he still plays music on weekends. Again known as Johnny Janot (with the *t*), he is a splendid supporter of South Louisiana music.

Jay Miller's commitment to rockabilly was never strong. After the failure of the Excello singles by Ferrier and Jano, Miller was unable to find a suitable outlet for his rebel rockers. Indeed, most of his recordings in the genre—by Milton Allen, Ervin Babin, Arnold Broussard, Tony Perreau, and Pee Wee Trahan—remained stubbornly on the shelf until the tapes were released by Flyright during the late seventies.

By the end of 1957 rockabilly was losing much of its country flavor, becoming just another facet of rock 'n' roll. This advanced metamorphosis mattered little to Eddie Shuler: "The rock 'n' roll days were some of my wildest times in the music world. The sound was new and different, everyone was a pioneer! I had the usual bunch of 'me-too' boys with doting parents, but I did manage to turn out some good records, which sold well enough to help me and the artists. Besides Al Ferrier and Johnny Jano, some of the more memorable people that I recorded in this field were Gene Terry and Larry Hart."

"Cindy Lou" by Gene Terry and his Down Beats was a wild, unforgettable sax-guitar-piano rocker that was a generation removed from the restrained bluesy original by Shelton Dunaway and the Boogie Ramblers, also on Goldband. In contrast, the selling side "Teardrops In My Eyes" was accorded a sensitive teen-vocal-group treatment, full of swampy feel. Nothing else Gene Terry recorded possessed the same supercharged energy—or magic.

Larry Hart had good Goldband singles in "I'm Just A Mender" and "Coffins Have No Pockets," but his true talents were not revealed until 1973. On an anthology album entitled "Bayou Rock," Eddie Shuler included six unissued 1958 tracks by Hart, ranging from the bouncy commercial rockabilly of "Oh Nelly" and "Good Rocking Joe" to the more classical primitive sounds of "Freight Train" and "Come On Baby." And that was not all: "Slim Needle" with Johnny Duhon's Yellow Jacket Band was compelling R&B, while "My Glass Is Empty" was heavy country. Larry Hart was portraying rockabilly at its varied best.

The other significant Goldband rockabilly singer was Little Billy Earl, who turned in romping performances on "Couple In The Car" and "Go Dan Tucker."

Why didn't the South Louisiana rockabilly artists make more impression locally? Johnnie Allan probably has a valid explanation when he says,

"People associate rockabilly so much with Elvis Presley and Carl Perkins, and anybody around here that would try to make it in that particular field, well, they were just second to them."

These were traumatic times for South Louisiana's Cajun and country musicians, as Lee Lavergne, the Church Point record man, perceptively recalls: "In 1953 I left the United States after joining the services, but when I got back in April '55, the whole scene had changed. Rhythm and blues and rock 'n' roll had taken over completely, I was shocked! I didn't know what was going on because in Korea things hadn't changed. Rock 'n' roll hadn't reached over there yet, it hadn't hit over there, the bands we'd hear over there were Koreans, Japanese playing like Glenn Miller stuff, the old stuff. And here I am back, rhythm and blues, rock 'n' roll! Very little French, it was still around, but very little, the French bands were for the old people and the dancers, you still had some but it had dropped considerably. But there was no country no more, what were once your country bands were trying to go rock and roll to survive."

For the older Acadian musicians survival came through perseverance with the original Cajun and Cajun-country format; for the younger artists, it came in the form of their own rock 'n' roll music—swamp-pop.

Atchafalaya River, 1980.   *Charley Nilsson*

Swamp Scene, 1980.   *Charley Nilsson*

Fais-dodo at Crowley, 1938. *Library of Congress*

Cleoma Breaux and Joseph Falcon, 1929. *Courtesy Johnnie Allan*

"Fe Fe Ponchaux," 1929.   *Bill Greensmith*

Leo Soileau (fiddle) with Crawford Vincent (guitar), 1946.
Courtesy Crawford Vincent

Leo Soileau and his Boys with Papa Cairo (steel guitar), ca. 1947.
Courtesy Chris Strachwitz

Hackberry Ramblers with Luderin Darbone (fiddle), Eddie Shuler (guitar, next to Darbone), Edwin Duhon (guitar, seated), and Lennis Sonnier (guitar), ca. 1945. *Courtesy Eddie Shuler*

Happy Fats (guitar, right) and the Rayne-Bo Ramblers, ca. 1936.

Courtesy Happy Fats

Harry Choates and Band, ca. 1947.　　　　*Courtesy Chris Strachwitz*

**Billboard
advertisement, 1947.**

"Jole Blon," 1946.   *Bill Greensmith*

Nathan Abshire and the Pine Grove Boys, 1967.
Mike Leadbitter

"Pine Grove Blues," 1949.
Bill Greensmith

"Evangeline Special," 1948.
Bill Greensmith

"Tolan Waltz," 1948.
Bill Greensmith

"Fais Do Do Breakdown," 1947.
Bill Greensmith

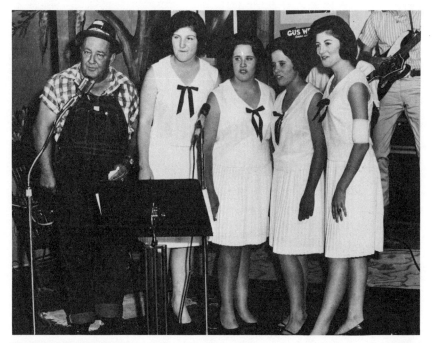

Happy Fats, ca. 1965.   *Courtesy Jay Miller*

Arhoolie album of Khoury's/Lyric masters.
Bill Greensmith

O.S.T. Nite Club, Rayne, 1980. *John Broven*

Lawrence Walker, ca. 1936.
Courtesy Pierre Daigle

Khoury's Record Shop, 1979.
Paul Harris

Goldband headquarters, 1979. *Paul Harris*

Iry LeJune and his Band with Robert Bertrand (drums), Wilson Granger (fiddle), Alfred "Duckhead" Cormier (guitar), ca. 1953.

Courtesy Eddie Shuler

North Parkerson Avenue, Crowley, 1979. *Paul Harris*

Al Terry and the Southerners with Bob Terry (steel guitar), 1950.
Courtesy Al Terry

Lou Millet, 1952.
Courtesy Rod Bernard

Jimmy Newman, 1954.
Courtesy Jay Miller

Doug Kershaw and the Continental Playboys with Rusty Kershaw (guitar), ca. 1953.
Courtesy Doug Kershaw

Billboard advertisement, 1961.

Country Band at El Toro club, Crowley, ca. 1960. Abe Manuel (fiddle), Pee Wee Trahan (guitar), Pee Wee Whitewing (steel guitar), Bobby McBride (bass guitar), Al Foreman (guitar), unidentified drummer.

Courtesy Jay Miller

Vin Bruce, 1967.   *Courtesy Leroy Martin*

"Dans La Louisianne,"
1952.   *Bill Greensmith*

**Gene Rodrigue (guitar), Harry Simoneaux (saxophone), Gerald Guidry
(drums), ca. 1950.** *Courtesy Gene Rodrigue*

"Jolie Fille," 1954.
Bill Greensmith

Southern Serenaders with Leroy Martin (guitar), Harry Anselmi (steel guitar), Pott Folse (drums), Dudley Barnard (guitar), ca. 1951.

Courtesy Leroy Martin

Leroy Martin, 1955.   *Courtesy Leroy Martin*

Al Ferrier, ca. 1955.
Courtesy Eddie Shuler

Gene Terry, 1958.   *Courtesy Eddie Shuler*

Part

II

ZYDECO AND BLUES

9

"Well, let the Bon Ton Roula!"

Zydeco is a black French country-dance music that evolved from Cajun, Afro-Caribbean, and Afro-American traditions. Songs are sung in a Creole dialect by "black Cajuns," to an insistent—often raw—bluesy backing. Sometimes called "Zodico," "La La" (referring to an earlier rural style), or "French" (to differentiate it from black R&B and soul sounds), this indigenous music is played throughout Southwest Louisiana and East Texas. During the 1970s zydeco surprisingly became one of America's better-known regional forms following the splendid success of Clifton Chenier and the crosscultural experimentations of rock musicians like Ry Cooder.

The term "zydeco" is generally thought to be a creolized variant of *les haricots* (snap beans), inspired by the title of an old one-step tune, "L'Haricots Sont Pas Salés" (The Snap Beans Aren't Salted). In a wider sense, a zydeco refers, like a Cajun *fais-dodo,* to a country party with plenty of eating, drinking, dancing, music, and fun. The accepted spelling of zydeco was originated by Houston folklorist Mack McCormick.

The roots of zydeco music can be traced to the second half of the eighteenth century, when most of the French-speaking black and *mulâtre* people of Louisiana came to the state as slaves for French planters or as *gens libres de couleur* (free men of color) both before and after the Haitian revolution. The new arrivals settled quickly among the close-knit Acadian family groups, easily adopting the Cajuns' customs, language, music, and religion; in turn they introduced to the Cajuns elements of their own cultures, including Creole folk songs. Through the years the immigrants' descendants—known variously as black Cajuns, black French, Creoles, or just *noirs*—evolved their own bluesy style of Cajun music within an Afro-Caribbean rhythmic framework, giving rise to the fast, distinctive syncopation of zydeco. Love in all its guises was the main subject, but there was also evidence of satire, ridicule, and mockery seldom found in Cajun music.

The predecessor of zydeco was "La La" or *la musique Creole,* which, like early Cajun music, was played at country dances and house parties. The embryo zydeco form developed rapidly during World War II when many French-speaking blacks took up jobs vacated by conscripted white workers in the Texas industrial towns of Houston, Galveston, and Port Arthur. For the first time the migrants' rural French music came into contact with the rhythmic blues sounds of the city. The shock waves of this musical fusion soon spread back to Southwest Louisiana by way of urban and rural clubs, church dances, and barbecue picnics.

Zydeco has continued to develop through the years. Musicians' repertoires are dominated by fast two-steps, blues, and—more recently—soul numbers, with few melodic waltzes. The traditional Cajun instrumentation has also been modified to give the music a heavy R&B bias: the focal point of most zydeco bands is the large piano accordion which allows a wide choice of harmony; the Cajun diatonic accordion, small and square by contrast, has buttons instead of keys and limited harmonic possibilities—the scale is ascended in whole steps. Another important instrument in zydeco is the rub board or *frottoir,* a relic from early Negro folk music which gives complex percussive figures when struck with the end of a fork or a similar metallic implement. Currently the saxophone is replacing the fiddle, while electric guitars and drums have become part of every group's equipment. But the dancing function of zydeco and Cajun music remains the same. "You can dance anything to zydeco," exclaims top artist Rockin' Dopsie, "you can disco to it, you can do the waltz on it, some people jitterbug, you can dance any way you like. Oh, they'll be kicking man, they'll be doing some high kicking!"

The first Negro-French recordings were cut soon after Joseph Falcon hit with "Lafayette" in 1928. The best-known early artist was Amadie (Amadé) Ardoin, who was affectionately called *Tite Nègre,* "the little black guy." On record he had a delightfully crisp, clean, crying sound; his singing and accordion styles were very much white Cajun. Ardoin was signed by Columbia in late 1928 after winning an accordion and fiddle contest in Opelousas with Dennis McGee, the fine Cajun violinist from Eunice. The tiny black accordionist went on to record for Brunswick, Vocalion, Decca, Melotone, and Bluebird, making such pure Cajun discs as "La Valse De Gueydan" (Brunswick), "Les Blues De La Prison" (Decca), "La Valse De Amities," "Les Blues De Voyages," and "Oberlin" (Bluebird). All told he made some thirty recordings, fourteen of which have been collated on a stunning Old Timey album; many of the songs are anguished laments to a woman named Jouline.

On his recordings Ardoin was often accompanied by Dennis McGee; in a way the two men were depicting the synthesis of the ancient Cajun and Creole styles. Between 1928 and 1930 McGee also cut some beautiful vocal and instrumental tunes in New Orleans with either Sady Courville or Ernest Fruge playing bass lines on "second" fiddle. An acclaimed Morning

Star album, "The Early Recordings Of Dennis McGee," features twelve numbers from these sessions. Included are the famous "Mon Chère Bébé Creole" and "Le Reel Cajun," where the spoken introduction is made in an amusingly self-conscious way: "Folks, this is genuine Cajun breakdown music as heard in the Evangeline country!" Since retiring from work as a barber, McGee has been booked at many folk festivals, performing an extensive selection of old Acadian songs in a classic fiddle style full of ornate melodic lines and cascading trills.

According to McGee, Amadie Ardoin was born around the turn of the century in l'Anse Rougeau, a tiny farming community between Eunice and Mamou. He was the seventh of seven sons. Ardoin and McGee met as sharecroppers on Oscar Comeaux's farm near Chataigner, and in 1921 their boss encouraged them to play together for house dances in the neighborhood. When Comeaux sold his farm, Amadie and Dennis moved to Celestin Marcantel's farm near Eunice and began to develop their musical partnership. Apparently Ardoin was not much of a worker in the fields, but his new boss considered his music an asset. Several nights a week after the day's work, Marcantel would hitch up the horse and buggy and transport Ardoin and McGee to dances in the country. After playing half the night for white dances, Amadie would return to the black community, sometimes alone, to sit in on dances that usually lasted until dawn. Canray Fontenot told fellow fiddler Michael Doucet: "Then Amadie would really get hot. After playing for the white folks—you know, two-steps and waltzes—he would get down on some blues and just sing and sing. He made up all those words and most of the songs he played, they didn't come from anybody else. He and my father Adam Fontenot would both play the old French songs, old African songs and hollers, and then make up something new, just their own."

Ardoin's popularity may have transcended racial barriers, but times were not easy for a black musician. Once he suffered a severe beating at a Eunice outdoor fair. Eventually he succumbed to alcoholism, and in the late thirties he was committed to the Louisiana State Institution for the Mentally Ill in Pineville, where he died. In June 1980 Amadie was justly honored, with Joseph Falcon, at the Second Acadiana Day at the Acadian Village in Lafayette. The crowds paid homage to the two musical heroes while enjoying the boudin-eating and pirogue-rowing contests, traditional Indian dances by children's groups, and, of course, the Cajun and zydeco music.

Amadie Ardoin had a mighty influence on many Cajun and zydeco artists, particulary Iry LeJune, Austin Pitre, and Clifton Chenier. A cousin, Alphonse "Bois Sec" Ardoin, is carrying on Amadie's tradition as leader of the popular Ardoin Family Band. Their traditional *musique Creole,* more Cajun than zydeco, has been recorded by several folk labels. Bois Sec recalled Amadie's impact on his career for writer Robert Sacré: "Little by little, I learned the different dances and practiced every day on my accordion. I continued practicing until I was good enough, but there is an enormous difference between playing for pleasure and at a ball. Then I followed my cousin Amadie, who traveled a lot. He was a professional musician and did not do any other work. I did not see him very often until we began to go to the balls together, I played all the balls he played in the neighborhood—*bals de maison* as they are called. One day it was one house, another day another, be it a wedding, birth, anniversary, or simply a Saturday night dance, *le fais-dodo*. Mamou, Basile, Lawtell, Eunice. . . . With him I learned to play really well. But that did not last long because my mother did not wish me to become a professional musician, and did not approve of these trips. Then Amadie became ill and he played less and less."

Fiddler Canray Fontenot joined Bois Sec Ardoin in 1948, and they played house dances as the Duralde Ramblers. Of the local fiddle style, Canray once remarked: "What I think makes our fiddle sound different is a special 'crying sound.' Like a baby. I remember how the old men used to shout at me, saying 'Make it cry like a baby, Canray!' Only Cajun or Creole fiddlers can do that. We do it by coming back on the high string and sort of choking it as the bow rubs over it gently. I can't say exactly how you do it, but I can do it. So can Mr. Dennis McGee and a few other old-time fiddlers."

Canray's father, Adam Fontenot, was a highly influential early black accordionist who was rated the equal of Amadie Ardoin as a musician but had a weak voice. Adam's second cousin, old-time accordionist Fremont Fontenot, is another member of the small, proud caucus of French-speaking black musicians from the Basile area. The Carrière Brothers, Bébé and Eraste, from nearby Lawtell are also important practitioners of the early, primitive zydeco sound.

After World War II, timid zydeco performances appeared on records by the famed folk singer Leadbelly (in the course of the Moses Asch sessions) and by bluesman Lightnin' Hopkins, who imitated the zydeco accordion on "Zolo Go" (a phonetic name for zydeco) for Gold Star. The first important record by a zydeco performer was "Bon Ton Roula" (Let The Good Times Roll) by Clarence Garlow, which made the nation's R&B charts in early 1950 on the Macy's label (slogan "Queen of Hits"). Over a foot-tapping rhumba rhythm augmented by a sturdy sax riff, Garlow exhorted his listeners to have a good time as he sang:

> You want to have yourself some real fine fun,
> Go down in Louisiana and you get you one.

You find them cutting cane all down the line,
I've got a cotton picker, she's-a really fine.
We let the Bon Ton Roula. . . .

And then he made a direct reference to zydeco:

At the church bazaar or the baseball game,
At the French La La, it's all the same.
You want to have fun, now you got to go
Way out in the country to the Zydeco.
Well, let the Bon Ton Roula. . . .

Clarence was influenced musically by his father, who was a country-dance performer. The young Garlow was born in 1911 in Welsh, a tiny town east of Lake Charles: "When I was a kid, about nine years old, I used to play my daddy's old fiddle, I can still play some now, I guess. He had a little old three-piece string band, he used to play the violin, bass fiddle, and the guitar. My daddy would play with his two brothers, and I'd sneak in and play with them—stomps and hoedowns. They never developed from that, they just had their fun, get together, you know. We were all much musically inclined, I was a black Cajun!"

After taking the migratory trail to Texas, he worked as a mailman in Beaumont, still playing music in his spare time. Then in 1949 he became a professional blues/R&B artist (there was little prospect of widespread success with a localized music like zydeco). He recalls: "About the year of 1949, I used to love to listen to T-Bone Walker, he was my idol. I only wish I could play guitar like that! He was father of the blues guitar, when he came out with that amplified guitar I thought, 'Well, I'm gonna try that!' I decided I would buy me a guitar and amplify it and do the same; I used to listen to the older records, try to strum like Lonnie Johnson. As T-Bone traveled through I made it my business to meet him, sometimes I'd catch them at rehearsal, sit around and listen to them and get pointers from them. One time T-Bone came through and said, 'Well, look at my old buddy, still got that mailbag on him instead of a guitar!'

"For some reason or another I resigned the post office and picked up a guitar. I couldn't really play it or front a band, but I went out and joined the musicians' union and got me some contracts and went out booking. I booked out several engagements and then I went to hiring me some boys. Most of them had their instruments in hock and I'd go and get them out! I had me some placards made, and made those engagements. My band was pretty versatile, we played blues, ballads, suites, waltzes.

"Well, I'd be doing alright to some extent but the boys would sometimes run me off the stand and say, 'Well, OK, bossman, you go down and meet the people while we keep the people dancing!' We kept that a-going, and I learned on the bandstand really, how to handle my affairs. I could whine on them strings, I could make a sour blues sound! I cleared more money in the first year after I picked up the guitar than I grossed in the whole eight years I carried mail. You know, I didn't ever regret that! In that year I had a '49 Buick, a '49 Cadillac, and a '49 Mercury station wagon. Plus I bought a guitar in 1950, well I guess I'd take a thousand dollars for it now—a collector's item!

"Then I happened to be coming through the town of Houston, and stopped at the Coconut Grove on Marshall Street on my way back to Beaumont. They had a little band with the guitar up the front, like blues 'n' rhythm—we was all playing blues 'n' rhythm—so I decided to ask the guy could I sit in. And I did, and the boys must have liked it for they split to the telephone and called Macy Lela Henry and Steve Ponchio from Macy's Recording Company to come to listen. They came over to hear, I didn't think I was good enough, but they thought differently. The first number was 'Bon Ton Roula,' kinda broken dialect, but it does have a memorable catchphrase. It was born right in the studio when we was trying to find something to record, it caught on like a shot in the arm, the crowds got bigger."

Shortly after the hit, Macy's—primarily a hillbilly label—collapsed, forcing Garlow to arrange one-shot deals with Feature and Lyric. The new releases were in a morbid Texas city-blues style, and lacked the distinctive hit-making qualities of "Bon Ton Roula." In the meantime Clarence set up his own small club, the Bon Ton Drive-In. "It was just dances," he says, "I used live gig bands Mondays and Thursdays, but I wouldn't use them Fridays and Saturdays because of the jukebox. They'd get the door, it would hold 150, 200 people. I never booked myself in there, the only time I'd play there would be one night if I was off. My band played other places, it wasn't big enough for me, I could beat that. I'd always get more people, I hate to sound too conceited but I was just too big for it. If I was playing in any territory, they'd be very careful about booking any big bands, 'See where that Bon Ton's playing tonight, 'cause if he's playing anywhere within fifty, sixty miles we're gonna have a bad night!' "

In 1953 he was signed by the prestigious Aladdin label of Hollywood. "A nightclub owner in Beaumont was going over to Orange to hear a band that was playing over there, to see if he wanted to bring them into his club in Beaumont," he recalls. "He asked me if I wanted to ride over with him, they had a band with the guitar player Arthur Prince. So I decided to sit in with them and after I did my little number, as a celebrity, like, Eddie Mesner of Aladdin Records asked if I was under contract to anyone. I said, no, I wasn't, then he asked me would I consider recording for his Aladdin label. I said, 'Yeah, certainly,' Aladdin was a big label! He asked me to meet him in New Orleans the next day and we cut the 'New Bon-Ton Roulay.' "

At a second session at Aladdin's home studio, Radio Recorders in Hollywood, Clarence was accompanied by the Maxwell Davis band, a prominent unit in B. B. King's early career. The cuts ranged bewilderingly from Rodgers and Hammerstein's "No Other Love" to the intriguing but unissued "Jumping At The Zadacoe" [sic]. Still in California, Clarence was introduced by songwriter Leon Rene to the Bihari Brothers of the Modern Records group, and made his best recording, "Route '90' "/"Crawfishin'," for Flair. On "Route '90' " he took an imaginary trip from the West Coast to his beloved Louisiana. It was almost possible to hear the crunching of the gears as he told of the *filé gumbo* and *bon ton jivin'* that awaited in *Jennings, Crowley, Lake Charles, and Rayne,* while *when you pass Lafayette, boy, you see them cutting cane.* Then, as he neared his destination,

There's Morgan City, where the shrimp boats land,
Put a nickel in the jukebox, hear a Cajun band.
Ain't you glad you came along, boy, to the Land of Dreams,
On old Route 90, on to New Orleans.

The same delightful scenario was retained for "Crawfishin'." It was party time down on the bayous, with the "Bon Ton" man excitedly imploring his friends to

Bring cousins by the dozen, and tell them to buy some wine,
We'll cook crawfish and have a real good time!

On both sides the scorching Louis Jordan–type R&B accompaniment seemed just right. But Clarence was looking for a more down-home feel, and his comments reveal how little control he had over the production: "There I had a big band, too much of a band for what I wanted to cut. I wasn't happy with cutting it much, but nevertheless, they paid for the session, so . . . It didn't bring out the story I wanted, what I wanted at the most was myself, piano player, bass player, and a drummer. Maxwell Davis did the arrangement, they told me, 'You can't miss with Maxwell!' But it really didn't take off like it should. I had a vocal group with me on 'Crawfishin,' but it wasn't what I wanted to do. I wasn't trying to get no big band, I was trying to get country boys, get the gut effect—all peoples, not just black but white and Cajun. That country feeling. But this was done with so much *weight!*"

Returning from the West Coast, Garlow recorded again for Jay Miller before making a deal with Eddie Shuler. On his first Folk-Star record, "Za

Belle," he played a rocking zydeco accordion and had reasonable sellers in the bluesy "No No Baby"/"I Feel Like Calling You" (Folk-Star) and the doomy "Sundown" (Goldband). In 1957 he tried to crack the rock 'n' roll market with yet another "Bon Ton Roule" (Goldband) but, for him, the musical good times had rolled to a grinding halt. He went back once more to Jay Miller who, while admiring Clarence himself, complained that he always brought along a dreadful pickup band. The new tapes remained on the shelf until the excellent "Foggy Blues" was released by Flyright in 1976.

Withdrawing gracefully from performing, Garlow concentrated on his disc-jockey duties at KJET Beaumont and neighboring stations (as a parting gesture he did record again, for the Bon-Ran label). In 1979 he had retired from music altogether and was happily involved in "TV repair, seafood sales, and invisible vinyl repair." It was a strange assortment of jobs, but his approach to music had been just as eclectic—from zydeco, city blues, and swamp-blues to R&B and rock 'n' roll. In a way Clarence had shown the opportunities that music offered to a poor country black man who had started out playing zydeco—and the constraints. With no defined audience for his kind of music, he had had to look towards the wider black music spectrum to make a living.

Despite its zydeco theme, "Bon Ton Roula" had a distinct R&B feel. Much more rooted in the traditional zydeco form was "Paper In My Shoe," an unexpected regional smash for Boozoo Chavis on Folk-Star in 1954. "Paper In My Shoe" (also known as "Pebble In My Shoe,") was adapted by Chavis from an old folk number. Boozoo's repetitive vocal chant in English and French was rough and unpolished, but his accordion, harmonizing with an unlikely saxophone, held the song together over a primitive, almost tribal, rhythm. The hilarious story behind this oddest of hits is related by Eddie Shuler:

"I came into contact with one Boozoo Chavis, a colorful character, to put it mildly. He talked in short, clipped sentences and was a natural-born clown. Boozoo played a German button accordion in a style known in this part of the country as zydeco and had no band of his own. I decided to record him and went out and found Classie Ballou, who then had the best R&B band in the area. I didn't know it, but Ballou's band had never heard of zydeco music, let alone played it, and after eight hours in the studio no mentionable results were forthcoming. Ballou's boys just couldn't dig Boozoo's music, and Boozoo didn't know that they weren't with him!

"At last someone decided to give Boozoo something stronger than water to help things along and we got a little jug and carried on rolling the tapes. The door to my studio was just an ordinary front door with no glass, so I couldn't see in from the control room, but I knew Boozoo was getting saturated. Suddenly there was a colossal crash in the studio, but as the take was the best so far I didn't check what had happened until the number was finished. When I opened the door there, before me, lay Boozoo. He had fallen off his stool but managed to keep his accordion in the air and play on without missing a note! Everybody's nerves were on edge at the time as can be imagined, but this broke us down. We laughed until we were hysterical. It was about the most comical sight anyone could hope to see!

"I realized by now that things had gone as far as they could, and after paying the boys a huge sum for the long session I found myself broke. I told them we would try again as soon as I raised more funds, but things were so bad for months after this that we never did have another try. Some time afterwards I played the tapes back to see if there was anything there worth all the trouble and expense. The number where Boozoo fell on the floor was still the best, so I thought I would edit it and then release it as a feeler to test public reaction.

"The song was 'Paper In My Shoe,' and it was just one of those natural hits that so seldom come along. I am used to surprises, but that was amazing! I had a friend called Johnny who was a salesman for A-1 Distributors out of New Orleans, and I got him to handle the record. He took it to Lew Chudd of Imperial, who leased it from me. It sold over 100,000 copies and at that time you had a hit if you sold 25,000. This was the biggest seller I had had so far!"

Cashing in on this surprise success, Boozoo toured the southern states with Classie Ballou before disagreeing with Eddie Shuler over terms for a follow-up. Eventually the excellent "Forty One Days" was released, with storming accordion, guitar, and saxophone work, but it was too late; the record buyers had forgotten him. Boozoo Chavis may have been responsible for relegating himself into the unenviable ranks of one-hit wonders, but with "Paper In My Shoe" he created a lasting standard—the song is still played by black and white musicians throughout South Louisiana.

While Boozoo was enjoying fleeting fame, Clifton Chenier was embarking on a recording career that would see him emerge as the undisputed King of Zydeco. Until he was sidelined by illness in 1979, he was easily the most popular and best exponent of zydeco music, appearing before capacity crowds wherever he played. Singing with a heavy French accent, he performed a tantalizing program of zydeco interspersed with low-down blues, good-time dance music, pop songs, R&B and C&W tunes, and two-steps and waltzes, abetted by his masterly accordion gliding over a rock-steady rhythm from an impeccable band. Of his music he says, "It is simply the traditional French two-step with new hinges so she can swing!"

Clifton was born on a sharecropper's farm near Opelousas in 1925. With elder brother Cleveland he helped his impoverished parents work the fields from sunup to sundown, riding mules and picking cotton. Fascinated by his father Joseph's accordion playing, Clifton started traveling with Joseph to Saturday-night suppers and house parties. When his father gave Clifton his first leaky, wheezy instrument, Cleveland borrowed their mother's rub board and they made music together, influenced by the records of Amadie Ardoin and local performers like Sidney Babineaux and Jesse and Zozo Reynolds.

In 1947 a newly married Clifton left home to join Cleveland in Lake Charles. Finding that the most remunerative employment was offered by the Gulf and Texaco oil refineries of Port Arthur, Texas, the brothers started driving refinery trucks while playing music in their free time. Clifton was broadening his repertoire by listening to leading blues singers like Clarence Garlow, Lowell Fulson, and Joe Liggins, but his career did not take off until he was discovered in 1954 by J. R. Fulbright, a Negro from Los Angeles who was on a scouting trip of the South for his Elko label. The late Fulbright told the story behind the first record, "Cliston Blues" [sic]/ "Louisiana Stomp," credited to Cliston Chanier:

"When I got started in the business after the war I used to find my own talent. That's how I met Clifton, I was looking for a harp player to kill Elmon Mickle [Drifting Slim], see old Elmo walked out on me. There's this town on the Lafayette highway, I saw this big crowd of people and I got out of my car and found Clifton. I thought it was a harp player! He was just a kid then, him and his brother were playing. I recorded him in Lake Charles but I preferred to bring my artists to the West Coast. There's prejudice in the South—they won't let you get anything if they can't get a share too. When I was recording Clifton at a Lake Charles radio station the white boy wouldn't do nothing to help. Wouldn't do no engineering work or test the machine. He got his cigar in his mouth and his newspaper and put his feet up on the desk. So I asked him, 'Ain't you doing no engineering work?' and he jumped up like I hit him and said, 'What the hell you talking about? You know where you at, you in Lake Charles!' Anyway, I didn't do much with the record, so we sold the masters to Imperial. I couldn't help Clifton much but they could, Imperial had nationwide distribution."

Clifton then recorded two singles for Post, an Imperial subsidiary label, before signing for Art Rupe's Hollywood-based Specialty Records in 1955. At Specialty Chenier had an immediate R&B hit with the rousing "Ay-Tete-Fee" (Eh Tite Fille), a considerable achievement with a French song. He even enjoyed a surprise success in the small Jamaican market with the stomping accordion instrumental "Squeeze Box Boogie"; the record had the right rhythm for the local dancers. The best Specialty efforts are included in the "Bayou Blues" album, a marvelous mixture of blues and boogie with a dash of zydeco.

Now an R&B star, Clifton was the "King of the South" as he toured nonstop with his band, the Zodico Ramblers. These hectic times are fondly recalled by his former guitarist Phillip Walker: "In 1953 I left Lonesome Sundown to go with Clifton Chenier. In 1954–55 we was booked out of the office of Shaw out of New York City and the southern route chief was Howard Lewis of the Empire Room in Dallas, Texas. And I think at that time, well, Howard handled a lot of stuff, the West Coast as well. Also we were touring at that time with Lloyd Price, the Clovers, the Cadillacs, the Dells, and we was the backup band for many of these artists.

"At the time, 1955, we had all the heavy load, Clifton would have his own spot, he never played behind the other artists. Chenier's home is Opelousas, Louisiana, but his headquarters was Port Arthur, Texas. We used to play around Port Arthur, our local territory when we wasn't on dates was Corpus Christi, Houston, Dallas, Oklahoma City into Louisiana, Lafayette, Breaux Bridge. Then when the big dates would come up they would send us a letter: 'Be in Dallas at the office on so-and-so date.' Most times, we'd have as high as a hundred one-nighters, then if we was off a couple of weeks we'd do our own gigs, but when the real booking would come up sometimes we would go from coast to coast before stopping. Yeah, we worked plenty, a whole lot! I'd be so tired I'd just be wishing for that day to come when we'd be off, that was the good old days—now they're the rough days! We played fifteen days at the Crown Propellor, I think it was burnt down, at Sixty-third and Cottage Grove, Chicago.

"I played in Memphis in 1956 with Rosco Gordon, he was with Clifton Chenier's band at the time, 'cause Rosco didn't have a band but he was a nice piano player. He was on the show with us, Etta James, Jimmy Reed, Lowell Fulson, all these artists that didn't have bands. Yeah, we was packaged together for three and six months at a time. Most times we may only have an hour to rehearse before the show, sometimes maybe a day, so it was a lot of work, you had to learn quick. I was with Chenier I'd say the last part of '53 to 1957. I did a lot of stuff with him for Specialty Records and Argo, that was made in Chicago at Chess across the road from Vee-Jay—'The Big Wheel.' I had some great times then, money, traveling . . . I could write a book. He was a great guy, Clifton, got a good band."

In the late fifties Clifton was still recording R&B rather than zydeco, although whenever he performed locally he included some French numbers in his program. After leaving Speciality he languished with Chess, receiving little promotional support for either "The Big Wheel" (Argo) or "Bajou Drive" (Checker), two strutting instrumentals. He lowered his sights by joining Jay Miller's tiny Zynn label, but of three singles only "Rockin' Accordian" caught the natural zest of his music—Chenier was a rare failure for Miller as a producer. In 1964 Clifton's faltering career was given much-needed direction by record owner Chris Strachwitz from Berkeley,

California. Chris had launched his Arhoolie label in 1960 by recording several Texas bluesmen, but soon branched out to cover all forms of ethnic music; he was particularly fond of the Cajun, zydeco, and blues sounds of Louisiana. A wonderful friend of American traditional music, he is a modest unsung hero who has preserved much on record that was neglected and in danger of early extinction.

Under Strachwitz's guidance, Clifton promptly returned to his zydeco roots. The first Arhoolie album, "Louisiana Blues And Zydeco," found ready acceptance in South Louisiana and East Texas, although Chris needed time to convince his regular blues customers about the merits of zydeco music. Albums were released periodically; besides the debut LP the best were "Bon Ton Roulet" (1966), "King Of The Bayous" (1970), and "Bogalusa Boogie" (1975).

Early on Strachwitz made a deal with Floyd Soileau of Ville Platte for singles to be culled from Clifton's albums for release on the Bayou label. "Louisiana Blues" was a real jukebox favorite and notched respectable sales, as did "Zydeco Et Pas Sale." In 1966 Clifton recorded briefly for Huey Meaux's Crazy Cajun label in Pasadena, Texas; from these sessions came the delicious, bluesy "La Coeur De La Louisianne" and the rollicking "Oh! Lucille," now a zydeco standard. On "Oh! Lucille," one of the most melodic zydeco numbers, Clifton's smoothly intricate piano accordion echoed his controlled vocal lines over a simple rhythmic backing; he was the rejected lover lamenting his loss: *"Oh! Lucille, oh! Lucille, tu m'as quitté pour t'en aller."*

Sporting a gaudy mock crown, the King of Zydeco was on the road all the time, playing his loud, socking music along the grinding Gulf Coast chittlin circuit. Clifton was received like royalty at such clubs as the Casino in St. Martinville, the Bon Ton Rouley in Lafayette, Richard's Club in Lawtell, John's Bar in Lake Charles, and all the way to Houston, where a vibrant zydeco scene supported such local artists as Lonnie Mitchel and Herbert "Good Rocking" Sam. The first step towards wider acceptance came with Chenier's appearance at the 1966 Berkeley Festival, which prompted further bookings on the West Coast. Canada and Europe beckoned next.

Clifton's full but relaxed life-style was caught sympathetically on film by director Les Blank in *Hot Pepper* (Flower Films, 1973). Clearly a star among his own people, Chenier is seen with friends drinking beer, indulging in back-porch accordion jams, just laughing and talking; there is also fine footage taken in clubs and bars, and views of the Chenier Zydeco-Blues Band station wagon hurtling along a highway into a beautiful bayou sunset to the unmistakable sound of his music. A companion film, *Dry Wood*, featured Alphonse "Bois Sec" Ardoin.

During the seventies Clifton Chenier's name became synonymous with zydeco. Personal talent aside, a key factor in his increasing prestige was his splendid group. The ever-present rub-boarding Cleveland Chenier and lively drummer Robert Peter (surname St. Judy) were joined by Blind John Hart, a thrilling sax player; guitarist Paul Senegal; and bass guitarist Joe Brouchet. Called the Louisiana Red Hot Band, they were just that— they sizzled! The best example of their work together can be found on the "Bogalusa Boogie" album. Chris Strachwitz is especially fond of "Bogalusa Boogie," Arhoolie's top seller with 15,000 copies: "Clifton loved the Bogalusa studio, it was a superb studio, they had a fine set of drums and everyone was feeling great. Cliff was in a separate room but they all could hear each other and he was turned on like at a good dance. Tunes just flowed out—he gets his songs from old R&B material and old Cajun tunes but reworks them to suit his style."

With Strachwitz's blessing, Clifton left Arhoolie because he was becoming too big for the label to handle. Most of the new recordings that followed were below par, except for the scintillating "Boogie & Zydeco" album recorded for Floyd Soileau's Maison de Soul label, with talented pianist Glen Himel sitting in to good effect. At the 1979 New Orleans Jazz and Heritage Festival, Clifton was showing disturbing signs of musical and physical fatigue. It transpired he had a kidney infection that required dialysis treatment; later he had part of a foot amputated. The next year he made a valiant comeback, but could only blow the harmonica until he acquired an easy-to-play electric accordion. In 1981 he seemed to be full of energy again; besides playing his usual venues in Louisiana and East Texas he was also booked for a fall tour of the West Coast. He had even added a trumpet player to his band.

Clifton, known affectionately in South Louisiana as "the blackest coonass," will always be the King of Zydeco. Chris Strachwitz has the last word: "Clifton is a real giant in his field, no doubt about it. When you hear all the dozens of Chenier imitators it becomes even more obvious. Clifton is a giant on his instrument—no one comes close—he has a great gutsy voice and a very expressive and emotional delivery when he feels like it. And his band is always good. I feel bad that no one has come and made a real star out of him. Clifton is not only a unique artist in the zydeco field, but he is a jazzman, an endless improviser. He sings the blues and he can do Cajun numbers better than anyone else. But in recent years he has not wanted to do much French stuff, he feels the kids like R&B and it sells better than any other types for him. I can't praise the man enough—he is a giant! There will never be another Clifton Chenier."

Clifton Chenier's success encouraged other performers to play zydeco and made record companies aware of the zydeco style. Of the current crop of artists, the most impressive are Rockin' Dopsie and the Twisters, Fernest Arceneaux and the Thunders, and Buckwheat and his Zydeco Ils Sont Partis Band.

Accordionist Rockin' Dopsie, born Alton Rubin in the country outside Lafayette in 1932, has a most energetic and sweaty—if limited—down-home style. Although he has been playing the rural dance halls since his late teens with rub-board friend Chester Zeno, he did not record until 1968, when zydeco was gaining prominence. After uneventful singles for Floyd Soileau's Bon Temps and Jay Miller's Blues Unlimited labels, he has recorded since 1976 for Sonet Records of Sweden and England, cutting lively albums in Baton Rouge, Ville Platte, Crowley, and Bogalusa, with Sam Charters as producer. In 1979 Dopsie made his first visit to Europe, astounding local music critics who were encountering his earthy zydeco sound for the first time. He had the considerable support of his R&B-oriented band, the Twisters, who were boosted by the towering presence of John Hart. The former Clifton Chenier tenorman gave a cosmic performance on the saxophone; he was a one-man horn section as he riffed and soloed with impunity, showing the influence of every tenor-sax master from Lee Allen to Lester Young.

Even if the French element was toned down, Rockin' Dopsie gave a good account of himself on foreign soil. He was clearly enjoying himself as he talked apocryphally of record sales of 200,000 back home. His assertion that zydeco was taking over in Louisiana from the dying disco craze also had to be taken with a pinch of snap-bean salt, but what a delightful thought!

The affable, gangling Fernest Arceneaux is another zydeco accordionist who has made the long trip to Europe, despite being unknown in most of Louisiana—many of his gigs are in the voracious zydeco area of East Texas. A talented, bluesy musician from Lafayette, he has the remarkable ability to make his instrument sound like a small orchestra, and he deserves his billing as "The New Prince of the Accordion." But his vocals, though soulful, lack power because of an asthmatic condition (on record he has recruited singers Gene Morris and Bobby Price). He is backed by the Thunders, a serenely unspoiled band propelled by the highly capable drumming of Clarence "Jockey" Etienne. On stage Arceneaux's program features a happy range of black music popular in South Louisiana, including songs by Clifton Chenier, Cookie and the Cupcakes, Guitar Gable, Guitar Slim, Earl King, Fats Domino, Jessie Hill, Ray Charles, and B. B. King—plus, of course, "Jole Blon."

In 1979 the career of this soft-spoken yet charismatic musician was stimulated by an excellent album, "Fernest And The Thunders" (Blues Unlimited). The LP provided an expansive view of zydeco, and included swamp-pop–type numbers like "Irene," "(Those) Lonely Lonely Nights," and "Mother Dear" and R&B favorites "You Can Make It If You Try," "My Girl Josephine," and "Send Me Some Lovin'." The lovely laid-back Louisiana swamp-sound was a feature throughout. But as an artist Fernest does not appear to be forceful enough to get to the top.

The brightest star in the zydeco firmament is Stanley "Buckwheat" Dural Jr., the Crown Prince to Clifton Chenier. His superb debut album "One For The Road," also for Blues Unlimited, was one of the most entertaining South Louisiana releases of 1979. Accompanied by his accomplished Zydeco Ils Sont Partis Band (named after the famous "They're off!" heard at the Acadiana Downs racetrack in Lafayette), Buckwheat, like Fernest, traveled deep into R&B territory. Besides his single "I Bought A Raccoon," standout tracks included "Madame Coco Bo," "You Got Me Walkin' The Floor" (a remake of Fats Domino's "Good Hearted Man"), and "One For The Road," a soulful instrumental. Singing appealingly in French and English, he played accordion (which he had not learned until 1978), piano, and a spine-chilling organ. His second album, "Take It Easy Baby," was a polished, more soul-oriented production.

Born in Lafayette in 1947, Buckwheat had his first professional opportunities during the sixties with the touring bands of Clarence "Gatemouth" Brown, Little Richard, and Barbara Lynn. He then formed the Hitchhikers, a "rock 'n' roll disco" band, and made local records. His biggest seller, "Miss Hard To Get" (Soul Unlimited), with Dennis Landry as featured vocalist, sold a modest "few thousand" copies in 1972. After he played in Clifton Chenier's band, Buckwheat turned to zydeco. On the basis of the Blues Unlimited albums, he can already be considered a major zydeco performer.

Other prominent zydeco artists include Delton Broussard and the Lawtell Playboys from Opelousas, Wilfred Latour and his Travel Aces from Lake Charles, and Hiram "Lune" Sampy and the Bad Habits from Carencro. Meanwhile, on the West Coast, Queen Ida (Guillory) and her Bon Temps Band are pumping out a popular mixture of zydeco, blues, and rock for the Creole community of San Francisco. But the most intriguing zydeco group is the Sam Brothers, a teen-age band from Scott that has already recorded for Arhoolie and Blues Unlimited. Directed by their accordionist father, Herbert "Good Rocking" Sam (who used to perform in Houston), the brothers not only sound like Clifton Chenier—they dress like him as well.

If Clifton is having that sort of effect on the younger generation, there must be hope for the future of zydeco. But by relying on jet-speed, syncopated rhythms, zydeco musicians are limiting themselves structurally; few permutations remain unused. Also, local soul radio stations seem to feel the music is too French to be played, while the Cajun music programmers consider it too black. In 1981, however, radio KEUN Eunice began broadcasting a full hour of zydeco music each Saturday morning from eleven to noon. According to the station "zydeco, traditional black Cajun music, has been neglected by South Louisiana radio stations for years . . . included will be works by musicians such as Bois Sec Ardoin, the Delafose Brothers [an upcoming group], Clifton Chenier, and others."

The truth is that it has never been possible to sustain a career strictly in zydeco music. In the early days Clifton Chenier and Clarence Garlow were forced to cross over into the R&B field, just as Rockin' Dopsie, Fernest, and Buckwheat are doing now. But thanks to King Clifton and his devoted disciples, the fresh, invigorating zydeco sound has richly earned its spell in the spotlight.

10

"If it wasn't for bad luck, Po' Lightnin' wouldn't have no luck at all"

As a folk music of the American Negro, the blues has roots that extend back to the days of slavery when European folk songs became intertwined with the traditional music of Africa. From the work songs, the field hollers, the ballads, and the country music of the American Negro, the blues emerged as a recognizable form towards the end of the nineteenth century. The music provided a vital emotional safety valve for performer and listener alike.

While blacks in southern states like Mississippi, Texas, Georgia, and the Carolinas developed identifiable rural blues styles, there was no parallel development in Louisiana, despite its large black population. This sparse blues tradition can be attributed in part to the French-Caribbean origins of some of the state's black population, allied to the unique social conditions that prevailed in Acadiana and New Orleans. As a result, the one-man-and-his-guitar rural back-porch sounds were confined principally to the small farming communities around Shreveport and Baton Rouge. Over the years a handful of commercial recordings were made by Shreveport artists like Oscar Woods, Leadbelly, Country Jim, and Stick Horse Hammond, but the Baton Rouge bluesmen were ignored until Lightnin' Slim was recorded by Jay Miller in 1954. As Slim Harpo and Lazy Lester began traveling along Highway 90 to Miller's Crowley studio, it soon became clear that Baton Rouge had been harboring many other talented performers.

Amazingly, the fast-fading styles of the old-time rural Baton Rouge bluesmen were not caught on record until 1959—by two academics, Dr. Harry Oster of Louisiana State University and Richard Allen of Tulane University. Acting under the auspices of the Louisiana Folklore Society, the dedicated archivists recorded such musicians as Robert Pete Williams, Smoky Babe, Butch Cage, Snooks Eaglin, Clarence Edwards, Hogman Maxey, Willie Thomas, and Guitar Welch, initially for the Folk-Lyric label; later albums appeared on Prestige-Bluesville and Arhoolie, among others. (At the same time Oster collated the classic traditional Cajun LP "Folksongs Of The Louisiana Acadians" featuring Chuck Guillory,

117

Wallace "Cheese" Read, Bee Deshotels, and Isom J. Fontenot, mostly with minimal instrumental support; the album offers a wonderful perspective on the folk roots of many popular Cajun tunes.)

Harry Oster's most famous blues release was the fascinating "Angola Prisoners' Blues" album, recorded at the notorious state penitentiary in Angola. Rather like a latter-day Alan Lomax (the pioneering fieldworking folklorist who had recorded Cajun music in the thirties with his father John for the Library of Congress archives), Oster had organized the Angola trip with the intention of documenting disappearing folk-blues and spiritual styles, which he hoped might have been preserved in the prison like some fossilized form. Instead, he found that almost all the inmates were mimicking the latest R&B sounds heard over radio WXOK Baton Rouge. But Oster did find a handful of prisoners still caught in a musical time warp, including the gem he was looking for—Robert Pete Williams. The unspoiled bluesman's heartrending version of "Prisoner's Talking Blues" made the entire visit worthwhile. It was a memorable statement from a despairing lifer:

Lord, my worry sho' carryin' me down,   (repeat)
Sometimes I feel like, baby, committin' suicide,   (repeat)
I got the nerve if I just had anythin' to do it with.
I'm goin' down slow, somethin' wrong with me,   (repeat)
I've got to make a change while that I'm still young,
If I don't, I won't never get old.

Like most of Robert Pete's blues, it was a deeply introspective personal statement colored by his unregimented vocal and guitar styles. "I had never played a twelve-string guitar before," he once recalled, "but Oster asked, 'Robert Pete, can you make up a talking blues about your family?' I sat down and played the 'Angola Prison Blues' [sic]. It's a sad blues, I wasn't happy in Angola. It sounded so lonesome and sad, the inmates had tears comin' to their eyes."

Robert Pete Williams soon became the leading exponent of Louisiana country-blues music. Born in Zachary in 1914, he moved with his family to Scotlandville, near Baton Rouge, in 1928. "I've been a hustlin' man all of my life," he said on one occasion. "I used to work at a dairy and then go pick moss and sell cow bones for fertilizer to make money. I farmed in Baker, cotton, corn, sweet potato. When I was eighteen I made my first guitar out of a sugar box. It didn't hold up so I bought an old guitar for $1.50, but the strings were too high off the bow. When I was twenty-one I went to a white lady's house a friend of mine cooked for, and I got a $65 guitar her son wouldn't play for $4.50. White folks started havin' me play at their parties, I got to rappin' good with the guitar. They used to call me Peetie Wheatstraw 'cause I could play all of his tunes. I also liked Dan Jackson, a man who could play so well that once when he was at the depot he started to play and they gave him his money back and a pass for the train! He could play all of Bessie Smith's records. I liked Walker Green and Willie Hudson, but Blind Lemon Jefferson was my man! I never heard him, but I did hear his records. During the forties and fifties I used to practice for a month or two and then lay up my guitar for six months."

Robert Pete's routine existence was interrupted in 1956 by a murder rap that led to the life sentence in Angola—he always insisted his action was in self-defense. Paroled for good behavior by Governor Earl Long in 1959, he spent the next five years on a work-release program share-cropping for a Denham Springs farmer before being granted a full pardon following representations by Oster, Allen, and other friends. Finally freed, he appeared at the prestigious Newport Folk Festival in 1964 and was then booked regularly at colleges and festivals at home and abroad until his death in 1980. Of his many recordings the Angola session remained supreme. Ironically, the time and place had been exactly right—his imprisonment had inspired his greatest blues.

After World War II, South Louisiana blues musicians started imitating the amplified sounds of the best-selling blues artists they heard on records. Inspiration came from the solo southern guitarists Lightnin' Hopkins and John Lee Hooker, and from the Chicago-based small-combo music of Sonny Boy (John Lee) Williamson, Little Walter, Muddy Waters, and especially Jimmy Reed. With harmonicas wailing and electric guitars booming over a wallowing swamp-beat (the drums had a muffled sound), the local vocalists lazily made their mark in the noisy juke joints; like all South Louisiana singers they seemed to have time to spare. By the late fifties many Louisiana bluesmen had begun to forge their own warm, recognizable style from the borrowed sounds. The style was the swamp-blues, and Baton Rouge became its spiritual home.

Baton Rouge, the "Red Stick" of the Houma Indians, is the second largest city in Louisiana, the site of the state capitol, and a focal point of business, culture, education, and finance. It is also a key industrial center with an immense chemical and petroleum complex served by a port on the Mississippi that caters to oceangoing ships and barges. The city has obvious attractions for the work-seeking rural populace, among them blues singers looking for daytime employment to supplement their musical incomes.

Lightnin' Slim, who started out as a Lightnin' Hopkins imitator, opened up the Baton Rouge blues scene after hitting with his first record, "Bad Luck" (Feature) in 1954. The popularity of Lightnin' Slim's song persuaded Crowley record man Jay Miller to step up his blues recordings, especially since his Cajun and country markets were starting to disintegrate in the face of competition from rock 'n' roll. Until then Miller had halfheartedly used a Feature blues series for occasional releases by Clarence Garlow and Richard King.

J. D. was well placed to record the bluesmen of Baton Rouge—he had no local rivals and his studio was only a short car ride away. Over the next ten years Miller was to help project the fresh Louisiana blues sound throughout the South—and even further afield—by flattering his artists with superior material and consistently good productions. Lightnin' Slim was his best bluesman, but Slim Harpo, Lonesome Sundown, and Lazy Lester were not far behind.

Jay recalls how he came to record Lightnin' Slim: "They had station WXOK in Baton Rouge, they had a colored DJ [Ray Meaders] there, his stage name was Diggy Do. So he called me one day, he wanted me to go over and listen to a band. We made arrangements for me to go over one particular night and after the station closed there, this band played. We listened to them through the night, they were about seven or eight pieces, but in my judgment they wasn't too much of a band.

"And I was just walking out the hall when I heard a guitar playing some of these low-down blues. So I just turned around, I said, 'Who in the world is that?' I hadn't heard the guitarist, you see the room wasn't very large and with seven or eight musicians, they had three horns, I had never heard the guitar once. I just thought he was so great so I turned round and went back in there, started talking to him. Had him show me some of that playing, I asked him if he did any singing.

"He said, 'I knows a few numbers . . .'—you know how he talked, real slow and everything. So I said, 'Why don't you sing?' So he sang two or three songs and I tell you what, they did things to me, I just knew right then and there we had somebody that would sell. At that time of course black people were buying this black music, they weren't buying the white music and the white people weren't buying the black music. But this was genuine, authentic colored blues, the roots of the colored music.

"I asked him if he wanted to make records. 'Yes, sir,' so I got hold of Diggy Do. 'Sit down, I can tell you for sure I'd like to record him but I'll have to let you know about this band.' At the back of my mind I wasn't interested [in the band], but I said I do want to record Lightnin'. So we made arrangements for Lightnin' to be recorded. And he sang for me the 'Bad Luck Blues,' that really did something to me. And it was a black new artist.

"I came back, told several of my friends that were very interested like me in blues music, so I told him to rehearse, get his tunes together, and we'd get together as soon as we could. So they called me one day, Diggy Do did, and said he was gonna be able to come on a Sunday. We were due to record on that particular Sunday, so that Saturday I had to start looking for a harmonica player. I needed a good harmonica player, so I got in my car and went to Beaumont. I heard they had a fellow by the name of Wild Bill Phillips that played real fine, harmonica players were real hard to find.

"This friend of mine, J. P. Richardson, the Big Bopper, told me Wild Bill was a good harmonica player. Well, J. P. was a DJ on the station over there, KTRM in Beaumont, and he put on what you might term a black show, you know a white man doing a black show, everybody thought he was black. So I went over there, and I'm gonna tell you it's awfully difficult to find a colored person when you go around asking for them because they won't tell you. So finally after everybody said they didn't know him I talked to a policeman and he said, 'Yeah, I know where he is. He's in jail!' So I went and bailed him out, it was either forty-one or forty-two dollars, I got him his bail and paid his fine and brought him to Crowley. Hadn't heard him, I didn't know what I was getting.

"Anyway, I brought this colored fellow back here, put him up in a colored hotel. Next day we wait for Lightnin', it's after twelve, no Lightnin', he was supposed to be there about nine o'clock. So what happened, somewhere around Church Point the damn car broke down. So they reached me by phone, said the car broke down, so I went over there with a pickup truck, brought a chain, and pulled their car in. But anyway, I didn't have any drummer, I was so caught up with trying to get a harmonica blower when we got down to record and for some stupid reason we had no drummer. Diggy Do had never played the drums in his life and we had an old piece of drum, a terrible thing, somebody had left it there, it wasn't ours. A band had come in to rehearse, listened to how they sounded on tape, and left this little drum there. So Diggy was the only one we had. I had to work the equipment, he was the only one we could maybe put in there to try to beat the drum! But it was so simple, I covered him up as much as possible, but you didn't do too much of that with this big old drum. Every time he hit it, it just went 'Boom!' It didn't have the resonance that you could control now with drums.

"Lightnin' was real funny. Although it was his first session he tried to convince Wild Bill he was a big record star. But when the tapes began to roll he turned around nervously and said, 'Bill, you'se go ahead and start, and I'se gonna contact you!'

"But anyway we cut this first record, I just knew we had a hit. And Ernie Young, he had Ernie's Record Mart in Nashville, I sent him copies to sell. I sent them to Randy's Record Shop in Gallatin, Tennessee, I don't know what the initial order was, not many, maybe 50 records. They started

ordering those things 500 at a time, which was something then. We started
getting calls for it."

Recorded in the spring of 1954, "Bad Luck" was the ultimate in self-
pity. The sparse guitar, crude harmonica, and simple drum beat provided
a suitably poignant backdrop as Lightnin' sang in his deep, rich voice:

Lord if it wasn't for bad luck
I wouldn't have no luck at all.
If it wasn't for bad luck
Po' Lightnin' wouldn't have no luck at all.
'Cause bad luck's been followin' po' Lightnin'
Ever since I began to crawl.

Lightnin' was to record this kind of endearing personalized blues
throughout his career. His highly promising debut was rounded off by a
relaxed, flowing version of the traditional "Rock Me Mama." The very
likable Lightnin' Slim was the archetypal slow-talking, down-home
bluesman, he was southern through and through. Yet he came from the
North: "I was born Otis Hicks in St. Louis, Missouri, in 1913 and grew up
like most any kid. After school I worked in a grocery store, sold newspapers. It was city living, but there wasn't too much live music around
that I remember. I listened to music on the radio a lot and bought myself an
old folk guitar and tried to play it. I'd take that old guitar with me fishing
and sit under a tree and play it all day. At the time I listened to Lonnie
Johnson, Blind Lemon Jefferson, and Ma Rainey. My folks got the records
and I listened to them. They made me want to play music too, my biggest
influence on guitar would be Blind Lemon Jefferson, then Lightnin'
Hopkins later. I went as far as the tenth grade and my father died so I had
to quit school and go to work to help the family. I got to see a few shows that
came through town, like the Rabbit Foot Minstrel shows. After my mother
died I didn't want to stay around St. Louis anymore."

In the late twenties the Hicks family moved south to work on a ten-acre
farm at St. Francisville in the Louisiana hill country. Somehow Lightnin'
survived the depressed thirties: "I growed cotton, corn, sweet potatoes. I
wasn't wanting for anything but the sun to go down so I could knock off."

In 1946 he left the farm to work in a fertilizer plant in Baton Rouge:
"There was a lot of music going on there and I got interested in it. I learned
to play pretty good, so me and a friend got together and went down to a
little town called Gonzales, it was just me and him on drums. That old boy
owned an electric guitar besides his drums, so I played it sometimes. We
played house parties and dances for two years." Then Lightnin' joined Big
Poppa (John Tilley) and the Cane Cutters and the radio station audition

followed. He was christened "Lightnin' Slim" by Jay Miller, who had a penchant for picking colorful artists' names. In Slim's case it was a wry observation on his painfully deliberate manner and thin, wiry frame, and it conveyed, indisputably, the impression of a *real* down-home bluesman.

After the "Bad Luck" hit another session was quickly arranged. This time Sammy Drake from Crowley sat in on drums, and when the unreliable Wild Bill Phillips failed to show Henry Clement was deputed to play harmonica. At 9 P.M. on that night in 1954 the trio settled down to record "I Can't Live Happy," very much in the doomy style of "Bad Luck," and "New Orleans Bound," a bright shuffle blues. On the next date, which produced "Bugger Bugger Boy" and "Ethel Mae," Cleve White took over the harmonica role. His playing was dirtily down-home, ideally suited to Lightnin' Slim's style.

At the session White himself sang a few earthy blues songs that led to the release of the "She's Gone"/"Strange Letter Blues" single on Feature, in the name of Schoolboy Cleve. One of the few harmonica players active in the area at the time, White came from Baton Rouge and was influenced by the popular Chicago blues harmonica star Sonny Boy (John Lee) Williamson. Cleve acquired his stage name when people asked, "Have you heard that schoolboy?" After playing in the bands of Lloyd Reynaud and Lightnin' Slim, he set out on his own. He recorded again in 1957 for Ace, but nothing was released; then his excellent "New Kind Of Loving" for Lloyd Reynaud's Opelousas-based Reynaud label evoked little response. Deciding to retire from music in 1960, Cleve headed for the West Coast, but resurfaced a decade later for occasional festival and recording dates.

Meanwhile Lightnin' Slim was arousing the interest of other record men, including Johnny Vincent, the head of Ace Records, who enticed him over to Jackson, Mississippi, for an illicit session. Jay Miller was not amused: "I think Johnny Vincent intentionally misled Lightnin' Slim into believing that I would not record him again. There was not too much of a disagreement except I told Johnny personally that if he ever caused trouble to me and my artists again, I would give him a whipping he'd never forget. I meant it then and I mean it now."

But Miller realized that Lightnin' Slim's records had to be leased to a bigger company to get better exposure and maximize sales; Feature simply did not have the right facilities to further Slim's recording career. Ernie Young's Excello Records in Nashville was the perfect answer: it was a blues label, had the right distribution network, and worked hand in hand with WLAC radio which beamed programs throughout the South. Moreover, Young owned Ernie's Record Mart, a highly influential retail and mail-order outlet "located in the record center of the South," plus a chain of jukeboxes. And Nashville was familiar territory to Miller through his Acuff-Rose links. "I went to a DJ convention over in Nashville in 1955," recalls Jay. "I went over to see Ernie and he wasn't what I expected, nor was I what he expected! I walked in there with cowboy boots and he said, 'That's strange, a guy that produces and writes for records walks in here with cowboy boots. I wouldn't expect that, I thought you'd have a zoot suit on or something!'

"But Ernie and I got along real fine, our deal was on a lease basis. I liked Ernie a lot, but he was real tough to deal with, you couldn't get no money out of him. When he promised to pay, he'd pay you, but he would not promise to pay you much. But I was here in the country, I didn't know too much about anything. He started off paying me a nickel a record for each one sold and that would include the artist royalty—and I'd pay some of them two cents depending on how long they've been with me. He got all the publishing and I had to pay all the expenses of recording. And finally after dealing with him about twelve years I got up to 6½ cents. It took me twelve years to get that. But I think Ernie will tell you, we did 90 percent of his sales, the records he sold were what we did here in Crowley."

Lightnin' Slim's early Excello singles like "Lightnin' Blues" and "Sugar Plum" were in the same archaic blues style as "Bad Luck." The essential commercial refinement came when Slim was partnered by harmonica player Lazy Lester, a superbly expressive technician whose mellifluous phrases saturated the many spaces between Lightnin's meager guitar figures. Lester always took short, stabbing solos that were inevitably preceded by Lightnin's unerring shout of "Blow your harmonica, son!"—a splendid gimmick. By 1958 Lightnin's records were selling steadily throughout the South among blacks who readily appreciated the honest messages in such gems as "I'm Grown," "I'm A Rollin' Stone," "Hoo Doo Blues," and "My Starter Won't Work." It was easy for listeners to conjure up images of humid Louisiana nights with crickets chirping, alligators barking, and fat-bellied frogs croaking—the real swamp-blues sounds.

In early 1959 the up-tempo "Rooster Blues" became Lightnin's only single to break into the *Billboard* R&B charts, climbing to No. 23, a remarkable feat for such a pure down-home blues performance. The flip, "G.I. Slim," using the familiar Muddy Waters "I'm A Man" riff (the Chicago blues were a continuing source of inspiration), portrayed a distinctly patriotic stance:

> *Now I want all you young chicks and grown-up hens,*
> *I just want to tell you about where I've been.*
> *From coast to coast, to the golden gates of Maine*
> *I've chatted with the Queen's maids, I've shot jokes with the King.*

I heard Hitler say to President Roosevelt,
We've got the fastest planes in the world.
I heard President Roosevelt say that ain't so,
'Cause we've got planes that climb like a squirrel.

That's why I'm goin' to join the Army
Just like any boy should.
I wanted old man Hitler to know
That po' Lightnin' didn't mean him no good.

Now when they raised the white flag and all of us came home,
I thought that I would settle down and no more would have to roam.
Now I understand there is more trouble with those Russians over there,
That fellow that they call Khrushchev don't want to do it fair.

Now I'm goin' to join the Army. . . .

"Rooster Blues" was a hit, and an album followed, but Lightnin' did not alter his down-home approach at all. The next single, "Tom Cat Blues"/"Bed Bug Blues," was bluer than ever. The consistent record sales ensured that Lightnin' was always in demand for personal appearances. Often performing with Lazy Lester, he played mostly in Baton Rouge clubs and at Acadiana venues like the Rickey Club in Duson, the Silver Slipper in Arnaudville, the Four Leaf Clover in Church Point, and the Hide-A-Way Lounge in Rayne. Lightnin' was even booked at Father Auclair's Immaculate Conception Church in Lebeau and Our Lady of Victory Church in Loreauville; occasionally he would travel to New Orleans and East Texas. In one instance Jay Miller asked his blues star if he wanted to perform at the University of Mississippi in Oxford. Lightnin' was not keen, explaining in his inimitable way, "But Mister Jay, over there you'se got to call a white mule 'mister'!"

During this period Baton Rouge drummer Jimmy Dotson used to sit in with Lightnin' Slim. Recalls Jimmy, who also recorded for Jay Miller: "Lightnin' had three pieces—himself, Lazy Lester, and a drummer. And the drummer in most cases tonight wouldn't be the one he used last night. You could only play one night with Lightnin', you had to rest a couple of days because your hand would swell up. He was a nut for the backbeat, and he wanted you to slam that backbeat in, he didn't want you to do anything but the backbeat . . . *whoom!* And you hit so hard, you had the stick laying the front way, you hit the drums so hard until by the time you got off your hand is swollen up. I got slick to him, I started holding my stick differently, I'd palm away. . . ."

In the studio Lightnin' was a model artist. "Lightnin' and I would generally get together and put the song together," says J. D. "I'd just tell him a story and tell him to tell that story, tell it whatever way he felt. We might have three or four cuts of one song, completely different to some degree. His words would be different, his phrasing would be different, and his tune would vary, too." For his part, Jay was always open to ideas from Lightnin', as he was from all his artists. On the next release, "Cool Down Baby"/"Nothin' But The Devil," a heavier electric sound was evident. *The Cash Box* gave the record a good review: "Vet southern blues standby Slim delivers one of his top efforts here. Harmonica highlights the infectious musical support to Slim's sturdy chanting. A murkier mood is quickly established [on the flip] by the deep-throated vocal work of the artist. Two strong stanzas for the right market." Throughout 1961 and 1962 Lightnin' was at his peak with flawless couplings of "Hello Mary Lee"/"I'm Tired Waitin' Baby" and "Mind Your Own Business"/"You're Old Enough To Understand." Best of all was "Winter Time Blues," a truly great twelve-bar blues which, encouragingly, sold well throughout the South in early 1963. In a song with fascinatingly irregular stanzas, a dejected Lightnin' bemoaned his lost love:

> You know winter time done rolled around,
> And here I am again by myself.
> Oh, winter time done rolled around,
> And here I am again all by myself.
> You know the little girl that I used to love,
> Well, she's lovin' somebody else. . . .
>
> You know the little girl is just sixteen years old.
> How you know, Lightnin'?
> Well, that's what I heard her mother said.
> Yes, the little girl is just sixteen years old.
> How you find out, Lightnin'?
> I eavesdropped and heard her mother said,
> You know she got a way of huggin' and kissin',
> She'll bring livin' back to the dead.

But the standard began to decline when Lazy Lester missed a few sessions; perhaps Slim had become overdependent on their musical empathy. To make matters worse, the blues market was falling away because of the changing tastes of Negro record buyers: they were now black and proud, and they wanted soul music. In 1964 Jay Miller desperately tried to introduce pop-style backings. "Things were flagging, I tried to improve sales, but it didn't work," he recalls. The familiar Lightnin' Slim sound was revived on a remake of "Bad Luck (Blues)," to no avail. Times had really changed.

Then, in 1965, Lightnin' wrecked one of Jay Miller's trucks—and lost his recording career at the same time. Fearing prosecution, he fled north, obtaining work in factories in Romeo and Pontiac, Michigan. Three years later his old friend Slim Harpo rescued him from a soulless production line by inviting Lightnin' to join his band. In 1970 Lightnin' was re-signed to Excello, now under different management. His first album under the new deal, "High And Low," produced grandiosely with a large backing group in Sheffield, Alabama, lacked the cozy down-home friendliness of a Jay Miller recording. Despite B. B. King's assertion on the LP sleeve that Lightnin' was "a qualified authentic blues singer who has finally arrived," Excello must have been hard pressed to recover its costs.

At least Lightnin's career had entered another positive phase. In 1972 he was summoned to Europe, where he became a regular visitor over the next eighteen months with harmonica player Whispering Smith. On each trip Lightnin's confidence grew visibly as a static but powerful stage act was replaced by a happy jiving routine. He was enjoying himself greatly, although in his attempt to entertain the European audiences he replaced many of his emotional down-home blues songs with inferior up-tempo R&B. Jay Miller was right when he said that it was necessary to make Lightnin' "blue" to get his best performance. Then Lightnin' developed a stomach tumor and died on July 27, 1974, at the Ford Hospital in Detroit.

Lightnin' Slim had given the Louisiana swamp-blues an identity where there had been none before. His musical influence was evident in the work of Slim Harpo, Silas Hogan, Guitar Kelley, and others, and he also introduced many Baton Rouge bluesmen to Jay Miller in Crowley. Miller was upset at the way Lightnin' had departed, but his admiration remains untarnished: "Lightnin' to me was the greatest, not only of my artists, but all of them. Low-down gutbucket blues!"

11

"Slim Harpo's generation was awful rough on the black man"

In 1956 Lightnin' Slim was established on Excello, and Jay Miller's leasing deal with Ernie Young was vindicated. Hearing of Lightnin' Slim's success, other bluesmen started arriving at Crowley hoping to be recorded. Miller, with his new contractual obligations to supply blues master tapes to the Nashville-based label, was happy to give opportunities to these ambitious musicians, who included Slim Harpo, Lonesome Sundown, and Lazy Lester.

If Lightnin' Slim was Jay Miller's most consistent bluesman, Slim Harpo was the most commercial. The harmonica virtuoso had three huge southern hits with "I'm A King Bee" (1957), "Rainin' In My Heart" (1961), and "Baby Scratch My Back" (1966), and his songs were covered by a galaxy of artists from Clifton Chenier to the Rolling Stones. But he was not a favorite of Jay Miller's: "Slim Harpo was playing harmonica, he was with Lightnin'. So Lightnin' asked me one day, he said, 'Slim would sure like to make a record on his own,' and I said 'Does he sing?' He said he sings some. So after we finished a session I listened; his singing was very, very poor. I liked his harmonica playing, but it was a different thing with his singing. And I've always found in music, like any other thing, sometimes you've got to have a gimmick. So, it was a little ridiculous to ask him to do it, but he did—I asked him to sing, kinda sing through his nose, with a nasal sound. You know who developed that? Hank Williams.

" 'I'm A King Bee,' that was his first record, very nasal. And it was different. I can't recall the session, but the buzzing noises I believe they were my idea. Like I say, you've got to work as many gimmicks as you can." Modeled on the macho theme that Muddy Waters was using to good effect in Chicago, "I'm A King Bee" was a lustful, evocative blues written by Harpo:

Well, I'm a King Bee buzzin' around your hive, (repeat)
Well, I can make honey, baby, let me come inside.

I'm young and able to buzz all night long. (repeat)
Well, when you hear me buzzin' baby some stingin' is going on.

The simplistic sexual imagery was richly amplified by the erotic musical backdrop: a booming bass line answered Harpo's command of *Well, buzz awhile!* while a biting guitar note greeted his cry of *Sting it, then!* The colorful scenario was completed by Slim's sensuous harmonica playing and a tantalizing swamp beat. Without doubt, "I'm A King Bee" was a vinyl masterpiece.

The atmospheric "I Got Love If You Want It" flip, with its complex Afro-Caribbean rhythms, confirmed the productional genius of Jay Miller. Slim was a King Bee no more. Although he was quick to assure his woman with her *fine brown frame* and *hair hung down* that he had *love if you want it, babe,* he realized, much to his chagrin, that she had *been ballin', the talk's all over town.*

Slim Harpo was born James Moore in 1924 at Lobdell in West Baton Rouge Parish. As an orphaned teen-ager he moved downstream to steve-dore on the New Orleans riverfront before returning to Baton Rouge as a laborer. Calling himself Harmonica Slim, he started playing in Lightnin' Slim's small band. Lightnin' once recalled: "Harpo, me, and a drummer teamed up in Baton Rouge, we'd just play for friends at a birthday party or wedding or something like that. We never really made any money at it, we had a lot of fun. I taught him how to play music. In fact I gave him his first set of instruments to play with. He could play one number and that was 'Blue Suede Shoes.' And we once went to a dance and I let him play it slow, then let him stay off, and then he came back in half an hour and I let him play it fast!"

Slim followed "I'm A King Bee" with the swamp-blues of "Wondering and Worryin'," "You'll Be Sorry One Day," and "Buzz Me Babe," without capturing the splendor of the first single. Then, in 1960, he recorded "Blues Hang-Over." Gliding over one of the moodiest bass lines ever, his wailing harmonica paved the way for a stark monologue that reflected all the melancholy despair of the alcoholic's world:

Lord, I wonder what could have happened,
Ain't nobody here but me.
All these empty bottles on the table here,
I know I didn't drink all this by myself.
I must have a Blues Hangover . . .

In the final verse, he looked to members of his band for support:

Well, I believe I'm goin' back on the stem now
With James, Rudolph and Tomcat,
Get my head bad again,
Don't seem like nothing's goin' right for me today . . .

But the sound was too down-and-out even for the southern markets of the time, where Jimmy Reed, Muddy Waters, John Lee Hooker, and Lightnin' Slim were selling blues records in large quantities. The flip, "What A Dream," was a more conventional twelve-bar blues, but a powerhouse for all that. The interplay between Willie "Tomcat" Parker's saxophone, the two guitars of Rudolph Richard and James Johnson, and Harpo's chilling harmonica was faultless. During this period Jay Miller was organizing bookings for Slim Harpo, and not just in Louisiana. An old contract reveals that on Monday, November 23, 1959, a Joe Carl in Birmingham, Alabama, contracted "Slim Harpo and his band . . . $250 . . . to play for two shows—one for the white and one for the colored. The first show is to begin at 7:00 P.M." Carl was asked to send a deposit to Miller while "the balance of $200 will be paid to Slim Harpo upon completion of the engagement."

On November 17 and 18 a year later Harpo was booked to appear in Chicago with Lightnin' Slim and Lazy Lester by Bill Hill's Colt Agency for $450, "the place of engagement to be at choice, but it is understood that each engagement will not be in excess of four hours." In an attempt to please the crowds, all three artists played the popular hits of B. B. King and others instead of introducing their new audiences to the unique Louisiana swamp-blues. The promotional purpose of the trip was therefore defeated.

In May 1961 a young Jonathan Foose, the New Orleans researcher and musician, saw Slim Harpo at his school's end-of-year "Midnite 'Til Dawn Dance" in Yazoo City, Mississippi: "The group that the seniors had hired for the occasion that year was Slim Harpo and his Band. I was a freshman and it was the first time I was allowed to attend this all-night rite. The dance was held in the National Guard armory, which was a cavernous building that houses Yazoo's crack military unit. The main drill hall was so large that the crepe paper seemed scant and lost. A parachute was suspended from the ceiling to give a canopied effect. The band arrived around 10:30. My memory has dimmed a bit, but I believe there were five pieces in the group. The main thing that sticks in my mind was Slim Harpo walking in, carrying a large metal fishing-tackle box. He put it in a chair by the vocal mike and it was stuffed full of harmonicas. The man meant business. His sax player was crippled and played while leaning on a crutch.

"The music was full and the large room gave it an echoing rawness. Slim had put out 'Rainin' In My Heart' and was touring behind it. It was a school favorite. The song that he did that I liked that night was 'I Got Love If You Want It.' He also played 'I'm A King Bee,' complete with buzz and sting, and a great version of Howlin' Wolf's 'Howlin' For My Darling.' Needless to say, the dance was a huge success and I had had my first shot of Louisiana swamp-blues. It would not be my last."

"Rainin' In My Heart" changed everything for Slim. For a start, *The Cash Box* warmed to the record: "Slow moaning, earthy blues proves the artist's meat as he takes the tune for a tuneful ride. A real weeper. Tempo moves up to jet speed [on the electrifying 'Don't Start Cryin' Now'] and Harpo follows the combo on a rafter-shaking journey. Both ends have the goods to deliver." The mesmerizing "Rainin' In My Heart" more than justified the reviewer's optimism. After climbing the R&B charts the record crossed over to the popular ratings and reached No. 34 on the *Billboard Hot 100* in the summer of 1961. Jay Miller knew the song was commercial, but he was not entirely happy with the finished production.

" 'I'm A King Bee' was nice," he reflects, "we sold a number of records, but it wasn't a national hit or anything like that. But it put us in a position where he had some name recognition and it made me feel a lot better about his ability. And finally we cut 'Rainin' In My Heart.' He was the one who gave me the title. He said, 'Mr. Miller, I got a good title for a song,' and I said 'Ah!' He said, 'I just can't put it together, I know you can,' because I used to write these quite often, I'd do it in the studio while we were recording. But anyway I put it together and I recorded it at three different sessions. And I really didn't get what I wanted, frankly speaking. When I say three different sessions I mean just that, at three different dates. I felt we had gotten all I could out of it so I sent it to Ernie Young with a letter apologizing. I thought it was a good song, but that was the best we could do. And it turned out it wasn't too bad, because it sold a lot of records!"

But Slim Harpo promptly took the bubbles out of the champagne by refusing to set foot in the recording studio because of a royalty dispute. Although Excello released a first-class album, "Rainin' In My Heart," it was not what was needed in a world governed by the hit single. Harpo soon lost his status as a "hot" artist. Jay Miller's disaffection with him is clearly rooted in this period: "You know how the business is, when Joe Blow is not doing any good, nobody wants him. But you let him taste a little success, then everybody is after him. Anyway Slim became in demand. Here we are, we're a little country outfit, and my wife and I and my family are given a trip to visit Randy Wood, president of Dot Records, on the West coast. Randy called, wanted me to go and work for him. I said, 'I don't know how to, I don't want to leave here ...' Well he said, 'Do this, get your family together and you come over and spend a week or two, Dot Records will pay all the expenses. Look the situation over.'

"So we got in our T-Bird and we went. And I got over there and got a call from Ernie Young telling me he had heard that Slim Harpo had cut a session for Imperial, Lew Chudd. And I said, 'Ernie, I want you to check to see if that's true.' He says, 'I've checked it as far as I know, I believe it is. You've got a contract on him?' I said, 'Sure ... I tell you what I'm gonna do, I'm gonna see Lew Chudd in Hollywood.'

"And I told him, 'I understand you recorded one of my artists, that I have under contract.'

"He said, 'Yes, he wanted to record for us.'

" 'Well!' I said, 'you do know, or you did know, or I'm sure you know now because I'm telling you, he's under contract to us.'

" 'Oh yes,' he said, 'but he's union and you're not.'

" 'Well, you know the fact that he's union and I'm not, when he signed up with me he didn't even know what a union was. And I'm quite sure that union bylaws and laws, rules, and regulations won't supersede our legal rights. I'm not gonna hassle with you, I'm going to tell you this, if you release anything by Slim Harpo before his contract is over with me I'm going to sue you. My lawyer tells me that I'll be in a lot better shape if you did release it because we'll sue you and get plenty in court after a hit.'

"I just left like that, I was bluffing then, I hadn't talked to my lawyer. You know, a strong offense is the best defense sometimes. But anyway when I got back to my room I called Jerome Stokes who was Ernie Young's lawyer and he says, 'Send me a copy of your contract,' so I called Crowley and had them send a copy of the contract. He called me back and said, 'Don't worry about it,' and he wrote a letter for me to Lew Chudd."

Nevertheless, two tracks from the Imperial session were later released on an anthology aimed at the white collector's market; they turned out to be competent but routine southern blues.

In 1963 the rift between Miller and Harpo was healed temporarily. But except for "I Need Money (Keep Your Alibis)"/"Little Queen Bee (Got A Brand New King)" the new singles were disappointing. However, in January 1966 the name of Slim Harpo graced the charts again when "Baby Scratch My Back" was a No. 1 R&B hit before crossing over to No. 16 on the *Billboard Hot 100*. The record was subsequently voted No. 3 R&B for 1966—at a time, it must be remembered, when Motown ruled the airwaves. This infectious rhythmic dance number with an arresting clip-clop sound was unmistakably a Jay Miller production. "Even when we had drums we used a lot of sound effects," recalls Miller with pride. "Like for instance 'Baby Scratch My Back,' gee wee, we had some percussion!" "Shake Your Hips" was an engaging follow-up in the same rhythm-dance format, but it inexplicably failed to make the charts.

During 1966 Ernie Young sold his Nashboro/Excello concern, which was moved from crumbling Third Avenue North to sparkling premises on Woodland Avenue in Nashville. Needing a hit artist—and not wishing to be constrained by the terms of a leasing agreement—the new regime proceeded to spirit Slim Harpo away from Jay Miller, together with new soul artist Johnny Truitt. This action angered Miller so much that he split with Excello: "The contract was for three years, so I stayed more or less dormant for the balance of the contract in respect to the production of blues records on which they had first option." Meanwhile Slim was flown to Memphis to record "Tip On In," a cute latin-tinged single that became a No. 37 *Billboard* R&B hit in July 1967. The attractions of "Te-Ni-Nee-Ni-Nu" were less obvious, but it still made No. 36 on the R&B chart in March 1968. Then Harpo's new producers immersed him in the heady world of psychedelia, flanked by fuzzed-up guitars, atmospheric organs, and funky bass guitars. Mercifully surviving the experience, he proceeded to record an outstanding blues album with brilliant guitar work from his old accompanists Rudolph Richard and James Johnson. When Slim was scheduled to visit Europe a few months later it seemed he was about to make a long-overdue breakthrough, but he died of a heart attack following a suspected drug overdose on January 31, 1970, in Baton Rouge General Hospital. "He Knew The Blues" was the hasty title for what turned out to be a memorial album.

Slim Harpo was a fabulous, original Louisiana swamp-blues artist who, even posthumously, has not been accorded the acclaim he deserves. John Fred, the Baton Rouge singer famous for the worldwide hit "Judy In Disguise," offers a fitting tribute: "Slim Harpo was a very good friend of mine. In fact I was there when he wrote 'Baby Scratch My Back,' he wrote that at the back of Tommy's Record Shop. Yeah, I knew all those guys, I played gigs with them. I was closer to the black people than the white people because in those days I used to go with somebody like Slim Harpo, we'd drive down to New Orleans and we had to go eat in the back. It used to really make me mad ... I didn't really understand it. But you had to do it, if you said anything about it you got a knock at the side of the head. You just ate back there and that was it. He didn't question it, I used to question it, it didn't make any difference to him.

"Slim could roll with the flow, you know what I mean? I loved him. He was great in person, he was Slim Harpo. He used to play a little place called the Glass Hat every Wednesday night, it was Slim Harpo, Rudolph his guitar player. Slim had a fairly big suitcase full of harmonicas, I mean, just like a guy with fish bait, that type of box. He used to have harmonicas everywhere, he was just amazing. To me, 'Rainin' In My Heart' was just so real, so soulful. You had to like him. If Mick Jagger was here right now he'd tell you that Slim Harpo was definitely a plus for him. On the Rolling Stones' first album he did 'I'm A King Bee.' I'll never forget, Slim Harpo came to me, he said, 'John Fred, John Fred, guess what happened, the Rolling Stones recorded one of my songs!' I said, 'Who in the hell are the Rolling Stones?' He said, 'Well, they said they're gonna be big.' But God rest his soul, he was right.

"Slim could have been big, it was like Leadbelly and those other guys, they were kinda trapped in the South, they were born just at the wrong time. They didn't have much influence locally, that's the amazing thing. For example, in my opinion the Beatles were imitating American music and the Americans were trying to play Beatles music. 'Dizzy Miss Lizzy,' 'Roll Over Beethoven,' man, I played those songs many a time, so it was just the generation you grew up in. Slim Harpo's generation was awful rough on the black man, you got to remember that."

Lonesome Sundown was part of that same oppressed generation. He was a versatile bluesman with a powerful voice and a commanding guitar style, but unlike Slim Harpo he never had hit records to establish any sort of national reputation.

His doomy blues music suited his splendid *nom de disque.* "I gave Lonesome Sundown his name," says Jay Miller. "Well, Cornelius Green didn't sound too commercial. We'd always try to pick out a fairly commercial name. I've always liked him. . . . The first one was the best one, 'Lost Without Love,' then he had a thing I wrote for him called 'My Home Is A Prison' that did quite well. I wrote that right on the session. Never had anything big, I think he had the potential if people had kept buying this type of record."

Lonesome Sundown spent nine years with Jay Miller, and had a total of sixteen singles and one album issued by Excello. He was born in 1928 on the Dugas Plantation near Donaldsonville, thirty-five miles south of Baton Rouge. As a boy he toiled in the sugarcane fields, but in 1946 he left for New Orleans, working at a hotel, in a rice mill, with a construction company, and in a gambling house. In 1948 he returned to Donaldsonville and took guitar lessons from his cousin; the first song he learned was John Lee Hooker's "Boogie Chillun." Then he left home again to drive trucks on a sugarcane plantation near Jeanerette, and in 1953 he moved to Port Arthur to work at the Gulf Oil refinery. In the evenings he jammed at local clubs. "There was a guy there playing Muddy Waters's 'Still A Fool,'" Sundown recalled. "The way he would introduce the number is where I got my style, but I already had a soul for the blues. I saw so many musicians playing on Saturday night that I got better and better. Then I met Clifton Chenier at the Blue Moon club in Port Arthur, he needed a band to go on the road to promote his hit record 'Ay-Tete-Fee' and I was hired with Phillip Walker as first and second guitar players. We traveled from Louisiana to California playing dances mostly. I got a chance to sing with the band and the people seemed to like the feeling I put into the blues more than my pop songs. So I decided to stick with the blues and perfect my style. After traveling we went to California to record and there I met Specialty representative Bumps Blackwell. I tried hard to get my own recording contract, but had no luck.

"When I married in 1955 I moved to Opelousas and started playing in a local trio led by Lloyd Reynaud, we played regularly at the Domino Lounge in Eunice. After hearing about Jay Miller I brought a demo tape to his studio. You should have seen that studio, it was like a radio repair shop and studio combined, so closely combined you couldn't hardly tell which was which! Jay Miller asked me to bring the band by, we recorded a couple of songs for him."

Sundown's first record, "Lost Without Love"/"Leave My Money Alone" introduced a promising young bluesman who was clearly molding his style on the popular blues singers of the day, notably T-Bone Walker and Muddy Waters. That style was perfected in "My Home Is A Prison," a plaintive blues classic:

My home is a prison and I'm living in a world of tears,   (repeat)
I've been in misery since the judge gave me ninety-nine years.

I had a real pretty woman who said she loved no one but me,   (repeat)
But I caught my baby cheatin', now my home ain't where it used to be.

I've got bread and milk for breakfast,
Milk and bread every suppertime,
And the food I got for dinner is a low-down dirty crime.

Yes it's true I shot my baby (lord have mercy),
But I did it 'cause she did me wrong,
Now the only thing I got is this lonesome jail that I call home.

Sundown confirms Jay Miller wrote the song at the session—a striking example of Miller's talent as a songwriter. "He would get an idea from an incident and begin writing," the bluesman said. "At that time my wife didn't like me in the music business and called the studio for me. Mr. Miller detected my agony and displeasure and began writing. That's the way a song is written."

With Lazy Lester often lending harmonica support, Lonesome Sundown maintained an impressive standard throughout 1957 and 1958 on "Don't Say A Word," "I'm A Mojo Man," and "Gonna Stick To You Baby," climaxed by "I Stood By"—an immaculate tour de force in which he regretted that he had *stood by and watched another man take my friend.* Although the fifties ended quietly for Sundown, he made a strong comeback in 1962 with "Lonesome Lonely Blues," a marvelous, hypnotic song enhanced by his smoky, husky voice dredging every ounce of meaning out of the despairing title phrase. The backing by Jay Miller's studio musicians was superb, especially the startling tenor-sax work of Lionel Prevost, a former Clifton Chenier sideman who recorded for Miller as Lionel Torrence. He was a saxophonist of cherishable individuality, with the tone, emotion, and creativity of a top jazzman.

Harry Simoneaux, a fellow sax player and J. D. Miller session man, recalls: "Lionel was fantastic in any key! His horn was a sight to behold, he always had more rubber bands holding it together than you could count. Perhaps that enhanced the beauty of his art. A magnificent musician and a wonderful person, he was open to any suggestion at a session and always quiet—he let his horn do the talking. It's a shame that such a talent was not more widely recognized. It was an honor to play with him, and my one regret is that we were never able to play together on a dance job. That would have been great! I hear Lionel may still be in Port Arthur, Texas. I hope he's still playing and perhaps influencing some younger musicians."

In 1964 Jay Miller tried to inflict the same pop gimmicks on Lonesome Sundown as he had on Lightnin' Slim and Slim Harpo. The results were aesthetically and commercially disastrous. Before Sundown stopped recording for Miller, he redeemed his self-respect with the pleasing "I Got A Broken Heart," "Please Be On That '519,'" and "Hoo Doo Woman Blues." Along with other Excello releases of the time, these recordings represent some of the last ethnic down-home blues 45s aimed exclusively at the Negro market.

Sundown decided to seek salvation in religion: "I wasn't totally satisfied, because after I recorded so many years I hadn't received no income, I didn't receive no check or nothing, and it began to discourage me. I joined the Church of the Lord Jesus Christ on February 7, 1965, and I thank God every day. It gave me a beautiful mind concerning my life and the things around me—things to be enjoyed, things to be admired, things to be appreciated."

This big, friendly man came out of musical retirement in 1977 to record a highly commendable blues album, "Been Gone Too Long" (Joliet), with Phillip Walker in Los Angeles. By 1979 he was back in Louisiana, working as a bulldozer driver for a Lafayette construction company. He took time off to play the important Jazz and Heritage Festival in New Orleans, but his set was ruined by an unrehearsed band. As he used to sing, it was a low-down dirty crime—his luck in music had not changed at all.

Lazy Lester arrived in Crowley in late 1956, hot on the heels of Lonesome Sundown and similarly intent on becoming a top recording artist. Although he helped to pioneer an identifiable Louisiana swamp-blues style through his accompaniment of Lightnin' Slim and others, he never tasted real success on his own. While his harmonica sound was unique— one phrase and it was unmistakably Lazy Lester—his monotone Jimmy

Reed–influenced vocals were not in the same class. For all his natural ability he did not possess the self-discipline to be a star; he was the joker in the pack. "I tell you I liked Lester," stresses Jay Miller, "but he just wouldn't leave that booze alone. He'd drink anything, anytime, anyplace! I had to quit sending him on the road because I got so many calls to get him out of jail, he'd get in trouble, see. A lot of talent, a fine, real real fine harmonica player, and I liked him personally."

Lazy Lester was born Leslie Johnson in 1933 in the small town of Torras near the Mississippi state border. Moving to Scotlandville, a suburb of Baton Rouge, he worked as a grocery clerk, gas station attendant, and woodcutter before taking up music: "I was working in a grocery store in Baton Rouge at that time and I bought a harmonica and a record while I was working there. I was sitting on the back of the bus going home and I revved the harp up a bit. By the time I got off the bus at Scotlandville I had it tuned down the way I wanted it. The record was 'Juke' by Little Walter. Jimmy Reed was my favorite, but I've got my own style. I just kept fooling around with it till I got the sound out of it that I wanted."

Lester helped form the Rhythm Rockers, a group that played the popular blues and dance tunes of the day at high-school dances and proms. In the band were the late Sonny Martin on piano and vocalist Eddie Hudson; both went on to record for Excello. For Lester, events took a noteworthy turn when he met Lightnin' Slim: "Well, I was living in Rayne at the time and I was on the bus and Lightnin' Slim was on the bus. So since I was going just seven miles from where he was going I decided I'd just ride on over to Crowley. And after he told me he was going to record some stuff I just went along with him. The guy that was supposed to play harmonica, he didn't show up, he was from Texas, Wild Bill Phillips I believe he called himself. We sat around that night and I told Slim, I said, 'Well, look man, you want someone to play harmonica, from what I hear on your records I believe I can do that.' So we got in the studio and it sounded all right."

Soon Lester started making his own records. Of his early Excello releases, backed by Guitar Gable's group, only the bright instrumental "Lester's Stomp" and the ironic "They Call Me Lazy" had a distinctive sound. There was a welcome improvement on "I'm A Lover Not A Fighter"/"Sugar Coated Love," a powerful boogieing double-sider that turned out to be his best seller. Just as dynamic was the follow-up "I Hear You Knockin' "/"Through The Goodness Of My Heart" from the same session. By chance, these were among the first recordings to feature guitarist Al Foreman, bass guitarist Bobby McBride, and drummer Warren Storm, who were all destined to play on countless Jay Miller sessions in the years ahead. They were white, but they were such good musicians, so steeped in the South Louisiana music tradition, that they enhanced rather than diminished the authenticity of the blues recordings. Quite simply, they swung.

Himself a constant presence in the studio, Lester was just as versatile. He accompanied every type of Miller artist, playing blues, R&B, Cajun, country, or rock 'n' roll with ease. In addition to his harmonica work, he was a reliable guitarist and also excelled as a percussionist (besides the standard drums, brushes, washboard, and wood blocks, he would often improvise on cardboard boxes or saddles, even bang walls and pat newspapers on his lap). Usually Lester was the anonymous figure behind Jay Miller's famous percussion sound.

Excello continued to release Lazy Lester's blues records—including one album—at regular intervals until 1966. There were some real firecrackers, like the 1961 coupling "You Got Me Where You Want Me"/"Patrol Blues" and "Whoa Now," arguably Lester's finest recording. Featuring the raunchiest of accompaniment from the magic saxophone of Lionel Prevost and the piano of Katie Webster, "Whoa Now" was a fabulously sculptured twelve-bar blues that saw Lester in a mean mood:

> *Whoa now, stop your runnin' around on me,*   (repeat)
> *Well, you're thinkin' crazy, baby,*
> *If you think that's how it's gonna be.*
>
> *I say like the little red rooster said to the little grey hen,*
> *You used to lay your eggs in another yard,*
> *But you can't do that again.*
> *Whoa now . . .*
>
> *Well you say that was your brother I saw you with last night.*
> *I've never seen a brother*
> *Kiss and squeeze his sister tight.*
> *Whoa now . . .*

By contrast, the mournful "Lonesome Highway Blues" from 1963 was a delightful minor-keyed opus with Lester on guitar and the underrated Sylvester Buckley of Silas Hogan's band playing harmonica. But Lester never set the charts alight, and his chance vanished when the Excello outlet was lost. Like Lightnin' Slim he moved north to live anonymously in Pontiac, Michigan, although he was momentarily hoisted out of obscurity to play at a blues festival in Holland in 1980. In a world short of great harmonica players he should have filled part of the void left by Little Walter, but, lacking direction, he seems to have missed his chance.

Without doubt the Crowley days saw him at his very best, and for him they remain a happy memory: "When we was working together Lightnin' would live with me in Crowley. I had a house rented over there, the whole band would stay. Lightnin' would stay over, he and his wife, or somebody else's wife most of the time, ha, ha. I had an eight-room house over there, I had plenty of room for everybody. Those were the good old days, didn't have to work at that time. All I did was wait for the mailman to bring my checks!"

For every bluesman who struggled to attain even modest success, there were many more who enjoyed less commercial recognition, talented though they were. Vince Monroe and Boogie Jake were two such artists. Besides recording for Jay Miller, both men were later signed by Joe Banashak, who operated the New Orleans–based Minit and Instant labels.

Monroe, a guttural singer and quality harmonica player, was first recorded by Jay Miller in 1956 on the uninspired city blues "Give It Up (Or Tell Where Its At)" for Excello. Much more worthy was his "Hello Friends Hello Pal"/"On The Sunny Side Of Love" (Zynn), a beautiful swamp-blues release credited on this occasion to Mr. Calhoun. The wayward Vincent was born in Woodville, Mississippi, in 1919, and was influenced like many of his generation by the harmonica-dominated records of Sonny Boy (John Lee) Williamson. After spending many years in military service Vincent settled in New Orleans in 1954 before moving to Baton Rouge, where he met the local Jay Miller artists. Although he made regular visits to Crowley the Excello and Zynn singles were the only positive results of his endeavors—Miller found him even more difficult to handle than Lazy Lester. However, when Bruce Bastin of Flyright Records in England started excavating the Crowley tape vaults in 1976 he found among the buried blues treasures several good Mr. Calhoun sides full of down-home character, including "Hey Mattie" and "Change Your Ways." (Bastin also discovered sufficient unissued material for albums by Lightnin' Slim, Slim Harpo, Lonesome Sundown, and Lazy Lester [see appendix I]. Obviously there was a limit to the number of songs that Excello could release; Miller has always maintained that he gave them "the best.")

After returning to New Orleans, the restless bluesman recorded "Ain't Broke Ain't Hungry" in 1963 for Instant as Polka Dot Slim—a name that finally stuck. The producer Sax Kari was credited with writing the song, which was in the true swamp-blues tradition:

I ain't broke, I ain't hungry,
And I ain't sleepin' out of doors.   (repeat)
I ain't dirty or nasty,
Always wearing clean clothes.

Check yourself baby,
You ain't got no fool,   (repeat)
Well now, you're overheated, baby,
I think you need time to cool.

Monroe followed this marvelous recording with an inferior version of
Earl King's "Trick Bag" for Al Michael's Apollo label of Baton Rouge.
Much of the time he played at Allen's Bar in uptown New Orleans. He even
made occasional appearances at the Jazz and Heritage Festival, but was
never able to capitalize on his unquestioned blues talent. He died in 1982.

Boogie Jake, from Marksville, breezed briefly into Jay Miller's studio in
1958, but his splendid recordings of "I Don't Know Why" and "Early
Morning Blues" remained cocooned in a dusty tape box until Flyright
released the "Gonna Head For Home" anthology LP in 1976. The tracks
were so good that it was hard to understand why they were not issued at
the time.

Jake rerecorded both songs in 1959 for the newly formed Minit label of
New Orleans. The "A" side, "Bad Luck And Trouble" (formerly "I Don't
Know Why"), was a compelling swamp-blues with lovely, loping piano and
guitar accompaniment, boasting the glorious line, *Yes, if bad luck was*
music I'd have the hottest band around . . . After strong initial sales the
single was picked up by Chess for national distribution, but it was ignored
by prudish northern deejays who objected to Jake's "offensive" cog-
nomen. As a result his real name, Mathew Jacobs, was used on the follow-
up "Chance For Your Love," an inviting swamp-pop performance. But his
music was out of tune with the funky New Orleans sounds producer Allen
Toussaint was perfecting at Minit and he was dropped from the label's
roster. In 1961 he settled in Berkeley, California, and he has since
appeared at blues festivals on the West Coast.

12

"I wonder what was bad about good blues music?"

Following Slim Harpo's national success with "Rainin' In My Heart" in 1961, Jay Miller began augmenting his stable of blues stars to meet the increased demands of a contented Ernie Young at Excello. J. D. found impressive understudies in Silas Hogan, Jimmy Anderson, Whispering Smith, Tabby Thomas, and Charles Sheffield. The Louisiana bluesmen had never had it so good.

Silas Hogan, the old man of the party, did not record for Miller until he was fifty-one, but his eight Excello singles over a four-year period were a remarkably consistent series of unadulterated laid-back blues. There were no gimmicks; there was no need. Hogan, who was born in 1911 in Westover, a hamlet just ten miles west of Baton Rouge, lived with his parents in the neighboring farming community of Irene until 1939, when he moved to his present home in Scotlandville, next to the Ryan Airport: "Until that time I'd been living in the country, there were some old people around there picking guitar. And I just followed them from one to another, rapping on the guitar. And that's how I learned, following them. The first man who taught me how to play guitar was Frank Murphy, he had a brother that could play good, too. They were real bluesmen, that old way-back stuff. When we were playing back yonder, we were playing them house parties, they didn't have as many joints as they have now. Way back yonder they'd give a dance under an oak tree, it'd be something like a picnic. We played all night too, I'd go to them house parties around eight o'clock on a Saturday night and didn't come back till Sunday morning. I played all night for seventy-five cents."

After performing much of the time with Guitar Kelley in a rural Lightnin' Hopkins style, Silas Hogan started gaining prominence in the Baton Rouge area when he formed the Rhythm Ramblers in 1956. Also in the group were harmonica player Sylvester Buckley, guitarist Isaiah Chatman, and drummer Jimmy Dotson. Recalls Dotson:

"I was playing with Silas Hogan and the Rhythm Ramblers for about six years, we never did change musicians. During that time we would play a song exactly like the record or we wouldn't play it, it had to sound just like the record. That was the Rhythm Ramblers' trademark, we would copy a record note for note. We played all the local spots around town, across the river in Port Allen, right up to the state line with Mississippi.

"One day we had a 'Battle of the Blues' contest with Big Poppa and the Cane Cutters out from Donaldsonville. The place was called Champ's Honeydripper Club, they were looking for a regular band to play on Sundays. So OK, the owner said, 'I want one band to play every Sunday, I don't want to switch because my crowd will be confused . . . the band that wins today is gonna be the band that plays.'

"Big Poppa had a way of blowing two harmonicas at once, he could blow one with his mouth and one with his nose. He had a six-piece band and they were sounding really good. So what would happen, they would play for an hour and we would play an hour. Then at the end of the show they'd come up and play one number; and they'd get the applause from the audience. Then we'd come up and play one number, and we'd get the applause. The one that got the better applause was the one that won the show.

"So Big Poppa and the Cane Cutters played something that was so fantastic I'd never describe it. I mean we just knew we had lost the show, they were so good, they had horns and everything. And we only had four pieces—two guitars, harmonica, and drums. I was playing the drums and singing a few numbers, and Sylvester was playing the harmonica and singing a few. So we had a meeting while Big Poppa was playing, they were jammin'!

"And Jimmy Reed had a new tune out called 'Honest I Do,' and the radio station had just started playing it within the last couple of weeks. It was hot, everywhere you'd go you'd hear it on the jukebox, everywhere. So we said, 'Let's play "Honest I Do" '—we had never played it, never rehearsed it, nothing. So we said, 'Let's play it anyway! It's basic, let's play it.' Sylvester hit the harmonica . . . *squeak, squeak, squeak* . . . and I just hit the drum rolls. And we got the show just from the first few notes!"

Silas Hogan was first recorded by Reynaud Records at the turn of the sixties, but his performance on "Born In Texas" and "Let Me Be Your Hatchet" was thoroughly uncommercial. He was signed by Jay Miller in 1962. The first Excello release, "Trouble At Home Blues," was equally uncompromising, but it was a far meatier production, a torrid low-down blues in the best Lightnin' Slim style:

Rats runnin' in my kitchen,
Roaches around my cabinet door. (repeat)
These rats have got so brave around here, people,
They've shut the gas off of my stove.

For the follow-up, "Airport Blues," he tackled an old blues theme with a refreshing modern approach:

Yes I'm standin' at the airport waitin' for your plane to arrive,   (repeat)
If I don't see your face I believe I'm gonna break down and cry . . .
When you left me little woman we were livin' in a one-room shack,
    (repeat)
Now I've got me a mansion and driving a new Cadillac.

Silas's middle Excello period was highlighted by the fine rhythmic coupling of "I'm Goin' In The Valley"/"Lonesome La La" and a menacing "Dark Clouds Rollin'." But in the final sessions he really outdid himself, performing exquisitely on "Baby Please Come Back To Me," "Out And Down Blues," "So Long Blues," and "If I Ever Needed You Baby"—all beautifully crafted blues of great charm, with Sylvester Buckley's atmospheric harmonica in sympathetic support. In the early seventies Hogan took part in the Baton Rouge "revival" sessions that yielded the albums "Louisiana Blues," (Arhoolie) and "Swamp Blues,"and"Blues Live In Baton Rouge" (Excello). He was a class above the other participants, but due to uncertain health he has been restricted to playing in the Baton Rouge area since. Although he never outshone Lightnin' Slim or Slim Harpo, Hogan has been another important torchbearer of the Louisiana swamp-blues.

Jimmy Anderson, a younger artist from Baton Rouge, was too much in Jimmy Reed's shadow to succeed. Sticking rigidly to the same upper regions of the harmonica, he used identical walking-bass rhythms, and even slurred his words like the bossman of the blues. Yet his records had a compelling charm. Anderson's first single, the easy-paced "I Wanna Boogie," did well enough locally on Zynn in 1961 but faded when Dot was unable to find any sort of market after taking up national distribution. The next release, "Naggin'," rightly appeared on Excello along with Miller's other blues recordings. On this occasion Jimmy's exemplary backing group, the Joy Jumpers, latched on to a wicked downbeat; "Naggin' " was a minor masterpiece. After a disappointing remake of "I'm A King Bee," played too straight and cool, Anderson bounced back with the sardonic "Goin' Crazy Over T.V.":

Well you get up in the morning babe,
Turn on your T.V. set.
I bought you a radio, woman,
And you ain't played it yet,

'Cause you're goin' crazy over T.V., baby,
Get it out of your mind,
If you don't it's gonna run you blind . . .
Saturday morning you got to check Mr. Popeye,
At night you wanna watch Gunsmoke.
But if you don't wanna treat me right, woman,
You won't watch T.V. no more . . .

A clever novelty record, "Goin' Crazy Over T.V." might have been a hit in the South a few years earlier, but in 1964—with the blues and R&B markets diminishing rapidly—it had no chance. Jimmy Anderson has not set foot in a recording studio since.

Harmonica player Whispering Smith was introduced to Jay Miller by Lightnin' Slim. His voice was so loud that in the recording studio he had to stand way back from the microphone; there was more than a hint of irony in his adopted name. Smith's declamatory vocals and strangulated harp sound were featured on four competent singles; the best were the doleful "Mean Woman Blues" and the rhythmic "Cryin' Blues." He says the records sold "quite well."

An easygoing, friendly man, Moses Smith came from the deepest South; he was born in a tiny farming community outside West Brookhaven, Mississippi, in 1932. Influenced by the early postwar hits of John Lee Hooker and Muddy Waters, he took up music seriously when he moved to Baton Rouge in 1957. During his time at the Crowley studio in the sixties he also acted as an accompanist, but he did not possess Lazy Lester's fluent virtuosity. After a bleak end to the decade, he joined in the Arhoolie/Excello "revival" sessions which led to his only solo album, "Over Easy" (Excello), an unlikely but tasteful blend of blues and southern soul produced by Lionel Whitfield at the Deep South Studio in Baton Rouge.

Smith's best moments came when he played behind Lightnin' Slim in Europe. With arms flailing, body weaving, and legs ducking, his performance was animation itself, a throwback to the country dance and juke-joint workouts of yesteryear. Although Lightnin' Slim's death was a setback, Whispering Smith is still active in Baton Rouge.

Tabby Thomas, yet another Baton Rouge bluesman attracted by the proximity of Jay Miller's Crowley studio, had a small southern hit with his 1962 recording of "Hoodoo Party" (Excello). The big-voiced singer received sterling harmonica support from Lazy Lester on this colorful carnival song:

Well the Voodoo King, Voodoo Queen,
Gave a little party down in New Orleans.

I heard a woman scream and I turned around,
Cadillac Slim had just rolled in town.
Boogie chillun, hey boogie chillun,
Well now boogie woogie chillun,
Boogie 'til the break of dawn . . .

The flip, "Roll On Ole Mule," based on the traditional hard-times theme, was driven along by a funky New Orleans second-line beat. The same irresistible New Orleans rhythms were used on the follow-up, "Popeye Train," a very commercial-sounding dance record. On the other hand, "Play Girl" and "Keep On Trying" some four years later were right down blues alley.

A great champion of the blues, Ernest "Tabby" Thomas made his musical debut as a twenty-three-year old airman at a 1952 amateur talent show in San Francisco with the young Etta James and Johnny Mathis. After returning home to Baton Rouge he became one of the top blues entertainers in the area, playing clubs like the White Eagle and the Streamline, both in Port Allen, and the Esquire in Baton Rouge. In 1953 Thomas cut his first record, for Delta Records of Jackson, Mississippi, with credits to Tabby and his Mellow, Mellow Men. He gave "Church Members Ball" the swinging treatment popularized by Roy Brown; "Thinking Blues" was in the early Fats Domino blues style. "I heard a record on the Delta label," Tabby recalls, "and I found out the company was in Mississippi. So when I played up there I looked up the fellow that had the company, Jimmy Ammons, and I made the record with some of Buddy Stewart's musicians. The owner knew what to do because that record had a good sound!"

Two years later Tabby recorded in Crowley and had a local hit with the tuneful "Tomorrow" (Feature). A more refined artist than many of Jay Miller's bluesmen, he had further releases in the city-blues idiom on Miller's Rocko and Zynn labels prior to the Excello sessions. During the seventies he recorded for his own Blue Beat label, "but the studio was a drag." In 1979 he put on an excellent show at the New Orleans Jazz and Heritage Festival. Sitting at the piano, he led his tight five-piece band— with gifted guitarist Melvin "Big Boy" Hill—through a varied program of city blues including a rocking "Stagger Lee," the twelve-bar blues of "Candy (I'm The Sweetest Thing In Town)" and the crowd-pleasing "Hoodoo Party." Visibly encouraged, Tabby proceeded to record an album of honest merit for Blues Unlimited in Crowley with Whispering Smith, Stanley "Buckwheat" Dural Jr., and the Moore Brothers, poign-antly entitled "25 Years With The Blues." A little later he opened Tabby's Blues Box in Baton Rouge, featuring blues artists live, four nights a week. This friendly club is providing a vital outlet for local bluesmen.

The big-voiced Charles Sheffield came from the Lake Charles area, and had little connection with the Baton Rouge bluesmen. On his highly proficient 1961 Excello debut, "It's Your Voodoo Working," he showed he was not averse to dabbling in the eerie folklore of Louisiana. The mood of mystery was neatly captured by Jay Miller's studio band, which was hitting new peaks at the time. The *Billboard* reviewer was entranced: "Showmanly vocalizing by Sheffield on solid rhythm-novelty with infectious tempo. Side could happen if exposed." It was not exposed, and it did not happen. On the flip, "Rock 'N' Roll Train," Sheffield took a breezy excursion on the latest model of that familiar blues vehicle, the *mean old train movin' down the line.*

The follow-up was even better. "I Would Be A Sinner" was given a romping R&B treatment with a scorching sax break from Lionel Prevost; on "The Kangaroo," a beguiling New Orleans–influenced number, the blues-shouting singer (he also recorded for Goldband and for Jay Miller's own labels) hinted at his Gulf Coast background:

Down in Houston on Dowling Street,
In Beaumont, Texas, on Urban Street,
At the high school prom they're doing it too,
The brand new dance called the Kangaroo.

But "the brand new dance" lost out to Chubby Checker's "The Twist" and a thousand others, and Sheffield drifted into undeserved obscurity.

Jay Miller's blues productions, mostly 2½ minutes of jam-packed creativity, always had an impeccable sound. "I guess it's love more than anything else," he says modestly, "I'm not an audio technician as such, but I did get to knowing the technical end of it. I just kind of went by my ears, we played with it and we got what sounded right to us, hoping it would sound right to others. But I have to admit we got some pretty fair sounds for that day. Especially on Lightnin' Slim, it was a lonesome sound."

Among the outstanding musicians contributing to the classy sound on Miller's sessions was pianist Katie Webster. Curiously, she never had an Excello release herself, although she did have an unworthy pop single in 1966 on a new subsidiary label, A-Bet. Despite her awesome talent for blues, R&B, swamp-pop, and rock 'n' roll, Webster has had little success as a solo artist. The closest she came to having a hit record was in 1959; "Sea Of Love" (Decca), "On The Sunny Side Of Love" (Rocko), or "I Need You Baby, I Need You" (Zynn) could all have broken through. A brilliant pianist, Katie also impresses vocally. "I have a funky left hand and a rolling right," she says. "There is also that church in there that stems from my early childhood, where it was church in the morning, church in the evening and church at suppertime! So you will hear that and then you will get that little sound out of my voice because when I am singing and I am souling, I close my eyes and just drift off. Then I can feel the electricity from my body flowing in there, I feel it floating in my mind and I get these chills. Then I start doing funny things with my voice. . . ."

One of the ten children of a mailman who became a pastor in the Pentecostal church and a mother interested in missionary work, Katherine Thorn was born in Houston, Texas, in 1939. A religious upbringing was inevitable, but did nothing to dampen her desire to play the heretical music of the day: "The way I learned, well my daddy told me that when he was a young boy he used to go playing the honky-tonks, he'd play in these smoke-filled rooms all night long, just a piano playing boogie-woogie and blues, Fats Waller–type stuff, and my daddy still plays a mean piano, he's eighty years old now.

"I was into the church, but when my parents were out the radio would be blasting and I'd have somebody standing on the corner watching to see if my mother would turn the corner. As long as my mother hadn't turned the corner, well I would play Fats Domino and Chuck Berry and who else was out at that time, Little Richard. I would be tearing that piano up and I would pay this little girl a quarter a day to stand on the corner and watch for my mother. And when my mother would turn that corner I would start to play *Amazing Grace, how sweet the sound . . .* and when she walked in she'd say 'Well, my baby's playing some beautiful music this evening!' But if she'd have stepped up two minutes earlier and heard me playing 'Please Don't Leave Me,' well you know, this piano was a sanctified piano. I just wasn't supposed to be playing that kind of music on that piano. So that's what really made me go from the gospel music to rock 'n' roll and whatever."

Before Katie married Sherman Webster, "a terrific gospel piano player," she went to live with an aunt in Beaumont, Texas. Removed from the strict home environment, she started wearing fancy dresses and makeup, going to parties, and playing music in a high-school band called the Hylites. After gigging with "two blues guys," she joined a progressive jazz band at Papa's nightclub, billed as "Big Mama Cat." Then she had a spell with New Orleans R&B star Smiley Lewis before teaming up in 1959 with Ashton Savoy, a guitarist from Opelousas who recorded for Eddie Shuler. Surprisingly, Shuler was not interested in recording Katie as a solo artist, so she went to see Jay Miller. At Crowley she cut an early session with Ashton Savoy (listed as "Conroy") that yielded a minor blues classic, "Baby Baby" on Kry (retitled "No Bread No Meat" on her excellent Flyright album). With Savoy's guitar setting up a hypnotic Jimmy Reed walking-blues groove, her piano rippling in the background, she scowled:

Look at him, comin' down the street with his hand in his pocket,
I don't know what he's holding, it sure ain't no money.
Look at him walkin' that jive walk and talkin' that jive talk.
I don't want to hear that yakety-yak.
They say I talk too much, but at least I tell the truth.
Somebody done fooled that child, honey, and made him think he's cute.
Just look at that walk, ain't that something,
A-clumpity clump, a-clumpity clump, I'll say!

Arriving within Katie's earshot, Ashton innocently called out in a lazy Jimmy Reed drawl:

Hello baby, it's so good to see you now . . .

Katie Webster continued recording for Jay Miller until 1966, but she is reluctant to talk about her time in Crowley. "I did some songs and I recorded there for years and I didn't get anything moving," she says grudgingly. "I never received any royalties off these records, so I never knew what they really did." For his part, Miller says her debts outstripped royalties due.

During the early sixties Katie played with Bill Parker and the Showboat Band before forming the Uptighters. Her break came in 1966 at the Bamboo Club in Lake Charles: "They used Otis Redding one night, I was sitting in the audience and the customers wanted me to sing. I kept saying well, this is his show, let him do his show, but they kept on. So finally I decided I would sing one song and the band boys, they looked at me and thought, 'Well, she's not going to do nothing much anyway, so we'll let her come up here and do one song,' so I got on the bandstand and did a song that Gene Chandler had out at the time called 'Rainbow '65.' And Otis Redding was in the dressing room in his shorts and when he heard me sing he came out with just his shorts. He said, 'Don't let that woman get off the bandstand, keep her there, she's going with us tonight!' So that's how I got my chance with Otis Redding, and that opportunity led me to working with other great artists like James Brown and the Famous Flames, Arthur Conley, Sam and Dave, but Otis was always my favorite."

With Redding Katie toured all over the States, but the good times ended when Otis died in a mysterious plane crash on December 10, 1967. His death brought down the curtain on the golden era of soul music, especially in areas like South Louisiana where such national stars as Bobby Bland, Wilson Pickett, and Percy Sledge were well known and liked. "They had the kind of melodic blues style that sold around here," says Johnnie Allan. Except for Lil Bob and the Lollipops there were few local soul acts of note; this situation was largely brought about by the weak gospel music tradition in Cajun South Louisiana. Explains Rod Bernard: "This is primarily a very big Catholic area and for some reason gospel music is more associated with Baptist and Methodist churches."

After Redding's death Katie returned to the bars and lounges in the Lake Charles area, much of the time playing an unsuitable portable electric organ. With personal problems mounting, she eventually tried her luck on the West Coast, working at clubs in Los Angeles and San Francisco. She also performed in Reno, Nevada, with old R&B star Jimmy Beasley, and for a short while was on the "Gong Show" out of Hollywood. By 1979 Katie was back in Lake Charles, recording for Eddie Shuler at the Goldband studio. The audition tapes revealed that she had felicitously rejected the latest disco sounds for the South Louisiana music she performs so well; included were appealing swamp-pop ballads by Lil Bob, Guitar Jr., and Sticks Herman. But something went wrong in the production stage, and "Katie Webster Has The Blues" was a disappointing album; the follow-up "You Can Dig It" was even worse. However, Katie's fortunes began to improve when she was invited to Europe in 1982. Perhaps she is about to find fulfillment in music at last.

In 1967 the Crowley blues sessions were almost at a standstill. "The blues sales just dropped off as we got into the civil rights affair," says Jay Miller. "The blacks didn't want to have anything to do with the old days, regardless of what it was, good, bad, or otherwise. I wonder what was bad about good blues music?" The contractual dispute with Excello, precipitated by the loss of Slim Harpo, did not help Miller's situation either. One of Jay's few blues releases of 1968 was Joe Johnson's "Otis Is Gone" (Cry), a soulful tribute to Otis Redding with backing from Guitar Grady and his Strings of Rhythm. "Got My Oil Well Pumpin' " on the reverse was more in the blues groove. Johnson, a harmonica player from Independence, had previously recorded a rather lifeless "Dirty Woman Blues" for A-Bet, the Excello subsidiary, but he showed how good he could be on the stunning "Alimonia Blues," rescued from Miller's vaults by Flyright. In the early seventies Johnson and Grady were still churning out the hits of the day in and around New Orleans with their group the Blue Flames.

The blues stirred again in Crowley in 1970 when Jay's son Mike, briefly involved in recording, produced Henry Gray's magnificent Blues Unlimited single "I'm A Lucky Lucky Man"/"You're My Midnight Dream" with Lazy Lester and the Moore Brothers. At the session Henry had an unfortunate tendency to forget both lyric and melody, yet the finished product was almost flawless. By this time Gray had already achieved fame as pianist for the great Howlin' Wolf in Chicago, but his roots were in Louisiana: he was born in Kenner, near New Orleans, in 1925 and raised in the hamlet of

Alsen, outside Baton Rouge. Starting in music as an organist at the local Baptist church, he was soon entranced by the blues records of Big Bill Broonzy, Tampa Red, Roosevelt Sykes, and Memphis Minnie. After serving in the Philippines during World War II, Henry headed for Chicago—the sweet home of the blues—where he became friendly with the classic Windy City pianist Big Maceo Merriweather and his disciples Johnny Jones, Otis Spann, and Sunnyland Slim. The influence of these men is evident in Gray's exciting, driving style; he has a solid left hand and fast trilling right, although his timing does waver occasionally. After a short spell with Hudson Showers's Red Devil Trio he played with such blues luminaries as Little Walter and Jimmy Rogers before embarking on his twelve-year stint with Howlin' Wolf. He was also featured on many important Chicago blues recording sessions for Chess and Vee-Jay.

In 1968 Henry returned home to be with his sick father in Alsen. Easily settling down to the more relaxed way of life in the South, the blues pianist became an expert in roof repairs and coatings. He began performing with a group called the Cats at local juke joints, bars, suppers, and picnics, and he also made regular appearances at the New Orleans Jazz and Heritage Festival. After the Blues Unlimited date Gray took part erratically in the Arhoolie/Excello Baton Rouge sessions, but he did not record again until 1977, when he cut a solo album for the German Bluebeat label while touring Europe. In London two years later Henry confirmed that his piano work was as enthralling as ever, although he was very derivative vocally, leaning more to Chicago than Louisiana.

The 1970–71 Baton Rouge sessions had been set up independently by Arhoolie and Excello to capitalize on the growing awareness of the blues among college students and other young people. Despite good intentions, the attempts at recapturing the old Crowley sound with Silas Hogan, Whispering Smith, Henry Gray, and others were not successful. The music no longer seemed alive, and the productional skills of Jay Miller were badly missed. Nevertheless, the sessions did provide long-awaited opportunities for both Clarence Edwards and Arthur "Guitar" Kelley. Although Edwards, born in Linsey in 1933, recorded country blues for Dr. Harry Oster's Folk-Lyric label in 1960, the guitarist never made the trip to Crowley. One wonders what he would have achieved under Jay Miller, for he exhibited an unusual power and presence on the new recordings, especially "Let Me Love You" and "Cooling Board" on the Excello "Swamp Blues" double album, produced by Englishman Mike Vernon.

Clinton-born Arthur Kelley did not exude quite the same freshness. Molding his style closely on Lightnin' Slim's, he had been playing at house and country parties since the late forties, sometimes with Lightnin' himself or with Silas Hogan. When he made the 1970 recordings he had never appeared before a white audience or traveled outside the environs of Baton Rouge. After the "Swamp Blues" session he found local club jobs easier to secure.

During the early eighties Henry Gray, Silas Hogan, Whispering Smith, and Tabby Thomas were showing considerable enterprise by pooling resources to form the Blues Possie. It was as if these veteran Baton Rouge bluesmen intended to ride into the sunset together, taking with them warm, glowing memories of the golden era of the Louisiana swamp-blues. But despite the brave efforts of these artists the future looks uncertain. There are not many other blues performers of quality active in South Louisiana, and the music has lost its appeal to the mass black audience, including the young black musicians (the excellent Neal Brothers—sons of local harmonica player Raful Neal—are rare exceptions).

That there was any cohesive Louisiana blues scene in the first place was due to Jay Miller and his artists. Miller's many fine Crowley recordings of Lightnin' Slim, Slim Harpo, Lonesome Sundown, Lazy Lester, and Silas Hogan stand as permanent memorials to their combined talents. Nor did Miller's involvement with black music end with the swamp-blues. He was also keen to record the natural stylistic progression, rhythm and blues. Not surprisingly, the local R&B artists gave their music a special South Louisiana flavor.

13

"Rhythm and blues had a big effect on the music down here"

Rhythm and blues, a loud, rocking, urbanized music, evolved from a variety of black styles, notably big-band swing, piano boogie woogie, country blues, jazz, and gospel. The term "rhythm and blues" itself was first used by *Billboard* magazine in 1949 to replace the unflattering "race" moniker ("hillbilly" was superseded by "country and western" at the same time).

In South Louisiana, a largely rural area dominated by Cajun and hillbilly music and without a strong blues tradition, acceptance for R&B came more slowly than in many other regions. But in the early fifties visionary disc jockeys started picking up the melodic "white" sounds of Fats Domino and tuneful R&B hits like "Lawdy Miss Clawdy" by Lloyd Price, "The Things That I Used To Do" by Guitar Slim, "Pledging My Love" by Johnny Ace, "I Hear You Knocking" by Smiley Lewis, and "A Mother's Love" and "Those Lonely Lonely Nights" by Earl King.

Naturally, it was the New Orleans brand of R&B that exerted the strongest influence in South Louisiana. Other than the mighty Fats Domino, the major early New Orleans figure was Guitar Slim, an extroverted character who helped to popularize the dominant electric guitar sound in R&B. His one big hit, "The Things That I Used To Do" (1954), had a truly memorable melody line that endeared it to South Louisiana fans; the song is still performed regularly in Acadiana. Earl King, another top New Orleans artist who was a disciple of Guitar Slim, explains how he slanted his own hit records toward the South Louisiana market: " 'A Mother's Love' for Specialty was influenced by Guitar Slim, because down in South Louisiana and places like that, that was Slim's haven down there. Anywhere in there, you say 'Guitar Slim' and that was everything, that was it. That part of the country was behind Slim, whatever band you had, whatever artist, you had to contend with the people, their expectations. Slim related to them in numerous ways.

" 'Those Lonely Lonely Nights' for Ace was a change of structure for me. When I wrote the song in 1955 it was geared towards those people in that area out there. It was a country/rhythm and blues–type song. We've got a piano part in there where Huey Smith is playing a solo and it was predominantly a guitar/mandolin type solo to get that country flavor, so he gave that type of tone to it. The record broke first in South Louisiana and the person really responsible for it was Don Robey, head of Duke/Peacock Records in Houston. He promoted the record although it was on a competitive label as he was my booking agent. South Louisiana jumped on the disc quite naturally because I used to work that area so much and they were familiar with me. And during those times I used to do songs on a gig before I'd record them, and see the people latch onto the songs.

"There's so many clubs down there and we used to play maybe twenty dates a month, and every night we'd play a different club in a different little town. And sometimes two clubs in the same night. And some of the standard ones, like in Lafayette they had Landry's Palladium, which was one of the big spots to play in, Ball's Auditorium in Lake Charles, and a bunch of other places in Lake Charles. It's just so fast down there, it's unreal to even think that you got so many places all along the community out there. You had places like Robinson's Recreation which had a lot of entertainers went down there in Abbeville. One of the big places where all the big acts from all over the country came down in Opelousas was the White Eagle, Bradford's White Eagle. All the big names came there, T-Bone Walker, Ray Charles. Frank Painia of the Dew Drop Inn in New Orleans was booking some dates through there.

"People would drive twenty, thirty, forty, fifty miles in buses to go hear a particular group, it was common for them to do that. They did it frequently, every week. It could be any day. . . . I'm talking about the area from Opelousas into bits of Texas, then back into Louisiana. Even Orange, Texas, that bites on the borderline, you're dealing with the same people. Most of the people down there are French, and that's an interesting concept. I had a chance to play with Percy Sledge out of Port Sulphur about four years ago, and Percy went down there trying to sing some songs that were kinda up to date, and the people they panicked! They wanted him to do the type of things that they knowed well. Down there I found 'A Mother's Love' on a [juke] box and I said 'Wow!' "

In the mid-fifties there were still few South Louisiana artists playing R&B, except for the zydeco-oriented Clifton Chenier and Clarence Garlow. Jay Miller, with his Excello output, did his best to take advantage of the commercial R&B trend as it infiltrated the area. From 1956 to 1958 he had some reward with Guitar Gable and Carol Fran, but he was not so fortunate with Classie Ballou, Jay Nelson, and Leroy Washington. On his R&B sessions Miller generously dispensed stirring musical accompaniments featuring chunky sax sections, tripleting pianos, and romping rhythms. The sound was clearly influenced by Fats Domino's music, but it was not a mere copy of New Orleans R&B.

Guitar Gable and his Musical Kings scored on their first attempt in 1956 with "Congo Mombo," a percussive guitar workout. The tuneful blues-ballad flip "Life Problem" introduced the plummy-voiced crooner King Karl (Bernard Jolivette), who was a songwriter of some potential:

I have always had a problem,
All my life I've been so blue.
Something in my life was missing,
Now I learned that it was you.

"The recording happened accidentally with J. D.," Gable recalls. "I just came through one day going towards Lake Charles to record at a studio there, Goldband. When we got to Lake Charles we weren't able to record because the fellow, Eddie Shuler, wasn't there, so we came on back. We found out in Crowley on the way back there was a studio over there, so we drove in and talked to Mr. Miller about it. We put a couple of tunes on tape and that's the way it started. 'Congo Mombo' was quite a big hit. We were on the bandstand one night, I started fiddling around with it and the drummer started beatin', the bass got in and did its little part and we put it all together. It had something to do with the African beat. I used to watch TV a lot and I would see them beating on the drums, doing different things, it was influenced from that background. And I put some music to that beat . . . Made the 'Congo Mombo'!"

Gable, a quiet, affable man, was born Gabriel Perrodin in Bellevue, near Opelousas, in 1937. "My first memory of music was in 1953, when I first started trying to play the guitar, I was influenced by Guitar Slim and B. B. King," he recalls. "There were not too many local artists I knew at the time—Cookie and the Cupcakes, Good Rockin' Bob, and Clifton Chenier—we'd play Clifton's tunes and I'd go out to hear him." In late 1956 Gable followed his instrumental hit with "Guitar Rhumbo," but this proved to be a tactical error since the tune was too similar in concept to "Congo Mombo." However, singer King Karl deservedly succeeded with the flip side "Irene" (*the sweetest girl I've ever seen*). "Irene," a melodic ballad in the Fats Domino vein, was an important influence on swamp-pop music and the direct inspiration of "Just A Dream," the million-selling national hit by Baton Rouge teen idol Jimmy Clanton.

"King Karl sang on dance dates," says Gable, "he sang with the band for about ten years. I'd sing on the bandstand, but not on record. I never could get my voice to mature to the point where it would be acceptable on record, we put it on tape but there was always something about it that was not quite right. And we just let King Karl do the singing and I'd arrange the music and play the music to his writings—he wrote the songs and we made the music up to it. We played regular barrooms, we played teen-age parties, we played private parties, we'd just break it up and play around. Anything that came up, that wanted us, we were there. The Southern Club in Opelousas, Seven Seas in Lake Charles, in Baton Rouge we had the Carousel."

An excellent guitarist, Gable was used by J. D. Miller as a studio musician with other members of his group, brother Clinton "Fats" Perrodin on bass guitar and Clarence "Jockey" Etienne on drums (Clarence was a well-known racehorse jockey who later played with Fernest and the Thunders). The trio kicked up a storm behind artists like Slim Harpo, Lazy Lester, Classie Ballou, Skinny Dynamo (T. J. Richardson), and Bobby Charles.

Gable and Karl had another minor hit with "It's Hard But It's Fair," followed by "What's The Matter With My Baby" and "Walking In The Park," "but they wasn't that big, they went fair." In 1958 the duo cut "This Should Go On Forever," a typically lazy blues ballad, but the record was not released until the song was well on its way to becoming a national hit for Opelousas singer Rod Bernard. Gable "got a little disgusted with the business somewhere's along the line," and he and King Karl stopped recording. After serving with the armed forces, Gable continued with his own band before joining Lynn August. He now plays two or three nights a week with Lil Bob and the Lollipops. But his flirtation with musical stardom seems to be a thing of the past. As for King Karl, "he now lives in Opelousas, he's retired. I see him occasionally but I'm not sure if he's ready to fool around with music anymore."

Carol Fran, from Lake Charles, enjoyed some action in the R&B markets in 1957 with "Emmitt Lee," a straightforward South Louisiana blues ballad amusingly described by Excello as "R&B (Borderline)." The flip, "One Look At You Daddy," veered into commercial R&B territory and featured lovely "doo-wah-doody-wah" vocal-group support. The latinish follow-up "I Quit My Knockin'" maintained the same high standard.

During the early sixties Carol moved to George Khoury's Lyric label, giving the world an unforgettable version of the Platters' standard, "The Great Pretender." With her crystal-clear, soulful voice, Carol Fran was a top-class artist, part of a long line of great women blues singers stretching from Bessie Smith to LaVern Baker and Ruth Brown. Tragically, her enormous talent has never been widely recognized.

In 1957 Classie Ballou, the respected Lake Charles guitarist of "Paper In My Shoe" fame, recorded the chirpy instrumental "Hey! Pardner"

(Excello) but failed to emulate Guitar Gable's success. He did no better with "Confusion," a rocking instrumental inspired by Bill Doggett's "Honky Tonk," or with the appealing Mardi-Gras chant flip "Crazy Mambo." The latter single was the first release on Ernie Young's Nasco label, a new subsidiary aimed primarily at the popular markets. Another early Nasco record, "I'm Gonna Kill That Hen," was a hard blues by Blue Charlie (Morris), also a Miller artist.

Jay Nelson was a competent South Louisiana singer and guitarist from Jeanerette who attracted modest attention with "A Fool That Was Blind" (Excello), a sentimental blues ballad with the same droning horn sound heard on Rod Bernard's "This Should Go On Forever." But after recording a fetching, bluesy "Rocka Me All Night Long," also for Excello, Nelson had little impact on the local recording scene.

Influenced by Roy Brown's brand of soulful blues, Leroy Washington from Opelousas had a rich voice and was a real favorite of Jay Miller's. Generally his records were good, blues-laden R&B, but that vital ingredient labeled "hit" was missing. His first Excello release, the rousing "Wild Cherry" (*You're just an old alley cat*) was his best, with the lazy, laid-back "Everyday" (Zynn) a close second. Both songs were included in the valuable 1981 Flyright album "Leroy Washington," which contained many previously unissued sides, the most noteworthy being the very bluesy "Baby Please Come Home" and the highly amusing "Long Hair Knock Knees And Bow Legs." A reputable guitarist and an underrated singer, Leroy died in 1966 following a club performance at Oakdale, near Kinder.

Goldband's Eddie Shuler never had Jay Miller's commitment to the blues. He admits that he did not fully understand ethnic blues music or its markets, and his few recordings in the genre came about when bluesmen casually knocked on his studio door seeking auditions. But he did enjoy some success with commercial R&B. Eddie explains how he saw the local development of blues and R&B in the fifties: "For many years, blues and rhythm and blues wasn't really popular. It was a situation where fifteen or twenty blacks would gather in a home somewhere out in the boondocks, out on the bayous someplace and they'd have a ball. And they'd play the guitar and have a time like everybody else. A lot of those Cajun things they had back then were going on in the homes, and it was only later that the clubs came into existence. And so the blues was a participating music, not too many blacks were buying records. Then about the mid-fifties the blacks started making records and the blacks started buying [their own] peoples' records. That's when I came into the scene when these boys came to me. 'Cause I always loved the music, but until that point I didn't know too much about it."

The first black artist to record for Goldband was James Freeman from

Orange, Texas. His Rockin' Rhythm band, which included drummer Bill Parker and guitarist Chester Randle, became well known in the Lake Charles area. Before Freeman dropped out of music in the mid-fifties he cut "You're Gonna Need Me," a good strident city blues number with jazzy trumpet and tenor sax solos; the record was leased by Eddie Shuler to Bob Tanner's T.N.T. label in San Antonio, Texas.

As word spread that there was a recording studio in Lake Charles, a few blues artists, mainly from Texas, started arriving at Goldband. Hop Wilson was easily the best. His first recording, "Chicken Stuff" in 1958, was a startling instrumental that had all the bounce of an old country dance number. "Hop recorded 'Chicken Stuff' for me," says Eddie Shuler, "and you have to hear it just to appreciate how original and well produced it was. I doubt if I or the musicians could ever duplicate that number, and that makes it original! It is unique in the blues field, he played a Hawaiian guitar—six strings of blues soul. Hop lived a hard, meager, and lonely life, and this was very evident in his music."

At the time Hop was touring Texas and Louisiana with Ivory Semien's band. He had a second Goldband release, the stark "Broke And Hungry," before recording three impressive singles for Ivory Records in the early sixties. But his reticent, uncharismatic personality was an insuperable hurdle to stardom and he was reduced to playing the rough clubs of Houston's ghetto areas. He died in the summer of 1975, an embittered old man. In 1981 Eddie Shuler released a nice tribute album, "Hop Wilson Blues With Friends (At Goldband)."

Juke Boy Bonner from Austin County was another talented Texas artist. He first came to the attention of blues enthusiasts through his 1960 Goldband single "Call Me Juke Boy"/"Can't Hardly Keep From Crying." "Juke Boy had been playing club dates in and around Sacramento, California," recalls Eddie Shuler, "and had just had a record released by a small local label [Irma] when he noticed a Goldband record on the jukebox. He liked the name of the label and told everyone that was the company he would record for next. Working in his usual way from town to town, he wound up in Lake Charles, where Goldband naturally recorded him."

Known as a one-man band—he played guitar and harmonica (in a neck harness)—Juke Boy was influenced by Lightnin' Hopkins and Jimmy Reed. He cut ten songs for Goldband in 1960, eight of which appeared later on an excellent Storyville (Denmark) anthology of Goldband blues. His sparkling efforts indicated that he was a folk poet of the highest order, if musically derivative; he confirmed this impression when recording for Arhoolie and touring Europe, successfully, in the late sixties. Unfortunately drink was a problem and he died a broken man in his uncaring hometown of Houston in 1978, still only forty-six years old.

Tal Miller gave Eddie Shuler a rare blues success after the up-tempo "Baby" was leased to Don Pierce's Nashville-based Hollywood label in 1957. This Opelousas pianist's most memorable record was "Life's Journey" (Goldband), a poignant, reflective slow blues; he also did session work for Jay Miller. Another Opelousas musician, Morris "Big" Chenier—Clifton's late uncle—made several commendable blues recordings for Goldband, including "Let Me Hold Your Hand," "Please Try To Realize," and "Going To The City." As a guitarist and violinist he was highly regarded locally, but music took second place to his Chenier Barbecue And Smoke House on Enterprise Boulevard in Lake Charles.

Eddie Shuler's early R&B star was Guitar Jr., who had two regional hits. In 1957 he scored with "Family Rules," a tuneful Guitar Slim–styled antiparental blues ballad (*family rules, family rules, how they can be so cruel*), and in 1958 he did well with "The Crawl," a classy rhythm-dance rocker. These recordings were finely honed to the chart requirements of the day, and helped to establish Goldband as a professional concern. "Roll Roll Roll" and "I Got It Made (When I Marry Shirley Mae)" were other outstanding releases.

Guitar Jr. was born Lee Baker in 1933 on a small farm near Dubuisson. He became interested in music after moving with his parents to Port Arthur, Texas: "In those days I listened a lot to T-Bone Walker, he was the favorite up to B. B. King started. B. B. used to play in Port Arthur every couple of months, so I had a chance to go and see him. My first record was for Goldband, it was called 'Family Rules.' I quit Goldband in 1958, got tired of playing because of the separation between me and my wife. I left to Chicago and was just living off my royalties. Before I started playing music again in the early sixties, I accompanied Jimmy Reed on his hit record 'Big Boss Man' in 1960 and then Eddie Shuler's son, Wayne, he wrote my mother and he came to Chicago and found me. He got me a contract with Mercury. Wayne wanted to use the name 'Guitar Jr.' for Mercury, but I had changed my name to Lonnie Brooks, because when I got to Chicago I found they had another Guitar Jr. I didn't use my own name Lee Baker because it's much too dangerous in Chicago being famous under your own name! The Goldband and Mercury sessions were about in the same style."

As Lonnie Brooks he had a soul blues hit in 1967 with "Let It All Hang Out" for Chess. Blending his easygoing South Louisiana R&B music with the harsher blues of Chicago, Brooks was defying musical categorization. Two years later he confirmed his all-round ability by recording "Broke An' Hungry," an album of southern blues produced by Wayne Shuler for Capitol; the title track was Hop Wilson's number and there were several Louisiana songs by Lightnin' Slim, Guitar Slim, Elton Anderson, and Professor Longhair. By then, however, he had progressed musically and there was an uneasy air about the session. Even the name Guitar Jr. was revived, "and I didn't like that at all!"

Lonnie Brooks has become a respected figure in the Chicago blues establishment; so has top guitarist Buddy Guy from Lettsworth, who started out with the Big Poppa band in Baton Rouge in 1953.

In 1958 Goldband had its biggest hit to date with Jimmy Wilson's "Please Accept My Love," a charming R&B ballad with the wonderful line *I'm like the picture on the wall, please don't let me fall.* The record was leased to Imperial for national distribution and sold promisingly before running up against a cover version from B. B. King. Wilson was first discovered in 1951 by Aladdin Records, while he was singing on the West Coast with the Pilgrim Travelers gospel group. Two years later he cut a magnificent series of doomy blues for Bob Geddins in Oakland; particularly unforgettable was "Tin Pan Alley" (Big Town). He was brought to Goldband by Clarence Garlow, who wrote and produced "Please Accept My Love," but this hit failed to save Wilson's declining career; he died in Dallas in 1965.

Like all record men, Eddie Shuler also had his share of failures. In 1959 the supremely confident Big Walter Price, billed exotically as "The Thunderbird from Coast to Coast," burst into Lake Charles from Texas with two R&B hits under his belt, "Calling Margie" for T.N.T. and "Shirley Jean" for Peacock. His two Goldband singles, "San Antonio" and "Oh Ramona," good rumbustious efforts that they were, never made the charts, and he was forced to retreat to Houston. Another disappointment was "Sticks" Herman (Guidry) from Lake Charles, who failed with two potential R&B hits, a mournful "Crying Blues" (Goldband) with the Marcelle Dugas Combo in 1957 and the beautiful original version of "Lonely Feeling" (Tic Toc) in 1961. Local R&B artists Good Rockin' Bob (the late Ed Thomas) and Little Ray Campbell might also have done better with "Take It Easy Katy" and "Why Why Why."

Eddie viewed such setbacks philosophically: "To produce a record in a given field is no problem, but to produce one that will sell is a different matter. There are overnight sensations in any form of business, but to be a real A&R man in any given category you had to have been down that road, produced your share of dogs and survived while doing so!"

A major factor in the nationwide success of R&B was that it came to be promoted as rock 'n' roll music. By 1958 there was no doubt that R&B had made its presence felt in South Louisiana, even if it was by way of the national stars. "Rhythm and blues had a big effect on the music down here," confirms Floyd Soileau. "Basically you had the Cajun and country music, *strong* country music. Rhythm and blues started making it, the Fats Dominos, the Little Richards, the Chuck Berrys—especially those—and they began getting radio play. And people started going to that type of music and leaving that country and Cajun stuff behind. It was really a low day for country and Cajun music when rhythm and blues first made its imprint here."

The growing influence of R&B music on young Cajun musicians is remembered by Doug Kershaw: "I was one of the first that started using a drum kit. And the bass fiddle. Before that it was just men with rhythm guitars and fiddles and accordions and triangles, all portable instruments, because the drums and bass were too heavy to carry around. But with rhythm and blues coming up so big in the fifties it was so obvious: you either had that rhythm or you were in trouble. That changed the whole thing."

But the Cajun and country traditions were too deep to be completely cast aside by R&B—or, for that matter, by rockabilly. For the young Cajuns, at least, the natural solution was to blend all these forms to create their own South Louisiana rock 'n' roll. Only now it was saxophones and electric guitars that occupied the stage, rather than accordions and fiddles. . . .

Amadie Ardoin, ca. 1936.

Courtesy Pierre Daigle

Dennis McGee, ca. 1960. *Courtesy Pierre Daigle*

Canray Fontenot and Alphonse "Bois Sec" Ardoin, 1979. *Paul Harris*

"Bon Ton Roula," 1950. *Bill Greensmith*

Clifton Chenier, 1954. *Courtesy Mrs. Boneau*

Clifton Chenier, ca. 1956.　　　*Courtesy Blues Unlimited*

"Oh! Lucille," 1966.
Bill Greensmith

Bon Ton Rouley club, Lafayette, 1980. *Charley Nilsson*

Zydeco Posters. *Bengt Olsson*

Buckwheat, 1979.   *Paul Harris*

Sam Brothers at the Bon Ton Rouley, Lafayette, 1980.   *Charley Nilsson*

Louisiana State Penitentiary, Angola, 1980.   *Charley Nilsson*

Robert Pete Williams, 1972.   *James La Rocca*

Lightnin' Slim, 1958.   *Courtesy Jay Miller*

"New Orleans Bound," 1954.

Bill Greensmith

Schoolboy Cleve, ca. 1957.

Courtesy Blues Unlimited

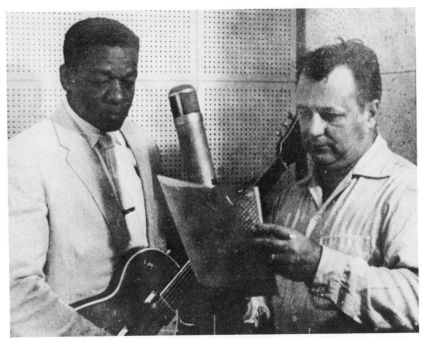

Lonesome Sundown and Jay Miller, ca. 1958.   *Courtesy Jay Miller*

"I'm A King Bee," 1957.   *Bill Greensmith*

ON *THE CASH BOX*
R&B CHART

"RAININ' IN MY HEART"

SLIM HARPO
Excello 2194

ALL SOUTH DIST., NEW ORLEANS
SOLD 7000 IN TWO WEEKS

NASHBORO RECORD COMPANY
177 3rd Ave., N. Nashville, Tenn.

The Cash Box advertisement, 1961.

Slim Harpo, 1961.   *Courtesy Excello Records*

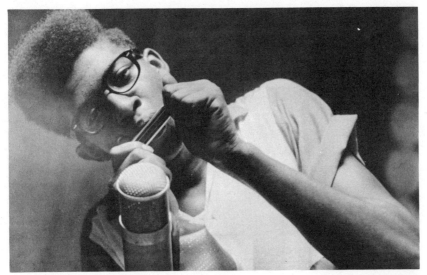

Lazy Lester, ca. 1958. *Courtesy Jay Miller*

Silas Hogan, 1972. *James La Rocca*

Jimmy Anderson and the Joy Jumpers, 1961. *Courtesy Silas Hogan*

"Church Members Ball," 1953. *Bill Greensmith*

Katie Webster, 1979. *Paul Harris*

Guitar Gable, 1958.
Courtesy Jay Miller

King Karl, 1958.
Courtesy Jay Miller

Carol Fran, 1958.
Courtesy Jay Miller

Classie Ballou, 1958.
Courtesy Jay Miller

Jimmy Wilson, 1958.
Courtesy Eddie Shuler

Juke Boy Bonner, 1961.
Courtesy Eddie Shuler

Guitar Jr., 1958.   *Courtesy Eddie Shuler*

Part

SWAMP-POP
AND THE CAJUN REVIVAL

14

"See you later, alligator!"

"Swamp-Pop," a term currently gaining acceptance in its homeland, was coined by a small group of English researchers to describe the colorful rock 'n' roll music of South Louisiana (known locally as "South Louisiana music"). Ironically, swamp-pop became established as a distinct musical entity in 1958, at a time when rock 'n' roll was becoming a uniform entertainment with few regional nuances. The South Louisiana version was created with typical ingenuity by teenage Cajun musicians, who integrated segments of their musical heritage with the latest popular sounds. The end product was instantly recognizable, a unique combination of Cajun emotional feel, lingering hillbilly melodies, and refined New Orleans–style R&B musical backings featuring plenty of solos from saxophone, guitar, and piano. The songs were sung in English.

Like the Cajun-born country singers before them, the young Cajun rock 'n' rollers were entering the American mainstream with a vengeance. The teenagers were now able to compete on equal terms with singers from the rest of the nation, an impossibility with the French lyrics and "old-fashioned" sound of traditional Cajun music (which proceeded to lose a generation of musicians as a result). In developing and projecting the new South Louisiana music through the medium of the hit record, aspiring singers and musicians were greatly assisted by the small circle of local record men. New Orleans studio owner Cosimo Matassa was particularly intrigued that "there were a lot of [swamp-pop] records, when they first hit the street you didn't know if the artist was black or white, they both sounded the same."

Swamp-pop was at its creative peak from 1958 to 1963 until suffering, like rock 'n' roll, from the musical changes wrought by the Beatles. The South Louisiana sound remained at a low ebb for the rest of the sixties and most of the seventies, but toward the end of that bleak decade Freddy Fender did enjoy success in the country markets with a swamp-pop approach. By the early eighties, however, those swamp-pop singers who were still active were uniting at concerts to present their music to audiences old and new.

179

Most swamp-pop songs were vehicles for presenting true-to-life situations; love was the favorite subject. The musical sound centered on gentle, melodic ballads cast within a narrow format, a format that New Orleanian Earl King called "a I-V structure, one chord to five progressions." Another New Orleans artist, Mac Rebennack (also known as Dr. John), described this ballad style as "a classic South Louisiana two-chord—E flat, B flat." But the up-tempo rock 'n' roll outings were still an essential part of any swamp-pop repertoire.

"Our swamp-pop style is half Fats Domino and half *fais-dodo*," says saxophonist Harry Simoneaux. "The reed backgrounds in our style of music make up for the violin sections that we didn't have, and also make up for the organ that was not popular at the time. They helped to fill in the empty spaces. Our style of music is very fundamental, nothing fancy, and certainly not very technical. With very few exceptions, like Jay Miller's session players Katie Webster and Lionel Prevost, there were no outstanding musicians. None of the singers had the quality voice—that is, with a vibrato. None of the singers had any formal training. However, they made up for this by singing what they knew about and what they lived through, same as for the French singers. You have to remember that all of the singers who made a little splash in show biz from this area are—or were—not very far removed from the Cajun-French bands. If there had been no French Cajun bands, there would definitely be no swamp-pop.

"It is common today for partygoers who dance to Johnnie Allan's music on Saturday night to go to the Triangle Club in Scott on Sunday afternoon and dance to French Cajun music only. Fans who like one type of music will generally like the other too. One thing about the swamp-pop style is that there are few musicians that ever play it right if they are not born and raised in South or Southwest Louisiana."

Without doubt the major catalystic influence on swamp-pop was Fats Domino, the New Orleans superstar who had been creating a stir for some time in South Louisiana with songs like "Goin' Home" and "Please Don't Leave Me." If a single recording served as a model for the new music, it was his unforgettable 1956 rendition of "Blueberry Hill." Young Cajun and black artists were quick to imitate Fats's lazy Creole-French vocal phrasings, tripleting piano, and riffing band arrangements. There seemed to be a natural empathy between their styles and his.

The importance of Fats Domino and New Orleans R&B generally is stressed in Johnnie Allan's description of the advent of swamp-pop: "During 1957 Fats Domino was real, real popular. He has always been one of my idols, I've always loved his music because it closely resembles the stuff I grew up with. And guys away from New Orleans started to copy his style of music, like Jimmy Clanton and Joe Barry. Clanton's 'Just A Dream' is not the exact Fats Domino beat, but there is a resemblance . . . Jimmy Clanton to my knowledge does not come from a Cajun family and somebody like Freddy Fender comes from West Texas, but there was something about playing in South Louisiana that made them take some of what Fats Domino had to offer. If they were going to sell to the people of South Louisiana, there was going to have to be a sound that everybody could relate to.

"And I think the guys working the board, the A&R people, guys from the record companies [in South Louisiana], when they would hear a sound that was almost identical to what Domino and Clarence 'Frogman' Henry and all these guys were doing, they'd say, 'Hey, let's change this a little bit.' Because if you notice Fats Domino and Clarence Henry, the instruments they used on their records, they're almost identical to those used on my recordings and the other guys. But there is a difference between swamp-pop and New Orleans R&B. The guys that own the record companies, like Floyd Soileau, Jay Miller, and Eddie Shuler, they all grew up with Cajun music. And they had their own idea of what South Louisiana rock 'n' roll should sound like. It was not that farfetched from Fats Domino, but it was different because there was more thrown into it. As Floyd likes to relate, there was more put into the gumbo than they did in New Orleans!"

That hillbilly music also made a valuable contribution to swamp-pop is affirmed by Rod Bernard: "Hillbilly music in the early fifties was very, very big. . . . We sang hillbilly music, all of us started out the same, Johnnie Allan started out singing French and hillbilly music, I did, T. K. Hulin, all the singers you can think of except the black guys. And then the rock 'n' roll thing came along, we kinda went with that, we blended rock 'n' roll, country, and French into that South Louisiana sound, that swamp-pop thing. . . . It's really a blend. But most of these songs, 'Just A Dream,' 'This Should Go On Forever,' 'On Bended Knee,' 'Please Accept My Love,' 'Mathilda,' 'Got You On My Mind'—they could all be beautiful hillbilly songs, just add a steel guitar and a couple of fiddles. . . ."

The musical integration implicit in swamp-pop was facilitated by a racial climate that was more relaxed in South Louisiana than in much of the South, although the Cajuns, being white, were obliged to observe certain social ethics and traditions governing their southern neighbors. "I never did have any racial problem," confides Earl King, "maybe some places for some people. The only problem I ran into was with state troopers, with bands speeding through those towns, you can't get away with that too much. We'd be leaving New Orleans about 4:30 in the evening to get to Lake Charles! I used to hear a few bands had racial problems . . . I think it was in certain areas of the South, but South

Louisiana, no. They're just fine, those people are just so interwoven into one another."

Echoes Rod Bernard: "You know, we read about the riots in Mississippi and the riots in Arkansas, we never did have any riots right down here. You see, the university here in Lafayette, Southwestern, was integrated way before, even in the fifties. Black people went to college here with white people. Now when I was in high school we were segregated, in Opelousas High there were no black students. They had a black high school and we had a white high school, and the same with elementary schools. And it was very segregated, but there was no trouble. During that same period of time I would go listen to black bands play in white nightclubs. Like Guitar Gable's band was all black, Good Rockin' Bob, Lil Bob and the Lollipops. When Jimmy Reed and Fats Domino would come in town, they'd come to white clubs and play. The black people went to their own nightclubs, and the white people went to theirs.

"Back in the fifties, the black people didn't try to come in the white man's clubs, I don't think they even wanted to. We never thought about that, I mean we didn't think about going in theirs. But occasionally I would go to black clubs to listen to black bands. One night after work at the radio station I went to listen to Lonesome Sundown and his band at a black club near Lawtell, they invited me over and I went around the back and went in the back entrance. And I sat there, he introduced me to the crowd and this was in 1956. There was no trouble or anything. We liked Fats Domino, the white people danced to his music and bought his records and went out to see him play. And looked forward to him, it was a treat to have Fats Domino come and play in a white club. We never thought of it being a black-white thing, there was just good music that everybody enjoyed."

With "(See You) Later Alligator," Bobby Charles became the first Cajun rock 'n' roller to have a significant hit. His classic song, coupled with "On Bended Knee," was released by Chess in late 1955. Charles was a most talented writer; his slow, melodic blues ballads, especially, proved prodigious prototypes for swamp-pop music in the years ahead.

"Bobby Charles, as well as Fats Domino, really had so much to do with swamp-pop," says Rod Bernard. "But Bobby particularly. 'On Bended Knee' was a typical South Louisiana ballad—*Please forgive me if I cry . . .* It was just a typical, beautiful South Louisiana song. And a lot of those things we did are based on the same tune, you could take that same music track and sing maybe a hundred South Louisiana songs. You had the same type of music, the piano triplets . . . it's almost identical, the phrasing, the structure of the song. Musically they're almost all identical, and the melodies are a little different to each one. Bobby Charles wrote 'See You Later Alligator' when I was in high school. He wrote 'But I Do' that

Clarence 'Frogman' Henry recorded [a No. 4 national hit], 'Walking To New Orleans' and 'Before I Grow Too Old' that Fats Domino recorded, and of course all the things that he recorded on Chess."

The enigmatic Bobby Charles was born Robert Charles Guidry in 1938 in the pretty town of Abbeville, the seat of Vermilion Parish. Like most swamp-pop artists, he used an anglicized stage name and English lyrics; it was assumed that a Guidry singing in French would never make the *Hot 100*. The writing of "Later Alligator" and his signing for the black-oriented Chess label of Chicago, historic events both, are described by Charles himself: "I had played this high-school dance in Crowley and this guy named Charles Redlich, they call him 'Dago,' he had Dago's Record Shop. Leonard Chess had passed through there a couple of years before, Leonard was a hustler. He'd go out and travel all over the South and he'd hear people singing songs, picking cotton, and he'd go in there with his little tape recorder and just tape it all. He'd passed through Crowley doing some promotion for his record company, and he stopped at Dago's Record Shop and told him that if he ran into anything he thought was worthwhile or worth anything to give him a call. Dago heard me and gave him a call and we got together. That's how it all started.

"Well, I had the phrase 'See you later, alligator,' and I had this local band back here in Abbeville I started back when I was fourteen or fifteen. We had finished a dance job one night, we were walking out of a restaurant one night after a dance job and I turned round to my piano player and I told him 'See you later, alligator!' Then they had two couples sitting in a booth in front of us, they were pretty loaded and she said something to my ear. I was walking out and I walked back in and asked her what she had said. 'You said, "See you later, alligator," and I said, "After a while, crocodile." ' I said thank you very much, that was it. I went home and wrote it in about twenty minutes. We called the group Bobby Charles and the Cardinals. Then we had to drop the name and chose the Clippers because they had another group out called the Cardinals at the time. When I got to Chess Records the only reason they signed me up they thought I was black. And when I got off the plane it kinda shocked them a bit. But everything was smooth, there wasn't any problem or anything. It was one of the best things that ever happened to me. I really enjoyed my time and stay with Chess."

"Later Alligator" was recorded in New Orleans in the fall of 1955, with Bobby's own band in support. Harry Simoneaux, who took the sax rides, says they spent an entire weekend recording just two titles—"Alligator" was finally subdued after about twenty-five attempts. The time was not wasted. Although "Later Alligator" was similar in concept to Guitar Slim's "Later For You Baby," Charles's song—with its unforgettable catchphrase and shuffling New Orleans rhythm backing—was a natural for the new rock 'n' roll market:

Well, I saw my baby walkin'
With another man today.   (repeat)
When I asked her what's the matter
This is what I heard her say.

See you later, alligator,
After a while, crocodile.   (repeat)
Can't you see you're in the way now,
Don't you know you cramp my style?

The record was covered by Bill Haley and his Comets, who proceeded to enjoy a worldwide hit at Bobby's expense with a more professional performance. Although Charles did benefit from writer's royalties, he was caught in a musical no-man's land—a white artist singing an R&B type of song on a black label (at that time R&B records were bought primarily by blacks). Singer John Fred explains: "He was the only white artist Chess had at the time and it was very unusual for a white guy to sing a black song. The record was like up and down, it was going real good, the song was selling, No. 30 in the R&B charts. Then Stan Lewis in Shreveport put out a picture in *Billboard* and the next week it wasn't even there. So there's a little racial prejudice both ways."

Bobby's early Chess records were produced by New Orleans bandleader Paul Gayten. "Bobby liked me," Gayten recalls, "he used to sing with me at the Brass Rail on Canal Street, and the people liked him. Bobby was a great writer, but as far as his singing went he didn't have the feeling the people wanted during that time [his warm voice was somewhat lacking in range], I guess today he could make hit records. I was father and mother to him, helped him get started and went with him to buy his first Cadillac."

Besides "Later Alligator," Bobby recorded other jump numbers for Chess, including "Take It Easy Greasy," "Laura Lee," and "One Eyed Jack," all with full-throttled New Orleans R&B backings. But his most satisfying releases were the bluesy swamp-pop ballads "On Bended Knee," "Why Did You Leave," and "Why Can't You." Apart from inspiring young Cajun musicians, Bobby was also paving the way in the broiling New Orleans R&B community for white teen-agers like Jerry Byrne, Jimmy Clanton, Frankie Ford, and Mac Rebennack. But Bobby was unable to sustain his bright start and a move to Imperial did nothing to arrest the decline in his record sales, despite the release of New Orleans–recorded gems like "Four Winds," "I Just Want You," "Bye Bye Baby," and "Those Eyes." He also cut sides for Jay Miller in Crowley which remained unissued at the time. After Bobby set up his own short-lived Hub City label in 1963 he was contracted briefly to Jewel, but then his recording career went into a self-induced vacuum.

In 1972 he came out of singing retirement temporarily to record the "Bobby Charles" album for Bearsville. This excellent contemporary rock LP confirmed Bobby's brilliance as a songwriter. A real highlight was "(Before I) Grow Too Old," a glowing testament to living life before it passes by (the number had been superbly recorded by Fats Domino in 1960). Another standout was "Small Town Talk," a loose, languid ballad about malicious gossip—the wicked murmurs on the front porch or behind the screen door, the whispers in the bars and restaurants on Main Street. Bobby's dignified response was masterly:

We're only two people trying to live together,
Trying to make something work.
Who are we to judge one another?
That can cause a lot of hurt.

"Bobby's style of writing is a kind of a unique style within a unique style in Louisiana," says Johnnie Allan. "Some of the songs that he's written, they've got the South Louisiana flavor to it, but he kinda bends them a little towards the New Orleans blues. Fats Domino has recorded several of his songs, also Clarence 'Frogman' Henry. So he's a Cajun Louisiana boy, he speaks French too, by the way, but he kinda bends his songs towards New Orleans music.

"I've been to his house recently, he's still writing and I know he's still along that type of music, he's still trying to bend it towards the rhythm and blues. He lives out in a secluded area of Abbeville, way back in the woods. Bobby's always been a loner. Fact is he's been to some of our dance jobs sometimes and I've practically begged him, 'Bobby, get up there and do a few songs!' He won't do it, he says, 'I'm strictly a writer. . . . ' "

Roy Perkins helped to galvanize the swamp-pop movement when he had a local hit in 1955 with "You're On My Mind," a sublime, wistful ballad recorded for Meladee. Through the years, Perkins—the "Boogie Boy"— has gained a reputation as a mystical rock 'n' roll artist, and his singles for Meladee and Ram are prized and expensive collector's items. Today his style can be seen as embryo South Louisiana, with plenty of melodic feel on numbers fast and slow. "Roy wrote several good songs," observes Rod Bernard, "but he never worked very hard at doing music professionally. Actually he played piano and bass in various dance bands in preference to recording and writing—he wrote 'You're On My Mind,' which I recorded for Argo."

Despite his affinity for swamp-pop, Roy Perkins was not raised in the Cajun tradition. Born Ernie Suarez in 1935, he became interested in music in the forties when his father, a poor Lafayette barman, brought home used jukebox 78s; Roy can recall hearing Cecil Gant's boogie-woogie records and copying them on the piano note for note. "I could play music just like the black man, I had it in me," he says. At the Lafayette Catholic high school, Roy started playing swing music with the Modern-aires, a student band. Then he heard Lloyd Price's classic New Orleans R&B recording of "Lawdy Miss Clawdy" and was mesmerized "by its brilliant, dazzling piano introduction and middle break [by Fats Domino]." Perkins managed to convince his classmates that R&B was the music of the future. In 1953 the Modernaires incorporated a special 45-minute spot by Perkins in their act, becoming one of the first white bands to feature R&B songs alongside the stock swing arrangements. Their show was enthusiastically received at all the big colleges.

At this time Roy started to perform two of his own songs, "You're On My Mind" and "Bye Bye Baby," and quickly noted the positive reaction they aroused. "It was obvious that we had a hit there," he says, "but we didn't know what to do. In those days making a record was so farfetched an idea. Just big stars made records ..." After discovering that it was easy to make a demo record, Perkins approached Carol Rachou of the local Music Mart store; Rachou, who later owned La Louisianne Records, introduced the band to Mel Mallory of Meladee Records in New Orleans. Mallory promptly rerecorded the two demo songs, with the result that "You're On My Mind" was No. 1 in New Orleans for six weeks and also broke in the rest of Louisiana and parts of Mississippi and Texas. The less distinguished follow-up "Here I Am"/"You're Gone" had a pronounced black sound with vocal-group support. But Perkins was a very reluctant star. "I was just as happy to be playing for myself," he admits.

In 1956 Roy went into the armed services. After a year away from music he joined Bobby Page and the Riff Raffs as bass guitarist; the group accompanied him on his Ram single "Drop Top," which was leased to Mercury. Perkins also did session work for Jay Miller—he played piano on Warren Storm's hit "Prisoner's Song"—and later recorded for Dart and Eric. In the sixties he appeared with the Lafayette-based band the Swing Kings and also played with Johnnie Allan. Roy is now a draftsman for an oil company; on Sundays he preaches at a small St. Martinville church. "I was never aware my music was an innovation," he says, "I just played and sang the way I felt. I get a degree of satisfaction looking back, those were good years, but life goes forward and hopefully upward!"

After the early swamp-pop hits of Bobby Charles and Roy Perkins, Bobby Page scored regionally with "Loneliness" in the spring of 1958.

An enchanting swamp-pop ballad, "Loneliness" was recorded for Myra Smith's Ram Records of Shreveport; the flip "Hippy-Ti-Yo" was a rock'n' roll version of the old Cajun song "Hip Et Taiaud." Bobby "Boogas" Page (Elwood Dugas) fronted the Riff Raffs band that included saxophonist Jimmy Patin from the Modernaires; guitarist Bessyl Duhon, currently playing accordion with Jimmy C. Newman; and pianist V. J. Boulet, who later owned Boo-Ray records. Roy Perkins, who was also in the group at the time, remembers: "Bobby was a real showman, he just cut it up; he was a wild man, great personality, beautiful smile... the band was a lot of fun." The Riff Raffs remained popular throughout the Gulf Coast until the early sixties. But Bobby Page never found another number to match "Loneliness," and after several lesser recordings he became a plumber in Lafayette.

In the summer of 1958 Jimmy Clanton of Baton Rouge set a glamorous example for young South Louisianians when he had a Top Five national hit with "Just A Dream" (Ace), a teen ballad with swamp-pop influences. Warren Storm promptly breached the lower regions of the *Billboard Hot 100* with "Prisoner's Song," produced by Jay Miller for Nasco. And then Cookie and the Cupcakes recorded "Mathilda."

If swamp-pop has a signature tune, an anthem, it has to be the quintessential "Mathilda." Recorded for George Khoury's Lyric label and leased to Judd (owned by Judd Phillips of Memphis), the single climbed to No. 47 on the *Billboard* chart in early 1959. "Mathilda" would surely have gone higher with a bigger company behind it. Cookie's crying vocal was stunning. *Billboard* was right when it noted that the "cat has a sound and he belts it, as tho' from the swamps." The Cupcakes' instrumental backing—baying saxes, tripleting piano, and swirling guitar over a wallowing beat—was just as majestic, while the song itself was memorably melodic:

> *Mathilda, I cried and cried for you,*
> *It's no matter what you do.*
> *Yes I cried and cried in vain,*
> *I want my baby back again.*

There was one particular verse that seemed to appeal to brokenhearted young lovers, and helped to sell the record:

> *You gave me love when there was none,*
> *You know you're the only one . . .*

Even today everybody accepts that if a local band plays "Mathilda" and nobody dances, the musicians may just as well pack up and go home.

" 'Mathilda' by Cookie and the Cupcakes is probably the all-time, super-strong, No. 1 South Louisiana hit record," stresses Rod Bernard. "That's the song we still get requests for, you start playing 'Mathilda' on the bandstand today and people go wild. If you took a vote 'Mathilda' would be the all-time South Louisiana smash. It was very, very big at the time. I remember it because it was always No. 1 and 'This Should Go On Forever' was No. 2 . . . it was a big record."

Johnnie Allan agrees: "If there's any guy in Louisiana that had an influence on a lot of us, it's Cookie. Because when his song 'Mathilda'—brother, that's swamp-pop down to a tee!—when that song came out you could put your radio on any station, on any station, I don't care if it played Cajun music, country and western music, rock 'n' roll music, or rhythm and blues, they were playing 'Mathilda.' This song was really popular, it really went big, big, big. It's another song like 'Jole Blon.' Cookie had a good band, they were very popular, extremely popular. They played a lot around Lafayette as well as East Texas. They played the Green Lantern club in Lawtell for years, they used to play there on Thursdays and Sundays. They played over here at Landry's Palladium on the old Scott Highway between Lafayette and Scott, about three or four miles out of Lafayette, every Saturday night and that place would hold over 600 people. . . . They started at nine o'clock and if you wanted a table and a chair you had to be there about seven o'clock. They were just that popular."

Cookie and the Cupcakes were led by Huey Thierry (Cookie), who came from Jennings, and Shelton Dunaway from Lake Charles; they shared the vocals and both played tenor sax. The other group members were Sidney "Hot Rod" Reynaud, tenor sax; Marshall Laday, guitar; Ernest Jacobs, piano; Joe "Blue" Landry, bass guitar; and Ivory Jackson, drums. As the Boogie Ramblers, this black group cut its first record, "Cindy Lou"/"Such As Love," for Goldband in 1955. But there was no follow-up, much to the dismay of Eddie Shuler: "In those days I just didn't worry about fixing contracts for artists and with this group this was the one thing I should have done. The fellows were excellent musicians and had a good show. The sales of the record were quite good for a new group's first release, and realizing their potential I tried to get them back into the studio to cut a follow-up. One day I heard a record called 'Mathilda' on the radio and then I knew they never would. One cannot blame them for finding a better deal, for that's human nature, but I did blame myself for not conducting the business properly. I made it a point from then on to never record anyone without a contract."

"Mathilda" was recorded at KPLC radio station, Lake Charles; later sessions were held at ACA studios, Houston, and Bill Hall's Beaumont studio. The Cupcakes' slew of gorgeous swamp-pop releases included "Until Then" (the follow-up to "Mathilda"), "I've Been So Lonely," "Trouble In My Life," "Even Though," "I Cried," and personalized versions of "Breaking Up Is Hard To Do" and "Sea Of Love." At times it was possible to detect the clean, melodic tones of R&B star Chuck Willis in the vocals; on other occasions a strong New Orleans instrumental sound was evident. Despite their prolific output, the group had just one other *Hot 100* entry, the tuneful "Got You On My Mind" (Chess), a meager No. 94 in the early summer of 1963.

Cookie and the Cupcakes never completely adjusted to the soul era of the sixties. But Shelton Dunaway, Marshall Laday, and Ivory Jackson have stayed together to play the old hits in Lake Charles (Cookie is tragically confined to a wheelchair following two automobile accidents in California, while the great pianist Ernest Jacobs left the group in deference to his wife's wishes). The wonderful but hard-to-find Khoury's singles have been assembled in two essential Jin albums released by Floyd Soileau.

In the slipstream of "Mathilda" George Khoury landed a second smash hit with Phil Phillips's "Sea Of Love," another important swamp-pop record by a black artist. On this occasion Mercury handled nationwide promotion and distribution, and helped to propel the single to No. 2 on the *Billboard Hot 100* in the summer of 1959. Locally "Sea Of Love" is not as revered as "Mathilda," but the record was the biggest national hit yet for a South Louisiana release.

"Sea Of Love" was simplicity itself, the tune just hung in the mind. With immaculate support from the tripleting Cupcakes band and the serene harmonies of the Twilights vocal group, Phillips meandered his way smoothly through the seductive lyrics:

> *Come with me, my love,*
> *To the sea, the sea of love,*
> *I want to tell you*
> *How much I love you . . .*

The hit recording was produced by Eddie Shuler, who remembers it with pride: "My million seller was 'Sea Of Love' by Phil Phillips. On February 23, 1959, my friend George Khoury brought Phil and his guitar into my studio for an audition. George wanted me to go fifty-fifty with him on the song, with me producing the record and of course putting up the money for the initial release. I didn't go so well for this at the time, but now I wish I had.

"I finally came to an arrangement where I should arrange and produce the song in exchange for the publishing rights. When I heard the song I really liked it and figured that it would sell. So we really took our time with it, literally building up a vocal group to do the background and changing musicians more times than I care to remember. After three months' work we had the finished product ready for release on George Khoury's label. As soon as we put it out the record sold so heavily that we had to lease it to Mercury, and the result was a No. 1 hit on all the national charts [except *Billboard*]. It's a two million–plus seller, it's still going, and we're still getting money. You just produce it one time and if it's a hit, it goes on forever. You don't fight it!"

Phil Phillips, born Phillip Baptiste in Lake Charles in 1931, was a member of the Gateway Quartet and a bellhop before he recorded "Sea Of Love." After the hit Mercury promoted him as a pop singer, which he was not. He turned out to be the archetypal one-hit wonder; nothing else he did ever came close to making the charts. A man of intense pride, he found it hard to accept the return to normal life after enjoying the trappings of success. He remained in the music business by becoming a disc jockey at KJEF Jennings, where he still introduces himself unabashedly as the "King of the whole black world!"

By 1960, with two huge hits under his belt, George Khoury was able to step up his output. Little Alfred (Babino), a tortuously bluesy singer, had a minor hit with "Walking Down The Aisle" while Carol Fran made the venerable "The Great Pretender" her own in a shatteringly soulful performance. The remainder of the Khoury's catalog consisted of an interesting if poor-selling selection of R&B and swamp-pop from Marcus Brown and the Continentals, Little Ray Campbell, Frankie Lowery and the Golden Rockets, Jay Randall, Jerry Thomas and the Rhythm Rockers, and Margo White. Mickey Gilley breezed in with the fine rock 'n' roll of "Drive In Movie."

Meanwhile Khoury's Record Shop was important enough to have its best-selling record charts listed regularly in *The Cash Box*. A November 1960 Top Ten, somewhat after the initial swamp-pop surge, highlighted the customers' broad musical tastes:

1. "Last Date," Floyd Cramer.
2. "Let's Go, Let's Go, Let's Go," Hank Ballard and the Midnighters.
3. "My Girl Josephine," Fats Domino.
4. "Walking Down The Aisle," Little Alfred.
5. "Save The Last Dance For Me," The Drifters.
6. "You Talk Too Much," Joe Jones.
7. "Am I The Man," Jackie Wilson.
8. "North To Alaska," Johnny Horton.

9. "Move To Kansas City," Harold Dorman.
10. "Don't Be Cruel," Bill Black's Combo.

The chart emphasizes the strong national competition encountered by local artists; other than New Orleans artists Fats Domino and Joe Jones, the only South Louisiana entrant was Khoury's own Little Alfred. But the listed records were a rich mixture of R&B, rock 'n' roll, country, and swamp-pop, and they lend credence to Rod Bernard's observation that "South Louisiana was a unique area, the things that sold here a lot of times didn't sell anywhere else. And things that were selling everywhere else weren't selling here."

In 1966, after a long period without a hit, George Khoury quietly wound up his recording activities to take up the post of deputy sheriff in Lake Charles, leaving his brother in charge of the record shop. There is little room for George's casual approach in today's highly pressurized music business, but the gold disc of "Sea Of Love" hanging in his office is an enduring symbol of his musical achievements.

15

" 'This Should Go On Forever' . . . I just knew it was a hit song"

The fledgling swamp-pop movement gained momentum in 1958 after Floyd Soileau founded his Jin label in Ville Platte. Drawing on the music of the South Louisiana locale, Soileau put swamp-pop firmly on the map with hits by Jivin' Gene, Rod Bernard, Johnnie Allan, Joe Barry, Tommy McLain, and others; Rod Bernard actually made the national Top Twenty. Initially most of Floyd's recordings were produced at Jay Miller's Crowley studio, which was to play an important part in the development of swamp-pop music, just as it had in the evolution of the South Louisiana Cajun, country, and blues sounds. At the same time, Floyd set up the Swallow label to record his native Cajun music.

As a friendly young disc jockey, Floyd Soileau became involved in the retail side of the record business when he opened a tiny record stall in 1956. From such humble beginnings he has built up a thriving enterprise, incorporating the Jin, Swallow, and Maison de Soul labels; Floyd's Record Shop; pressing and printing plants; and mail-order, music publishing, and distributing companies. He has diversified into other business interests as well, but music is his real love, the preservation of the Cajun tradition his passion.

Raised in the rural French area of Grand Prairie (just outside Ville Platte, the commercial center of Evangeline Parish), Floyd was unable to speak English until he was six, but once he started school he learned quickly. While in high school he worked occasional disc-jockey stints at the local radio station, KVPI, thus kindling his interest in music: "At that time there was a show called 'Juke Junction' and it was probably the most listened hour of broadcasting in this area as far as 250 watts would carry, Lafayette was really tuned in to this program at the time. The guy doing the show was Bootsie Cappelle, and he recognized the influence of the black rhythm and blues in the area. So he was quick to get the station to program it and I think they were probably the first radio station in the area that played some of that music, real strong, and had the listeners really beaming in. It helped to push this music that was on Chess, Specialty, Aladdin, and some of these early rhythm and blues labels that were being distributed in New Orleans by A-1 Record Distributors."

In 1956 Chris Duplechain, the KVPI manager, gave Floyd a full-time post. Because the low-watt station had to finish broadcasting at sundown due to nighttime interference, Duplechain told Floyd, "By the way, when the daytime hours get shorter I'm gonna have to cut some of your hours, why don't you get a part-time business or something, like maybe a music store?" Liking the idea, Floyd obtained a loan from his parents and went into partnership with J. L. Sylvester, the radio station engineer: "With the $500 in my pocket I went up to New Orleans and I bought a demonstrator phonograph for $50 and I purchased $300 worth of records from the local distributors. And I set up shop in a little one-room office—the station is on the second floor of the old bank building and they had two or three one-room offices to rent. So I set up my inventory in there, and when I was on the air the shop was closed, but when I was off the air I was in there peddling records. And through ads with the radio station it helped things to roll along and got people to know that there was a place in Ville Platte where they could buy records."

In the summer of 1957 Floyd left the radio station to concentrate on his record business. The choice was not entirely his: "I had four or five customers waiting while I was on the air. They could hear me doing the news and I got to thinking there's all these people wanting to buy records and I'm stuck on this miserable newscast for fifteen minutes, they're gonna get tired of waiting, they're *gonna leave.* And I couldn't wait to finish that newscast 'cause I knew I had fifteen minutes to wait on them after, because it was one of these long transcriptions, 'Meet the Navy, the Air Force' or something. So I grabbed the long transcription just as quickly as I could and just slapped it on, put the needle on, and I ran back out there. So I went back and sold them the records they wanted, everything was fine. And they had just walked out the door and Chris Duplechain, he's a relatively small person but he stood in that doorway, he looked like a *giant.* Beaming fire! And I couldn't imagine what the hell was wrong. And he said, 'Son, you gonna have to make up your mind, 'cause you're either gonna be selling records or else you're gonna be on the air. But this business of running Christmas programs in the middle of July, this has got to stop!'

"Eventually I dropped out of the radio thing completely and just went pushing on with the record business. While I was at the radio station I would receive samples, and Don Pierce of Starday Records always sent a piece of literature with his sample packets that said, 'If you've got a tape, we can press a record for you.' And I was selling quite a bit of Cajun music at that time and I was getting it mostly from George Khoury. And every time I would order he would send me a list of what was available and the list got shorter. And I said, 'We—somebody—has got to start making some more Cajun records or we ain't gonna have no Cajun records to sell!' And I mentioned this to a friend of mine, Ed Manuel, who was one of the first jukebox operators to come around and buy his records from me."

Later Ed Manuel told Floyd he had taped Milton Molitor with Austin Pitre's band at a party and wanted to press a few records. "He said, 'We're gonna call this "Manuel Bar Waltz" and "Midway Two-Step" ' because those were two nightclubs he had an interest in, and he wanted some publicity. So we put that out on Big Mamou Records c/o Floyd's Record Shop, Ville Platte. And I sent the tape to Don Pierce at Starday and he had it pressed in Nashville and sent it down to us. I think there were five hundred 78s and three hundred 45s done. [Accordionist Milton Molitor also recorded with Austin Pitre for Dr. Harry Oster and Chris Strachwitz in 1960; these recordings appeared on Prestige and Arhoolie.] And Ed introduced me to some other operators who were in the business so we could sell wholesale some of these records too. Also we sent some samples to the radio stations in the area we knew were programming this music. Word got around that there was a new record company that had opened up in Acadiana, in Ville Platte of all places, because we had this one record out.

"Then the late Lawrence Walker came in one day and says, 'I know you got a record company started, you making records. I did four sides at the radio station in Eunice and I'd like for you to release them. One of them, "Bon Ton Rouley," is going to be a real hit, I know—they're all good, but this particular one I've got a lot of hope for.' "

After some hard bargaining, Floyd purchased two sides from Lawrence for sixty dollars with a forty-dollar option on the other two if the first single was a success. But Ed Manuel was no longer interested in the recording business, he had obtained the publicity he needed for his clubs. Floyd was on his own: "So I changed the label to Vee-Pee Records c/o Floyd's Record Shop, and that issue was 'Bon Ton Rouley' and we used a 102 number on that because that was the second record release we had. I think I had seven hundred 45s and three hundred 78s done, and it started selling very well. It got me in touch with some more operators and music stores. In fact, we got a good relationship built up as a result of this. Then the third artist to see me was Aldus Roger out of Lafayette, he was also a Cajun artist. We went to J. D. Miller's and the record was later called 'The Cajun Special'—it was listed as Vee-Pee 103. RCA pressed that one, it was a green label, and it started selling pretty well. Then I had Adam Hebert, another Cajun artist, come to see me."

In September 1958 Floyd Soileau put his recording operations on a more businesslike footing by setting up the Jin label for popular releases and Swallow for Cajun music. At the time rock 'n' roll was pausing for a second wind and Cajun music was showing remarkable resilience in the clubs and dance halls.

"We called the label Jin because I was going out with my wife, we weren't married then, her name is Jinver and I thought I'd get a few points!" Floyd says. "I wanted something a little different, and that's where the J-I-N comes from. But 'Swallow,' my old man gave me hell about that because my last name is French! I said, 'Uh, uh, away from this area they may not know how to pronounce this too well, I'm gonna have hell, it's gonna have to be easy. I remembered RCA had Bluebird, I said, 'Hey, I'm gonna have a bluebird too, I'm gonna call mine the swallow bird and it's also the pronunciation of my last name. We gonna call this Swallow.' And for a logo I found a little old bitty mockingbird thing and we put that on for the label. Then an artist friend of mine teased me about it and eventually he designed a swallow bird and we got the mockingbird off. The guy's name was Jessie Gary, he designed some of the earlier jackets on my albums, and came up with this 'Always in the Spotlite' subtitle for Jin. We still use it on some of the older cuts we come up with and I guess we should never have changed it. The more modern logo I have just doesn't have the feeling or the meaning of the one-man operation we've been, more or less. You know, no big label type of thing.

"Jin 101 was 'Southland Blues' by a group of young white musicians calling themselves the Boogie Kings. They were led by Doug Charles [Ardoin] with Elbert Miller and Skip Morris as vocalists, they were very, very popular in the Eunice, Opelousas, and Ville Platte area and they had not recorded yet. So I called them one day, I said, 'Hey, if you want to make a record, let's go down to J. D. Miller's and we'll get a session done.' The Boogie Kings were the first local group who were doing a sort of blue-eyed soul, a white band playing black music—or trying to play black music.

"And about that time Rod Bernard was in Opelousas and he was playing music with a group called the Twisters. . . . He had done his first record with Jake Graffignino on the Carl label. And after the Boogie Kings' record came out there was a rivalry between the Twisters and the Boogie Kings. I guess Rod, being the head man for the Twisters, decided, 'Hey, we ought to look into recording with Floyd because he'll spend a little bit more money on the session, we'd go to J. D.'s to record it.' . . . Jake was doing his in the back room of his shop. So we got together and we decided we were going to do a session. And he said, 'I've got this song which I think is going to be a hit, I got it from Bernard Jolivette,' at that time he was known as King Karl, playing with Guitar Gable and his bunch, and he was quite a good writer. And he said, 'He's given me this song to record, it's gonna be a real good song, it's called "This Should Go On Forever," I really like it.' He sang a few bars of it, I thought it was nice."

In fact, "This Should Go On Forever" was swamp-pop at its melodic best. Fronting a brooding horn section, with elegant triplets from piano and guitar, Rod tearfully explained his dilemma in love:

This should go on forever,
It should never ever end.
If it's wrong to really love you
I'll forever live in sin. . . .

If it's sin to really love you
Then a sinner I will be.
If it's wrong to hold and kiss you
Oh my soul will never be free.
This should go on forever . . .

Although the lyrics were bold for the time, the record burst through to No. 20 in the *Billboard Hot 100* in the spring of 1959, after being leased to the Chess Brothers' Argo label for national distribution. By hitting the national charts, Rod Bernard had fulfilled every dream in the bayou country. His timing was faultless: Rock 'n' roll was starting to mellow after its frantic onslaught, and swamp-pop with its tuneful melodies was suddenly selling beyond South Louisiana. Besides "This Should Go On Forever" there were three other major swamp-pop hits in 1959: "Mathilda" by Cookie and the Cupcakes, "Sea Of Love" by Phil Phillips, and "Breaking Up Is Hard To Do" by Jivin' Gene. Rod Bernard's story provides an intriguing insight into the anatomy of a hit record during the rock 'n' roll era.

Rod was born in the historic town of Opelousas in 1940. "Opelousas is a very old town," he says, "it was once the state capital many years ago. It's the home of Jim Bowie, he fought at the Alamo, he was a frontiersman and there's a Jim Bowie museum. He's the greatest thing that ever came out of Opelousas! It's an agricultural town, there's not much industry there. There's a very heavy black population, it's about 70 percent black, the population is about 40,000. It hasn't grown much.

"Of course I was raised with Cajun music from the time I was a kid. My grandfather owned a big Cajun nightclub in a little town called Port Barre, which is near Opelousas, and I used to go there when I was seven or eight years old. We'd go there on Saturday nights, I'd just hang on the bandstand and listen to those French accordion bands, Papa Cairo, Clifton Chenier, Jimmy C. Newman, and Aldus Roger. And I never did learn how to speak French, that's one unusual thing from being around here, my mother and father both speak French. When I started school in Opelousas most of the kids in my class spoke French, but there was a thing going on back then, for some reason people thought that those who spoke French, or just French, were a little ignorant. So they tried to make everybody not speak French, in fact they'd punish anybody if they were caught speaking French. And for that reason I never did learn it, which is a real shame."

Rod started in music when he was ten, singing on the Saturday morning radio program sponsored by Dezauche's Red Bird Sweet Potatoes over KSLO Opelousas: "I had to stand on some feed sacks with my guitar and sang. And they invited me to come over every Saturday, and from there I wanted to have my own radio program. So I went down after school one day, I didn't tell my parents anything, I walked down to KSLO and talked to Johnny Wright who was a program director." Wright told him to find a sponsor, which was a polite put-off. But the youngster bounced back with the support of the Main Motor Company, the Lincoln-Mercury dealer in Opelousas: "It kinda floored Johnny Wright, I found out later this was one client they had trouble selling radio to, this guy didn't want to buy any radio commercials! So they started sponsoring my program on Saturdays, 4:15 to 4:30 every Saturday afternoon. I played my guitar, it was country things—all of the Hank Williams songs, 'I'm So Lonesome I Could Cry,' particularly 'Jambalaya,' naturally that was always first. And Cajun things like 'Colinda' and 'Diggy Liggy Lo' and things like that which we ended up recording later."

At the youthful age of twelve he became a disc jockey at KSLO, playing the country and western hits of Hank Williams, Lefty Frizzell, and Ray Price every Tuesday evening. He was tasting, firsthand, the intriguing inside world of radio broadcasting, a fascination that stuck.

In 1954 Rod moved with his parents to Winnie, Texas, where he met Huey Meaux, a hip Cajun barber who was to play a considerable part in the development of the South Louisiana swamp-pop scene in the early sixties: "I went to school there in the ninth grade and Huey was my barber, he used to cut my hair every couple of weeks. And Huey was managing a French band and he had a radio program on KPAC in Port Arthur at the time every Saturday. He'd play real French music, there's a lot of French-speaking people around East Texas. And I got to know Huey pretty well, but at that time I didn't think anything about recording, I just played my guitar and sang at school functions and things like that."

A year later, the Bernard family returned to Opelousas. Rod reenrolled at the local high school and resumed part-time disc jockey duties with KSLO: "Back then we had a lot of white guys that would get on the radio, they would try to talk like black guys, that was in back then. In fact J. P. Richardson, the Big Bopper who was killed in the plane crash, he had a show, that's where he got his Big Bopper name from. He was program director of KTRM in Beaumont, Texas. He had a radio show there where he'd do the same thing, he'd get on the air, he'd talk like that and play all the blues records. And I was doing the same thing in Opelousas, playing records by Fats Domino, B. B. King, and Jimmy Reed. I took over Jinkin' Rene's rock 'n' roll show, his name was Rene Fontenot. I was called 'Hot Rod,' that was my radio name from 3:30 to 5:30, and after that I became Rod Bernard. I did the news and things like that, I went from one accent to another. During that time I was working at the radio station, then on Friday and Saturday nights we formed a little band called the Twisters and there were four or five others in high school then. And we played dances at teenage centers, we weren't playing any nightclubs back then, we were all fourteen, fifteen, sixteen years old."

In 1957 Rod and the Twisters cut two youthfully enthusiastic singles for Carl Records, operated by Jake Graffignino, the benevolent owner of Jake's Music Shop in Opelousas. Rod recalls: "We recorded 'Linda Gail' and 'Little Bitty Mama' on a tape recorder, one microphone, at the Southern Club in Opelousas. The second record we did for him was 'Set Me Free,' we recorded that in his music store. We were just standing around the counter with the guitars and all, and one microphone, and recorded that. And he took the tape, sent it off, and had a few records pressed." Jake Graffignino maintained a low profile in the record business until 1961, when he signed Jay Randall, Joe Richards, and Lil Bob and the Lollipops. Although sales were nothing special, Graffignino did finally earn some reward when he received writer's royalties for the big Dale and Grace hit "Stop And Think It Over."

Rod Bernard's Carl singles never exceeded their modest expectations, but "This Should Go On Forever" for Jin in October 1958 was quite a different story. Rod explains how he came to record his big hit: "Whenever I got through with the radio station we would go down on weekends and listen to bands from around here and one of the most popular bands at that time was Guitar Gable, and he had a singer, King Karl. They made a lot of records under the name of Guitar Gable and his band. And King Karl had written and recorded a whole bunch of songs, 'Irene,' 'It's Hard But It's Fair,' 'Life Problem'—things like that, songs that were popular around here. And I was playing them on my radio show every afternoon. It was a really good band. Anyway, we went in this place called the Moonlight Inn, one night Karl acknowledged the fact that I was there, he said, 'Old Hot Rod's here from KSLO, I'm gonna dedicate this next song to him, it's gonna be our new record!' And he sang 'This Should Go On Forever.' And it just floored me, it was one of these things, when you hear that song. . . . I just knew it was a hit song.

"I couldn't remember the name of it, but every time I'd see him or he'd come up to the radio station I'd say 'Karl, when's that song I like, when are you gonna put it out?' He said 'It's gonna be our next record.' The next record would come out and it wouldn't be that. And I kept asking him, and finally he told me that the people he was recording for, he'd cut all these songs for J. D. Miller at Crowley but they'd come out on the Excello label out of Tennessee, and he said the people in Tennessee didn't like 'This Should Go On Forever.' And I kept telling him how much I liked it, that was when Floyd called me. And asked me to make a record, told me to find a couple of songs. And I immediately thought about that song. I couldn't remember the name of it, but I just knew it was a good song. So I went over to Karl's house and I told him what the deal was. I ran it all down to him and told him I would like to make this record, and I'd really like to record this song that he had written [with Jay Miller], that he had sung for me that night, and would he teach it to me. He said sure.

"So we sat down on his front porch, he sang 'This Should Go On Forever,' I wrote the words down—I can't read or write music, I just sat there and learned it. And I hurried on back home to try to keep singing it so I'd remember it. Somewhere between his house and my house I changed it a little bit without realizing it, I thought I was still singing it exactly like he did, but it was just a little different, not very much. Anyway, I learned the song, Floyd didn't have a studio then naturally, he was just beginning. And so the only studio around here was in Crowley, J. D. Miller's, so Floyd called J. D. and told him he wanted to start his own record company and he had this little band from Opelousas that was going to record for him. J. D. said, 'Send them on down here.' So we lined up a night for this session and I took my band down there and I had rehearsed two songs, 'This Should Go On Forever' and a song I had written, 'Pardon Mr. Gordon,' which ended up being the flip side.

"We got in there and started recording, back then there was just a single-track tape and you did everything at one time. And we were all amateurs by a long shot. Several times the saxman would hit an off note, I kept hitting off notes the whole time, and every time we had to stop and redo it again. And we started at 7:30 one night and we finally finished at 3:30 the next morning, just one time after another. Over and over and over and over trying to do this thing, trying to get it better. When we finally got the final cut, I had a terrible nosebleed and I sang the same thing with a towel all wrapped around my face and that's how we did 'This Should Go On Forever.' Maybe that was the key to it, maybe I should have kept singing with a towel around my face. Maybe that's what happened.

"It was a coincidence, since King Karl recorded for J. D. Miller, J. D. had his own publishing company, Jamil Music Company, and he had the publishing to all the things that King Karl wrote. Now I never had anything to do with J. D. directly, but he A&R'd this session, all I knew was that he was sitting in the control room running all the controls. But he'd come in and say, 'Why don't y'all do things this way?'—Floyd wasn't even there that night. He couldn't make it. J. D. really had a lot to do with how we did it. We learned it a certain way, like he made us take the breaks, which we hadn't done, we'd just sing it all the way through. Things like that, he added to it. We had my band the Twisters, but they were kinda weak, there was something missing that night. So I think about 10:30 or 11 o'clock J. D. finally called in a couple of his studio musicians, Bobby McBride and Al Foreman. Al played guitar and Bobby played bass, we switched my brother Rick Bernard from bass to rhythm guitar. That's how we ended up getting the final cut on it, and Floyd put it out on his label."

The flip, "Pardon Mr. Gordon," is rightly recognized as a minor classic of the rock 'n' roll era, with amusing lyrics, a foot-tapping rhythm, and exciting saxophone and guitar breaks. But the record's elevated status perplexes Rod: "It was just a song that I wrote in high school, it was just a novelty-type tune with a good beat to it. I don't remember why I wrote it, I had really truly forgotten about that song. We just needed something to put on the other side of 'This Should Go On Forever' and I gave Floyd half-writer's royalty on it."

Once "This Should Go On Forever" was recorded there was still the hit-making riddle to solve. In his vivid recollection of ensuing events, Rod conveys all the romance and deception of the era—from the grandeur of overnight success to the extremes of exploitation: "We did some really unique things to publicize the record. I went to the post office and bought a bunch of postcards from my dad and I wrote on all of them, 'Please play "This Should Go On Forever" by Rod Bernard' and we mailed it to the radio stations. We got it played right away on KVPI Ville Platte and KSLO in Opelousas, because Floyd worked at one station and I worked at the other! But we had trouble getting it played elsewhere, KVOL in Lafayette wouldn't play it, stations in Baton Rouge wouldn't play it, they said it was too bad.

"But it started selling, we started getting honest requests for it. We got it in a few jukeboxes and it started being the most-played song. It was one of those natural things, we really didn't have to hype it. It was unusual, being in effect a first record, we really didn't realize how fortunate we were at the time. I'd give anything to go through that again, to have a problem like that. Floyd couldn't get the records pressed fast enough, first from RCA in Indianapolis, then United Record Distributors out of Houston. I think he ordered two or three hundred the first time, and they were gone almost immediately. After it started selling so well in this area we got a distributor in New Orleans, Henry Hildebrand's new All South Distributing

Company, and they put salesmen out on the road and they got it played on stations fifty, sixty, seventy-five miles from here that we had not been to yet. Just on the strength of it selling here in South Louisiana. And then one thing led to another, and a station in Lake Charles started playing it, and then the station in Baton Rouge started playing it, and KVOL Lafayette finally started playing it after it was really, really popular. That song and 'Mathilda' were the two hottest things around here, they were No. 1 and No. 2 on all the jukeboxes.

"With the record starting selling well around here, Floyd said we really need to get this thing going in Texas. He said, 'I'd love to get it going in Houston and Beaumont, do you know anybody over there?' And the only person I knew was Huey Meaux, and at that time Huey was managing a couple of little bands around there. One of them was a guy named Gene Bourgeois who later became Jivin' Gene and had 'Breaking Up Is Hard To Do,' and another was Johnny Preston who later had 'Running Bear,' but all this was prior to that. I called Huey, reminded him who I was and I told him what was going on with the record. He said, he talks with a heavy Cajun accent, 'Tee boy, send me a box of them records and I'll see what I can do with that over here.' So Floyd sent him a box of them and Huey got in his car, and in between his barbering duties and managing these bands, he went around the radio stations of East Texas and one of the people he visited was J. P. Richardson, who was program director of KTRM Beaumont. And Huey bought him a copy of the record and J. P. started playing it on his show. And that was the first chart that it was ever listed on, KTRM's 'Pick of the Week.'

"And the thing started selling real big and of course All South told Capitol, Columbia, and all these about this little old song down in Louisiana that was doing so well. So all of a sudden I started getting calls from companies like MGM . . . I told them all to call Floyd in Ville Platte. And of course that didn't do any good, because Floyd would talk to them, but we didn't realize what was going on. They wanted to lease our record and we got mad as hell, we didn't want anybody to have it, that was ours. Floyd wanted to keep it on Jin and make Jin another RCA! He was a good-thinking businessman, even back then. So anyway they'd say that if we wouldn't lease it to them they would cover it, and we didn't know what that meant until records started coming out by other people. I have some of them. . . . Then Guitar Gable's record started coming out and Excello finally released it. You see, I was working at the radio station and I was getting these records in the mail, all these different singers, and it was all my song. And they all tried to sing it as badly as I did, the bands were trying to play all the off-keys and all! The Boogie Kings cut one, J. D. Miller had them in there, Gene Terry, they had eight or nine covers. About that time I think Floyd started talking to people and J. D. was as happy as hell because he had the publishing on it. The more records that came out the better! And I kept calling him, 'What about this, I got another record of "This Should Go On Forever." ' He said, 'That's good!' I could never understand how that was good, it was good in his eyes, he owned the publishing company! So we almost lost it because of that. And Floyd didn't want to lease it, and I wanted Floyd to do whatever he wanted to do. Floyd and I have a very, very good relationship, he's one of the few people I know, he as a producer and me as a singer, that have retained our friendship through the years, through all this. We've never had a cross word, he's a great guy.

"And I left it up to Floyd because he knew more than I did what to do about things like that at the time. And we ended up to where Floyd finally worked a deal out with Leonard Chess. He had one of the hottest labels back then, he had Chuck Berry, Bo Diddley, and a whole bunch of people on Chess, Checker, and Argo. And Floyd worked a deal out with him, but I know Capitol was interested, Columbia, and a whole bunch of other people. There are many times I wish we had gone with one of those labels to see maybe what would have happened in the future. Anyway, Floyd went with Leonard Chess because he came up with the best deal. . . ."

"Well, Chess Records got wind of it," continues Floyd Soileau, "probably through Stan Lewis in Shreveport. Stan was a big contact man at the time who worked very closely with Chess. And I got a call from Chess, they said, 'Hey, you got a record, you need national distribution, we can take that record off your hands and help you make a hit with it!'—you know, the full story. And he says, 'We'll give you a thousand dollars advance.'

"I didn't think at the time, I said, 'A $1,000 advance, that's pretty good,' because the distributors weren't paying too fast and I had to keep on paying the pressing plant for the stuff. And I said, 'National distribution, sure, one thing I gotta ask you, if we lease that record can you guarantee us an appearance by Rod on "American Bandstand"?' And he says, 'Well, that's almost in the bag if the record continues to sell.' So I said, 'Fine!'

"As my distributors had been so helpful in making the record a regional hit, I called Lelan Rogers of United Record Distributors, who'd been breaking the Houston market. I said, 'Lelan, we're probably gonna lease this thing to Chess, how's that gonna affect you?' and he said, 'That probably shouldn't affect us very much because we're distributing Chess, but of course I've put a lot of time and effort into this thing. Why don't you give me maybe 1,000 records and I'll sell them and I'll get the money for that. That'll fix me up if that's OK with you.' I said that's fine. I also called Henry Hildebrand of All South Record Distributors in New Orleans, and

Henry didn't distribute Chess. I said, 'Henry, what can I do for you?' He said, 'Well, make sure you have enough records on the floor before you turn it loose, and I'll take those pressings and sell them through the distributors, I don't handle Chess.'

"So Paul Gayten drove down to New Orleans with a contract and that $1,000 check to pick up the master tape, and then drove away with it. And two days later I got a call from a Dallas distributor who wanted to buy 8,000 copies of that record and I could have kicked myself for turning it loose so darned fast! That could have been the start of Jin Records, maybe it could have catapulted way up higher and we could have been a much bigger company than we are today. But anyhow Chess kept on with it, they got the sales and they got it played over WLAC Nashville, they got it going all over the country. Rod went on to 'American Bandstand' and that was our first big record."

"Anyway, Floyd worked it out," resumes Rod, "and they sent me on a two- or three-week promotion tour right away. I was playing in Opelousas one weekend and the next week I was on a train going to Chicago to do this promotion trip. It was the first time, I was eighteen and just graduated from high school, scared to death. I had never been away from here except with my parents, I don't think I had been across the state line except to Texas.

"Incidentally, when 'This Should Go On Forever' started doing well around here, Floyd mailed a copy of it to *Cash Box* and *Billboard,* and I think it was *Cash Box*—I don't know if *Billboard* ever reviewed it until it was leased—they gave it a terrible rating, they said it was one of the worst records they'd ever heard, D minus, it really broke my heart. And to show you how money talks, after it was leased to Chess, Chess sent them a copy and they put it a big 'Pick of the Week,' the identical record, not a thing was added, the same master except it was on Argo.... 'Great new hit from the South, it's going to be a tremendous record...' I learned my first lesson in the music business right there.

"From then on, it came out and it started selling. So they sent me on this promotion tour. Back then 'American Bandstand' was on every day on national television and almost every major city had a similar program. There was 'Detroit Bandstand,' 'Chicago Bandstand,' 'The Buddy Deane Show' in Washington, 'The Milt Grant Show' in Baltimore, and of course Chess had contacts with all these people. All this was set up ahead of time, I'd fly in to New York and they picked me up, put me in a hotel, I'd visit a couple of radio stations. Then I did the 'Alan Freed Show' and then I'd go back to the airport, catch a plane, go to Chicago, do a TV show there, then to Baltimore, and did the one there. This was all in a two-week period, February–March, I think, in 1959. You see, 'This Should Go On Forever' came out in October 1958, but it wasn't until 1959 before it got leased, it took nearly six months for all this to take place.

"So I was on this promotion tour, finding these different cities, and I'd call home every day and my girl friend told me that Dick Clark had played 'This Should Go On Forever' on 'American Bandstand.' Of course that floored me, that was too much to believe. We did this in two weeks, we leased the record, I was gone and all these things, it was a lot to happen to somebody in that short a time, particularly a little old country boy that had never been anywhere, it was such a shock. And Dick Clark started playing it every day, that thrilled me. Of course, I didn't know it at the time but he had a record pressing plant, he was pressing all those Chess, Checker, and Argo records. There was a motive behind it, but at that time I thought Dick Clark, boy he's really being a nice guy to play my record like that. I couldn't wait, I'd hope one day to write him a letter and thank him.

"Then about the second week I was on this tour Chess called me and said I was going to be on 'American Bandstand,' the next week at the end of that tour. And man, I can't tell you in words what that was. I just sat down and cried, to be on 'American Bandstand,' goodness that was about the greatest thing! I never could even say that I wanted that because I never even thought that would happen, and it all happened so fast. So I flew into Philadelphia. One thing about 'This Should Go On Forever,' when Dick Clark played it on 'American Bandstand,' some man from somewhere up north wrote in a very hot stinging letter and said the song was immoral and it was a terrible song because of the line *If it's sin to really love you then a sinner I will be.* And Dick Clark got shook up, he called Leonard Chess and wanted me off the 'Bandstand.' They compromised, we would re-record 'This Should Go On Forever' with new lyrics. Anyway we had no music track, you remember back then everything was on one track, so while I was on tour they got my band back together in J. D.'s studio and they cut just the music track and they flew it up to Chicago. I went upstairs to the Chess recording studio and we redid 'This Should Go On Forever' and changed it to say, *If it's wrong to really love you, then wrong I'll always be* instead of *If it's sin to really love you, then a sinner I will be.*

"We changed that one line on it and that's what I lip-synched to on 'American Bandstand,' you really didn't play it, you just pantomimed to your own record. I never told this story to many people until several years later, and yet today listen to what's on record. And we had to go through all that trouble for me to be on 'Bandstand.' (Unknown to Rod, the cleaned-up, musically superior version was released by London-American in England, where it failed to make any impression.)

"I did a lot of record hops, that's how the disc jockeys at the stations picked up extra money. They had these record hops at weekends, high schools were popular venues. The DJs would announce all week they would be there and they would have just a turntable and a sound system, not like the disco things of today. It was just a plain old speaker, one speaker or maybe two and a record player. And he'd play the current hit records and then we'd come on, he'd introduce us, and sometimes we'd bring our bands with us. But more times than not we would get up and just lip-synch with a microphone. He would play the record and cut the sound off the microphone. We would hold the microphone and just pantomime to our records. Also I went on a lot of these two- or three-week tours, in the record business when you're hot you're hot, when you've got a hit record everybody wants you. When you don't, nobody wants to answer your phone calls, that was lesson No. 2 I learned.

"Anyway, I got a chance to sing with a lot of these guys that I'd been playing their records through the years, and all of a sudden I was on the same bandstand with them, which was another big thrill. Like we went on this tour, Frankie Avalon had 'Venus' out then, it was No. 1, Chuck Berry had 'Almost Grown,' the Skyliners had 'Since I Don't Have You,' the Impalas had 'Sorry I Ran All The Way Home,' and Frankie Ford had 'Sea Cruise.' And we went on a big package tour one time in Illinois, we worked different things like this. Shows with a lot of these big singers, Brook Benton one week and Johnny Horton the next week. But I never got a chance to meet Elvis, that's one of my big regrets.

"But we didn't take advantage of a lot of things when we could have. A lot of people feel we really didn't make a lot of money out of 'This Should Go On Forever,' and we didn't. None of it was stolen, it was just that we didn't know what to do. It was really a shame, because there was so much more we could have done. And Floyd didn't know what to do, I didn't know what to do, J. D. really had not had a whole bunch of hit records at that time. Back in 1958 no one around here, no attorneys, no lawyers, they couldn't advise us, they didn't understand what was written in these contracts anyway. Anyway, we got paid on 475,000 copies, they wanted to give me a gold record, but everybody gets a gold record and I didn't want it because it really didn't sell even half a million. I ended up with something like a penny a record, which was a few thousand dollars. But the problem was I took off my work from the radio station to go on this promotion tour, and then I worked some other things like that. All of it was for promotions, so by the time I had got a royalty check I had already run up that much in bills. It took all that we made, it wasn't a very good business deal.

"Considering we didn't know anything I was more fortunate than many singers back then. A lot of other singers never had anything, I know many singers around here who either wrote or had hit records that never received a cent, nothing. Some of them even lost money by it, it really was unfortunate. The publishers and the record-company owners took whatever money there was. Leonard Chess, for example, was a very smart man, he was a very sharp man, he had a lot of contacts. . . . He had a promotion man called Max Cooperstein, and there was Leonard and Phil Chess. I remember when I was in Chicago I was in my hotel and I had my radio on listening to John R. [Richbourg] on WLAC in Nashville, you could pick up this radio station. And I was listening to him, they played 'This Should Go On Forever' by me, then a little while later they played 'This Should Go On Forever' by Guitar Gable.

"And we were eating breakfast the following morning and I happened to mention I heard 'This Should Go On Forever' by Guitar Gable and they dropped their forks, they looked at each other. 'You what??!!' I said, 'I heard "This Should Go On Forever" by Guitar Gable, he's a friend of mine,' and I didn't realize what I was saying. . . . He said, 'Max!' He said, 'Yes, sir.' So he jumps up and goes to the phone and he comes right back and says, 'All right, it's taken care of.' And I didn't realize, but now I know what had happened, the phone call said, 'Hey, "Hoss [Bill Allen of Radio WLAC]," stop that!'

"But Leonard Chess had things wheeling around the range, that was prior to payola, too. [Payola, a system that rewarded disc jockeys for plugging certain records, was widespread in the fifties. In a way payola contributed to the rise and growth of the independent record companies; if a small label owner felt confident about a record and was willing to pay the tariff, he could be assured that his record would be played.] When I'd get into Baltimore they'd take me up to a radio station, to the key man in Baltimore. And I'd get in there, they'd interview me for a minute, then when the guy would put another record on I'd say, 'I really want to thank you for playing my record,' I really thought the guy was just being nice doing that. When the payola scandal broke later [top disc jockey Alan Freed was made a scapegoat in 1959 following investigations by the Internal Revenue and the Federal Trade Commission] I found out why the guy was playing my record! However, Chess had a good organization, he had the promotion behind all this stuff and knew what it took."

"About that time one of the tragedies occurred," recalls Floyd Soileau. "The Big Bopper was killed in this airplane crash with Buddy Holly, and the Big Bopper's personal manager was Bill Hall, who was living in Beaumont. Bill had heard of Rod through Huey Meaux and had heard the record, and he had just lost his artist he was promoting and he was looking for another artist. So he drove to Louisiana and talked to Rod, and came over and talked to me. And he made certain there were no contractual ties, we had a handshake, that's what Rod and I had. And he saw the contracts that I had signed with Chess that guaranteed Chess at least one more record. He made sure that we had one more record on Rod that we could give to Chess. And then he signed Rod on to a personal management and contacted Leonard and said, 'I represent Rod, we have an offer from Mercury Records,' he was partial to Mercury because that was where the Big Bopper was. And he said, 'If you can meet it and beat it, we'll continue with Chess, but if you can't we have a guarantee and we're gonna take Rod over to Mercury.' So the Chess Brothers didn't like that too much, in fact I don't think they put much effort behind Rod's second record [Roy Perkins's 'You're On My Mind'], and he went on to Mercury and did fairly well with them."

Mercury, which was beginning to do big business by purchasing southern masters for national release, took a serious interest in the swamp-pop field. Rod explains their modus operandi: "Shelby Singleton was vice-president for Mercury then, in charge of the southern district. In fact Shelby, when he worked as a promotion man for Mercury, he used to come up to KSLO at night. He would visit all the little radio stations in the New Orleans area, he worked the New Orleans zone for Mercury as a promotion man prior to being vice-president. He was based in Shreveport and he'd come up to KSLO, we'd go drink coffee when I got off work at 10:30 at night and talk about the record business. This was before 'This Should Go On Forever.' And then Shelby, he got 'Chantilly Lace,' 'Sea Of Love,' and 'Running Bear' leased to Mercury, he's the one who found them down here, he got them on Mercury and that landed him a pretty big job at Mercury, he worked his way up to vice-president. I think he's the one that got George Jones on Mercury, and his contact with Bill Hall began. So all this kinda tied in.

"Bill Hall is from Beaumont, Texas, he went to school to be an attorney, a music lawyer, and he never finished. But he went into partnership with J. P. Richardson and formed Big Bopper Enterprises. And they recorded 'Chantilly Lace' and put it out on a little label, D. That's how he and Shelby met up and they got it leased to Mercury. And then Bill Hall had started signing up little bands around there, he signed up Johnny Preston. Johnny's name was Johnny Courville, which is a French name. Johnny was born around here, around Cecilia, but he lived in Port Arthur, near Beaumont. So J. P. wrote this song 'Running Bear' and Johnny recorded it and the record came out, it didn't do anything. About that time J. P. was killed in the plane crash and about six months or so later a DJ in Houston started playing 'Running Bear.' The thing started selling and all of a sudden it ended up on Mercury, too. It was a huge, huge record, a No. 1.

"Anyway, we were all in a group, Bill Hall had me, Jivin' Gene, Johnny Preston, a country singer named Benny Barnes, we were all with Bill Hall and Big Bopper Enterprises. They were starting going to Nashville and cut sessions, that's how I ended up going to Nashville. I had a real good contract with Mercury, they would pay for everything. And then I got like $100 a side whenever I recorded and they had to put out four records a year, I had to record something like ten sides a year. And when my contract ended I still owed them something like $8,000! All this was advance money and recording all these big sessions up there in Nashville. And Floyd Cramer played piano, Boots Randolph played sax, the Anita Kerr Singers, the Jordanaires, we used all these people. That was another thrill, going up there and being able to record. Unfortunately they didn't sell anything."

Of Rod's Mercury releases, only the first, "One More Chance," made any chart impression (it reached No. 74 on *Billboard* at the end of 1959). The rest were mainly vacuous teen ballads, complete with tedious violin sections and vocal choruses, that have not stood the test of time; they were more "pop" than "swamp." At its best (as in "This Should Go On Forever"), swamp-pop had a raw, attractive edge, but on occasions like the Mercury sessions the music became a limp self-parody. "That was when Brenda Lee and Johnny Tillotson were coming out with the strings and all that," says Rod, "so the local things we were doing didn't really happen. Also, Mercury had Brook Benton, the Platters, Dinah Washington, a whole bunch of big names, and they spent all their money promoting them. Jivin' Gene and myself were just one of two or three hundred artists on Mercury, and we just got lost in the pile. They just never put any money behind us, that turned out to be an unfortunate move. I should have stayed with Chess, they wanted me to stay with them, but I wanted to be on this big label on Mercury. That seemed to be the right thing to do at the time."

After the Mercury contract expired in 1962 Rod recorded for Bill Hall's new Hall-Way label. The improvement was relishable. Besides superb versions of minor swamp-pop classics "I Might As Well" (V. J. Boulet), "Loneliness" (Bobby Page), and "Forgive" (Steve Hebert), he cut a rousing "Fais Do-Do," which pinpointed a Cajun generation-gap problem:

> Now the girl in Opelousas, Louisiana,
> She's the Queen of the Teche bayou,
> Prettiest girl in South Louisiana,
> The youngest daughter of Rufus Thibodeaux.
>
> But she don't like to ride in my pirogue,
> Don't even know how to cook gumbo,
> She upsets her Cajun papa when she does the twist at the fais-dodo.

For Bill Hall, Rod had a regional hit with the catchy Cajun favorite "Colinda," sung in French and English. "One night we were doing a session in Beaumont," he recalls, "we had Johnny Winter and Edgar Winter there, they played on all the records that we did in Beaumont. They were from Port Arthur at the time, they played guitar, organ, piano, harmonica, or whatever, we had a four-piece band, we paid them each ten dollars to record. We recorded 'Loneliness' and 'Boss Man's Son,' that was inspired by Allen Toussaint, and Bill Hall said, 'Do that song that I liked, that Cajun song' and we just did 'Colinda' one time through, that was it. He put the thing out on his label and that was the next hit I had! A song I really didn't think that much of. It was real weird, it sold along the Gulf Coast in the southern states, then it sold a lot in Canada. I say a lot, the whole thing may have sold 80,000 or 100,000 records, but a lot of that was in Canada. Then I left to go in the Marine Corps and they wouldn't let me out of camp, not even for 'American Bandstand.' So it did what it did just on its own. Hardly no promotion at all."

In the meantime Bill Hall had been joined in Beaumont by Jack Clement, formerly of Sun Records. They produced two significant hits for Smash, "Defrost" by Texas blues guitarist Albert Collins and "Patches" by country singer Dickey Lee, before making their fortunes in Nashville with Charlie Pride.

After leaving the Marines, Rod decided not to follow Hall and Clement to Music City, U.S.A. Instead he took up his old job as a deejay and program director at radio KVOL Lafayette, a station he had first joined in 1960. He also started working for KLFY-TV Lafayette. Rod's musical activities were confined to the Shondels, a group he had formed in 1963 with drummer Warren Storm and Skip Stewart, a deejay at KVOL who had a minor Jin hit with "Take Her Back." The Shondels were best known for their appearances on "Saturday Hop," a KLFY-TV program based on "American Bandstand." In 1965 they had twelve rock 'n' roll tracks from the show issued on a La Louisianne album; the vocals were shared equally, and Bernard had the choicest cut with a version of Chuck Berry's "The Promised Land."

Rod did not find it easy working during the day and playing at night: "We played in different towns like Lake Charles, Opelousas, Morgan City, Lawtell, Alexandria, we played all around this area. So the only sleep I'd get would be riding back from a dance job, I'd sleep in the backseat of the car. I learned how to sleep while the record was on, when the record was ended I'd wake up, 'Hi, good morning, it's the Rod Bernard Show on KVOL . . . a beautiful day in Lafayette, sixty-five degrees and sunshine . . .' I'd die again and put a record on, go back to sleep. Those were tough days, I couldn't do that again!"

In the mid-sixties Rod launched the Arbee label with Carol Rachou of La Louisianne, and had one terrific Chuck Berry–type rocker, "Recorded

In England," a sardonic comment on the English beat-group domination of the time. The seventies were relatively uneventful, enlivened only by the occasional meritorious Jin album. "Rod Bernard" was a marvelous retrospective compilation drawn mainly from the Hall-Way recordings, while "Country Lovin' " contained new versions of attractive, molasses-thick swamp-pop ballads like Bobby Charles's "On Bended Knee," Jimmy Donley's "Born To Be A Loser," and Cookie's "Mathilda" and sold a commendable 15,000 copies. "Boogie In Black And White" with Clifton Chenier fared poorly by comparison. The idea of Rod and Clifton doing a pulsating album of R&B oldies was hard to fault, but in supposedly enlightened times their respective fans took polarized views and ignored it.

Today Rod lives with his family in an impressive new house, built in the Acadian style on the outskirts of Lafayette; he still works for KLFY-TV. Although he has made many excellent swamp-pop records, full of color and feel, he has never been able to match those heady days of '59. "This Should Go On Forever" was a unique passport into the exhilarating inside world of rock 'n' roll, where he was able to rub shoulders with legends; to make personal appearances in star-studded caravans, at modest record hops, on the hallowed "American Bandstand"; to see the good and bad in the record business, and in human nature generally; and to take pride in the role he played in spreading the South Louisiana swamp-pop sound throughout the nation. Rod's hit record had provided an epic, unrepeatable adventure, yearned for by many, attained by few.

16

"I went into a fever, called the South Louisiana fever"

After Rod Bernard's amicable departure for Mercury in 1959, Floyd Soileau badly needed other potential hit-makers to fill the void. He decided to enlist the help of Huey Meaux, the Crazy Cajun barber from Winnie, Texas, who became a formal partner in Jin two years later. With Huey introducing Jivin' Gene and Floyd signing Johnnie Allan, Rod Bernard was not going to be missed after all.

"Well, Rod was leaving," says Floyd, "so I had to find somebody else. With the records that we had going, Rod's record helped a lot and the name of Jin Records had been spread around quite a bit. And I got a call one day from a disc jockey in Texas who was a barber by trade, and he loved music and he loved musicians, Huey Meaux. Huey called me one day and he says, 'I've got a group of guys here that plays French music, called the Rambling Aces, I'm gonna send it to you.' So we started releasing a record on Huey Meaux and the Rambling Aces. 'Seventy-Three Special' and 'Dans Les Misere.' " The record sold about 500 copies.

Huey's musical talent was limited, but his promotional flair was not. A man of burning ambition and unlimited drive, he was intent on establishing himself as a national record force; as a Cajun, he was able to use South Louisiana music as a platform to accomplish this aim. Huey was born in 1929 in the small town of Kaplan, where musicians worked the rice fields during the week, playing house dances on weekends for beer and pass-the-hat. In his youth he played drums behind his father, Stanislaus "Te Tan" Meaux, a rice farmer who was also a fine accordion player. After Huey moved with his parents to Winnie, Texas, he had a spell in the services before starting work as a barber. A growing obsession with the music business led to his becoming a disc jockey and booking agent in his spare time, as Rod Bernard recalls: "Huey always loved music . . . On Saturday afternoons he had an hour show on KPAC in Port Arthur called 'The Crazy Cajun Show' and he would do the talking. He'd say, 'Eh cher, we're gonna play those Cajun records here for all our good Cajun friends listening in Lake Charles and in Winnie, Texas, here's Aldus Roger and the Lafayette Playboys . . .' And he'd play these French records and Huey would put on this real heavy accent doing this show, he still has an accent anyway. But it was a unique thing in Texas for him to do this, this Cajun French music playing on a Texas station.

"He'd do this every Saturday, then he started booking shows, like he'd book Fats Domino. Huey always found a way to make money. . . . He told me one time, 'Rod, there's money all ready to be made, all a guy has to do is do it. If they could take everything away from me, throw me out on the street, just give me about two days and I'll have money in my pocket, I'll have a car to ride in, and I won't rob anybody.' He just knows how to make money, he's a hardworking guy. And he booked the shows to pick up extra money, he'd bring us over to Beaumont and Port Arthur, like when 'This Should Go On Forever' was hot. And he'd bring Johnnie Allan and I over there, we'd go over there and work a thing for Huey, he'd have a record hop—that was the thing back then. But that's how he began."

With the Rambling Aces, Meaux was primarily involved as manager and as master of ceremonies at club dances. This very proficient Cajun band, which at various times included Andrew Cormier, Rodney LeJune, Dallas Roy, and Marc Savoy, was popular in East Texas and Southwest Louisiana. Their first single for Jin was recorded in late 1958; the session was produced at the KPAC Port Arthur radio station by local deejay Donald Lyons. Recalls Huey: "I didn't know what the hell he was talking about, I didn't understand what recording was, 'cause recording machines were just becoming something then. But he said, 'When I give you the finger, y'all start playing just like it was a Saturday night!' When we came on the air it just blew my mind . . . That was my first taste." After the Jin single, the Rambling Aces (without Huey) did well with "99 Years Waltz" on Swallow before scoring in the Cajun markets of the mid-sixties with "Musicians Waltz," "The Wedding March," and "Madam Sostan," for Huey's Crazy Cajun label.

In 1959 Huey started to edge into the big time after he recorded Gene Bourgeois, a Port Arthur refinery worker: "He walked in with blue jeans and bare feet and kinda like Clark Kent's version of Superman, with horn-rimmed glasses. And he wanted me to record his rock 'n' roll band. I told him I didn't know what the hell I was doing, but if he wanted to bring his band in, let's get down to it. In the KPAC studio there was an old Magnecord in mono—you never heard of stereo in those days—and two pots and a toilet in the corner of the room. And he had to sing in the toilet. I had a big old RCA ribbon mike, a diamond-shaped thing, and I hung it up on the boom and put my amplifiers in a horseshoe shape. The drums had to be way back. I thought I was gonna have to put them out in the street before it was over 'cause it was getting too loud. I called Floyd, saying, 'I think this guy has got potential, I did a tape on him at the radio station, I think you're gonna like it. The guy's name is Jivin' Gene Bourgeois, we call him Jivin' Gene. He's got a thing called "Going Out With The Tide," listen to it, I think you'll like it. I can send him over and you can run him by the various radio stations.' "

"So he sent him over," Floyd recalls, "and we put out that one record, Jin 109, as Jivin' Gene and the Jokers. It made a little dent in the area, looking good, you know. And Huey says, 'I think we ought, you ought to spend a little bit more money and get a nicer session and I think we can sell this guy. So we booked a session at Jay's studio and went there and did 'Breaking Up Is Hard To Do.' *Not* the Neil Sedaka song, ours was out before he had that title, it was about Gene's wife problems. We did a Fats Domino–type thing and put the record out. Right away Huey started getting airplay on it over East Texas, and I got airplay on it down in this area, and things started happening. And Bill Hall still had his eyes open, and we made a deal with him to get it in on Mercury Records. And as a result his Big Bopper Music got the publishing on the original sides and that was his compensation. And Huey managed the artist and I had the record label and the record company, so I had my compensation. We had a three-way thing going there for a while, and Mercury took on with Jivin' Gene and did fairly well with him."

On Mercury Jivin' Gene's admirable "Breaking Up Is Hard To Do" ambled to No. 69 on the *Billboard* charts in the fall of 1959. This swamp-pop ballad was a classic of its kind, pleasantly melodic and gently mesmeric. With a musical backdrop featuring a barroom piano, Gene wistfully sang:

Breaking up is hard to do,
Breaking up is sad and blue.
Making up is the thing to do,
Don't you know what I say is true?

Like I told you once before,
This fussin' and fightin' there'll be no more.
I will make this promise to you,
Just to prove my love is true . . .

Jivin' Gene also had a minor hit with a violin-laden remake of the sumptuously tuneful "Going Out With The Tide" on *The Cash Box* (but not *Billboard*) listings in late 1960. Recording much of the time in Nashville, Gene managed to overcome Mercury's frequent productional excesses with strong, gutsy performances in the Fats Domino mold. He continued making good records for Chess, Hall-Way, and TCF-Hall until the mid-sixties. In 1982 Gene Bourgeois was still living and working in

Port Arthur, and had started to perform again, some twenty years after his initial brush with fame.

In 1959 Jin had another regional hit with Johnnie Allan's "Lonely Days And Lonely Nights," a typical swamp-pop ballad in the familiar two-chord South Louisiana format, but MGM was unable to turn the record into a national hit after taking over distribution. Today Allan is still not widely recognized outside South Louisiana and East Texas, a situation that hardly matters to this engaging entertainer since he continues to enjoy tremendous popularity locally and racks up respectable sales with his Jin albums. He is also an ardent campaigner for his native Cajun and swamp-pop music.

A great-nephew of the revered Joseph Falcon, John Allen Guillot was born in Rayne in 1938. He grew up surrounded by Cajun music, and at thirteen he was playing rhythm guitar with Walter Mouton and the Scott Playboys. In 1953 Johnnie joined Lawrence Walker's Wandering Aces as steel guitarist, spending five happy years with this top Cajun band. In 1958, feeling there was little future in playing French music, he formed a rock 'n' roll group called the Krazy Kats with the rest of Lawrence Walker's band: guitarist Al Foreman, pianist U. J. Meaux, and drummer Bhuel Hoffpauir— plus tenor player Leroy Castille (who recorded for Jay Miller as Lee Castle). Allan still recalls the awkwardness he felt in breaking the news of their mass exodus to Lawrence, who replied with hurt dignity, "So that's what happens when you put an old horse out to grass. . . ."

But it was a necessary step if the young Cajun singer was to realize his ambition to join Jimmy Clanton on the national charts. The first step was to prepare material for a record. "I was going to USL, the university of Lafayette," remembers Johnnie, "and I said, 'Doggone, if I'm gonna make anything out of the music business, the one thing I'll have to do first of all is to write.' So I sat down and started popping ideas in my head and wrote two songs, 'Lonely Days And Lonely Nights' and 'My Baby's Gone.' And I went to Floyd Soileau's in Ville Platte, he liked them. We went to record at J. D. Miller's in Crowley, in those days he was doing the sessions. J. D. had a very good studio sound at the time, it was a mixture of his skill and the equipment he had. You see he had cut several songs, Guitar Gable's, Rod had just cut 'This Should Go On Forever' there, and about that time that kind of swamp-pop sound was getting into the picture. So he had a pretty good idea of what was marketable, what the people would buy. So we took it from there and it's been down that road ever since. I've derived a lot of songs from that particular sound.

"Regionally the first record sold very, very good, that is the Gulf Coast from Houston on to Florida. In fact within the first three months the sales were so good that MGM picked it up, and they released it nationwide. It never did catch on like some of the other songs in South Louisiana and I hate to say it, I really think it was because the payola bit was big in those days, and some companies just refused to go along with it. But I went on tour from Florida, through Texas, Arizona, and into California, it was partly promotional and partly paying. The disc wasn't a monster, it was 'bubbling under,' but never did crack the '100' mark.

"Then Floyd and Huey Meaux made an agreement with Bill Hall on the next release. Bill Hall was with Mercury at that time, and they released 'The Letter Of Love,' which didn't do anything. Then I left Floyd for a while and went over to Viking, which was owned by Dago Redlich from Crowley—his brother Hank was lead guitar with me then. That's when 'South To Louisiana' was released. There are three names in the credits, 'Redlich-Trahan-Sam.' Sam came up with the idea of writing swamp-pop lyrics to the tune 'North To Alaska,' and sent it on to Dago Redlich, who added a couple of ideas to it. Redlich then turned it over to Pee Wee Trahan, who should be credited with the majority of the lyrics. Pee Wee told me the other two got bogged down for the appropriate words, he came to the rescue and finished it. 'Your Picture' written by Bobby Charles was another minor hit, those songs were recorded at J. D.'s."

Viking Records was never a commercial success. Except for Johnnie Allan, who had signed more or less as a favor to his guitarist Hank Redlich, the only noteworthy act was Randy and the Rockets, featuring Den Norris. (Owner Dago Redlich also ran the Chamo label to promote the rising young Cajun accordionist Belton Richard.) Disappointed by the comparatively poor sales of the Viking singles, Johnnie decided to support his growing family by teaching, and obtained an appointment as assistant principal at the Acadian Elementary School in Lafayette (he was able to retire on pension in 1981). On weekends he still played the local clubs and lounges, where he built up a solid following. He also continued making records. After Viking he had an isolated session for Huey Meaux in 1964 before returning to Floyd Soileau and Jin. Following several modest sellers Johnnie had a substantial regional hit in 1973 with "Somewhere On Skid Row," a country-flavored record that was on every jukebox in Acadiana. But a year later his musical ambitions were rekindled in a big way when he almost had a surprise English hit with a rip-roaring rendition of Chuck Berry's "The Promised Land," featuring Belton Richard on accordion. The record was an intriguing swamp-pop adaptation of an R&B song, enlivened by the Cajun accordion sound.

Floyd Soileau was as astonished as anyone by the reaction: "I got a call from a promoter in New York, 'I've just come back from the Ronettes, my, you've got a hit going over there in London!' And I'm going, like, 'What hit?' Charlie [Gillett of Oval Records] hadn't got back to tell me he had lifted 'The Promised Land' from the album. I knew I had an album over there, 'Another Saturday Night,' but I didn't know I had anything else. And he says, 'Man, they were playing this record coming and going, have you assigned the U.S. rights to it yet?' And I said, 'Well, no, not yet, but I'm interested.' I was still wondering, I was hoping he would tell me. He says, 'You know what hit I'm talking about?' I says, 'Well, er, no, I got several things working.' So finally he tells me, and I'm going, like, 'I still can't believe this . . .' I think it was the following day I got a letter from Charlie explaining what was happening. And here is a record that came out a year or so back. Then Elvis's version comes out and throws us out and we figured, 'Well, we've had it now, that's it.' Lo and behold, four years later—resurrection again."

Gillett rereleased "The Promised Land" in 1978, this time flying the Lafayette schoolmaster to London to promote the record. Johnnie was overwhelmed by the reception from the English record business, music press, and swamp-pop enthusiasts. "I don't know what your English folks did over there," says Floyd, "but you treated him so royally. He came back and I swear he didn't come off that cloud for at least two months! And he's still got all the clippings and the tapings of the interviews and everything else. He can just float in that for years."

Johnnie remains Jin's best selling artist. By 1982 he had eight albums to his name, including the "South To Louisiana" greatest-hits compilation containing many of the Viking sides; the superb "Johnnie Allan Sings" with standout versions of "You Got Me Whistling," "Please Accept My Love," and "The Promised Land"; and, most recently, "Cajun Country," an enticing selection of country numbers sung in English and French. Allan continues to showcase a rich variety of South Louisiana music at his classy performances at clubs, concerts, private functions, even country fairs. Says Johnnie: "We have drawn more crowds in the last six years or so than in all the past years put together. Just to cite as an example, we played at this place between Raceland and Golden Meadow recently, I booked this a few months before. There was not a single word of advertisement on radio or TV or nothing, the guy called me up, we booked it and within a week and a half, just by word of mouth, it was sold out. Eight hundred people! Seventy-five percent of the music is swamp-pop, we have to throw in some Cajun music, we have to throw in some country and western, mix it up. It's a mixture of a crowd, we draw anywhere from twenty-year-olds to sixty-year-olds. So we have to play some of the latest national hits, but I'll limit them to about three or four a night."

On September 27, 1981, Johnnie Allan's longtime dream of staging large-scale swamp-pop concerts became reality when he promoted the "South Louisiana Music All-Star Show" at the Civic Center in Thibodaux.

The roster of artists read like a Swamp-Pop Hall of Fame: Rod Bernard, Grace Broussard, Van Broussard, T. K. Hulin, Jivin' Gene, Charles Mann, Clint West, and of course Allan himself. Johnnie was sufficiently encouraged by the response to plan similar concerts, an indication of his confidence in the future of swamp-pop.

Besides the big-selling Jin artists, Floyd Soileau recorded several other swamp-pop singers between 1959 and 1961, including Rockin' Dave Allen, Phil Bo, Prince Charles, and Billy Lewis. While these artists were secondary in terms of sales and did not manage any national hits, they did occasionally breach the Top Ten charts in a few southern cities, especially in New Orleans, Beaumont, and Houston.

In 1960 Rockin' D. A. Stich had a small regional hit for Jin with his relaxed swamp-pop version of Big Walter Price's "Shirley Jean." Raised in Franklin, Texas, he was one of the first whites to play the blues in Houston; his friend Joe Barry says Dave could really make the guitar cry—his fingers were so long that he was able to hit the most obscure notes. Dave's quality Jin singles, ranging from the wailing "What's Left For A Fool" to an engaging bluesy version of Jimmy Reed's "Can't Stand To See You Go," had a definite R&B edge within a swamp-pop format. (In 1980 his Jin releases were repackaged in an appealing album oddly entitled "Southern Rock 'N' Roll Of The 60's" [Rock-a-Billy Productions].) For a while Dave worked in the studio for Huey Meaux, teaching guitar licks to Joey Long, a renowned Meaux session man from DeQuincy who had a minor hit in 1962 with "I'm Glad For Your Sake" (Tribe). Dave's career fizzled after he recorded a blues album for International Artists, and he is now a roughneck on the oil rigs in the Gulf, his rockin' days behind him.

Phil Bo (Boudreaux) from Houma was a superbly expressive vocalist who sang his English lyrics with an unmistakable Cajun accent. In 1961 he recorded a magnificent "She Wears My Ring" for Jin in a romping New Orleans R&B style, but the song was unaccountably relegated to the flip of the swamp-pop ballad "Don't Take It So Hard." Phil also had a brace of ravishing, quality swamp-pop singles for Huey Meaux: "Oh! What A Mistake"/"Mr. Train" with the Vikings (Som), and "My Sea Of Tears" (L. and K.). Later he cut a zestful version of Sugar Boy Crawford's New Orleans R&B number "Morning Star" for Smash. For all his praiseworthy releases, Phil Bo never made a breakthrough as a recording artist.

Another Jin act, Prince Charles (Fontenot) and the Rockin' Kings, featuring singer Charles Veillon, had a minor hit with the melodic "Cheryl Ann." But Billy Lewis failed to occupy pressing-plant time with either the rafter-shaking "Show Me How To Twist" (Jin) or a worthy Fats Domino—inspired "Growing Old" for the Hart label out of Leeville.

Joe Barry was a cut above his Jin contemporaries and his class showed when his recording of "I'm A Fool To Care," leased to Smash, climbed to No. 24 on the *Billboard Hot 100* in the early summer of 1961. "Mercury just started a new label called Smash," he says, "and we busted right away. Me, and Joe Dowell had 'Wooden Heart,' Rick and the Keens had 'Peanuts.' Three in a row, boom, boom, boom . . . Oh baby!"

"I'm A Fool To Care" was a wonderful record written by western-swing man Ted Daffan from Beauregard Parish, who was also responsible for writing another country classic, "Born To Lose." With the Vikings contriving a beautifully controlled New Orleans R&B–style musical backdrop, Joe Barry gave the old Gene Autry hit a sensitive swamp-pop rendition, his broad Cajun tones caressing the tender lyrics:

I'm a fool to care
When you don't care for me.
So why should I pretend,
I'll lose in the end,
I'm a fool to care. . . .

Joe Barry is a twenty-four-carat Cajun with an accent as thick as cane syrup, a splendid character who has seen life from the bottom to the top and down again. His story is a Cajun odyssey: "I was born Friday July 13, 1939, in Cut Off, Louisiana, my parents were Josef and Josephine Barrios. My father was a boat captain all his life, worked on the Mississippi River and bayous, and my mother worked in the fields. We trapped and hunted, we did just about everything we could for a living. We didn't even have gravel roads, there was mud roads, it was pretty primitive.

"My daddy was my first musical influence, he played an old mouth harp, and I tell you what, he did the prettiest version of 'You Are My Sunshine' you ever did hear, so that fascinated me. I had a cousin back then that was on Columbia, Vin Bruce. I'd go listen to him strum the guitar, boy, to me it was like the harps of the angels when I heard the guitar! Naturally a guitar was all I wanted. So I'd get me a cigar box, ruin the screen porches by pulling all the wires off, and then about the age of five, right before I started school, on my birthday—we were pretty poor, so it took Daddy and Mommy some pretty saving—they bought me a guitar. Believe you me, the only time I'll ever be as happy is if I make it to heaven, 'cause I tell you what, this was heaven that day! And every second I was beating on it, and I bugged Vin Bruce, my cousin, so much that he started showing me a couple of chords.

"Back then country and French was about the only thing. Ernest Tubb was the king and Happy Fats and Doc Guidry, and quite a few of the old Cajun stars. One thing I used to get fussed at a lot, we had an old radio and on Sunday I'd hear Negro gospel singers and I got fascinated. And my sisters and brothers would throw a fit because, man this is crazy, all this gibberish, but it just did something, it really freaked me out. I was Catholic-born, Gregorian chants and all that, it was so different. So I discovered a little bit of church and down the street was a little black church. So what I'd do, we'd walk to the Catholic church, wait until everybody walked in, then I'd boogie down to the black church. I was the only white dude in there, but I'd clap and shout with them, boy, and get it going! And I really got a deep feeling inside for this music still today, and it really inspired me.

"And I was about eight before I went to my first club. They were very relaxed on laws because at *fais-dodos* all the families would come. I mean at the *fais-dodo* you would bring all the children and the whole family to the dance hall and when the kids would fall asleep, they'd push all the tables in the corner, lay the kids on the table. And the music just went on, boy, that was it until daybreak. I was one of those that didn't want to sleep, I wanted to play! So I got to doing this for years, playing with jazz bands, country bands. Oh my God, by the age of thirteen I was pretty well educated in music and bandstands. There were some pretty wild clubs, my mommy and daddy had to come with me. My daddy was called the Bull of the Pampas, they wouldn't mess with me as long as he was around! But these were clubs out in the Indian parts, Golden Meadow, Leeville, and Grand Isle. Cut Off was pretty primitive back there, you had one house every two or three miles. It was a fishing village, later on oil boomed, but fishing was the main thing then. The Indian part was a no-no, I mean it was pretty rough, they'd chop you to pieces in a second. But as scared as everybody was to go down there, when I went there with my music these people loved it and I loved them. Because music I believe is the greatest communication in this world, music don't know no hate or race or anything.

"And this thing kept developing. I listened to the black gospel and I listened to Cajun, and I had a feeling that there's gotta be some way this can be put together. Then, in 1955, I'll never forget, Ray Charles had a song out called 'Come Back Baby,' boy, I said, this is it, this is solely what I'm looking for! To me it combined both the Cajun wild beat with the black gospel sound, and that was closer to what I was looking for. But I had problems, though. I went into a fever, called the South Louisiana fever, which had a little beat in the country songs which the country entertainers back then did not go for. So they said, 'Well Joe, you can sit in, but you gonna play the funny stuff?' and I said, 'Yeah, I'm gonna sing that funny stuff!' And they'd laugh at me, poke fun. So I'd take an old Gene Autry song like 'I'm A Fool To Care' and I'd hit a little different note on it, you know, with the beat. And the kids started liking it, which was the new generation to come and some of the grown-ups started liking it. So finally all the guys that were the big stars in the local bayou country wouldn't let me sit in with their bands because I kept singing this funny stuff—the club owners were asking me to replace them!

"Then rhythm and blues started getting hot, rock 'n' roll was on the fringe," says Joe, readily recalling influential New Orleans R&B hits of the late fifties like "Cha Dooky Doo" by Art Neville, "Lights Out" by Jerry Byrne, "One Night" by Smiley Lewis, plus the Fats Domino and Little Richard smashes. By hanging around important New Orleans spots like Cosimo's Studio and the Dew Drop Inn, Barry was able to jam with local stars Big Boy Myles, Sugar Boy Crawford, Smiley Lewis, and Tommy Ridgley. His swamp-pop education was finally complete.

"Meanwhile South Louisiana music was developing," Joe adds, "I wasn't the only one. I thought I was a creator but it had been happening in different parts of South and West Louisiana. A lot of artists like Jivin' Gene, Rod Bernard, and Warren Storm had been doing the same thing. That was when Floyd came up with the Jin label. So by that time I needed a band, and I finally learned how to organize a band. And what I did, I went nuts! Because I got a nine-piece band the first time, and in those days it was unheard of. We split like three bucks apiece, we'd rather suffer and starve and have good music, but soon we started getting our price. The first band was called the Dukes of Rhythm, we sacrificed pay and everything else to put a tight sound together. We became one of the best bands in the state along with the Boogie Kings. And had a more solid sound, I might add, the sax players were all equal to Lee Allen [from Fats Domino's band]."

The Dukes of Rhythm were named after the well-known Dukes of Dixieland from New Orleans and the "solid sound" came from their large horn and brass sections. Joe Barry was featured as "Rockin' Roland," but after a dispute he left to form the Delphis. The new group accompanied him on his first record, "Greatest Moment Of My Life"/"Heartbroken Love" for Jin in 1960. It was not an inspiring debut, as he recalls: "We tried to cut it at station KLFT, Golden Meadow, and we couldn't get a sound, so Floyd said to come down there. So we all saved up our pennies and drove down to Ville Platte, we cut it in his studio, which was tiny. Can you imagine eight pieces in there? One of the guys had a big bass sax and that took up a quarter of the room! Then we had a release on 'Greatest Moment,' we were all excited, it was No. 1 on KLFT in Golden Meadow of course, it made the charts! All you had to do back then was send in a card and request it, which I think netted the post office about a billion dollars because between our families we bought every postcard under the sun!

"And Joe Carl was in opposition and he had half of my old band, the

Dukes of Rhythm. He had a song out on Top Rank which was an English label, it was called 'Don't Leave Me Again,' so we were battling back and forth. Our record was a huge success in Cut Off, but it sold about 927 copies in total!"

Next, Joe recorded two competent R&B singles for Sho-Biz, owned by New Orleans disc jockey Jim Stewart (according to Stewart, Barry was a good artist but lacked stage presence). Floyd Soileau agreed to record Joe again after being impressed by a tape of a new song, "I Got A Feeling," submitted by producer Leroy Martin. Recalls Floyd: " 'I Got A Feeling' was a perfect copy of Ray Charles! And Ray Charles was just as hot as all hell back then down in this area. And I said to Leroy, 'Well, you know, these things are good for at least one hit, when you come out of left field with one of these soundalikes. God, we're gonna do all right with this, yeah, we want to record him again. I tell you what, I'll give you carte blanche to go to Cosimo Matassa in New Orleans, get the musicians you need and record him.'

"And he did, and I couldn't wait to get the master tape back 'cause Leroy had been doing all the Vin Bruce things for me, and producing for me, and it was working out great. And I got the master tape back and I couldn't wait to put it on the reel. I listened to it and I said, 'Well, gosh . . . where's Ray Charles, this guy doesn't sound like Ray Charles, he sounds like Joe Barry! There's nothing on this, you know.' But as the song played out and 'I'm A Fool To Care' came on, I said, 'Oh my, I lost Ray Charles, but I picked up Fats Domino, that's not too bad.' Cosimo had engineered so many Fats Domino sessions he couldn't help but record this song with the same arrangement and everything else. It was a natural, I don't know why Fats Domino never recorded this particular song [before Joe], although he did it later.

"So I called Huey [Meaux], I was all excited, so Huey came down to see me and listened to me. He says, 'Look, why don't you and I get together and start running this label as a partnership? I can help you, you don't have time or you're not taking time and not getting out.' And I'm basically a shy person, I didn't like to get out and mingle—and he was single, I had just got married. He liked nothing better than to go out, wine and dine the fellows, and talk to the disc jockeys, spend all hours of the night with the bands, and I could see that it would be a good combination for us. So I said OK and he said, 'Well, let's go to New Orleans and we're gonna break this record in New Orleans, we're gonna stop at every radio station on the way and let them hear our new Fats Domino record!' And by the time we came back from our trip I was getting calls for the record from the distributor and Huey took it over to Beaumont in East Texas, started getting it played up there.

"And our Mercury contact at the time got wind of it, and Charlie Fach from Mercury called in and said, 'Hey, we're coming up with a new label called Smash Records and we need a hot record to kick this label off, I understand you've got one and we want it.' So there went Joe Barry, we signed him off to Smash Records and we continued recording a whole bunch of things on him. And 'I'm A Fool To Care' went on to be a pretty big record at that time."

"I couldn't believe it," Joe says, "because I was still an awestruck country boy. This was just getting too big for me, it was out of my scope. I was like numb, you know ..." With Huey Meaux's help, he appeared on "American Bandstand," thus realizing yet another dream; but he lost the Negro market when he was seen to be white. It was a repeat of Bobby Charles's experience with "Later Alligator." Nevertheless, Joe thinks "I'm A Fool To Care" sold in excess of one million copies, although he is not absolutely certain; he even cut a French version for the Canadian and overseas markets. And he is still astonished by the uncanny Fats Domino sound: "It was so accidental it wasn't even funny. 'Cause I had no intention, I didn't even sing Fats Domino songs back then. I did Ray Charles and local things but I rarely did Fats Domino unless I had a request. It just came out that way. I was more surprised than anybody else because I could never hear any resemblance. Till today I can't, but everybody else can. So it must be."

The follow-up, "Teardrops In My Heart"—an old Sons of the Pioneers country hit—was another gritty swamp-pop record, but it only reached No. 63 on *Billboard* in the fall of 1961; the sound was too close to "I'm A Fool To Care" to succeed. Smash might have done better to promote the "B" side, "For You, Sunshine," a lively slab of New Orleans R&B. "I wrote that for Sunshine Tucker," says Joe, "her husband was Gabe Tucker, a DJ in Houston which used to manage Ernest Tubb at one time. They helped me and Huey a bunch back then, getting us started, because we were green. Huey had had some local success, but everything that went big Bill Hall had handled nationalwise and Huey had never been on a big national thing. But Sunshine and Gabe really gave us a big hand and the great thing is they had nothing to profit, nothing to gain. Just because they liked me and Huey, they made trips for us, called up people, talked to people, got us going. You see, me and Huey were down-home boys and you can imagine when we went to New York and met the echelon of the record companies, music barons that didn't know what they were talking about! And old Huey cracked me up, we'd go to receive an award or something and everybody would be wearing their tuxedoes. And Huey would have his shirt outside his pants, and just walk up in a short-sleeve shirt with everybody else wearing a tie. He always refused to be anything else but Huey, and that's one thing I've always loved and respected about him."

Occasionally Joe would play the black clubs in New York: "Everybody would go to the Copa and the big plush places and you know where me and Huey would head for? Harlem! They said, 'Man, you gotta be crazy, man, you got three million blacks around you!' And I said, 'So what, they've got two coonasses around them . . .' That's how a coonass thinks, that don't shake you up. So we went down there and Wilt the Stilt, he's a great guy, he booked me in at Small's Paradise and I sang. And Mickey and Sylvia had the Blue Morocco and I used to sing there. I guess I was the only white artist playing Harlem back then. Then we had more hits on Smash, 'You Don't Have To Be A Baby To Cry,' 'Little Jewel Of The Veaux Carre,' 'Till The End Of The World.' And 'Little Papoose'! Phew, she was something else, man, little jivin' genie! Huey still laughs about it, she was a little papoose, what a papoose! Every chief would be proud to have one like that!"

After the Smash sojourn, Joe had an arresting series of singles for Huey Meaux's Princess label. Among the releases, which stressed the close connection between swamp-pop and New Orleans R&B, was a rollicking version of "Big Mamou" with Barry in duet with Mary McCoy (who also recorded for Jin). But Joe was being lured into a twilight world of drugs and booze: "Things got better and then they got a little worse. Then I started pretty heavy into some heavy stuff, you know, drugs and everything. Got strong, real strong, shooting up and just going out of it. And I was getting harder and harder to handle. I wouldn't admit it at one time but I'd disappear for weeks at a time and Huey would be frantic. Unfortunately I was an outlaw back then, I really was, long before the outlaws ever thought of being outlaws. Huey Meaux would have to bail me out of motels because the tendency of getting so bored and I was so wild to start with—when I hit a motel Huey would try to subdue me by locking the doors on me. So what I'd do, I'd shoot out television screens. I learned a trick that used to always work, usually the phone connection had a wire that led up the plaster, and I just kept pulling it, the plaster would just . . . Matter of fact, the guy at Holiday Inn in Houston, I destroyed the room so bad that he won an award for The Most Destroyed Room in the Holiday Inn, he really did!"

It seems that everyone, including Rod Bernard, has an outrageous Joe Barry story: "Joe's crazy! We worked a show in San Antonio one night and they saw a big pile of smoke coming from the other side of the motel and we all ran over there. And Joe had taken the curtains down and had built a fire in the threshold of the motel room—he was sending smoke signals to his girl friend, some Indian girl he had met in San Antonio!"

And Joe's good friend, Mac Rebennack: "Joe's so crazy, a real problem kid! When I was working with Joe, many's the night I spent in jail because Joe did something. Like the night we were playing in Galliano, Joe pulled a gun out on the high sheriff! In pulling out the gun he had a pocket full of pills that fell out all over the floor, and the sheriff arrested him for pills. I'm the bandleader and I say can I help Joe. 'You go to jail, too!' I can't tell you the nights I spent in jail from working gigs with Joe, but I still to this day love Joe."

For a while Joe Barry stayed in Houston, playing with Joey Long at the Esquire Ballroom and backing many black acts that came to town, including Bobby Bland. In 1965 he returned to New Orleans to a regular gig at Papa Joe's on Bourbon Street with Freddy Fender, Skip Easterling, Mac Rebennack, and Ronnie Barron. Not many tourist bars could match that lineup. Then Joe drifted out of music to work in the oil fields. "A man's got to feed his family," he sighs, "I couldn't earn much of a living singing, so I picked up money doing what I could. And I picked up a lot of blues. All through it all, I went back out of it, went back into music, started again, came back out of it. But I could never get quite enthused, did a little stretch here and there . . ." During this barren period he made one record for the Houma label in exchange for a guitar and tape recorder.

His trip to Nashville in 1968 with manager Randy Daniels was more productive: "I thought I was forgotten and buried, and to my surprise a lot of big companies were interested in signing me up. But big companies never did impress me." So he turned down offers from mighty Columbia, Decca, and RCA in favor of Fred Carter Jr.'s novice Nugget label. Although he cut fabulous versions of "Today I Started Loving You Again" and "Chantilly Lace," the records sold only moderately and Joe admits "it wasn't sound thinking going with them, but you know, that's coonass thinking!"

He returned to Cut Off and the oil fields, "I became a Christian and I put music away forever, or so I thought. I was very content." Then in 1976 Huey Meaux, riding on the crest of a wave with Freddy Fender, tempted Joe into his Houston studios and recorded him out of context singing country ballads on the introspective "Joe Barry" album (ABC/Dot). The LP had many good qualities, but it soon found its way into the cut-rate bargain bins. Today Joe is based in Galliano and devotes his life to the church. Religion has been a real salvation for him, and he started repaying his inspirational debt by recording a gospel LP privately in Dallas, Texas, in September 1980. If asked by guests, he will still play his guitar and sing the songs of his formative Southeast Louisiana years, including "Dans La Louisianne" (Vin Bruce), "Jolie Fille" (Gene Rodrigue), and "Chere Cherie" (Doc Guidry); he will also slip in medleys of swamp-pop tunes by Bobby Charles and Jimmy Donley. Any casual listener lucky enough to catch such a meaningful performance must wonder why he has not used his vast talent to better advantage. The name of Joe Barry should be associated with more than "I'm A Fool To Care" and broken motel rooms.

Floyd Soileau and Huey Meaux decided to dissolve their year-long formal partnership in the summer of 1962. Floyd was left with control of Jin Records, which continued to hold its own through Tommy McLain's 1966 national hit "Sweet Dreams" and sporadic local hits by Johnnie Allan, Clint West, Rufus Jagneaux, and others. But the genuine excitement of the early years was never fully recaptured. Meanwhile, Huey Meaux departed with contractual rights over Joe Barry, and proceeded to set up his own recording organization. "The timing was again wrong for me," sighs Floyd, "because a week later Huey started hitting big with a new artist he had found, Barbara Lynn, a black left-handed guitarist from Beaumont. And that brought about his first big mother of a thing, 'You'll Lose A Good Thing' on Jamie. But I was happy for him and he was on his own running Crazy Cajun Enterprises as he saw fit. I was maybe too ultraconservative at that time, I think that's probably what caused us to split our partnership."

Barbara Lynn's agreeable "You'll Lose A Good Thing," a bluesy swamp-pop ballad, rose to No. 8 on the *Billboard Hot 100* chart. She became a regular visitor to the lower regions of the *Hot 100* during the next three years. Between 1962 and 1963, two other Huey Meaux signings broke into the national charts: Big Sambo (James Young) had a modest No. 74 hit with a wistful South Louisiana ballad, "The Rains Came" (Eric); then the Texas group Sunny and the Sunliners nearly breached the Top Ten with their version of Little Willie John's "Talk To Me" (Tear Drop). During this fertile period Meaux was holding frequent sessions in New Orleans, sometimes assisted by Leroy Martin. Among Huey's artists was the tragic figure of Jimmy Donley, a superb songwriter who had a genuine feel for swamp-pop. Before he committed suicide in March 1963, Donley had some success with the soulful "Born To Be A Loser" (Decca), "Please Mr. Sandman" (Tear Drop), and "Think It Over" (leased to Chess). Most memorable of all was "I'm To Blame" (Tear Drop):

Have you told your new friend about me?
I bet you never, never speak my name.
I close my eyes and see you with some stranger,
Oh how it hurts me, for I know I'm to blame.

Sweet memories of you come back to haunt me,
That's why my life can never be the same.
With broken heart I'm sending you best wishes,
Oh how it hurts me, for I know I'm to blame.

There's no room for me in this old world without you . . .

In the sleeve notes to Jimmy's memorial Starflite album, Huey wrote: "Born August 19, 1929, in Gulfport, Mississippi, Jimmy had to be the most lonesome guy on earth. He reminded me so much of the late Hank Williams, he wrote songs and sang them in a 'heartbreak' key. At times he could write as many as eight songs in one day. You could give him an idea and boom! He had you a song that could be recorded in any style.

"But like most artists he was the type of guy that would rather have $10 today than $10,000 tomorrow. By this I mean that he would sell his rights in his songs for peanuts. Like he always told me, 'I need the money now. I can always write more songs tomorrow.' Many of Jimmy's songs became hits for Fats Domino, like 'What A Price,' 'Rockin' Bicycle,' 'I've Been Calling,' and 'Bad Luck And Trouble,' some of which he co-wrote with Pee Wee Maddux."

Floyd Soileau also had a lot of respect for Jimmy Donley: "He would have been a very big artist had it not been for that tragedy. Every one of his songs had so much feel and meaning, and I think eventually they'll all get redone, they're getting a lot of records on them now. His records were hot at the time, everything he came out with, he was something like Johnnie Allan was around here except he was from Mississippi. He was selling back home as well as selling here. People here loved him right away, they took him as one of their own, like maybe he was from Lafayette or something. But he was selling all over."

Jimmy Donley is still remembered in South Louisiana. In swamp-pop terms, his songs are as durable as those of Bobby Charles.

Cookie and the Cupcakes and Phil Phillips had shown that swamp-pop could be performed with ease by black artists; indeed, there was little stylistic difference between swamp-pop and the R&B music of South Louisiana. Although Floyd Soileau continued to rely mainly on white Cajun singers to keep Jin "always in the spotlight," he also had some success with the R&B-oriented Rockin' Sidney and Margo White. In 1962 Rockin' Sidney had a small Louisiana hit with "No Good Woman," a light, melodic song based on Slim Harpo's "Rainin' In My Heart," with a similar backing of harmonica, guitar, bass guitar, and drums. Sidney's sweet voice contrasted with the cautionary lyrics:

Every day gotta work like a slave
'Cause my baby don't try to save.
A no good woman can ruin a man's life. . . .

Every weekend she calls me honey
Just to get her hands on my money.
A no good woman can ruin a man's life.

A talented and versatile artist, Sidney Simien was born in 1938 in the tiny hamlet of Lebeau in St. Landry Parish, a few miles from Ville Platte. He started playing professionally in his late teens and cut his first record, "Make Me Understand," for Carl in 1957. After uninspired releases for Fame, Jin, and Rod, he returned to Jin with the captivating "No Good Woman." The flip, "You Ain't Nothin' But Fine," and the follow-ups "If I Could I Would" and "It Really Is A Hurtin' Thing" had the same charm as the hit; they all came on like wafts of balmy southern breezes. (Flyright has since included these enjoyable singles in a definitive Sidney Simien album, "They Call Me Rockin'.") As Count Rockin' Sidney, complete with a Chuck Willis turban, he signed for Goldband in 1965 and dabbled mainly in the soul sounds of the day, without much distinction. In the mid-seventies, trying to emulate Clifton Chenier, Sidney bounced back with two delightful zydeco-flavored songs, "Louisiana Creole Man" (Bally Hoo) and "Let's Go To The Fais Do-Do" (Goldband). But in his desire to pursue the latest trends he seems to have lost the individuality he displayed on his later Jin singles. He still plays in the bars and lounges of Lake Charles.

Margo White did reasonably well in 1963 with "Don't Mess With My Man" and "I'm Not Ashamed." "She came through my door," recalls Floyd, "she was an attractive black girl from Franklin, her real name was Marguerite Wright. Already she had recorded for George Khoury ['Down By The Sea' with the Cupcakes]. She got a little reel-to-reel thing at the time, and I listened to her voice and said, 'Yeah I'd like to record you for sure.' Margo had one song she had written, and as she had no band I hired the Boogie Kings and we went down to Carol Rachou at his studio in Lafayette and we did a couple of sides on her.

"We redid the old Irma Thomas thing 'Don't Mess With My Man' and it sold some, but I just couldn't get it going. And the next thing I wanted her to do was a female R&B version of the Bobby Bland classic 'I'm Not Ashamed.' That was a Bobby Bland favorite for years over here, people still asked for it and couldn't buy it anymore. So I said, 'Now a black female version of this thing, maybe we could find a place,' you wouldn't want to compete a male artist against the Bobby Bland cut, no way. But my mistake was I had a white musician group. She was putting everything into it, but the musicianship, the background, wasn't just right. It turned out more of a pop side, it didn't have black soul feeling like it should have. But it turned out to be a pretty good seller anyhow, still selling. And she took on with a fast-talking promoter ... when this thing was there, he recognized there was some money to be made with it. See, I never did fool with booking, I had enough irons in the fire without going into that, that's a full-time job, promoting and booking. Anyway this guy came on, the first thing

I knew they went to California someplace and I've yet to hear of Margo White again, that's been it."

Floyd attributes Jin's poor showing with black artists to Jay Miller's local dominance; without an Excello fairy godmother he never could find a market for the occasional blues and R&B releases by Otis Smith, Junior Cole, Donnie Jacobs, Al Prince, and Lil Bob and the Lollipops. Nor has Soileau had outstanding commercial success with his current Maison de Soul label, despite good zydeco by Clifton Chenier, J. J. Caillier, and L. C. Donatto supplemented by fine New Orleans R&B from Clarence "Frogman" Henry and Irma Thomas.

In the mid-sixties, Floyd expanded the scope of his music operations: "I got into the wholesale distribution of records from my small retail store, and then gradually I got into being a one-stop distributor for various labels—I got into that through the help of Henry Hildebrand in New Orleans. He needed some help in getting someone in the rural area to promote some of the record labels he represented in the city, he was not getting out to the rural area too well. So he arranged for me to do that, and through his help I got started in one-stop and record distributing along with my own labels. And I was selling everybody else's labels at the same time. The distributing business got pretty big, not necessarily local labels, we represented any label that was hot—anything that was happening in the States, you could buy through our one-stop. And we serviced jukebox operators, it gave me a better introduction to selling to the operator, most of the singles go to the jukebox operators.

"So all the time the records were going on, this was also happening. Thank God I had a beautiful staff that stayed with me all these years and mustered up all the business, and kept the business going whilst I was away from the wholesale end of it. They were pushing it and it was still going strong, and I was concentrating on record manufacturing and promoting."

In the summer of 1966 Floyd surprisingly landed another national hit when Tommy McLain's ethereal South Louisiana adaptation of Don Gibson's hit country ballad "Sweet Dreams" rose to No. 15 on the *Billboard Hot 100.* Swamp-pop had been in rapid decline since the arrival of the Beatles in America; McLain was reminding fans that the musical past need not be entirely rejected. The song had powerful lyrics with a strong melody to match, and was given sympathetic instrumental support by Clint West and his Boogie Kings. More than a million copies of the single were pressed on the MSL label, and Floyd has the confirmatory gold record hanging in his office. "It's a good talking point," he quips, as he tells the story behind the Jonesville musician's tuneful hit:

"I stayed with trying to record the local talent and one of the groups was called the Boogie Kings and when they split half of them went to S. J. Montel in Baton Rouge and the other half stayed with Clint West. And this shop that I was selling to in Alexandria which is about sixty miles north of here, Modern Record Shop, well, the owner Effie Milligan told me of a young man there who had recorded a record on his own and it was selling quite well in the Alexandria area. She thought maybe I ought to call him and maybe see if I can handle some of the records for him. She sent me a copy of the record, and I could tell it was poorly done—it had been recorded with a trio at the radio station and yet it had a lot of feel in it. It was still a good sound. So I tried to locate him, but I couldn't find him, the phone numbers I had, I just couldn't reach him.

"Then I had a session scheduled for Clint West and his Boogie Kings, lo and behold this guy turns out to be the bass player with the group, he had just joined them. And they introduced him to me and they said the name was Tommy McLain and I said, 'I've been trying to reach you for some time, and here you turn up in the studio!' At the time the studio was right here where my office is with the control room next door, 40 feet by 22 feet, and we did a lot of Boogie Kings stuff in here. And I said, 'I wanted you to do this record for me that you did in Alec, but I'd like for you to rerecord it,' and he says, 'OK we can use the band and we can do it here.' So we did the session, 'Sweet Dreams' and 'I Need You So,' and after the session I kept playing the tape back and forth, and for some reason I was not satisfied with what I had on that tape. And I kept that tape on the shelf for six months or better, and every time he'd come in to do a session with Clint and his Boogie Kings, he'd ask me, 'When are you going to release my record?' And I kept telling him, 'No,' I kept making one excuse or another, I just couldn't see why I could release this record at this time. Finally after saying no so many times I said I can't face this guy anymore without putting this record out, I'm gonna have to put the record out.

"Don't ask me what I didn't like about it because it was something I wasn't happy about, the sound or what we had done with the multiple voices, and this kind of stuff, I don't know, I just wasn't happy with it. Then I finally consented to releasing the record so I did, and let's see, that was done in the mid-sixties and at that time the parish here still had a few houses of prostitution operating in the wooded areas, the outlying areas. It was not wide open as it had been way back then, it had calmed down, they were not as prominent. But everybody knew they were there. And the operator who had the jukebox in this particular place, he bought all his records from me, and I convinced him one day to buy some records. And he bought this one record here and went back and put the record on. One day he came in, maybe a week after, he said, 'Floyd, God almighty, do you have a hit!' I said, 'I do?' He says, 'Yes, that "Sweet Dreams" does not quit playing on the jukebox in that house, them women just play this thing over and over again. And the women really know what's going to sell in a record, and if this is any indication this is going to be one hell of a record for you!'

"He was correct, because this thing just kept mushrooming, it just kept building and building and building, and finally one day I called my old buddy up, Huey Meaux, and I said, 'Huey, I've got a record here and I can't seem to get anybody convinced that it is a hit and I need to get it out with someone. Could you put a word in for someone for me?' Well, at that time he was working with Harold Lipsius of Jamie Records with Barbara Lynn. So I sent them a copy of the record and they said, yeah, they would take it. But it was not their type of record because it was basically a country-flavored type, it was a country song, but it was done a little different. But they took the record, started working it, and the sales kept building up, and Acuff-Rose was very interested because it was their song, and they did a hell of a lot of promotion.

"But they were not happy evidently with what Jamie was doing, so I got through the grapevine, because they took Roy Orbison into a studio and had him do the same arrangement of the song, and then, so they say, they called Jamie Records and talked to the promotion man and played the session on the phone to him and said, 'If you don't get off your ass and get "Sweet Dreams" going in some of these major markets like you're supposed to, we're gonna release this record, turn around and lease this master to another label and get them working it.' They were not satisfied that New York and some of the bigger cities just were not playing the record, really getting the record sold. So they finally did move on the record and finally did get it sold, and to date it has sold the most singles of any single we had.

"The label was MSL—Meaux, Soileau, and Lipsius—and we have maintained selling rights within the southern region and Jamie has U.S.A. and world rights on it. They were also pressing in Houston and so Glasper has sent a gold record to Tommy and myself because they had actually pressed over a million copies of that single in the pressing plant. You know, back then they had the usual deal where if a distributor ordered 1,000 records he got 300 for nothing and you start talking about 1,300 instead of 1,000. All these freebies and promotions, it just added up. And that's the only gold record that was presented to me, unfortunately. But I was very disappointed that 'Sweet Dreams' went from No. 15 in the national charts and I think it dropped down to No. 20 or so, and then it dropped completely out of the picture. And I never had a particular love of charts for that reason. Of course I was happy that ours did not climb overnight like some things did, we were climbing four or five notches at a time. I think 'Sweet Dreams' stayed on the charts for about a year, and it gained strength and sales right along with it. But I was very disappointed in the fact that I can't see how a record can get up to the Top Twenty in the charts and then within a week's time be completely off the charts. You've got to take two or three weeks to come down. The national charts, to start off, are compiled from disc jockey plays first and then retail sales—that's the way I see it, what I've been told. At Jin, we haven't had very much chart rigging!"

Tommy McLain failed to find a chart-making follow-up, but continued recording class soulful material for Jin, including Bobby Charles's "Before I Grow Too Old," the Righteous Brothers' "Try To Find Another Man" in duet with Clint West, and a raunchy version of "Sticks And Stones," the old Ray Charles hit. He is still active with his Mule Train band throughout Louisiana and Texas.

Tommy McLain's former bandleader Clint West has been a stalwart of the Jin label. West cut his first record in 1958 as lead vocalist with Red Smiley (Bob Shurley) and the Veltones on the rousing rocker "Take A Ride"; under the name of Bob and the Veltones, the group then scored locally with a version of Smiley Lewis's "Jail Bird."

Clint, born Maurice Guillory in Vidrine in 1938, became interested in music at an early age. "I thought there was something wrong with me," he said, "because when everybody else was playing sports, I just wanted to stay inside and listen to the radio." Although his parents were not very musical, they did introduce him to the dance halls. By the age of twelve he was playing drums with Gilbert Mayeaux's Vidrine Playboys. After working with Red Smiley, Clint became drummer with the Monroe-based Roller Coasters. In 1962 he joined the Boogie Kings, who had become popular at high-school proms throughout South Louisiana. This ten-piece dance band was shown at its brash best on the Jin album "Clint West And The Fabulous Boogie Kings," which included lively versions of R&B favorites "Boogie Chillun," "Honky Tonk," "Okey Dokey Stomp," and "Night Train." In 1965 West and the group parted acrimoniously; for a while there were two sets of Boogie Kings traveling the state. Staying with Jin, Clint turned to a country-based style and had minor local hits in the early seventies with "Mr. Jeweler," "Shelly's Winter Love," and "Sweet Suzannah (C'est La Belle De La Louisiane)." Although he is a truly professional and respected performer, he has never been able to break into the big time outside of Louisiana.

With conditions in the recording industry continually changing, Floyd has followed the trend into albums, issuing almost as many LPs as singles. "Other than a super hit, the only singles that are sold now go into the juke-boxes, that's it. I would say as much as 80 percent of the singles that are released here are consumed by the jukebox operators," he reflects.

Since the Tommy McLain national hit, Floyd Soileau has had only a handful of decent-selling singles. The record with the biggest potential of all was the extremely catchy "Opelousas Sostan" by Rufus Jagneaux. This simple pop number, sung in English and French, had all of South Louisiana humming in 1973, but was totally unknown elsewhere:

Ol' Opelousas Sostan used to come this way,
On his way to sing his song,
I can hear the jukebox play.

I can hear the jukebox play,
Allons avec moi, bon temps rouler! (repeat)

Rufus (Benny Graeff), from Lafayette, had composed "Opelousas Sostan" while wintering in a hippie commune in the hills of Tennessee. Recalls Floyd: "I thought with a name like 'Opelousas Sostan' it couldn't miss. So he brought over his tape recorder and closed the door, he didn't want anybody to hear it. He put it on, real secretive, and I started listening to it. I can't analyze this thing, it's just a happy song, that's all it was. And I said, 'Yeah I love it, get your guys down here, let's go into the studio and cut this thing.' We went into the studio and did it first time in, mono cut, that was it. Put the record out and it took off like a storm. The first month that this thing was out we had done maybe over 30,000, it was unbelievable. The little bitty kids, three or four years old, they could just learn some lyrics on the radio, they were singing the song, the mamas were buying it for them. The secretaries were buying it, the hip cats, the blacks, everybody was buying it, this was the in thing.

"But yet out of Cajun country I didn't have a radio station with the *guts* to play it. I had a guy, a musical director at Shreveport, I called him, he said, 'I've heard about the record, I've heard of the phenomenal growth, the popularity it has, but I'm not gonna play this thing. I can't stand it! And if I put it on the air, they'll be bugging me every five minutes to play it.' And I said 'God bless, what are you supposed to do, you are supposed to be doing what your audience wants!' He said, 'I'm sorry, I'm not gonna play it,' and he never did play it. And we couldn't break it out of here. And to this date I guess we might be doing about 60,000 in sales, it still sells every year. I still think it's a jewel of a record."

On the tougher but still infectious "Downhome Music," the long-haired Rufus came on like a South Louisiana Mick Jagger, without the Rolling Stones' Midas touch. "I'm a one-record company, I guess," surmises Floyd ruefully, "I can come up with one hit, then when the time comes to repeat the performance I just fall flat on my ass. I don't know why, we just haven't been that lucky, we've missed with everything we've come up with." A lame "Poboy Rufus And The Sostan Band" album sold 16,000 copies in the wake of the hit, but would surely have done better if "Opelousas Sostan" and "Downhome Music" had been included.

Nevertheless, of all the South Louisiana record men, Floyd Soileau has remained the most loyal to the swamp-pop sound, regularly releasing albums and singles by such artists as Johnnie Allan, Rod Bernard, Tommy McLain, and Clint West, plus a successful "Golden Dozen" oldies anthology series. "I guess I just rode a good horse and I didn't want to get off him," he says, chuckling, "I knew he was good to win a few races and I just stayed with him. And being that I wasn't a musician, I just went along with something that I thought had some place in the record market. And I still judge a lot of the things I do today by that. If I think I can market the sound, I'll gamble on it. And if it's something totally strange to me I may be a little more reluctant to put it out, but if they can prove me wrong I'll go along with them!"

17

"And now we've got a good representation of some of the early Cajun things"

Throughout Jin's eventful history Floyd Soileau has been supporting his heritage in the best way possible, by making authentic Cajun music available on the Swallow label. By 1982 the Swallow catalog boasted more than 40 albums and 250 singles featuring Cajun-French vocalists singing exuberantly and sadly in their own language to musical accompaniment led by accordion or fiddle.

During the sixties Floyd was concerned only with the Cajun-French market in South Louisiana and East Texas. Always hoping to create a Cajun "hit" by selling a few thousand copies, he kept the younger audience in mind and opted for a contemporary Cajun sound. This "modern" Cajun music reflected the continuing Americanization of the Cajun life-style; most of the band instruments were amplified, including the accordion and fiddle. Traditional Cajun numbers were still being performed alongside Cajun versions of pop, country, and R&B hits, but there were few memorable new songs.

Floyd gradually realized that a market was developing for the traditional Cajun root styles, not only in Louisiana, but also in French-speaking Canada, France, and elsewhere. There was a definite need to document old-time Cajun music, soft and dreamlike compared with the modern sounds, not only for the new audience but also for posterity. Now the Swallow catalog has a commendable balance, with artists of the caliber and variety of Nathan Abshire, the Balfa Brothers, Vin Bruce, D. L. Menard, Belton Richard, and Beausoleil. One of the earliest Swallow hits was Austin Pitre and the Evangeline Playboys' "Flumes Dans Faires" in 1959. This irresistible two-step is better known as "Les Flammes D'Enfer," a Cajun classic that Pitre made his own; it is a desperate plea to a loved one to *pray for me, save my soul, I am condemned to the flames of hell.* The heartfelt flip, "Opelousas Waltz," was just as popular and helped to form a glorious single—the old-time Cajun sound was lovingly redolent of a bygone era. The same high standard was maintained in the ensuing releases, "Two Step De Bayou Teche" (with vocal by Menier "Cabrie") and "Mamou Blues," a variant of "Grand Mamou" with an impressive musical arrangement borrowed from Leo Soileau.

Austin Pitre had an enviably unspoiled style as a vocalist, accordionist, and violinist. Besides Leo Soileau, his major influence was Amadie Ardoin. Born in Ville Platte in 1918 to poor sharecropping parents, Pitre had been a prominent figure at rural dances in the Mamou area since the age of eleven. He claimed he was the first person to play the accordion standing up, rather than sitting down; his specialty was to squeeze notes out of his instrument from behind his back, over his head, and between his legs. . . . With his group the Evangeline Playboys, Austin was particularly prominent in the late forties when he recorded for Feature, broadcast every Sunday afternoon over radio KSLO Opelousas, and had a long engagement at the Chinaball Club in Bristol, between Opelousas and Rayne. By day, he ran an automobile repair shop on the Elton–Basile stretch of Highway 190.

After recording intermittently for Swallow between 1959 and 1971 and performing at local dances, he was invited to appear at the 1973 Smithsonian Festival of American Folk Life in Washington, D.C., and to return for a repeat performance in 1976. At the 1980 Louisiana Freedom Festival in Elton he was presented with an award in appreciation of fifty years of contribution to—and promotion of—Cajun music. In the same year, Sonet issued his first album, "Back To The Bayou," followed by a wonderful Swallow compilation of his old 45s. But Austin died in 1981, before he'd had a chance to reap the benefits of these releases.

Pitre's Swallow success with "Flumes Dans Faires" coincided with two popular releases by Adam Hebert and the Country Playboys from Church Point, "North Side Door" and "Cette Le J'Aime." But these well-received ethnic records were overshadowed by Vin Bruce's refined Cajun-country rendition of "Le Delaysay" in 1961, and by Badeaux and the Louisiana Aces' "The Back Door" with its perfect Cajun accordion sound. Says Floyd Soileau, " 'The Back Door' is getting to be a classic. That thing has been recorded over and over again and we've even got an English translation cut by the Rufus bunch. And I'm hoping some day some rock group or somebody wants to do something a little different, wants to do something from Louisiana, is gonna do 'The Back Door.' Because I think the rhythm is there and I think with a little imagination somebody can come up with a hell of a record. And someday this is gonna happen. Elias Badeaux was the accordion player and he led the group. But 'The Back Door' was D. L. Menard's record, he was the guitar player and the guy who wrote the song and did the singing. And D. L.'s still playing, he's come up with some other nice songs also, but that one is the one that stood out."

"The Back Door," cut in 1962 as a follow-up to "Valse De Jolly Rogers," was a riveting record performed with enormous enthusiasm by the Louisiana Aces, with Badeaux's splendid accordion gliding over an incessant stomping rhythm. The joyous Cajun yells were an added embellishment, as D. L. Menard sang his amusing and perceptive satire on the Cajun stereotype:

Moi et la belle on avait été-z-au bal,	We went to the dance, my girl and I,
On a passé dans tous les honky-tonks.	We passed through all the honky-tonks,
S'en ont revenus lendemain matin,	We got ourselves home next morning,
Le jour était après se casser.	The day was just about to break.
J'ai passé dedans la porte dans arrière.	I went in through the back door.
L'après-midi moi j'étais au village,	I went to town this afternoon,
Et je m'ai soûlé que je pouvais plus marcher.	I got myself so drunk I couldn't walk anymore.
Ils m'ont ramené back à la maison,	They led me back home,
Il y avait de la compagnie, c'était du monde étranger.	We had company there from out of town.
J'ai passé dedans la porte dans arrière . . .	I went in through the back door . . .
J'ai eu un tas d'amis tant que j'avais de l'argent,	I had many a friend while I had money,
À cette heure j'ai plus d'argent, mais ils voulont plus me voir.	Now there's no more, they'd rather not see me.
J'ai été dans le village, et moi je m'ai mis dans le tracas,	I went to town and got into a brawl,
La loi m'a ramassé, moi je suis parti dans la prison.	The cops hauled me in and now I'm off to jail.
On va passer dedans la porte dans arrière!	We'll go in through the back door!

The Louisiana Aces were formed in 1950 by Elias "Shuk" Badeaux. An older man, he was influenced by the early Cajun recording artists; he can recall learning "New Iberia Polka" from Dewey Segura of the Segura Brothers, who recorded the number for Columbia in 1929. Badeaux discovered that when he used the treble side of the accordion he was able to play in virtually any key, enabling him to work in both the Cajun and honky-tonk styles. In 1952 D. L. Menard joined the band, which also featured drummer John "Papa Bear" Suire as host, comedian, and sometime singer; the remaining members were the versatile steel guitarist Archange "Coon" Touchet and the equally adept fiddler Joseph Lopez. After recording "The Back Door," the Louisiana Aces continued cutting records for Swallow and playing local dances before starting to disband in 1967. D. L. (Doris Leon) Menard—known as the "Cajun Hank Williams"— has remained active since, promoting Cajun music at many festivals in the United States, Canada, and France, even traveling to South America and Southeast Asia. A father of seven, D. L. runs Menards Chair Factory in Erath with his wife Lou Ella; the plant produces handcrafted chairs and rockers. D. L. applies different skills with equal diligence to his music, which has been neatly showcased in a 1980 Swallow album, "D. L. Menard Sings 'The Back Door' And His Other Cajun Hits."

In 1962 Floyd had two other Cajun hits that have become enshrined in Cajun folklore: "Tracks Of My Buggy" (originally issued as "Les Traces De Mon Boghie") by Doris Matte and the Lake Charles Ramblers, and "Cajun Twist" (also known as "Le Tortillage," a variant of "Keep A Knocking") by the Cajun Trio with accordionist Harrison Fontenot. The irrepressible "Jole Blon" was also successfully revived by Vin Bruce.

In 1963 Joe Bonsall and the Orange Playboys, one of the two most popular Cajun bands in East Texas (the Rambling Aces were the other), scored with "Step It Fast" (Swallow), a frantic tune that must have left two-step dancers immobile with exhaustion! Accordionist Bonsall, from Lake Arthur, had the considerable support of veteran fiddler Floyd LeBlanc, who had recorded for Opera and O.T. back in the forties. Previously Joe had recorded for Goldband; after three singles and two LPs for Swallow he joined Cajun Jamboree, formed in 1965 by his producer, John Lloyd Broussard. At the time Broussard, known as "Tee Bruce," was broadcasting his "Cajun Jamboree" program over radio KOGT in Orange, Texas. For Tee Bruce's label Joe recorded an enthusiastic selection of Cajun numbers ranging from the traditional "Church Point Breakdown" and "Circle Club Waltz" (named after a club in Vinton) to the rocking "Going To Louisiana" and the swamp-pop of Bobby Charles's "Your Picture."

The best-selling Swallow act to date has been Belton Richard and the Musical Aces. Technically a very proficient accordionist, Belton spear-headed a fresh approach to Cajun music. By adopting a smoother, updated sound, he brought the music into the late twentieth century, although his cool, detached vocal style lacked the deep emotional qualities that are the hallmarks of Cajun music. Richard often released two slow waltzes back to back on the same 45, in contrast to the long-established practice of coupling a waltz with a fast two-step. His most successful records have been "Un Autre Soir D'Ennui" (Another Sleepless Night) and "The Cajun Streak," a Cajun version of the Ray Stevens hit made at the suggestion of Floyd's recording engineer Joe Avants.

Belton was taught the accordion by his father Cleby, who used to perform at the old Saturday night *fais-dodos* and later fronted the Welcome Playboys. From Rayne, Belton started out playing rock 'n' roll with the Cajun Rockers before forming the Musical Aces in 1959. With the Aces he began appearing at clubs like the Mid-Way in Breaux Bridge, Club L'Acadienne in Crowley, and Bon Ton Rouley in Lafayette. His first recordings were made for Dago Redlich's Crowley-based Chamo label; "Just En Reve" sold well. The move to Swallow established him as a top Cajun artist—he even had his own TV show. "The timing was right for Belton," explains Floyd Soileau. "The younger Cajuns were looking for something in French to associate with a little rock 'n' roll beat, it just catapulted him way up there. We had hit after hit, we had a big Cajun following with him, it was real good." The best overview of Richard's work can be found in his Swallow LP "Modern Sounds In Cajun Music."

Like Belton, Camay Doucet performs up-to-the-minute Cajun music. A very popular disc jockey, Camay had a double-sided Swallow hit in the mid-seventies with the novelty "Hold My False Teeth (And I'll Show You How To Dance)" and "Mom I'm Still Your Little Boy"—a "heart classic," according to Floyd. The deejay also had a minor hit with "Me And My Cousin" (Kajun). Doucet's most representative album is "Cajun Goodies" (Swallow) with Jimmy Thibodeaux Et Musique.

The more traditional weekend dance band Lesa Cormier and the Sundown Playboys acquired local notoriety in 1972 when their Swallow single "Saturday Night Special" was leased by the Beatles' philanthropic Apple label, initially for issue in Britain. Apple became interested after receiving a copy of the 45 audaciously mailed by Pat Savant, the group's young accordion player. The record notched only moderate sales, but it was quite unprecedented for a Cajun single to enjoy such wide distribution and publicity. Floyd Soileau still smiles at this unlikely episode: "It was a typical French group from Lake Charles, typical record, there was no big thing about it. Even when I had a call from Apple's New York office I still couldn't believe what was happening. I have a back-page ad they ran in *Billboard*, I've got the sample promotion kit 'Back to Mono' with the 78 copy and the 45 copy and the promo stuff they had inside. And I love to tell the story because it's one of the craziest things that can happen in this business!"

The Sundown Playboys, formerly with Feature and Goldband, were originally led by accordionist Lionel Cormier, Lesa's father, who died of a heart attack while pumping out "Church Point Two-Step" at the Bamboo Club in Lake Charles in 1971. Among the other Cajun artists to benefit from Floyd Soileau's loyalty to his own music were such staunch, dependable performers as Maurice Barzas, Sidney Brown, Louis Cormier, Cleveland Crochet, Allen Fontenot, Bobby Leger, Nathan Menard, Marc Savoy, and Dunice Theriot.

Soileau's best-known performer was Nathan Abshire, whose singles in the late sixties were beyond reproach. After enduring an uneventful decade since the success of "Pine Grove Blues" in 1949, Nathan saw his fortunes improve when he recorded for Jay Miller's new Kajun label during the early sixties. With a modern Cajun band lineup augmenting his stunning accordion work, he had a most pleasing series of releases for the Crowley record man, whose productions were as good as ever. "Popcorn Blues," "Hey Mom," "Pine Grove Blues," "Jolie Catin'," and "La Banana Au Nonc Adam" (with vocal by Robert Bertrand) were all infectiously up-tempo, while "The La La Blues" (with La La Laverne) was a haunting swamp-blues chant. Nathan and the Pine Grove Boys gave a particularly evocative performance on "Mardi-Gras Song," one of the oldest numbers in the Cajun repertoire to come from France and French Canada. (Of medieval origins, the famous Mardi Gras festival came to rural Louisiana in the 1780s when groups of French and Spanish settlers in the Opelousas country gathered together a week or so before Ash Wednesday to make celebration plans for "Fat Tuesday.") On the Kajun recording, Abshire's accordion wailed eerily, the percussion created the trotting sound of horses' hooves, and Dewey Balfa sang of the *capitaine* and his masked riders who sought offerings for the communal Mardi Gras gumbo:

Le Mardi Gras ça passe une fois par an,	The Mardi Gras comes once a year,
Tout autour et de toute manière,	All around and in every way,
Ça passe une fois par an pour demander la charité,	It comes once a year to ask for charity,
Quand même si c'est une patate,	Even if it's a potato,
Une patate et des gratons.	A potato and some cracklins.

The song ends with an invitation to *venez nous joindre au gumbo ce soir!*—come join us at the gumbo tonight!

The familiar Cajun waltzes in the classic heavy I-V-chord progression were still being recorded, including "Gabriel Waltz," "Dreamer's Waltz," and "Trouble Waltz." Nathan sang with a refreshing lack of inhibition and shared vocals with Junior Benoit, Ed Junot, Will Kegley, and Darius

LeBlanc who performed under the umbrella of the Pine Grove Boys. The best Kajun singles have been assembled in an impressive Flyright album, together with some unissued material, including the beautiful and moving "La Valse De Theo."

Nathan was already reaching new heights, but his recordings for Swallow with the Balfa Brothers hit truly stratospheric levels. It would be hard to think of a better sequence than "Sur Le Courtableau," "Tramp Sur La Rue," "Lemonade Song," "A Musician's Life," "Offshore Blues," "Valse De Bayou Teche," "Games People Play," and yet another "Pine Grove Blues." This time the vocals were shared with Thomas Langley. The two most exuberant tracks, full of Cajun adrenaline, were "Lemonade Song" and "Sur Le Courtableau." In the traditional "Lemonade Song" Thomas Langley wanted nothing but a "glass of lemonade" on Sunday after partying on Saturday night; the tune is based on the New Orleans jazz favorite "Eh La Bas." "Sur Le Courtableau" was Nathan's delightful tribute to life on the Courtableau bayou:

S'en aller sur le Courtableau tit monde,	Let's go to Bayou Courtableau little folk,
Pour ramasser des écocos, yé yaī,	To collect dry wood, yé yaī,
Pour faire du feu, bébé,	To light a fire, babe,
Pour faire bouillir les écrevisses.	To boil crawfish.

On all Nathan's Swallow singles the accompaniment was immaculate, with steel guitar, fiddle, and accordion blending together, then breaking out individually into smooth, successive "rides"; in particular the steel guitar contributed handsomely to the band's flowing, melodic sound (the steel guitar was only out of place when the whining Nashville-type chords were favored). Most of the best Swallow numbers have been included in the superb "Pine Grove Blues" album, a Cajun classic. A second Swallow LP, "The Good Times Are Killing Me," was a most enjoyable release, again with the Balfa Brothers in support. The title phrase was Nathan's professional motto.

Floyd Soileau looks back on this artistically prolific period with justifiable pride: "Nathan came to see me one day and he wanted to record for me, at the time he had been doing some records for J. D. Miller. And I told him, 'Nathan, I can't record you as long as you are recording for J. D.,' so he went to see Paul Tate, I think, an attorney back then, and got together with J. D. and got his release. Then he came to me with a release in writing and said, 'I can now record for you!' And I said, 'Well, let's get into the studio and do it.'

"We got the Balfa Brothers to help out on some of the first sessions and that first album I had on him with the Balfas is still selling. To me we have a fine version of his 'Pine Grove Blues' and some of his earlier numbers that were very popular, and are still selling. It's a good sound and I'm very proud of that one. He did a version of Joe South's pop hit 'Games People Play,' surprised the hell out of me one day. He came in, had his accordion, he says 'What do you think this sounds like?' He was playing a piece, I said, 'I heard that melody somewhere,' but I couldn't think what it was. And I never imagined Nathan Abshire coming up with a French version of 'Games People Play.' And there he was, he liked this thing, he was playing it, so I said, 'Well, let's go cut it!' Now we had built the studio downtown in 1970, got him in, put this thing out, and it started selling very well. I was always looking for some idea to get people interested in buying Cajun records sometime."

In the studio he was perfect to record. "He'd bring in his little coffee jug, and that was it. And he was just as cool in the studio as could be, he would do his thing, if it wasn't right he'd go back and do it again. He just sat there nice and cool as could be. Very easy to work with, just a jolly good fellow."

During the early seventies Nathan enjoyed great popularity with festival and college audiences; he was the Professor Longhair of Cajun music and they adored him. In 1972 he did a session with the Balfa Brothers for Sonet Records; released on "The Cajuns" LP, it showed that he was playing better than ever. His six-minute version of "Pine Grove Blues" was his wildest yet, with spine-chilling fiddle from Dewey Balfa and stomping steel guitar from the great J. W. Pelsia. In 1975 Nathan starred as the hapless antihero in "Good Times Are Killing Me," a Public Broadcasting System videotape documentary. But then his career slumped alarmingly in an alcoholic haze.

In the late seventies Nathan made occasional but inferior recordings for Folkways and La Louisianne. He continued to draw on traditional sources; songs like "Chere Toutou" (Folkways) and "J'ai Été Au Bal" (La Louisianne) had similar roots to "Dans Grand Bois" (Kajun) and "La Noce A Josephine" (Swallow). Abshire was still pouring out his gutsy brand of bluesy Cajun music at local dances, smiling graciously, his enormous potbelly serving as a precarious support for his accordion. Few Cajun musicians make a living from their music, and Nathan was no exception; he spent much of his working life doing a menial job at the Basile town dump. Like all the best Cajun artists he was admired as a well-known local figure rather than as a star.

After a prolonged period of bad health he died on May 13, 1981. Cajun music had lost a great artist and its most colorful character. Also lost was Nathan's intimate knowledge of traditional Cajun folk songs. He is totally irreplaceable, but his memory—and his records—will live on.

Floyd Soileau's most devoted artist has been the much-loved Dewey Balfa, the sterling fiddle player on so many Nathan Abshire recordings. With Doc Guidry and Rufus Thibodeaux, Dewey has helped to make the Cajun violin sound fashionable again. Moreover, he has done much to inform his audiences, near and far, about the broad spectrum of Cajun music. One moment whooping it up with a contemporary band, the next returning to the quaint old-time sound, he straddles the modern and traditional scenes with ease. It was Dewey who convinced Floyd to change his direction and record some of the older Cajun styles. "We were selling Cajun recordings in between the hits on Jin," says Floyd. "We were doing what I call the 'now' sound of Cajun music, especially with Belton Richard. I was hardheaded at that time and thought that was the only way we could record and sell Cajun music. And fortunately for me there was another gentleman, Dewey Balfa, that saw it otherwise, and he kept coming over here.

"I was always working in the front counter because I could get a feel of what kind of records my people wanted to buy, what kind of songs they wanted, especially with Cajun music. A lot of these things were no longer available, so when I had a Cajun group come in to do a session, if they didn't have something already planned, I would make sure that they would record some of these songs that I had been getting calls for and you couldn't buy records of anymore. And I wanted to record 'La Valse De Bon Baurche,' but nobody knew it. And Dewey Balfa came to see me many a time trying to convince me that I should record him and his brothers. I said, 'No, I want something with an accordion, if I don't have an accordion I don't want it,' and the final time he came over, we got to talking, he happens to mention that he had recorded 'La Valse De Bon Baurche' many years ago. I said, 'Why didn't you tell me this in the first place! I have been trying to get somebody to do this song for the longest.' [sic] So we went in and we did 'La Valse De Bambocheurs' [sic] (Drunkard's Sorrow Waltz); 'Indian On A Stomp' was on the flip. From then on we went on doing the Balfa Brothers, and they convinced me that there was another side of Cajun music that was not being recorded for the future, and that was the traditional side."

The reaction to the single was good enough to encourage Floyd to release an LP, "Balfa Brothers Play Traditional Cajun Music." Perhaps to appease Floyd, the Balfas drafted the superb accordionist Hadley Fontenot to supplement their usual acoustical lineup of two fiddles, two guitars, and triangle. Rodney, his voice full of plaintive hurt, was lead singer, and Dewey also vocalized. The result was an exquisite album that showed the Balfas at their very best, their entrancing lonesome sound reflecting the magnificent sorrow of the Cajun people and their noble survival. Standout tracks included the hypnotic "La Valse De Bambocheurs," the startlingly poetic "T'Ai Petite Et T'Ai Meon," and the marvelously fluent "Lacassine Special." The next album, "Balfa Brothers Play More Traditional Music," did not have quite the same magic.

The Balfa Brothers were raised in the heart of rural Acadiana. Their parents, Charles and Euna, were a poor farming couple living on Bayou Grand Louis in Evangeline Parish near Mamou. The family was caught in the iniquitous sharecropping system: in return for a third of the crop, the landlord would provide land, lumber for a fence around the yard, and building materials to make their wooden shack habitable. Dewey can remember one typical cabin so ramshackle that in rainy weather the furniture had to be moved to a dry spot to avoid leaks from the roof.

Of the large family of six boys and three girls, Dewey, Rodney, Will, Harry, and Burkeman picked up old Cajun folk songs from their father while learning to play the fiddle, harmonica, accordion, *petite fer* (triangle), spoons, and guitar. Dewey became a virtuoso on the fiddle, his flowing style technically correct yet full of emotion. "I learned songs from my daddy and also from some other musicians, too," he told Barry Ancelet in a *Louisiana Life* interview. "I was influenced by J. B. Fusilier, Leo Soileau, Harry Choates, and I think Bob Wills and the Texas Playboys had a little effect on my fiddling. And I can play a song and tell you whose influence is showing. This has developed to be my style from different influences."

During the forties Dewey and his brothers started playing together for family gatherings and house parties. Then they graduated to performing at dance halls, which were enjoying a great burst of popularity. "We sometimes played eight dances a week," recalled Dewey, "Sunday afternoon, Sunday night, and Monday through Saturday night. Some of the places we played were very small and couldn't afford a full band. And Mr. Hadley Fontenot, who was our accordion player at the time, was farming and couldn't play every night, so Will and Harry and I would just go as a string band." Dewey also played with the respected J. Y. Sabastian from Grand Prairie and performed with the Louisiana Rhythmaires led by Maurice Barzas and Elise Deshotel. In 1951 this group cut the original "La Valse De Bon Baurche" and the high-flying hokum of "Le Two Step De Ville Platte" on a home recorder for release on a Khoury's 78. The young fiddler began accompanying Nathan Abshire, and was featured on the accordionist's records for Khoury's, Kajun, and Swallow. But music was—and still must be—an enjoyable pastime; Dewey runs Balfa's Discount Furniture store in Basile, and also drives school buses on weekdays.

In 1964 Dewey's musical career took a considerable upward turn when he was "discovered" by folk musicologist Ralph Rinzler. At the time Rinzler had been sent to Acadiana to scout for talent for the Newport Folk

Festival; his visit was prompted by concern that traditional Cajun music needed support in the face of competition from modern musical influences. Dewey was booked as a late replacement to play guitar at Newport with accordionist Gladius Thibodeaux from the Point Noir area and fiddler Louis "Vinest" Lejeune. Newport was an awesome experience for Dewey: "I doubt if I had ever seen 200 people at once, in Newport there were 17,000 people who wouldn't let us off stage." The rapturous reception was a surprise to the cynics who foresaw only embarrassing consequences if Cajun music were performed at such an august venue. "I can remember people saying, 'They're going out there to get laughed at,' " said Dewey.

Three years later Dewey returned to Newport to even greater acclaim, performing with brothers Rodney and Will, daughter Nelda, and accordionist Hadley Fontenot. Thus revitalized, the Balfa Brothers band became a formidable unit, playing numerous club, festival, and college dates, touring Europe, broadcasting and recording frequently. They also appeared in the film *Spend It All*, a study of the Cajuns in Southwest Louisiana by Les Blank. The Balfas were splendid ambassadors of Cajun music. Much of the time they were giving a history lesson in the old traditional style to their audiences—and to schoolchildren as well. "I had my doubts that this music, language, and culture could survive," said Dewey. "Because there was nobody who would come back and sit on the back porch or sit by the fireplace and play their instruments and tell stories from grandmother and grandfather. Instead, kids would come back from school and do their homework and watch television. A lot of artificial things, instead of the real down-to-earth values. And I thought that the only way it would survive, could survive, was to bring this music into the schools for the children."

On other occasions, the Balfa Brothers played modern Cajun music with their "nightclub orchestra," as Dewey called it. They had become symbols of a renewed pride in Cajun music, but a triumphant decade turned sour in February 1979 when Rodney and Will were killed in a tragic automobile accident in Avoyelles Parish near Bunkie while on a family visit. Then in the next year Dewey's wife Hilda died of trichinosis. Dewey showed great fortitude in continuing to perform with Rodney's teen-age son Tony and close friends like Dick Richard, Marc Savoy, and Ally Young. He still calls his band the Balfa Brothers: "Will and Rodney were my blood brothers and my musical brothers. So were these other people my musical brothers. I think of the Balfa Brothers band as a brotherhood of musicians, not just as the three or four blood brothers. I have a big family. . . ."

Encouraged by the response to the Balfa Brothers' first single and LP, Floyd Soileau proceeded to record Cajun albums in the traditional style by Ed and Bee Deshotels, Sady Courville and Dennis McGee, Cyprien and Adam Landreneau, and Sleepy Hoffpauir. Soileau still regrets his belated involvement in this aspect of Cajun music: "There were a lot of people away from here who were learning about Cajun music, they wanted that root sound. And they would come in and inquire about some of the musicians and then later—I could still kick myself about this—it took fellows like Chris Strachwitz who came out of California to discover Joe Falcon, who was still alive at the time, he was living in Jennings—I didn't know about this—and some other talented musicians that they dug up and recorded. They were there, but they weren't playing dances anymore and because they didn't come to me . . . I don't know, I guess I had too many irons in the fire. I'm trying to find excuses why I didn't dig these people up back then. But fortunately somebody had the foresight to come in and dig around and find these people and record them. And now we've got a good representation of some of the early Cajun things and even some of the old 78s have been reissued. We've got a good spread now for future generations to be able to know what Cajun music was all about. And I'm happy about that!"

Today Floyd's musical empire is in good shape. Besides working with Johnnie Allan, Belton Richard, and Jim Olivier (a popular Cajun-country artist and broadcaster), he is able to offer local record men package deals incorporating manufacturing and marketing facilities, although he no longer feels the need to have a studio. The present trend toward the preservation and promotion of all forms of South Louisiana music pleases Floyd: "I want people to know this music is from Louisiana and we're proud of it. We've got a lot of talent in Louisiana and I just want it to stay alive, to be available. And at the same time I make a buck or two for Floyd!"

18

"I spent five years trying to find a Cajun band that could play rock 'n' roll"

While Floyd Soileau was busy establishing himself, veteran record men Jay Miller and Eddie Shuler were recording prolifically, and not without success. Miller had a national hit in 1958 with Warren Storm's "Prisoner's Song" followed by Slim Harpo's "Rainin' In My Heart" and "Baby Scratch My Back" in the sixties; Shuler made the *Billboard Hot 100* charts with Cleveland Crochet's "Sugar Bee" in 1961.

Jay Miller's Crowley studio, the home of the swamp-pop sound, remained a hive of activity until the mid-sixties. Besides swamp-pop Miller was recording blues for Excello, rock 'n' roll and R&B for his Rocko and Zynn labels, Cajun music (even comedy) for Kajun and Cajun Classics, and political material for Rebel. He was also arranging leasing deals with such national companies as Top Rank, Dot, and Decca. Miller's best-selling swamp-pop artist was session drummer Warren Storm, who scored first time out with "Prisoner's Song" (Nasco). Storm's attractive Fats Domino–influenced adaptation of Guy Massey's old country hit was one of the early swamp-pop successes, climbing to No. 81 on the *Billboard Hot 100* in the late summer of 1958. The charming, easy-paced flip "Mama Mama Mama (Look What Your Little Boy's Done)" was almost too good to be on the same single; it was a hit in its own right. On both sides a highlight was the insistent, reggaelike rhythm.

"Warren's 'Prisoner's Song' was very big," says Johnnie Allan. "Fact is nobody had heard of Warren Storm, and when I first heard him people referred to him as the 'Little Guy from Abbeville,' they couldn't remember his name. He had a band in those days called the Wee-Wows. Then all of a sudden overnight 'Prisoner's Song' comes in, it was cut for J. D. Miller in Crowley. I wouldn't say it was as strong as 'Mathilda,' but it was played quite a bit on radio stations throughout Acadiana. He did good with that song, it kept a very simple beat, it was very simple."

Warren Joseph Schexnider was born in Vermilion Parish in 1937. First introduced to music by his father, a drummer with the Rayne-Bo Ramblers, Warren had an early hero in Hank Williams, whom he met in 1948 on Dudley J. LeBlanc's famous Hadacol show. Recalls Warren excitedly,

"The only way you could go on is if you had ten box tops from the product, so I went all over the neighborhood and gathered up all the box tops that I needed to go!"

The immensely popular Dudley J. LeBlanc, a banty rooster–sized Louisiana state senator, had a truly remarkable product in Hadacol, a "tonic for every ill" that tasted like Seven-Up—with a dash of alcohol. Such was its success that for 1951 sales were forecast to exceed $100 million, while the monthly advertising budget was approaching $1 million. A vast Hadacol Caravan, a grandiose medicine show, toured the entire South; besides Hank Williams it featured such diverse entertainers as Roy Acuff, Sharkey Bonano's Dixieland Band, George Burns and Gracie Allen, Bob Hope, and Chico Marx. LeBlanc shrewdly sold his Hadacol business for a fortune before the tonic was banned as bogus by the federal Food and Drug Administration. In October 1954 he attempted to market a similar product, but Kary-On never got off the ground because of the poor publicity surrounding its predecessor and the persistent interest of the federal agencies. In his later years, the ebullient senator made riveting political broadcasts as Couzin Dud over KROF Abbeville.

Warren Storm had made his musical debut in 1952 when he sat in for his father on a dance job, and he continued playing country and Cajun music throughout his years at Abbeville High School. Occasionally he would visit the Brass Rail club in New Orleans with school-friend Bobby Charles and listen to Paul Gayten's R&B band featuring tenor sax star Lee Allen and—at different times—world-class drummers Earl Palmer and Charles "Hungry" Williams. "I think I picked up a lot of the New Orleans style of drumming and brought it down to Lafayette," Storm says. Through the years he was to give a new dimension to the art of drumming in South Louisiana.

In 1956 Warren formed the Wee-Wows: "I called my first group the Wee-Wows because the people would get excited and shout 'Wee-wow!' and I got my last name, 'Storm,' from a star back in 1956, her name was Gale Storm, and it matched my initials W. S. My first group was some local boys and later on we got a chance to play on Jay Miller's sessions, Al Foreman played guitar, Bobby McBride bass, and Merton Thibodeaux piano, with myself on drums. We played everything from Cajun, country, Fats Domino rhythm and blues to Elvis Presley music, and were booked at all the nightclubs around Lafayette, Crowley, Kaplan, and Ville Platte."

Warren was introduced to Jay Miller by Clifford LeMaire, a former Hot Rod and Khoury's artist who owned the Rainbow Inn club in Kaplan. At the audition Storm sang songs by Fats Domino, Hank Williams, and Elvis Presley: "So Jay said, 'Well, that sounds good,' and he had 'Prisoner's Song' in mind back then, so he said, 'Why don't we set up a recording session?' This was in May 1958. He had written some new words, and I knew the melody, so I started singing it to get familiar with it. So then he said, 'We are going to need a flip side,' so he sat down and wrote 'Mama Mama Mama' in thirty minutes. We set up a session one night in May 1958 and it took us just about all night long to record it.

"Surprisingly, my first record was a hit. It broke in Louisiana—New Orleans; then it went to Houston and Birmingham, Alabama; and Memphis, Tennessee. I got a spot on a local TV station in Memphis and Wink Martindale was there. It was similar to 'American Bandstand,' but it was on a smaller scale. So I did 'Prisoner's Song' and it got me exposure in that area. Wink Martindale after the show gave me a pass to see Elvis, Elvis happened to be at his house in Memphis in 1958 and I got a chance to meet him for a couple of hours. And he really gave us a very warm welcome and he was really a super King of Rock 'n' Roll, as everybody called him. I later on went to Birmingham, Alabama; Florida; Texas; and Tennessee. I think it sold over 250,000 records, which in 1958 was almost like a million seller today. At this time, I changed the name of my group to the Jive Masters."

Then Warren had minor hits with "Troubles Troubles (Troubles On My Mind)," "So Long So Long (Good Bye Good Bye)," and "Birmingham Jail." After the Nasco contract expired he had modest local success with "I Thank You So Much" (Rocko) before signing with Top Rank in 1960. An expensive session was arranged in Nashville with top musicians Floyd Cramer, Boots Randolph, and Hank Garland, but these country stars were unable to grasp the unique feel of South Louisiana swamp-pop; "Bohawk Georgia Grind"/"No No" was a dismal single. Warren's subsequent releases on Zynn and Dot had a nice, relaxed R&B approach, but did not achieve chart status.

An extremely fast and positive drummer, Warren Storm was working constantly as a session man for Jay Miller, accompanying Lightnin' Slim, Slim Harpo, Lonesome Sundown, Lazy Lester, Carol Fran, and many others. "It was really fun to record with them," he says, "because everybody would drink a few beers and get to work, and after we would record four or five songs we would drink a few more! We really had a ball doing all the sessions. Jay Miller's studio was very active because the blues records were in demand and they were selling, he had to furnish Excello with a certain amount of masters. I didn't find it difficult as a white person because we were into the music, we felt the music, we worked so long in the studio we got real tight, real good. In fact Lightnin' Slim didn't want to use any other drummer except me, I did some personal appearances with him, too. I really enjoyed doing all these sessions!"

Recalling the Miller sessions, star accompanist Katie Webster says:

"When you go into J. D. Miller's studio you have to cut *perfect* records. Folks used to tell him that perfect records don't sell, you have to have a flaw in them somewhere, but in his studio you do *not* cut a flaw, a record has to be perfect. You cannot make not one mistake, he seems to have microphones in his ears . . . he hears the least mistake, you cannot get away with nothing in that studio . . . He will back it up and play it and show you exactly where you have fouled it up. Yes, he was a good producer. . . ."

It is easy to imagine J. D. working the controls, feeding in the echo, adding and varying reverb, even changing reel speeds as he sought to achieve the right sound. But he was also indebted to his talented studio musicians. With Warren Storm, the red-hot rhythm was inevitably generated by Al Foreman on guitar and Bobby McBride on bass guitar; the occasional stand-ins were Rufus Thibodeaux on bass guitar and Austin Broussard on drums. Before Katie Webster's time the Crowley piano stool was occupied by Merton Thibodeaux, who had played upright bass on Miller's early country sessions. His bluesy piano style is heard to good effect on "The Snake" (Flyright), a sensational late-fifties dance record which for some reason remained unissued at the time. Now partially paralyzed, Merton still performs in Happy Fats's band with his father, "Uncle" Ambrose, the traditional Cajun fiddler. Other excellent Miller pianists were Benny Fruge (early country), Sonny Martin, U. J. Meaux (who also shared organ duties with Katie Webster), Tal Miller, and Roy Perkins.

In the horn section Lionel Prevost (Torrence) reigned supreme, while other saxophonists included Leroy Castille, Louis "Boobay" Guidry, and Harry Simoneaux, who doubled on tenor and baritone. Peter Gosch was another baritone man and Ned Theall blew trumpet. Steel guitar duties were usually handled by Pee Wee Whitewing. Being a session person for Jay Miller was not easy. Bobby McBride can recall playing electric bass all day and into the night before staggering home, his fingers bloody and sore. . . .

By 1966 most of the session musicians, including Warren Storm, had drifted away from Jay Miller's temporarily depressed Crowley organization. After recording the La Louisianne album "At The Saturday Hop" as a member of the Shondels (with whom he was making personal appearances), Warren joined Huey Meaux's promising emporium. Of his many recordings in Jackson, Mississippi, New Orleans, and Lafayette, only "The Gypsy" (Sincere) and "Tennessee Waltz" (Tear Drop) sold in any quantity. Years later Huey released two Crazy Cajun albums from this period, "Family Rules" and "Warren Storm & Johnny Allen [sic]," with many fine cuts by Warren in the South Louisiana idiom, including "Jack And Jill" and "Daydreamin'."

"Then Huey had a misfortune with his business and everything," says Warren, "so I stayed idle from 1969 until 1973, when I went back to J. D. Miller. J. D. had a new label called Showtime and I recorded a country and western song which was named 'Lord I Need Somebody Bad Tonight.' Around this area alone it sold like 7,000 copies, but I wish we could have broken it nationwide. Anyway it led to the album which is called 'At Last Warren Storm' with my group Bad Weather, featuring Pee Wee Whitewing on steel guitar. We had waited so long for this album, that's how we got the title!" Another good seller was "My House Of Memories" in 1975.

An ebullient, genuine person, Warren Storm has talent to burn, both as a convincing swamp-pop singer and as a top drummer. But he still has to earn a living as a printer. In 1979, in an effort to beef up his musical career, he joined forces with Rod Bernard for personal appearances before forming a new group, Cypress, with saxman Willie "Tee" Trahan. Managed again by Huey Meaux, Warren continues to make records and perform in South Louisiana clubs. His many fans believe that, given the breaks, he could still be a national star.

Although he signed artists of the caliber of Warren Storm and Katie Webster, Jay Miller promoted and distributed his Rocko and Zynn labels only locally. Since he was spending much of his time in the studio, it was not surprising that he could not pay more attention to the marketing side of the business. Local sales were not what mattered to Miller: his master plan was still to provide his artists with a window on the world in the hope of landing a national leasing deal—or getting a song he had published covered by a major artist.

The Rocko label, which started life as Rocket in 1958, was aimed initially at the lucrative rock 'n' roll market, blasting off with the prime record-hop sounds of "Jump And Shout" by Guitar Jeff and the Creoles, "Talk To Your Daughter" by Skip Morris with Doug Charles and the Boogie Kings, and "Nervous And Shakin' All Over" by Tommy Strange. Another early Rocko single, Joe Carl's "Don't Leave Me Again," was a routine swamp-pop ballad that justified Miller's strategy when it became a regional hit in 1959 after being leased to Top Rank. Joe Carl was backed by the Dukes of Rhythm featuring tenorman Harry Simoneaux, who recalls: "Joe's first record, 'Don't Leave Me Again,' was written by me and was originally released on Miller's label and later picked up by Top Rank for national release. The solo on this side was performed by me on tenor sax and Raoul Prado, also on tenor sax. After I left Vin Bruce's outfit, Joe Barry and I formed the Dukes of Rhythm and we lasted for a few years. But Joe proved to be undependable and would frequently fail to show for jobs. Because of this we split. Then the band got together with Joe Carl and we retained our original name. Joe Carl was an outstanding performer, knew how to keep things alive, kept up a constant rapport with the audience, and had a fine-quality pop-style voice. His real name is Nolan Duplantis and he comes from Houma."

Following the Top Rank excursion Joe Carl returned to Jay Miller, showing he could rock with the best on "Rockin' Fever" (Rocko) and "You're Too Hot To Handle" (Zynn), a name inspired by a chapter title in a sleazy paperback novel. But with no hit records to sustain his personal appearances, he dropped out of music to work as an internal auditor at the Avondale Shipyard near New Orleans.

After recording rock 'n' roll and swamp-pop for Rocko, Jay Miller began using the label for a harder form of R&B from Sonny Martin, Joe Mayfield, Charles Sheffield, Tabby Thomas, and Leroy Washington, who all graduated to Excello, the ultimate target for J. D.'s black artists. Zynn had a more popular ambience. Pianist Rocket (Rodney) Morgan was the label's most frequently recorded artist, and his releases alternated between the stomping rock 'n' roll of "Tag Along" and "You're Hum-buggin' Me," the swamp-pop of "This Life I Live," and the sprightly blues of Jimmy Reed's "I Know It's A Sin." He gained some local recognition before becoming a preacher.

Henry Clement, Zynn's leading vocal-group specialist, started out as Little Clem fronting the Dewdrops (he was also known as Little Henry). Excelling at slow-burning R&B ballads like "Please Please Darling" and "What Have I Done Wrong," both with surreal doo-wop support, Clement was just as adept on the finger-snapping "I'm So In Love With You" and "Jenny Jenny Jenny." Also a talented musician, he played harmonica on an early Lightnin' Slim session. His biggest success was with the romping R&B chant "Trojan Walla" (Spot), ironically not a group number. The general scarcity of vocal groups in the area was probably due to the lack of vocal harmonies in French music and to the weak gospel tradition in South Louisiana—the singer sang and that was it. Nevertheless, Jay Miller was expert at capturing the greasy street-corner sound whenever it was required. The Zynn single "Plea Of Love" by the Gaynotes from Baton Rouge was a supreme example of this skill.

Other notable Zynn releases included Clifton Chenier's "Rockin' Accordian," Lionel Torrence's "Rooty Tooty" (and a "Rockin' Jole' Blonde"), and Jerry Starr and the Clippers' "Side Steppin' " with Al Foreman on guitar—all solid examples of the fast-fading art of the rock 'n' roll instrumental. The most successful record was Jerry Morris's swamp-pop ballad "(Make Me) A Winner In Love," while the catalog was rounded off by singles from bluesmen Jimmy Anderson, Jimmy Dotson, Mr. Calhoun, Tabby Thomas, and Leroy Washington; Cajun-pop artists Rick Fontaine and Terry Clement and the Tune-Tones; and a nonrocking Al Ferrier.

During the busy early sixties, Jay Miller started recording Cajun music again; he was probably impressed by Floyd Soileau's involvement in the Cajun market with Swallow Records. J. D. reserved the Kajun label for Nathan Abshire and the Pine Grove Boys, and placed other acts on Cajun Classics and a revived Fais Do Do. One of the most commercial Cajun releases was an enthusiastic version of Chuck Berry's "Memphis" (Fais Do Do) by Robert Bertrand and the Louisiana Ramblers, on which the promising young Joel Sonnier vocalized and played accordion. Earlier, Bertrand and the Lake Charles Playboys had cut the hilarious "Drunkard's Two-Step" (Fais Do Do), humorously conjuring up woozy images of inebriated Saturday-night revelers absentmindedly tripping over the dance floor. A former drummer in Iry LeJune's band, Robert also played fiddle and went on to record for Goldband with Joel Sonnier. He died in 1974.

The Cajun Classics label offered a rich profusion of Cajun sounds, from the archaic music of Moise Robin (who had played accordion with Leo Soileau way back in 1929) to the Cajun-country of Jimmie Choates. The mainstream Cajun performances predominated; the best were "Roseland Two-Step"/"Tolan Waltz" by Floyd LeBlanc and his Cajun Fiddle, "Oson Two-Step" and "Crowley Two-Step" by Aldus Roger and the Lafayette Playboys, and "Les Filles Mexie" by Terry Clement. Except for the Nathan Abshire and Aldus Roger singles, Miller's Cajun sales were generally poor. "Cajun records were strictly local consumption," J. D. explains. "When you pass Port Arthur, Texas, in the west, Opelousas in the north, and Thibodaux in the east, I've never been able to find a market. If you sell a couple of thousand Cajun records right now you're doing well, unless you get an exceptional thing like Jimmy Newman's 'Lache Pas La Patate,' they've sold in excess of 200,000 in Canada."

Jay Miller was willing to record almost any kind of material as long as it had commercial potential. He had an acclaimed comedy album by Frenchie Carte (Cajun Classics), and enjoyed a huge left-field success with the unsubtle humor of JEB and Cousin Easy's "The Golf Game" (Par T), which sold throughout the greens and fairways of America. Then, in 1966, came Rebel Records, with its explicit insignia of two Confederate flags. The first releases, "Flight NAACP 105" by The Son of Mississippi and "Dear Mr. President" by Happy Fats, each sold more than 200,000 copies; "Kajun Klu Klux Klan" and "Looking For A Handout" by Johnny Rebel were also big sellers. Clearly Miller had found another underground market.

The liner notes of the solitary Rebel album, "For Segregationists Only," spelled out the label's philosophy: "These selections express the feeling, anxiety, confusion and problems during the political transformation of our way of life ... Transformations that have changed peace and tranquillity to riots and demonstrations which have produced mass destruction, confusion, bloodshed and even loss of life; transformations that have changed incentive for self-improvement to much dependency on numerous federal 'Give away' programs, under the guise of building a 'great society.' For those who take a conservative position on integration, this 'great society' program, the controversial war in Viet Nam and the numerous so-called 'Civil Rights' organizations, this record is a must!"

Over a three-year period the principal Rebel artists were "The Son of Mississippi" (Joe Norris), "Johnny Rebel" (Clifford "Pee Wee" Trahan), and Happy Fats, all country-oriented singers. Their protests were directed mainly at President Lyndon Johnson; they felt his policies were betraying the southern heritage and usurping personal freedom. Jay Miller himself had been involved in Louisiana politics for many years, and had acted as Jimmie Davis's campaign manager for Acadia Parish in the state gubernatorial elections. He is well aware of the controversies surrounding his Rebel label: "Of course we had a lot of fingers pointed at us, and I'm sure by a lot of people that are less friendly to blacks than I am. I've always been friendly with blacks and we never did hide the fact we were recording these records. We had blacks sitting in on the sessions and a lot of blacks agreed with what was said. We're not hypocritical about it. You'll find my address on there, I didn't try and hide it. There were others coming out of Bogalusa and other places, but they wouldn't put their address on the labels like we did, there's no way of tracing them!

"I never had any black people object to our records, I had some white people that were amazed at what we did. I met some white hypocrites that tried to stir up some trouble with it, they wouldn't dare sit down and eat with a black. I just ignored them. I've been eating and drinking with blacks since 1946, since I've been making records. It was nothing new, but I didn't have anybody telling me I had to do it. That makes a big difference, I choose my friends. And I don't choose them based on their color. The Rebel records were at the time of the civil rights disputes. The best seller we had was 'Flight NAACP 105,' there was nothing detrimental about that. I tell you what, you had a black radio station over in Port Arthur and Beaumont playing it. It was a kind of an Amos 'n' Andy skit by Joe Norris, a very talented person, done spontaneously—that's tough to do. That was the first one I did, my friends thought I was nuts when I decided to put that out. But I thought it was good, after all we're in the record business—none of those records were filthy, none of those records were vulgar, you never found one vulgar record. They were expressing a person's opinion."

When Jay Miller became housing director for Crowley in the late sixties he started handing over his music interests to his sons. At the time the recording industry was veering away from regional music with a vengeance: the traditional blues, country, Cajun, and swamp-pop markets were in a parlous state. For J. D., the contractual impasse with Excello was the last straw.

Although he is now effectively in musical retirement, Miller's past recording activities still attract occasional criticism at the expense of praise for his many achievements. In defending himself, he reflects on some of the problems inherent in running a small "country outfit"—from finding suitable artists, arguing over royalty payments, and ensuring the financial stability of the business to keeping up with the latest musical trends: "I don't know anyway that I'd do it any differently. . . . I've never been in a position where I got an artist that was already made, I'm not like a major or someone that's financially able to say to an artist, 'Well, you sold records over there, I'm gonna give you so much front money, you come and record for me.' I've never been in that position. My position has always been that there's a guy that comes in there in his old torn-up shoes and clothes, and an old torn-up guitar or whatever, and an old rattletrap car, and he starts singing for me and I thought he had potential. Everything was on. They had nobody else to turn to. So it's a different setup altogether.

"I always listened to everybody. If I wouldn't have done that I wouldn't have got anybody, because I never heard them anywhere else. They weren't on record. So I made it a policy all during my life to listen and I heard some terrible, terrible artists. But on the other hand I picked up some good ones. And I tell them in advance, I'm gonna be honest with you, I'm gonna tell you exactly how I feel.

"We had problems by being a little local outfit. Some of the French artists were probably the worst, really. We put out a French release and we'd pay them 2 cents, 2½ cents [per record], which was the going rate then. Not a damn one of them would have paid us to put the record out, but we were paying them; we used to have package deals for people, five hundred, a thousand records, we can't record everybody that comes in and pay them royalties. [Such deals covered the cost of using the studio facilities and of pressing the records; two beneficiaries were Cajun-country singer Dunice Theriot (Sportsman) and bluesman Joe Rich(ards) (T-Bird).] Anyway, they'd go into the New Cajun Lounge and everything, they'd hear their record on every damn Cajun phono, delusions of grandeur, you know. They don't stop for one moment and realize just in what a very small area that record is popular. When they get a statement showing they've sold one thousand or two thousand records, and if it's a big one they've sold three thousand, they just don't understand that. They heard their record on the radio all over, but they don't get out of this area.

They heard it on all the jukeboxes, and all these record stores had it. Goddam he just put the screws to us, lying to us!

"So you just don't have much of a chance one way or the other. I had the same trouble with the other [blues] artists, too. The fact that they heard their records over WLAC Nashville, 50,000 watts, more or less made them feel that their thing had to be selling 100,000 records with no problems. They'd get a statement for 12,000 records, I've done did it to them, see. So your producer, he's behind the eight ball all the time, no kidding. The only thing I can possibly see where anybody could have ever said that they didn't get their money from me was because we deducted, and they knew it. We deducted perhaps some of the money for payolas, or money they had gotten for equipment which was part of our deal. I don't feel that I have been misunderstood by my artists, they knew, but by some of these other guys. In the years where I was really active in this you could be certain we were always behind the eight ball.

"How did we prosper? Really it wasn't in the record business. Probably it was through the songs I wrote and I just put it right back into the record business. I had this other No. 1 song which I did not write but I owned, called 'Wondering.' That was Webb Pierce's first hit, a number of big artists did it, that was the old Joe Werner song. And of course I had 'It Wasn't God Who Made Honky Tonk Angels' for Kitty Wells, I had a number of lesser hits, but the royalties began to accrue. I've got 403 songs of mine on record. Of course the big, big majority of them did nothing to speak of, but all of that added up. I still do get a pretty fair income on royalties through my Jamil publishing company—I wrote a lot of blues songs as 'Jerry West' because of my given name identifying me as a country writer, which would not be acceptable to the black trade.

"But the trends changed to a point where I lost a lot of interest in it. What people refer to as country music now, I have a new *Billboard* there and we could go through the Top Hundred and I would say twenty years ago if anybody would call 80 percent of those country records they'd be laughed out of the room. They call them country records, they're not country records—not by country standards. You don't need an arranger, you don't need sheet music and all this to cut country music. The word 'country' more or less denotes the fact that somebody's not supposed to know too much about music. They'd come in and sing what they felt. Today it's not in the same category compared with your Ernest Tubbs and these other guys who really sing country.

"Country was big in the fifties, but then shortly afterwards came rock 'n' roll, followed by the Beatles next—they just upset our whole deal. Prior to that you had all your Fats Dominos, which I liked very much. . . . We had a great emphasis on what we term rock 'n' roll, Fats Domino, Little Richard, and some of the others. And the Beatles just tore the hell out of country music over here, same with the blues. It wiped that phase of business out. So I have slowed down. I figured out anybody who was in the business as long as I was was rather set in their ways. There's no question of it, things change as time goes on and I just figured it was time to bring in new blood, new ideas into the business. I was very fortunate to have my youngest son, Mark, who was interested. Of course he was brought up in this, but he's very interested, very very competent musician, he's excellent as an engineer. I don't participate much and I'm tired, really. . . ."

Still advised by their father, Mark and Bill Miller manage the family music interests, including the fine $300,000 Master-Trak Sound Recorders studio (first opened in 1967) and the large Modern Music Store. Both premises are located on North Parkerson Avenue in Crowley. To date Mark has produced albums by Al Ferrier, Warren Storm, and western-swing veteran Cliff Bruner for Showtime; and by Buckwheat, Fernest Arceneaux, Tabby Thomas, and the Sam Brothers for Blues Unlimited. There have also been several Cajun singles on Bayou Classics and on a revived Kajun label, featuring the respected Joe Bonsall, Camay Doucet, and Blackie Forestier and promising young artists such as Ricky Bearb and the Cajun Ramblers, Pat Savant, Wayne Toups and the Crowley Aces, and the Cajun Grass Band with Harold Fontenot (who have recorded a splendid version of Louis Noel's "La Cravat"). Encouragingly, the studio—with twenty-four tracks, Neumann mixers, and several outboard extras—is also being patronized by outside producers, including Floyd Soileau with Johnnie Allan, Sam Charters with Rockin' Dopsie, and Rounder Records with Joel Sonnier. Once again Crowley has every right to call itself the recording center of South Louisiana.

During the late fifties, Eddie Shuler's successful Goldband forays into rock 'n' roll and R&B with artists like Gene Terry, Guitar Jr., and Jimmy Wilson meant that he no longer had to rely on Iry LeJune's Cajun sales. Inevitably he was attracted to swamp-pop music, and he promptly produced his biggest hit—"Sea Of Love" by Phil Phillips, for George Khoury.

Eddie was assisted temporarily by his son Wayne, who also ran the Trey label, distributed by Goldband. Wayne's main artist was Elton Anderson, a gifted black singer and guitarist in the classic South Louisiana swamp-pop mold. Anderson had a modest regional record for Wayne in 1959 with "Shed So Many Tears," an attractive blues ballad released on Johnny Vincent's Vin label. Even bigger was "Secret Of Love," a melodious swamp-pop tune (very much like Clyde McPhatter's "Treasure Of Love") that became a No. 88 hit on the *Billboard Hot 100* after it was leased to Mercury in early 1960. Both records were cut at the Goldband studio.

Elton had another hit two years later with the old King Karl song "Life Problem," which was handled by Lanor (run by Lee Lavergne of Church Point) before being taken up nationally by Capitol. *Billboard* liked the record: "This is a salty rock ballad that is sung by the young lad. Side features staccato combo backing that gets a good sound." The "staccato backing" was, in fact, a beautiful Chuck Willis–type arrangement by producer Wardell Quezerque. Most of Elton's classy Lanor sides were cut in New Orleans with Mac Rebennack in support.

Then, according to Lee Lavergne, Anderson became "difficult to manage" and defected to California. Wayne Shuler also went to the West Coast—he was invited to join Capitol Records. "I almost had to break his arm to get him to take the job with Capitol," says father Eddie. "Then I almost had to break both arms to get him in a state of mind so that he could accept the transfer. Then they wanted to move him up the totem pole."

Having shared "Sea Of Love" with George Khoury and "Secret Of Love" with son Wayne, Eddie Shuler had the belated pleasure of seeing Goldband's name grace the national charts when "Sugar Bee" by Cleveland Crochet and his Hillbilly Ramblers became the first Cajun record to break into the *Billboard Hot 100*, climbing to No. 80 in early 1961. Distribution was handled by Bill Lowery's National Recording Corporation (NRC) in Atlanta, Georgia, and sales were particularly strong in the South and in California.

Eddie was always striving for new sounds; this time, with Cajun rock 'n' roll, he accomplished his aim. The song was deceptively simple, with vocalist Jay Stutes continually rasping out the hook line *Sugar Bee, look what you done to me.* Mike Leadbitter was aware of the hit qualities of the record in his review in the first issue of *Blues Unlimited* in April 1963: "Singer is a guy named Jay Stutes whose hysterical shouting vocals and powerful steel guitar make this Cajun-cum-R&B disc into a masterful performance. Crochet is heard only briefly on 'Drunkards Dream' for a short solo. Roaring accordion backing by Shorty LeBlanc." In the final analysis "Sugar Bee" stood apart from other Cajun records because it was sung in English and because the accordion sounded like a blues harmonica. Although a local disc jockey once introduced the group sarcastically as "the New Iberia Symphony Orchestra," "Sugar Bee" turned out to be the biggest triumph for Cajun music since "Jole Blon"— both as a public relations vehicle and as a hit record.

Eddie Shuler loves telling the background story: "Cleveland Crochet recorded his fabulous and big-selling 'Sugar Bee' for me and left the world another great sound. During the rock 'n' roll days I spent five years trying to find a Cajun band that could play rock 'n' roll. Everyone thought I was nuts, and I tried so many bands that I became really discouraged. I had just about given up when one day in 1960 Cleveland, Shorty LeBlanc, Jay Stutes, Charlie Babineaux, and Clifton Newman walked into my office. They had something they wanted me to hear, and we went out to the studio. They all sat down and played a number called 'Sweet Thing' and told me they had spent three years developing the sound. I knew that at last I had found the sound I was looking for! We set a date and the result was 'Sugar Bee' and 'Drunkards Dream.' I told them we had us a hit, but they were naturally skeptical. All we had done was to take a French song and give it a driving steel guitar and a rock 'n' roll backbeat, but the wailing sounds over the speakers told me the record was chartbound!

"I soon found that although I said the record was a hit, other people did not agree. For an illustration, I took it to the biggest Lake Charles DJ, promised him an exclusive and pointed out the benefits of being the first to put a needle to a hit. All he said was that I had a good song but had given it the wrong arrangement and treatment. As far as he was concerned it just wasn't modern enough. I met the same man in a record hop in Galveston some time after 'Sugar Bee' got in the charts and in the presence of eight other DJs he said he was taking his hat off to me, for I had proved him wrong. He added that he had been forced to play it due to public demand and now appreciated how good it was. Six months later it was the No. 1 on his station!

"But I had all kinds of trouble trying to get some airplay, though I knew that if it was only played once, the requests that poured in for it afterwards would solve my problem. I took it to the stations in Lafayette and Baton Rouge, but they said it didn't have the right sound for their particular areas, it was Cajun but it wasn't. In desperation I took it to Beaumont where I hoped KJET, a colored station, would help. This station is a great place if you want airplay and thus exposure for a new record. I had a great friend who was a DJ with the station and he promised to play 'Sugar Bee.' The result was like a snowball going down a mountain, it just got bigger and bigger. The DJ was my old associate Clarence Garlow, the great songwriter and bluesman! He and the public proved how right I was about that record. Once it hit the turntable that station switchboard lit up like a Christmas tree and stayed that way for weeks!"

Cleveland Crochet, an undistinguished fiddle player, had recorded previously for Folk-Star and Lyric. His group owed its original, modern sound to the raucous vocals and fearsome steel-guitar work of Jay Stutes, a truck driver for a Jennings beer distributor. Another key musician was the late Vorris "Shorty" LeBlanc, a magnificent accordionist who also played on record with Jimmy Newman and Rufus Thibodeaux. He was a machine-shop worker from Lake Arthur.

The "Sugar Bee" follow-ups "Sweet Thing," "Hound Dog Baby,"

"Come Back Little Girl," and "Coming Home" were in the same Cajun rock 'n' roll format as the hit, but the element of surprise was gone. When Jay Stutes took over as leader from Cleveland Crochet the band was renamed the Sugar Bees and reverted to a more traditional style of Cajun music, playing venues like Bailey's Fish Camp in Bridge City, Texas; the Palomino Club near Orange, Texas; and Club Lafitte in Lake Arthur. The Sugar Bees split when Shorty LeBlanc died in 1965. Jay Stutes joined Blackie Forestier and the Cajun Aces, and resurfaced on Joel Sonnier's Rounder album in 1980.

After "Sugar Bee" the Goldband studio was in constant use throughout 1961 and 1962 with a variety of good South Louisiana music being put on record. There was swamp-pop from the Fats Domino–influenced Jay Richards and his Blues Kings, teen rock 'n' roll from Charles Page, and rockabilly relics from Jay Chevalier. At the same time Joe Bonsall, Sunny Dupin, and old favorites the Hackberry Ramblers were striving for their own Cajun-French popular hits. The R&B representative was drummer Bill Parker, who had a string of gimmicky releases with his Showboat Band. A veteran of the Lake Charles scene, Parker worked with James Freeman and Clarence Garlow before organizing his own popular band featuring vocalists Jesse "Blues" Palmer, Little Miss Peggy, and Claude Shermack; guitarist Chester Randle later made soul records for Eddie Shuler's Anla label. Bill Parker himself eventually moved to Oklahoma City, where he operated the Showboat label.

Eddie Shuler also set up the Tic Toc subsidiary, releasing two classic swamp-pop ballads, "Lonely Feeling" by Sticks Herman and "You're Lonesome Now" by Charles Perrywell and his Fairlanes, both hauntingly beautiful records. But the benefits reaped by "Sugar Bee" evaporated suddenly when the distributors, NRC, crumbled and almost took Goldband with them. Although Shuler will not talk about this unhappy episode, thousands of unsalable NRC singles fossilizing in his attic hint at the wretched deal involved. He escaped battered and bruised, and was forced to retrench. For the rest of the sixties Eddie labored in vain for a hit. A major disappointment was Rockin' Sidney, who never fulfilled the promise of his Jin days; bluesy records like "Shed So Many Tears" and "Something Working Baby" had some merit, but the banal "Soul Christmas" was typical of his indifferent soul-music outings. The young guitarist Danny James had every chance of making the big time with "Boogie In The Mud," a steamy slab of swamp-rock written by Rockin' Sidney and inspired by Tony Joe White's "Polk Salad Annie." But the record foundered when James inexplicably refused to promote it. Swamp-pop artists Lee Bernard and Van Preston were also unable to make any significant commercial impact. Like other local record men, Eddie Shuler must have cast envious glances at the international success of Creedence Clearwater Revival with their borrowed Louisiana swamp sound.

During the sixties Shuler was still recording such traditional Cajun musicians as Hobo Bertrand (whose "Starvation Waltz" did well), Robert Bertrand, Nolan Cormier, Ed Kershaw, and the veteran J. B. Fusilier. "While I was turning out this rock 'n' roll, R&B, and everything else you can name," Eddie says, "I was still steadily releasing Cajun music. This stuff is still my bread and butter! By that I mean that Cajun music will always sell for anyone in this part of the country, and more important will continue to sell well long after it has been issued. There are even occasions when a Cajun record will remain inactive for months and then just take off along-side your newest releases. Now the thing that intrigued me about it and still does is that here I was in the richest country in the world, you know, tech-nologically speaking, monetary, et cetera, et cetera, and we have right here in our midst this authentic, truly undiscovered music. You know it was un-real, nobody knew it was here. I didn't really proceed to say, "Well I'm gonna make the world come down here, accept Cajun music'... the reason I wasn't wanting to do that was because I was smart enough to realize that you couldn't understand what they were saying, no way. But I said, 'Well, I can preserve the music, supposing that the world changes tomorrow and there won't be any Cajuns around to play this music.'

"My thinking turned out to be pretty correct, because today they don't have any more Cajuns that will play *authentic* Cajun music. That's like trying to ask one of the biggest names in the business and ask him to go out and play folk music like it was way back when, there ain't no way he's gonna do that. And of course the Cajuns today, they feel that they're above that type of thing, so they want to bring in the steel guitars and the electronics and all this stuff. And consequently you don't have any more of the Cajun music, you have a hybrid Cajun music today which is influenced by country music, by rock music—it depends which artist it is. They follow the whole spectrum."

With Cajuns showing renewed pride in their heritage, Eddie's com-ments are now open to some debate. Perhaps he was thinking of Joel Sonnier's uneven career. A superbly accomplished and delicate accor-dionist, Sonnier was Goldband's brightest star until he migrated to California in 1972, misusing his talents playing bass and drums in country-and-western dance bands. In the mid-seventies he was awarded a contract by the country division of Mercury, prompting a move to Nashville. But in 1980 the prodigal son returned home to Cajun country in heartening style with an outstanding album for Rounder.

Sonnier was born in Rayne in 1946. Influenced by the great Iry LeJune, he won many accordion contests before recording the tension-packed

"Tee Yeaux Bleu" for Swallow. At the time he was justifiably known as "The thirteen-year-old wonder." Then Dominic Dupre of Ville Platte formed the Dupre label specifically to give Joel extra publicity for his personal appearances, recording the boy accordionist with Les Duson Playboys in a country shack. Although the old hunting-dog song "Tayeaux Dog Tayeaux" (better known as "Hip Et Taiaud") had much youthful energy, the poor sound defeated all of Dupre's good intentions.

When Joel finished school he moved to Lake Charles, where he joined Robert Bertrand's Louisiana Ramblers. He sang and played with this group on the memorable "Memphis" (Fais Do Do) and duetted with Bertrand on the old Louisiana-French folk song "My 50 Cents" (Goldband). His solo recordings for Goldband as Jo-El Sonnier were bewilderingly mercurial, with the traditional "Jump Little Frog" (based on the well-loved "Saute Crapaud") and the bittersweet "I'm Leaving You" standing out as the better Cajun items. The albums were "full of electronics and all this stuff," for which Eddie Shuler as producer must shoulder part of the blame. As a publicity gimmick, Sonnier flaunted himself unworthily as the Cajun Valentino, complete with headdress. Joel did himself belated justice on the Rounder LP "Cajun Life," engineered by Mark Miller in Crowley. With a star-studded backing group including accomplished fiddler Merlin Fontenot from Eunice, "Sugar Bee" Jay Stutes playing dobro, and renegades from Nashville forming an innovative, sympathetic rhythm section (with a lovely, thumping upright bass), Joel sparkled on favorite Cajun numbers like "Allons A Lafayette," "Perrodin Two-Step," "Lacassine Special," "Les Flammes D'Enfer," and "Bayou Teche Waltz." On one or two tracks the country element seemed too strong, emphasizing the potential pitfalls of the Cajun/country alliance, but generally the LP was an encouraging testimony to the future of Cajun music—and of Joel Sonnier. As he commented in the sleeve notes, "I think ethnic music, roots music, will come back in, music that has love and inspiration, music that is real, not camouflaged. I am proud of my roots and proud to be recording what I believe in. I believe that people in the eighties will accept honest music. I fully believe that Joel Sonnier will be part of that. . . ."

During the seventies Eddie Shuler was unable to recapture Goldband's earlier musical glories. Some artists died, retired, or disappeared, while others updated their styles. Eddie concentrated his resources on repackaging his old recordings (notably Cajun, blues, R&B, rockabilly, and swamp-pop) in album form for the collector's market, which he tended to misjudge by adding unnecessary bass-guitar overdubs to the prime original cuts. In 1982 he was hoping that Katie Webster would resurrect Goldband's fortunes, but in typical unpredictable Shuler fashion found himself distributing "the number one in sales in South Louisiana at this point in time!", the controversial "A Coonass From Ville Platte" by Hebert Fontenot and the Super Country Cajuns, with vocal by Don Lafleur (Jador).

Still the salt of the earth, Eddie is the best person to put his recording activities in perspective: "Goldband has come a long way from its beginning, and in spite of many mistakes and disappointments I feel it has all been worth it. Above all I helped a little guy named Iry LeJune leave his wonderful talent on record for the world. I will be forever indebted to that man and the faith he had in me. I am very proud of my country background and it has been a tremendous influence in my choice of songs for recording. In country music, be it blues, Cajun, or western, one comes to realize the value of a good song and its effect on the public. In other fields too much attention is paid to an arrangement or tricky passages and not enough to the song. Some like to rely on electronic miracles rather than people and ability, and while electronics are a great advance I feel they should help to provide only a part and not the whole. I do try to make a record different in as many ways as I can, but I still try to make it compatible to the public's taste.

"I am now getting letters from all over the world asking me about my records, and this gives me great pleasure indeed. At last the message in blues and Cajun music is reaching for a long way! My goal is to bring national attention to bear on the great talent in Southwestern Louisiana."

19

"Why can't I go into the record business and produce these guys?"

As the sixties began, the established South Louisiana record men were facing fresh competition from Sam Montel (Montel), Lee Lavergne (Lanor), and Carol Rachou (La Louisianne). The most commercially successful new label was Sam Montel's Montel Records. Headquartered in Baton Rouge, Montel had national swamp-pop hits by John Fred in 1959 and Dale and Grace in 1963.

"Sam Montel's real name is Sam Montalbano," says Rod Bernard, "he's an Italian gentleman in the fruit and vegetable exchange business. His parents were in that, but he liked the music business. He changed his name to Sam Montel because it was easier to pronounce. S. J.—we call him 'S. J.'—had a music store in Baton Rouge in the fifties. He and Jimmy Clanton went to school together and were good friends. When Jimmy hit with 'Just A Dream,' S. J. went on the road as his road manager for a couple of years. And he started this Montel Record Company and Red Stick Publishing."

The first Montel release, "My Girl Across Town"/"Take It Home To Grandma" by Lester Robertson and his Upsetters, was scintillating New Orleans R&B and an immediate regional hit. (Previously Robertson had recorded for Jay Miller in 1957 as lead vocalist with Joe Hudson and his Rocking Dukes on the swampy Excello release "Baby Give Me A Chance.") Robertson's quest for stardom was blocked when the Montel follow-up "My Heart Forever Yearns" failed to make the charts. But Sam Montel was soon hitting again with John Fred and the Playboys' "Shirley," which nudged into the *Billboard Hot 100* at No. 82 in the spring of 1959. Singing in a pronounced Bobby Charles style, John Fred—like Bobby—was combining South Louisiana swamp-pop and New Orleans R&B.

"I was only seventeen," recalls John Fred, "Sam was only about nineteen, just out of high school. And he came by and he had put out Lester Robertson's record, he was interested in records. He heard our band one night, he thought we were really good and asked if we had our own songs. I said, 'Yeah, we have some songs we've written,' so we had a couple of songs and one of them was 'Shirley.' And we came down to New

Orleans, but we didn't use our band. Our sax player played, but we used the regular studio band, Charlie Williams, Red Tyler, Lee Allen, the whole thing. It was really freaking for me because when I walked in the studio there was a session before me, it was Fats Domino cutting 'Whole Lotta Loving' and 'Margie.' I got to meet Fats for the first time and played with the same band that played with him, I was only seventeen years old!

"I was born in 1941, John Fred Gourrier, I lived in Baton Rouge all my life. I was never really aware of music, I was a big basketball player, a big baseball player, a big athlete. One day I rode a bicycle to school, in those days Baton Rouge wasn't a very big town, and I heard this song going *They say No no no no no, your daddy knows* . . . I just stopped my bicycle and I said, 'Man, what is that?' So I went over there and it was a song called 'Hearts Of Stone' by the Charms, must have been 1955. So I kinda started listening in, there was no black station except for Poppa Stoppa in New Orleans, who was the only one playing those so-called Negro records because, like my mother would say, 'Will you please cut off that Negro music!' Well, I didn't understand it, because I really wasn't into Doris Day, Pat Boone doing 'Tutti Frutti,' that really turned me off.

"I started a band in the latter part of 1958, actually the guys were all singers at high school, I was only in the tenth grade. That was Catholic High School in Baton Rouge. We really started playing, our influence was New Orleans, like Fats Domino was a great influence. Every record he'd make I'd go to the record shop!"

With "Shirley" a hit, John Fred made a proud appearance on the "Alan Freed Show" in New York, but he lost ground when the excellent follow-up, "Good Lovin' " (written by Bobby Charles), missed the charts. John felt his genuine liking for black music was something of a handicap: "It was rough for the first five or six years, it wasn't long hair, it was that you were playing Negro music. We did 'Long Tall Sally,' 'Rip It Up'—you name it, we did it. We just weren't reworking the hits, we did everything from Joe Turner to James Brown, all of them."

John Fred's musical career went into wraps when he was awarded a basketball scholarship at Southeastern Louisiana College in Hammond. In 1965 he came back with a strong version of the old John Lee Hooker song "Boogie Children," which was picked up from N-Joy Records of Monroe by veteran Shreveport record man Stan Lewis. Lewis was an integral part of the national independent record company setup. From miniscule beginnings as a jukebox operator with five boxes in Negro locations, he built up a thriving record store and an important distribution network, establishing close links with the influential Chess Brothers; he was responsible for making North Louisiana Dale Hawkins's "Susie Q" a 1957 Checker hit. In 1963 Stan formed his own Jewel label; later he added the Paula and Ronn labels. Aiming primarily at the blues, soul, and gospel markets, he had early hits by the Uniques and Toussaint McCall. But there was little South Louisiana music in Lewis's catalogs, except for scattered singles by Cookie and the Cupcakes, Bobby Charles, Johnny Jano, the Boogie Kings, and Skip Stewart.

Then, in 1967, John Fred and his Playboy Band literally struck gold— for Stan Lewis and themselves—when "Judy In Disguise" (Paula) became an enormous international pop hit in a Beatles-influenced rock style known as "southern beat." The song referred to the sunglass craze of the time, and was indirectly inspired by the Beatles' "Lucy In The Sky With Diamonds." "The rest is history," says John Fred. "It sold 2½ million records, it was No. 1 in every foreign country but two, so it was a giant record because of the foreign market. In America it was No. 1 for two weeks, but at that time if you were there for more than two weeks you were lucky. We knocked the Beatles' 'Hello Goodbye' out, which was really something because the Beatles always had No. 1 records. I think 'Judy In Disguise' had a lot to do with what's happening now. It started people dancing, we had so many protest songs in 1966, the San Francisco business in 1967, 'Judy In Disguise' made people say, 'Hey, let's get happy again!' Because if you take away the lyrics it's just a rock 'n' roll tune for a track, and one of the best reviews I ever got was in a London newspaper which said, 'Although this group may never go down in history as having anything, their song "Judy In Disguise" may have brought rock 'n' roll back.' "

Neither John Fred nor Stan Lewis has enjoyed such heady times since. John lingered on as an artist until 1975 before going into record production and receiving early acclaim for his work with Irma Thomas. His last band helped to form the popular group La Roux.

After the first John Fred hit, Sam Montel scored regionally with the lilting swamp-pop of "Crazy Baby" by Buck Rogers and his Jets, but he had to wait another four years before Dale and Grace snuggled together at the top of the charts with "I'm Leaving It Up To You" in the fall of 1963. Sam was delighted at having the No. 1 record in the nation. "It was a wonderful feeling!" he told Lee Lavergne.

"I'm Leaving It Up To You" by former Jay Miller artist Dale Houston (from Hattiesburg, Mississippi) and diminutive Cajun-born Grace Brous- sard was cast firmly in the swamp-pop mold, although the production was marred slightly by an obsessive rock-a-string violin arrangement. Dale and Grace's starry-eyed version of the old Don and Dewey R&B song became a hit after Huey Meaux negotiated a national distribution deal with Jamie/Guyden Records of Philadelphia. The infectious follow-up "Stop And Think It Over" wasted no time in climbing the *Billboard* charts to No. 8, but the magical spell ended when "The Loneliest Night" faded at

No. 65 in the early summer of 1964. Dale and Grace's dreamy legacy has been preserved for posterity in an album on Michelle (an associated Montel label), since reissued by Floyd Soileau. The LP shows how strongly the pair was influenced by famous R&B duets like Shirley and Lee, Mickey and Sylvia—and Don and Dewey.

Following their breakup, Dale's name has faded into musical history, but Grace still sings superbly with her brother Van Broussard at Cal's club in Prairieville. Van has been a popular swamp-pop performer in the Baton Rouge area for over two decades, but he has never had a big hit record. However, in the late seventies he had sizable local hits with "(Lord) I Need Somebody Bad" (previously recorded by Warren Storm) and "Feed The Flame" for James M. Rogers's Bayou Boogie Records. The ensuing album "Van Broussard" was a revelation; it was one of the best—and most encouraging—swamp-pop releases in years. Van's voice was reminiscent of Bobby Charles's, and his material ranged from classic swamp-pop to New Orleans R&B; the band harked back to the heyday of Joe Barry, with high-flying trumpets, fruity rich baritone sax, and riffing tenor saxes.

After Dale and Grace parted, Sam Montel had moderate success with local country favorites Larry Brasso and the Rhythmaires, and with the blue-eyed soul of the Boogie Kings. Eventually Montel ceased recording to devote his time to the family fruit and vegetable company.

Lee Lavergne, a friendly likable Cajun, is head of Lanor Records. He lives in Church Point, a rustic, unspoiled town north of Crowley that is the home of several influential Cajun musical families, including the Bergerons, Cormiers, Heberts, LeJunes (Lejeunes), Mattes, and Thibodeauxs. Lee formed Lanor in 1960 as a sideline to his clerical job in a wholesale grocery. If enthusiasm and determination had counted for anything he would have had many hits in the swamp-pop and Cajun markets, but after two decades his label is still not widely recognized despite a catalog that contains quality releases by Shirley Bergeron, Bill Matte, Elton Anderson, Charles Mann, and others.

Lee is the son of poor farming parents who grew cotton, corn, and sweet potatoes on three acres of land, with another twenty acres shared. His love of music dates back to his childhood in the Acadiana of the late thirties and early forties when the roads were either gravel or dirt tracks, and the horse and buggy was still the main means of transportation (cars did not become widely owned until the fifties). Lee's story offers an illuminating overview of the evolution of Cajun music seen through the eyes of a Cajun: "I can remember when I first heard accordion music, it really got to me. And it was something I grew up with, I don't think I ever sat down and realized we had something different from any other part of the world. It was like a way of life. Speaking French, just about everybody around us where I lived always spoke French, something you accepted. I was raised speaking French because my mother and father spoke French, they knew very few words in English, just what they had picked up, because neither one had gone to school. My daddy had gone, I think, two days to school, he learned how to count to 100 and was able to recite his ABC, which he taught me. When I started school that was kinda the only thing I knew, I had picked up a little bit of English by playing with the other kids, but I knew very little. A lot of your teachers don't speak French so it was a hard start, but as a kid you have an open mind and I guess a lot sharper than as you grow older. And you pick up pretty fast, that was no problem.

"Cajun music was different, it was the greatest. I liked it, but I saw a lot of people that didn't like it. At each school a lot of the girls didn't like it, they looked down on you if you liked French music. So I guess you felt you was a little out of place if you were a Cajun-music lover, but I always did like it. The girls liked classical music because it was more dignified, but just about all the boys was taking to country, we liked country music and French music. The girls liked 'Harbor Lights,' possibly some of your Patti Page, they had to pick a certain music.

"I was heavily influenced by the cowboy movies. In the movies there was Gene Autry which would play the guitar and sing, and Roy Rogers, Tex Ritter. The great thing you wanted for Christmas was a holster with a gun, a cowboy hat, and play cowboys. Then when you got a little bit older you could have a horse. Boy, when you had a horse you were just like one of the cowboys in the movies. We would ride our horses into town, watch the movies, and pretend to be cowboys on the way home! Through the cowboys I really fell in love with the guitar and would take an old cigar box with wires that I could rig up, make a guitar. What a horrible sound! Just pluck the string and sing along with it, which was a very poor way of somebody starting out.

"At first the music I was hearing was strictly on records. We didn't have no record player, no radio, but one of the neighbors had a gramophone and he had some records 'cause he was an accordion player. One of them that I do remember by hearing him talk about was Amadie Ardoin. Later on I started hearing about Joe Falcon on old 78 rpm records. As time went on we were exposed I guess a little bit more to music and people started getting radios. You'd hear some country music, there wasn't all that much. And then after a while there started being some Cajun bands that started broadcasting. I'm talking about somewhere around 1947, that's when I can remember KSIG in Crowley opening up, and KSLO in Opelousas. And they started promoting local talent, like Nathan Abshire was coming in— that was on one of the Lake Charles stations, he had an afternoon program from 3 to 3:30, something like that.

"I can remember back, probably around '53, the Continental Playboys, which consisted of Doug Kershaw on fiddle, Rusty on guitar, and Pee Wee on accordion. They were broadcasting in the afternoon on KSIG. Then on Saturday night KSIG started an amateur talent night, they had a KSIG Barn Dance and they would have local guys—there was Joe Werner, he played guitar and harmonica, his kid would sing along with him, they had a French band there by the name of Louis Spell [who recorded for Feature], accordion, guitar, and drums. There were others, they'd switch around. And we would walk over to the neighbors, which was probably a quarter of a mile down the road, and gather round the radio and listen to that. That was fantastic! You could get 'Grand Ole Opry' too. You'd just sit around, listen and talk, no drinking, people seemed to enjoy it. But you couldn't listen too long because you had battery radios. Batteries wouldn't last too long, so you were rationed to about how much you could listen. You picked your best programs!

"I can remember there was Aldus Roger, he had a band and he broadcast too. J. B. Fusilier, he had a program around 10 or 10:30 in the morning, it wasn't every day, and I can remember Lee Sonnier. Then you had Chuck Guillory and Papa Cairo, it was a kinda string band, wasn't too much Cajun. These guys were recognized as big stars, you had very little recording. There was another group from Lake Charles, Shuk Richard and Marie Falcon, she was a girl that played guitar and sang, she was good. And Austin Pitre came along and of course Shirley Bergeron with Alphee Bergeron and the Veteran Playboys, they were holding their own very successfully. Some of the dances I went to, too. I remember Lawrence Walker playing, I went to one dance that Iry LeJune played. I thought he was good, but he was just another French band, I really didn't know that much about him at the time. He had had that big record, 'Love Bridge Waltz,' I guess it made us take notice and pay attention to him because the guy had a record out and that was something at the time. I never did see any records sold at dances.

"And I started developing a liking for country music, too. Evidently I liked [almost] any kind of music, but there was a lot of classical music on the radio because all day long it was mostly classical, and that I didn't like. Now and then maybe you'd have a country program, Happy Fats would come on and have his fifteen-minute program, some of the other artists, but it was here and there. But I guess my biggest ambition was to be in the Cajun French, but we went more and more into country as I started listening to some of the country artists, Gene Autry, Roy Rogers. Back in 1949 Hank Williams started coming along and I really liked him, he was about the greatest. Some people would go back as far as Jimmie Rodgers, even Ernest Tubb at the time, but to me Hank Williams was my idol. I remember ordering his songbook through the mail, getting enough money, fifty cents for a songbook. And about that time I got my first guitar, a Gene Autry guitar, by selling packs of garden seed, you'd order forty packs and sell that at ten cents each, the money you'd get for that you'd send back to the company with an extra $4.25 in cash to get a guitar. That was a great thing, I had a guitar, man! Didn't know how to tune it, or anything. Very cheap and not a bad guitar. But how can you learn when you're not even tuned? Everything was the hard way, I never had it that easy, nobody to show me.

"I just kept up with Hank Williams a whole lot, he had a radio program in the morning, I listened to him, he kept getting more and more popular. Then he died, but I have always been a good fan of his, I always thought he was great. His writing was terrific and I liked his singing. I never collected records because I didn't have a record player—I collected autographed pictures of cowboy stars given away over radio. Also we had no TV. It started coming in in the fifties.

"In 1953, when I finished school, I went into the service, Korea. My plans on coming back were for getting into country music, because to me that was the thing. Because before that we had kind of played around, we'd get together and play around house parties and stuff."

On his return from Korea, Lee found to his horror that country music had been devastated by rock 'n' roll: "Well, I was kinda down, like with no direction what to go. So I went to school awhile, got a job, but I wasn't happy because I wanted to be a part in the music business. So it went on two or three years, so I decided well, I don't know if I can fit in that type of music, but maybe I could be a disc jockey. So I applied to go to school in Chicago for three months and be a disc jockey, but before I went I talked with different people, they all advised me not to get involved in radio because there wasn't no money. If you were exceptionally good, you could make it, but you had to be good. Possibly I would never have been that good, so I reneged on it, didn't go. So I started going out to listen to the bands, started kinda understanding and liking the rhythm and blues and rock 'n' roll. I think rhythm and blues was what I liked the most because rhythm and blues has a trace of country, only it's done more bluesy and with different instrumentation. . . . We heard Jimmy Reed, Lightnin' Slim, anything with guitar always fascinated me. Rock 'n' roll, I can remember Rod Bernard going rock, he had his little group, the Twisters, then there was Jivin' Gene, Gene Terry and the Downbeats, Cookie—that was a big group around at the time. Then '58, '59, you had Elton Anderson, Phil Phillips's 'Sea Of Love' a million seller, then Rod Bernard came along, he emerged with 'This Should Go On Forever' which shot him up, a big deal for him, Guitar Gable, Guitar Jr.

"Somewhere in 1959, one night I was sitting in the club listening to some band from around Ville Platte, Prince Charles, and decided, 'Why can't I go into the record business and produce these guys?' I was starting to understand the music and taking a liking to it. Go into the record business. Well, it stayed in my mind, a few weeks later I was in another place, the same thing, listening to the band. I started laying out my plans and everything, getting ready for it. One day I started talking to Shirley Bergeron, who was playing in a French band at the time with his father, Alphee. I knew that he had done some recording but had never been released. Thinking he was familiar then to some extent with the recording business, I talked with him. He said, 'Yes, I'll take you to somebody that can tell you something about the business, the people who I recorded for, they can tell you all you want to know, I don't know that much.' He also told me, 'If you want to go in the business, we got something we'd like to record, we get an odd request for it, I think it could be a good record.'

"So we ended up in Crowley, talked with Jay Miller. I can recall he asked me what type of work I do.

" 'I work in an office, do bookwork.'

"He said, 'You'd better stick to that! You make a living, otherwise you're gonna starve, maybe, the other way.'

" 'Well, possibly so, but I still think I wanta go in the record business.'

" 'Well,' he said, 'whatever you want, if you decide to go into it, we got a studio and we'd be very glad to have you record with us.'

"So I asked him how much it was—twenty-five dollars an hour—what the details were about it, how to put out the records and everything. 'Y'all come on over!' We set it up and recorded, he processed sending in the tapes and everything, got my records, 'J'ai Fait Mon Ede'e' by Shirley Bergeron with his father, Alphee Bergeron and the Veteran Playboys. We were all very excited, started distributing the record, the record did good. We had a hit record, very encouraging, keep on!"

Accomplished steel guitarist Shirley Bergeron was born in 1933 and raised in the remote Point Noir area of Church Point, where tiny Cajun farm holdings dot the flat, open landscape. After joining his father's Veteran Playboys band, Shirley became one of the most popular local musicians. Like Dewey Balfa he can remember playing dances every night of the week in the late forties; he also broadcast regularly over radio KSLO Opelousas. Times were good, soldiers were returning to Acadiana with money, and the farmers were all doing well. But during the rock 'n' roll era, his dance dates suddenly dwindled to Saturday nights only.

Shirley's musical fortunes were revived in 1960 when he recorded "J'ai Fait Mon Ede'e" for his former school friend Lee Lavergne. To waltz-time accompaniment led by father Alphee's old-style accordion and his own steel guitar, Shirley sang of his decision to leave the family home:

J'ai fait mon idée, en faisant mon paquet,	I made up my mind in packing my bag,
Ma bonne vieille maman elle s'a mise à pleurer.	My dear old mother started crying.
Elle m'a dit, "Quoi faire t'es comme ça?"	She said to me, "Why are you doing that?"
Moi, j'ai répondu, "Moi, j'ai fait mon idée."	I replied, "I've made up my mind."

After consolidating his position with follow-ups "Chez Tanie" and "French Rocking Boogie," Shirley received acclaim for his debut album, "The Sounds Of Cajun Music." The LP was also Lanor's first. In his sleeve notes Lee Lavergne reminded listeners of the basic qualities of Cajun music: "The contents of Cajun-French Music all bear a realistic view of everyday life; may it be happy songs, sad songs, comedy songs, or folk songs. In our lives there are often tragic overtones . . . thus from these incidents are derived the material for most of the sad songs. Though the arrangements of the song material may be simple, the music speaks directly from the heart and accounts for a true view of life and love. I guess sincerity is what we like best about our Cajun singers. They mean and feel what they sing so much that we know this sincerity and feel it with them. They are in some respects 'song poets' putting the people, places, life, and times that they know into music."

Unfortunately Shirley's second album, "Cajun Style Music," sold disappointingly. Due to family commitments he has retired from music and is now an insurance salesman, but he is frequently hounded by friends to make a comeback. Certainly Cajun music would benefit from his early reappearance. In October 1980 everyone in Church Point was saddened by the death of Shirley's father Alphee. He was born in 1912 on the small family farm in Point Noir and by 1924 he was playing the accordion at local house parties and at dance halls like the Dupre LeBleu in Marais Bouleur and the Alcee Richard in Grand Marais. Through the years he performed with many famous musicians, including Nathan Abshire, Amadie Ardoin, Joseph Falcon, Happy Fats, Mayuse Lafleur, and Lawrence Walker, and broadcast with the Veteran Playboys over KSIG Crowley, KSLO Opelousas, KEUN Eunice, and KVPI Ville Platte. After recording for Brunswick in the pre–World War II era, he had just one single—"Chinaball Special"/"Eunice Waltz" for Feature—before he cut the Lanor sessions with his son. Happily, his beautifully archaic accordion style, sonorous and melodic, is preserved for all time on those Lanor albums.

"And so I was trying to make my rounds with Shirley Bergeron's 'J'ai Fait Mon Ede'e,' " explains Lee, "trying to place the record in different places, jukeboxes, stores, trying to find out who was in the business, who you could work with. Then I ran into a guy from Gueydan, Dizzy Richard, that managed a rock group, Elton [Hargrave] and the Rocking Eltradors. I agreed to listen to his group with possibilities of recording, and sure 'nough I recorded them with 'One Day.' And here was my second record, in the rock 'n' roll field. I was making advancements, huh? I kept getting more involved into rock. Then I met a guy in Opelousas, name of Lloyd Reynaud, which was playing with a group called Duke Stevens and the Sputnicks. He presented me with a tape of a song I took a liking to, "Nobody Knows," and I decided to record it. We recorded it, released it, didn't do too much."

In fact Lee issued two versions of "Nobody Knows," one recorded at Goldband that lacked "bottom" or rhythmic depth (a common fault with Eddie Shuler's productions at the time), the other at Jay Miller's. The contrast in sound was striking; the Crowley version was clearly superior. But through recording at Goldband, Lee struck up a friendship with Wayne Shuler which was to be of mutual benefit.

"At the same time as Duke Stevens," Lee recalls, "I had put out a record by Bill Matte, which was Shirley's uncle, called 'Parlez-Vous L'Francais.' We were working on it, but I was working the avenues of the Cajun-French market and it wasn't doing too much—it really wasn't considered a Cajun-French record, more rock 'n' roll. But I went down to New Orleans to promote Duke Stevens's record and I happened to take along a copy of the Bill Matte record, too. I got to New Orleans, I got in with Wayne Shuler and I played a DJ the Duke Stevens record. 'So-so.' I said I have this other record over here, he puts it on, he flipped over it. He said, 'That thing could be a hit record, let's go down and find a distributor for you!' So we went down, got it all lined up with the distributors, started getting airplay on the thing. It turned out to be a good-selling record. We sold several thousand copies." The catchy "Parlez-Vous L'Francais" was heavily influenced by Cleveland Crochet's "Sugar Bee"; the unlikely combination of Bill Matte's Cajun accordion and blues guitar (by a player from Lightnin' Slim's band) was particularly effective.

"Wayne and I's affiliation got stronger," says Lee, "we got to be friends and inclined to get involved with the business. So at about the same time he had put out a record on Elton Anderson that was out on Mercury Records, 'Please Accept My Love' [the Jimmy Wilson song], but it didn't do much and Mercury dropped him. So Wayne did a session, cut four sides on him, he had hopes of presenting it to Mercury, but they turned it down. So he approached me and asked me if I would be interested in working together, forming a partnership and putting out Elton Anderson. I said, 'Oh, yeah, fine,' because to me that was a big jump, I'd never had a fairly well known artist like Elton was known, he had had 'Secret Of Love' before, and 'Shed So Many Tears.' So out of that session we released the two records that we had, got some action on it, then we had put out what we had. So we needed to do more, we started scanning through material and I liked one record we were playing one day called 'Life Problem' by King Karl, I said let's do that. So we learned up 'Life Problem' with some other songs, we did a session in New Orleans, released 'Life Problem,' and it became an immediate smash hit. We ended up leasing it to Capitol Records, which I always felt they didn't do too much of a job with it, and I think we lost a fantastic record at the time. Should we have gone with somebody else, we had the opportunity of going with United Artists and I think Columbia also, I think possibly we would have emerged a lot better.

"We released another one, 'Shed So Many Tears,' which we redid, it didn't do that much, then Capitol dropped us. We went on our own again and recorded Elton some more, put out more records which were mediocre sellers, they sold just so much, then Elton skipped the country. Wayne and I had nothing left to work with and we drifted apart."

Meanwhile Lee had established a good working relationship with Lloyd Reynaud. Besides Duke Stevens, Reynaud brought Lanor Little Victor (Phillips), "a singer–piano player from Lafayette, did some stuff like Little Richard, had potential but didn't seem to have no interest in bettering himself," and Charles Tyler, a guitar player from Opelousas. Lee experimented with recording Tyler in the swamp-blues style at Crowley, with Jay Miller's session men providing an authentic Excello sound. Credited to Drifting Charles, "Drifting Cloud" was a pleasing excursion, but it was clear that in 1963 the blues was no longer a marketable commodity in Louisiana. Initially sales barely touched three figures, although they have been boosted considerably by subsequent European interest. Tyler's later New Orleans R&B recordings, good as they were, fared no better.

Manager Lloyd Reynaud, a distant cousin of Clifton Chenier's, had been operating on the fringe of the Louisiana blues scene since playing drums with Lonesome Sundown at the Domino Lounge in Eunice and sitting in on Sundown's first record, "Lost Without Love." Before linking up with Lee Lavergne he owned the Reynaud label and had worthwhile releases by Schoolboy Cleve and Roscoe Chenier. When the Lanor arrangement did not produce any hits, he went to work as an electrician at NASA in Houston.

In the early days of Lanor Lavergne was producing most of his records at the well-established studios of J. D. Miller in Crowley and Cosimo Matassa in New Orleans. "As a producer my object was to produce a *hit*," he states emphatically. "I listened very much for the proper combination of feeling, sound and the beat, I tried to get the proper blend between the artists and the musicians and the material of the song. I listen until I can feel everything is falling into place, I feel it's just like you bake a cake. You put the different ingredients which you gotta shake 'em up and stir 'em real good until you got that proper blend. Without that it's not a good cake.

"At J. D.'s, the old studio was very good, it goes back to three tracks and in those days with three tracks you could get a hell of a sound. The property was sold to the bank for a parking lot and he had to move. So he figures, well, instead of spending money buying property, he had enough property by his house and built right there. He built the studio in his home, that was about 1961, but never was able to achieve the sound that he wanted, he never had the sound he had in the old studio. Then he had his latest studio. I used Cosimo's because at the time he was getting a good sound, a lot of hits were coming out of there. One time I was going down to New Orleans to line up a distributor for my label and somehow or another I drifted over to Cosimo's to see what the studio sounded like. Met the guy, he was nice and everything, give me a rate sheet, I studied that and I had the feeling I was going to get what I wanted.

"Then I was scrounging around to find another artist to work with. One day I was in Lake Arthur, I ran into the same guy, Dizzy Richard, which had presented me with my first rock 'n' roll record, he told me he was still in the business. This was about in '64 or '65. He told me he had a band, he had an artist, listen to him, I think he's good. So I made arrangements to listen to him one Friday night at the River Club in Mermentau and I liked the guy, Charles Domingue. Boy, that's a long name, it's gonna be hard to remember. I baptized him Charles Mann, that was the birth of a star and a stage name. We went into the studio to record, but things didn't come out too good, people told me I was wasting my time. The band wasn't good, the singer wasn't good—they didn't like the singer, the guy can't sing. But I put out one record from that session, it was terrible, but I got reaction from it, in Lake Charles where the singer was from. At the time he didn't have any name, he just went by the name of the group, the Eltradors. But I was quite impressed by such a bad record that people would buy. We sold a couple of hundred copies, which made you think. It was bad! So I decided I was going to take him, we worked a lot harder to try to find a good band to back him up.

"That's when I called Huey Meaux in Houston, at various times I had given favors to Huey, different things, we had got to be good friends. 'I got a guy but I gotta have some help, I need to get a good studio sound and I need good musicians.' He said, 'Brother, you got it, you come over and don't worry about a thing. If it don't turn out right, we'll burn the tapes, won't look back, I won't charge you nothing, we'll go get drunk!'

"So I went, we cut a session, we were knocked out, Charles and I were very happy. We came back, put a record out, smash hit, 'Keep Your Arms Around Me.' We were on our way, and explored the possibilities of making it again. That record did very well for us in Louisiana and parts of Texas, not anywheres else, but we were happy, we had a territorial hit and it was big."

"Keep Your Arms Around Me" was a powerful record. Mann displayed an intense vocal style, while the bluesy, sax-led band used an arrangement similar to that on Elton Anderson's "Life Problem." The song, originally recorded by soul star Otis Redding, explored the aftermath of a bad hangover:

When I woke up this morning, oh I had an aching head,
The pain was so great, oh I almost fell out of bed.
Then you put your arms around me,
Then you kissed me three times,
And in a matter of seconds, I never felt so fine.

"After that we put out our second release which didn't do quite as good, it's always hard to follow up that first one," Lee says. "Charles was born and raised in Iowa, just outside of Lake Charles. He's a Cajun boy, his parents are Cajun, he has a brother that plays in a Cajun band. Charles's biggest record was 'Red Red Wine.' It was No. 1 in Lafayette and in Lake Charles with the help of disc jockey Buddy King. I tried unsuccessfully to break the record in Atlanta, Georgia, and when I told a local DJ it was a hit in Louisiana he said, 'Well, it would be, wouldn't it?' I was very proud that 'You're No Longer Mine' was played on 'American Bandstand,' it was quite a phenomenon for a little Cajun country boy like me. I remember that one night I lay down on the floor with a piece of paper and wrote the song. To think that some time later I was laying down on the same floor watching TV and I hear it played on 'American Bandstand'! It's a funny feeling.

"Charles's audience is like Johnnie Allan's, people are dedicated to each one; personally knowing Johnnie and being that close to Charles I think the reaction is pretty much the same. They are true individuals, both dedicated to their music, good entertainers, fantastic voices. They are sincere and honest in what they're doing and I think they have a high respect for their audiences and they have built up strong fans wherever they have played. I would say they could be classed in very much the same respect."

In the late sixties Lavergne tried to break into the southern soul markets. But he was unable to conjure up a single hit despite signing talented Georgia-based singers Willie Mallory (a superb Sam Cooke stylist), Ella Brown, and Hugh Boynton. Lee fared no better with Phil Phillips of "Sea Of Love" fame. Yet the Lanor boss was using the best musicians and recording at top studios like Fame in Muscle Shoals, Alabama, and Capricorn in Macon, Georgia.

During the seventies Lee put Lanor into cold storage, left his regular job, set up the impressive Sound Center music store in Church Point, and opened a second shop in nearby Rayne. He maintained his links with Charles Mann, and in 1980 released the pleasing "She's Walking Towards Me" album which showed the singer at his professional best (although the material could have been geared more to South Louisiana). A year later Lee decided to build a small studio at the rear of his Church Point store in order to pursue his recording ambitions. The first artists he recorded there were Cajun veterans Aldus Roger, Leroy Broussard, and Joe Bonsall.

How does Lee see his brave little label to date? "Lanor has been a lot of hard work, disappointing very much at times, like everybody goes through. You build up hopes and find yourself flat on your ass with disappointment! It's been an experience looking back, I don't regret it in the least bit. I have met wonderful guys, I've been up there with some of the top artists. I can sit back and say I knew him, I shook hands with him. I knew some that were nothing at the time, I had no idea that they would develop into the superstars they are today. It's been twenty years, never had million sellers, but we've had some hits to our credit, which have been a shot in the arm to keep going. Your hopes never die out because you always have something to keep you going. . . ."

The La Louisianne label was founded in 1959 by Carol Rachou, who owned the Music Mart store in Lafayette. Rachou first ventured into the recording business in 1956 when he formed the Jazz-Mar label; an early signing was a local swamp-pop act, Bobby Webb and the Jets. Promotion and distribution have always been a problem, but Carol has managed to build up a reliable catalog of Cajun and comedy albums by such recognized artists as Nathan Abshire, Vin Bruce, Aldus Roger, and humorist Bud Fletcher.

"Carol Rachou was a musician and he played in a couple of dance bands in the early fifties," says Rod Bernard. "He got interested in authentic Cajun-French music, but he didn't play that type of music, he played in a big band or the early rock 'n' roll things. He built this studio and formed his own record company here in town. At the time he had a music store, the Music Mart, but he didn't sell records so much as he sold stereo equipment, he had Magnavox stereos and television sets. He had a small record rack in it but it never was a big record store. Carol never produced any really big hit records on his label. However, the Dale and Grace song 'I'm Leaving It Up To You' was recorded in his studio, and I think he was the engineer, probably A&R'd the session. But it was not on his label and therefore he never got credit for it."

Still, Floyd Soileau can recall Rachou doing well with "Kidnapper" by Jewel and the Rubies in the mid-sixties: "That was a black rhythm and blues type of number, and I think he had leased it to Roulette at one time. But other than that he didn't have a Rod Bernard or Johnnie Allan type of artist, he didn't record too much of that type of music. I don't know why, but maybe it was the same reason that I didn't record too much black music, maybe everything was taken. He had Eddy Raven, Eddy turned out to be a terrific writer, he didn't sell records too much, he's still writing. He's under contract to Acuff-Rose, he's had many stars do a lot of his stuff."

In 1965 Little Bob and the Lollipops did make some impact with "I Got Loaded" and "Nobody But You," two old R&B favorites done in the popular southern soul style of the day. Both songs were featured in the warmly satisfying La Louisianne album "Nobody But You," which included Bob's versions of the latest soul hits. In the seven-piece band was the great tenor saxist John Hart.

Camille Bob was born in Arnaudville in 1937 and began playing drums as a teen-ager. He first recorded with Good Rockin' Bob for Goldband in 1957; a year later he formed his own band, which became popular at clubs and fraternity dances in the Lafayette area. In 1967 he left La Louisianne to record for Jin, and as "Lil Bob" he had another good album, "Sweet Soul Swinger." There followed many years in a recording wilderness, relieved only by isolated singles on Whit and Soul Unlimited. Finally, in 1980, he reemerged with a soulful local hit, "Harry Hippie," on Mark Miller's Master-Trak label.

At live performances Lil Bob performs almost any type of tune in his smooth soul style. When enthused he will reveal his South Louisiana roots by happily singing swamp-pop classics like "Mathilda," "Sea Of Love," "Rainin' In My Heart," and "No Good Woman," interspersed with a choice selection of New Orleans R&B favorites. With his well-rehearsed band (which sometimes includes Guitar Gable) Lil Bob always puts on an entertaining show. Because of his light, almost white vocals, he is one of the most consistently popular black singers in Acadiana, but his lack of original material will always be a handicap to wider stardom.

In 1967 Carol Rachou flirted with the blues when he released "Change My Way Of Livin' "/"Getting Late In The Evenin' " by Raful Neal, the Baton Rouge harmonica player. With horns and a lively bass rhythm, the production was well up to standard—Rachou always obtained a good sound—but like so many blues singles of the time it was a commercial disaster.

Raful Neal was influenced by harmonica stars Slim Harpo and Little Walter, whom he once witnessed in the fifties at a big Baton Rouge blues spot, the Temple Room. Neal made his recording debut in 1959 with a cover of Katie Webster's "On The Sunny Side Of Love" for Peacock. The session came about when he traveled to Houston with deejay Lester Foster to see the Junior Parker/Bobby Bland Blues Consolidated Show at Don Robey's Bronze Peacock nightclub. At Junior Parker's invitation, Raful was subsequently recorded with Parker's band, but his version of "On The Sunny Side Of Love" was withdrawn after a copyright dispute. Neal missed out on the Jay Miller sessions and the heyday of the Louisiana swamp-blues. After the La Louisianne date he recorded two pleasant singles for Lionel Whitfield's Baton Rouge–based Whit label, which was hitting with the soul-blues of Bobby Powell; more recently he made "Inflation Time"/"Tomorrow Night" for Tic Toc. Raful is now playing regularly with his sons' band, the Neal Brothers.

Meanwhile Carol Rachou had wisely followed the trend into albums. Apart from the occasional commercial LP by Little Bob and the Lollipops, the Shondels, and the Swing Kings he set his sights firmly on the specialist comedy and Cajun markets. His most consistent seller was Bud Fletcher, whose bawdy humor was heard on ten albums. Like his main rival, Justin Wilson, Fletcher is not full-fledged Cajun; both men have been accused of demeaning the Cajun ethos with their Cajun-English sketches. According to Revon Reed, himself a French Cajun humorist, "Among elite groups of people they're not very popular, but ordinary Cajuns like them." Reed believes that the delivery of a Cajun humorist is often more amusing than the story, which may last from five minutes to half an hour. "Cajuns love to put each other down," he says, "just for the hell of it. Of course, they'll put down any other ethnic group too!"

"Bud Fletcher is English-with-a-Cajun-accent-type comedy," explains Floyd Soileau. "He became more popular for his risqué stuff, his 'Outhouse' series was quite popular—some of them were really rough, they really were. Justin Wilson never did anything like that on record and he got some national exposure, which Bud didn't, he [Wilson] appeared once on an Ed Sullivan short spot. But these men weren't true Cajuns like Marion Marcotte. However, Marion's Swallow records never got out of Louisiana—a few sold in France—and unless you could speak French or else you've been in Cajun country and can understand some of the localisms we use, you cannot appreciate his down-to-earth humor. It's very unique and I'm proud to have it on record, it's something that had to be done."

The rest of the La Louisianne catalog is devoted to Cajun music: the Cajun-country sounds of Vin Bruce, L. J. Foret, Doc Guidry, Jimmy Newman, Eddy Raven, and Rufus Thibodeaux; the traditional accordion music of Ambrose Thibodeaux; and the mainstream stylings of Nathan

Abshire, Blackie Forestier, Lawrence Walker—and Aldus Roger. One of the most respected and precise accordionists in Acadiana, Aldus Roger became a firm local favorite through hosting the "Aldus Roger and the Lafayette Playboys" TV show over KLFY Lafayette from 1955 until 1970. His three La Louisianne albums, which feature the sterling vocals of drummer Fernice "Man" Abshire and steel guitarist Phillip Alleman, show modern Cajun music at its entertaining, energetic best.

Aldus's pedigree as a Cajun musician is impeccable. The son of an accordionist, he was born in Carencro, a few miles from Lafayette, in 1916. He started playing the accordion when he was eight years old, often hiding behind the barn to practice. In 1931 he performed at his first dance, and in the early years he played such numbers as "Johnny Can't Dance," "Lovesick Waltz," and "Over The Waves."

Aldus thinks his career peaked in the sixties. Besides the TV show, he had "my best band, had lots of bookings, and best-selling records." Also, in 1962 he was chosen to represent the state of Louisiana in the National Folklore Festival in Washington, D.C. His biggest-selling record was the first La Louisianne album, "Aldus Roger Plays The French Music Of South Louisiana." Prior to this 1965 release, Aldus had several popular singles, including "Diga Ding Ding Dong" (Goldband), "Lafayette Playboy's Waltz," and "Family Waltz" (Cajun Classics); he also had a minor hit with "Louisiana Waltz" for La Louisianne. For a while he quit performing because of personal problems, but he is now back in action again. "He kinda went off the deep end," says Johnnie Allan, "but he's in the groove again. He's got his band back together and he's doing real good. You can say he's very well known around here, very well liked. Aldus has had several albums out and numerous singles—as far as records as big as Joe Falcon's I would say no, but he had a steady market. Anything he came up with sold good each time, but there wasn't a big, big splash. By a steady market I mean anytime somebody records something you know for sure he's gonna sell 10,000 copies."

La Louisianne's activities slowed down in 1979 after Carol Rachou became seriously ill. Looking back, the highlight for the label has undoubtedly been Jimmy Newman's 45 rpm hit "Lache Pas La Patate." Overall, Rachou deserves much gratitude and respect for keeping the Cajun flag flying through good times and bad.

In terms of size Montel, Lanor, and La Louisianne—like all the South Louisiana labels—were real minnows in the national pond. But there were even smaller outfits in Cajun country trying to tap the wealth of local talent, labels like Drew-Blan, Richland, L. K., and Sportsman.

Record-store owner and jukebox operator Andrew Blanco formed the Drew-Blan label in 1961. Working from the oil and shrimping port of Morgan City, he was fortunate in having a regional hit with his first release, Jerry Raines's "Our Teenage Love," a graphic swamp-pop ballad that was later leased to Mercury. Blanco then arranged further, fruitless sessions in New Orleans with Jerry Raines, Jay Nelson, and Peter Buck. "While Drew-Blan was enjoying the Jerry Raines record it did fairly well," says Floyd Soileau, "but then it hit upon a few duds. And I guess that discouraged him, because that can be very discouraging—getting a whole lot of records back and filling up a warehouse, and not knowing what to do with them after that."

Richland Records, also based in Morgan City, had one of the best Little Richard R&B imitations around with the storming "Papa Lou And Gran" by Little Victor, who later recorded for Lanor. Another notable release was veteran Gene Rodrigue's equally energetic "Little Cajun Girl," which was reissued by Floyd Soileau with credits to Gene King.

L. K. Records, located in the peaceful and historic town of St. Martinville on Bayou Teche, was set up in 1958 to promote the recordings of teen-age prodigy T. K. Hulin. "There was a small studio in St. Martinville run by a guy named Robert Thibodeaux," says Johnnie Allan, "he wrote a lot of T. K.'s early songs. I think T. K.'s daddy, Elie, kind of took the reins and would distribute the records."

Alton James "T. K." Hulin's first release, "Many Nites," was an unexceptional swamp-pop tune with sparse backing from the Lonely Knights. After several singles the perseverance of Elie Hulin and Robert Thibodeaux paid off when T. K.'s relaxed "I'm Not A Fool Anymore" slipped into the *Billboard Hot 100* at No. 92 in the late summer of 1963. The important push came from the ubiquitous Huey Meaux, who arranged a distribution deal with Smash. Despite the chart entry, T. K.'s best-known record from this period is the tear-jerking "Graduation Night (As You Pass Me By)," a perennial favorite among local high-school students written by Robert Thibodeaux. During the seventies T. K. recorded country music for the Lafayette labels La Louisianne and Boo-Ray (which also had Coteau and Jay Randall) without repeating his earlier L. K. success. Over the years he has developed a slick stage act in which he tends to feature the latest national hits rather than the songs of his heritage.

The car drive from St. Martinville to Henderson is scenically pleasant, with the small towns of Parks and Breaux Bridge breaking up the lush green expanse of the sugarcane farms. Henderson, famous for its seafood restaurants, is the home of Dunice Theriot's personality label, Sportsman. Dunice is a Cajun-country singer who is a keen fisherman and hunter, and he has been recording mainly for Sportsman since the early sixties; the releases range from the heartfelt Cajun sounds of "Henderson Waltz" to the equally heartfelt swamp-pop of "I Lost My First Love." His tiny label is a perfect example of the gutsy South Louisiana "small label" philosophy—and of the indomitable spirit and flexibility of Cajun music.

20

"OK, hit me a lick, a South Louisiana lick!"

The meteoric rise of the Beatles in 1964 precipitated the end of a musical era in the United States. It was a time when youth asserted itself dramatically in the music business; the antiauthoritarianism of the fifties was tame in comparison. Rock 'n' roll was transformed into rock, and much of the innocence and charm of the earlier epoch disappeared overnight.

South Louisiana was not sheltered from the winds of change. Although the record men and Cajun musicians tended to stick to the music they knew and loved (thereby paving the way for the Cajun revival of the seventies), the younger artists felt that if they wished to retain their popularity it was necessary to set aside their regionalized music in favor of the latest national sounds. Suddenly the swamp-pop hits of the early sixties like "Secret Of Love," "I'm A Fool To Care," "Got You On My Mind," and "I'm Leaving It Up To You"; the Cajun rock 'n' roll of "Sugar Bee"; and the swamp-blues of "Rainin' In My Heart" had all become museum pieces. More than anything, the ascent of the Beatles underlined the awesome power of the modern communications media.

"The Beatles affected everything in the States," affirms Floyd Soileau, "whole bands didn't know what to do anymore. They didn't want to have to play the music, but if they didn't they weren't on the in thing. Sooner or later they found out that if they wanted to keep their audience and continue, they just had to adapt to it. So it didn't take much time for everybody to join the Beatlemania craze."

First came British groups, then American groups, all seeking rock superstardom. South Louisiana was further away than ever from Los Angeles and New York. Reeling from the effects of this musical revolution, the majority of the swamp-pop artists finally took refuge under the cozy umbrella of Nashville country music; they also fulfilled audience requests for golden oldies and performed the mandatory pop hits. But in 1975 Freddy Fender gave the bayou singers fresh heart with two successive national hits, "Before The Next Teardrop Falls" and "Wasted Days And Wasted Nights." Although Freddy was a Chicano from Texas marketed as a country artist, much of his formative career was spent in South

281

Louisiana; spiritually Fender's music was from the Louisiana swamps (swamp-pop was very popular with Tex-Mex bands).

Freddy's triumph was masterminded by Huey Meaux, who had been bustling away in the music business at the national level since his involvement with the small Louisiana labels during the early sixties. After the hits by Barbara Lynn, Big Sambo, and Sunny and the Sunliners, Huey had notched a regional success with Clarence "Frogman" Henry's splendid "Cajun Honey" (Parrot). Then in 1965 he had two Top Twenty smashes, "She's About A Mover" by the Sir Douglas Quintet (Tribe)— Huey calls it a "Mexican-Cajun sound with a Beatles flavor!"—and "Treat Her Right" by Roy Head and the Traits (Backbeat). Meaux's biggest discovery was Texas pop balladeer B. J. Thomas.

By 1967 Huey had accumulated a veritable conglomeration of labels, including Som, Eric, Tribe, Parrot, Crazy Cajun, Tear Drop, and Jet Stream. There was South Louisiana swamp-pop music from Johnnie Allan, Joe Barry, Jimmy Donley, and Warren Storm; Texas music from Link Davis, Big Walter Price, and T-Bone Walker; Cajun music from Joe Bonsall, Amidie Breaux, Pappy "Te Tan" Meaux, and the Rambling Aces; and zydeco from Clifton Chenier.

Huey had a natural touch in the studio, as Rod Bernard testifies, smiling at the memory: "The amazing thing about Huey Meaux is that he's produced records in every kind of music, and he can't read music. But he gets in a studio and he'll tell a piano player, he says, 'Hit and do something with that money-makin' octave!' and he talks about the triplets *da dada*... and he tells them what to do. He tells the guitar player, 'OK hit me a lick, a South Louisiana lick!' and then he'll say, 'I don't like that, try something else!' He'll try something else and then he'll say, 'Look, play that the first time and the second time play the second thing, do it halfway through and do it a little faster.' And that's how Huey A&Rs a session, that's how he tells everybody what to do. And the guy just gets one after another, he continues to have hit records."

In the early days Huey booked Cosimo's Studio in New Orleans; later he used facilities in Pasadena, Texas, and Clinton, Mississippi. Then he purchased Bill Quinn's old Gold Star studios in Houston, which he renamed the Sugar Hill studios. Shortly after this acquisition Freddy Fender's hits started rolling; they could not have been better timed.

Freddy was born Baldemar G. Huerta in 1936 in the South Texas valley border town of San Benito. He spoke only Spanish until his teens. Like many poor Mexican-Americans he followed the harvests to earn a living, working beets in Michigan, bailing hay and gathering tomatoes in Indiana, picking cotton in Arkansas. Occasionally he was provided with shelter, but usually he lived out of a truck, sleeping in the open air. In 1957, after three years in the Marines, Freddy started making Spanish-Chicano records for the local Texas market. His break came when he cut "Holy One"/"Mean Woman" in a heavy R&B style for Wayne Duncan in a Brownsville, Texas, radio station; the record attracted some attention when leased to Imperial. The swamp-pop follow-up "Wasted Days, Wasted Nights" (the original version of the song) did even better, climbing to No. 82 on *The Cash Box Top 100* in July 1960. But its progress was halted abruptly when news leaked out that Freddy had been busted for possessing marijuana while appearing in Baton Rouge on May 13. He was sentenced to five years in Angola State Penitentiary.

Producer Wayne Duncan recalled this traumatic period in his excellent sleeve notes to the GRT album "Since I Met You Baby": "I first met Freddy Fender in 1958 when his name was Baldemar Huerta. I was running a nightclub in South Texas and I hired 'Baldie,' as he was called, to sing in the club. People had trouble pronouncing and even remembering the name and so I gave him the stage name of Freddy Fender.

"It didn't take long for Freddy to gain local popularity at the club and we tried to get him a recording contract to see if we could get him some national attention. However no one wanted to take a chance and we finally recorded him ourselves and released 'Holy One' on the Duncan label. It became a hit in Baton Rouge and spread in popularity to New Orleans. All of a sudden most of the national record labels wanted to lease Freddy's record from us and I decided to make a deal with Imperial Records. But 'Holy One' was not the national hit we had hoped for, so Imperial released 'Wasted Days, Wasted Nights,' which was a minor hit.

"Imperial asked us to fly to Los Angeles to sign Freddy to an exclusive recording contract, but before we left something happened that changed both Freddy's life and my life. He was arrested for possession of marijuana and in 1960 that was a very serious offense. I am convinced Freddy was framed on the charges, but I got Freddy out of jail on $20,000 bail and we flew to Los Angeles. Suddenly the news of Freddy's arrest hit the wire services and was in newspapers across the country. By the time we got in to see Lew Chudd of Imperial Records the story of Freddy's arrest had killed 'Wasted Days, Wasted Nights.' Imperial said there was nothing they could do and they wished us success with Freddy at whatever record company he might go to next.

"While Freddy was out on bail we recorded a great number of tunes and we finally signed a contract with Chess Records out of Chicago and they released 'You're Something Else For Me' on Argo. But the story of Freddy's arrest was still in the minds of the disc jockeys and the public, and so nothing happened. We even tried releasing his records under other names, like Scotty Wayne, but without success. You might say that Freddy was a marked man."

Freddy's recordings from this period were ravishing R&B and swamp-pop, highlighted by a compelling version of Buck Rogers's "Crazy Baby" (Duncan), a magnificent "Wild Side Of Life" (Duncan), and a rollicking "I'm Gonna Leave" (Talent Scout) as Scotty Wayne. In 1962 an informal session was arranged in Angola, and a single later appeared on Goldband.

"I worked very hard to try to secure his release," Duncan continued, "though it took a long time. Eventually the Louisiana governor, Jimmie Davis, helped us get Freddy out, but three years of his life had been wasted and one of the conditions of his parole was that he get out of the entertainment business! For a while Freddy held various jobs and finally got back to singing in Louisiana and Texas."

"My time in prison was hard," recalled Freddy in the sleeve notes to his "Before The Next Teardrop Falls" ABC/Dot album. "But music made it better. I can remember when my bass player and I (we were busted together) walked into Angola, carrying our guitar and bass instead of our clothes. Then every Saturday and Sunday we would play on the 'walk' for our fellow convicts. I even recorded an album of Chicano songs on a portable tape recorder at the prison. In 1963 I headed for home from prison on a Trailways bus, made some records for Norco in San Benito, but soon came back to Louisiana, singing at Papa Joe's on Bourbon Street in New Orleans until 1968. It was there I played music with cats such as Joe Barry, Joey Long, Skip Easterling and Aaron Neville."

The Papa Joe's period has now assumed legendary proportions. Joe Barry remembers it well: "When Freddy got out of the pen, he couldn't work nowheres and matter of fact it was in a little patio one evening, I'd see these two Mexicans strumming a guitar *Oh yeah, ya ya.* And that boy's voice rang in my ears, I said, 'That voice sounds familiar.' And he'd come, he'd laugh, he'd come around the table.

"He said, 'Hey man, how you doing?'

"I said, 'Who's this?'

"And he said, 'My name is Baldemar Huerta . . .'

"I said, 'I don't know *Baltimore Walter,* go play your guitar over there.'

"So he kept on laughing and I kept looking at him, he said, 'Freddy, man, Freddy Fender.'

"I said, '*Freddy,* when did you get out the joint?'

" 'Shh, shh, shh . . .' he said, 'I just got out, man, but I'm not supposed to be working, I'm on parole, so I gotta do this Mexican bit.'

"I said, 'Well, you're lucky you're Mexican doing it!'

"And I couldn't stand to see a talent like Freddy just playing a troubador. I said to Freddy, 'Why don't you come and work for me at Papa

Joe's?' I had Skip Easterling playing with me, Joey Long, we had about four or five recording artists on the whole thing playing at Papa Joe's. Which was a great thing because when I came out I hadn't played music in a while and the guy who owned Papa Joe's then, Angelo DeFordo, told me he couldn't afford a band. I said, 'Well, I tell you what, me and my guitar up there, if it goes you pay me, if it don't you don't. Free booze anyhow, right!'

"But we built it up and in a matter of months that place was jam-packed. As a matter of fact we'd start sometimes at one o'clock in the morning on a Saturday on to Sunday sometimes at two or three in the evening without stopping. And they were dancing on the bars and on the ceilings and everywhere, the street was full. We couldn't quit, I mean this thing was big. And then Freddy, we went to talk to the governor in the end and got a permit for him to work while he's on parole. 'Cause I said to him, 'The only thing this man has ever done is to play music for a living, this is his life. And then you deny him his right to work in the club. They ain't got no clubs where they don't sell booze and if he works in one you're gonna put him back in jail. He's done his time.' So finally they let him work, but they harassed him all the time. And it would make me very angry, almost put me in jail a couple of times—I got so angry I punched one or two of these cops. But they got to like him, Freddy is a very likable fellow, he's very easy to like. He's crazy! So he won their hearts over."

In 1969 Freddy returned home to the San Benito Valley, where he took a regular job as a mechanic and obtained a high-school diploma. He gave up music for a while, but in 1974 he recorded again for Huey Meaux. After taping several R&B songs, Freddy cut the ten-year-old Charlie Pride country weeper "Before The Next Teardrop Falls," which—sung partly in Spanish—shot to the top of all the charts when leased to ABC/Dot. The hit-making remake of "Wasted Days, Wasted Nights" was pure swamp-pop; the tune was inspired by "Mathilda," "Breaking Up Is Hard To Do," and other early South Louisiana classics.

All of a sudden Freddy Fender was the darling of the country-music business. The trade magazines loved his rags-to-riches story—even the prison sentence was romanticized—and his hit sequence continued with "Since I Met You Baby," "Secret Love," and "You'll Lose A Good Thing." ABC/Dot deluged the market with albums of variable quality, but "The Best Of Freddy Fender" was just that; there were brilliant versions of Lazy Lester's "Sugar Coated Love," Big Sambo's/Sir Douglas Quintet's "The Rains Came," and Cookie's "Mathilda" nestling alongside the hit singles. Freddy's debt to South Louisiana was acknowledged directly in the "Swamp Gold" album that included loving renditions of Jivin' Gene's "Breaking Up Is Hard To Do," T. K. Hulin's "Graduation Night," Jerry Raines's "Our Teenage Love," and Jimmy Donley's "Please Mr. Sandman."

Throughout 1976 and 1977 Freddy Fender was a superstar, a living hero to his underprivileged race. But the predatory instincts of his former record companies were aroused as they rushed in to reissue his old material in inferior packages. By the eighties the magic was wearing thin; Freddy seemed to be at odds with his country-and-western image, and he badly needed a hit in any field.

Although Freddy Fender's period of superstardom appears to have run its course, which means that Huey Meaux is also taking a breather, there is no doubt that his startling success gave an overdue boost to the South Louisiana swamp-pop singers. Artists such as Rod Bernard, Tommy McLain, Charles Mann, and Warren Storm began featuring more and more familiar South Louisiana songs in zestful live performances. Johnnie Allan's All-Star Show was another encouraging sign of swamp-pop's new vitality. But stronger recordings, new material—and younger artists—are essential if the bayou rock 'n' roll sounds are to be lifted out of the "oldies" category and swamp-pop is to become an animated music once again.

21

"What'cha gonna do, jump in the bayou?"

Despite the substantial attractions of zydeco, blues, country, and swamp-pop, the future prosperity of South Louisiana music depends upon the well-being of its Cajun-music root sounds. Happily, Cajun musicians, young and old—from Michael Doucet to Dewey Balfa, Joel Sonnier to Aldus Roger—are currently enjoying unprecedented popularity. On the other hand, some of the greatest Cajun artists have passed away in recent years.

During the sixties Cajun music was kept alive by older musicians performing at weekend dances throughout rural Acadiana, cutting records for the local record men, and making occasional radio and TV broadcasts. In the seventies, however, the fortunes of Cajun music improved in line with an American trend toward "roots" music; there seemed to be a general reaction against the mindless progression of rock, which was no longer the music of the people. Suddenly there were blues festivals springing up in Mississippi, bluegrass festivals in the Appalachians—and Cajun music festivals in South Louisiana. For the first time in years, young Cajun musicians were proud to be associated with their cultural past, and they were greeted by receptive audiences wherever they played.

"In the early sixties you started getting the records of the Cajun bands," says Lee Lavergne, reflecting on the Cajun revival. "It created some excitement and a drawing card for them again in the clubs. In the mid-sixties some people wouldn't accept the Beatles, there was a gradual tendency to drift over to country and French. It started building up again. When I started in 1960, there were twelve radio stations in Louisiana playing Cajun and French music, some of them daily, some of them only Saturdays. Like KROF in Abbeville had Bradley Moore every morning, an hour show six to seven, and very much listened to. I think that helped out quite a bit, Happy Fats was in there plugging away. Since then Cajun music has kept increasing . . . You started having people promoting it more, realizing that it was here and it had a distinctive sound, it had a following, and that it could be accepted more and more.

"I think today it's even stronger than it's ever been, it's getting more and more accepted. I've seen it go nationwide, I've seen it go internationally and accepted. The people like it. I've shipped records to Australia, Thailand, Belgium, Amsterdam, England, some in France—not all that much, to my surprise, I thought France and Canada would be your biggest market, but it didn't prove that way [for me], why I don't know. You're also developing an interest amongst the younger generation to get involved with Cajun music, taking up the accordion. You'll find young bands in their late teens and early twenties, which is something years ago you'd never see. It used to be all your older guys."

The young Cajun bands, playing a modern form of Cajun music, tend to favor the fast two-step instead of the slow waltz, relying on a lively sound rather than lyrical content and emotional feel for effect. Despite the revival of interest in Cajun music, some danger therefore remains that a vital part of the traditional style may be lost. Moreover, little effort is being made to conserve the important Cajun-country string-band music of the thirties and forties. But by drawing upon a variety of outside sources, from rock, country, blues, and jazz to bluegrass, the new Cajun groups are giving the music fresh direction. Dewey Balfa, himself an improviser, considers that *legitimate* change is essential: "Things have to change, when things stop changing, they die. The culture and the music have to breathe and grow, but they have to stay within certain guidelines to be true. And those guidelines are pureness and sincerity. Some young musicians are playing Cajun music. Others are using it."

The most respected of the younger musicians is fiddler Michael Doucet, described by Arhoolie boss Chris Strachwitz as "the Leo Soileau of today, an amazing musician!" From Scott, Doucet started his career playing with Zachary Richard and Coteau before forming Beausoleil. The repertoire of this popular folk-oriented band is based on traditional Cajun material, but there are no premeditated barriers; on their Swallow album, called simply "Beausoleil," medieval songs are performed in tandem with the latest Cajun tunes. In 1981 Doucet boosted his reputation even further by recording a very accomplished Arhoolie album, "Dit Beausoleil," with members of his band in support. Other young groups perpetuating the Cajun music tradition include Bourré and Jambalaya. By contrast, Zachary Richard is playing a hybrid, rock-influenced form of Cajun music; while popular in Canada, he seems to provoke the sort of volatile reaction in Louisiana that is normally reserved for Doug Kershaw.

Typical of the younger generation is Charles Thibodeaux, a talented accordionist from Church Point. Before taking over as manager of Lee Lavergne's Rayne music store, he worked as a technician with John Deere Tractors in Crowley. Inspired to play Cajun music after attending local dances, he learned by listening to the records of Doug Kershaw, Marc

Savoy, Joel Sonnier, and Iry LeJune (Iry's "Love Bridge Waltz" is his favorite disc). Thibodeaux's special desire was to try to perform difficult tunes like Joe Bonsall's "Step It Fast" and Marc Savoy's "Silver Bells."

In 1973 Charles recorded two traditional numbers, "I Went To The Dance Last Night" and "The Waltz That Carried Me To My Grave," with Ivy Miller and the Church Point Playboys for Elton Cormier's Bee label. The accordionist was just fifteen at the time. "Almost every band makes a record," he says modestly, "mainly because they like having a good time making the record. They are mostly for sale at dances, you start by pressing 500 copies, if it sells you order more. I gave most of mine away!" Since 1979 Charles has been playing every other weekend with Jay (Collins) and the Traveliers at clubs like Bourque's in Lewisburg, the Triangle in Scott, and Pat's Showboat Club in Henderson. The band, which has made good swamp-pop records for the Tamm and One Way labels, plays an intriguing mixture of Cajun, swamp-pop, and country songs, from Aldus Roger's "Lafayette Two-Step" and Cookie's "Mathilda" to Hank Williams's "Hey Good Lookin'." This kind of enlightened programming is currently becoming more widespread.

Charles Thibodeaux is aware of Cajun music's changing fortunes since he started playing in 1972: "The music was just hanging on due to the old musicians and listeners. The youngsters were listening to country and western and rock music, they had no desire to listen to or play Cajun music. They were ashamed. Then the organization CODOFIL helped to put the music on its feet, the younger generation began to be proud of their heritage. The future looks good, there is still somebody around keeping it alive."

There is no doubt that CODOFIL (the Council for the Development of French in Louisiana), founded by James Domengeaux in 1968, has done much to inspire the encouraging revival in Cajun music, especially among younger people. Johnnie Allan confirms the views expressed by Lee Lavergne and Charles Thibodeaux when he says: "Right now, Cajun music is changed. Over the years, everything changes, it doesn't stay the same. Nowadays it seems to me like it's taking a little progressive turn. And strange as it may seem I've noticed in the last three to four years the younger people are getting into it, which is good, because it's keeping the culture alive. And when I say younger people, I've seen them on TV sometimes early in the morning where some of these guys, fourteen-, fifteen-year-olds, they're playing French accordion and singing in French. Which is kind of unusual because a few years back it started to die out. Then it was revived again. Now you've got your college-aged crowds that go for this—I wouldn't call it an extremely progressive type of Cajun music, they've got the accordion, they've got the fiddles.

"I would say the turning point was probably around the early seventies. Cajun music had kinda faded out of the picture, not entirely, but pretty close to it. And then we had this organization around here called CODOFIL and they started bringing in people from Canada, from France, from the French-speaking parts of Europe, to try to keep alive the French language in Louisiana. It's being taught right now in the schools, in the lower grades as a secondary language. And I think these people coming into here, it started stimulating an interest in French music in a lot of the younger people. The older people they already knew about it, it was there with them, but the younger people had not been exposed to it."

Floyd Soileau agrees: "For a while, until CODOFIL came around, some of the people that spoke French and all, they weren't too proud of the fact they were bilingual, that they had French ancestry or Cajun ancestry or what. And it took a little movement on the part of CODOFIL and some years and some changes, for people now are proud they are Cajun, they've got Cajun ancestry. For a while this wasn't so and there was a decline in Cajun sales."

But there are certain South Louisianians who feel that CODOFIL is trying to foist a standardized French culture on Cajuns instead of allowing them to develop their life-style naturally—and to hold on to their heritage at the same time. One such opponent is Happy Fats: "We've got some people who are pushing the French influence. You get the Cajun kids here, they try to teach them Parisian French. And it's a mess, because it's all different. We've got our dialects, and I believe they should leave it alone."

The Cajun cause has attracted many supporters, including Professor Glenn R. Conrad, director of the Center for Louisiana Studies at the University of Southwestern Louisiana in Lafayette and author of many books and articles on Louisiana folklore. A similar missionary zeal is exuded by two Mamou residents, attorney Paul Tate, Chairman of CODOFIL's annual Tribute to Cajun Music, and Revon Reed, a retired high-school teacher.

Every Saturday morning from 8 to 11 A.M. Revon Reed hosts "The Mamou Hour," a program of Cajun music and fun broadcast by radio KEUN Eunice direct from Fred Tate's lounge in Mamou. The resident traditional Cajun band is led by fiddler Sady Courville, and usually includes accordionist Ambrose Thibodeaux and guitarist Preston Manuel; guest performers are welcome. Repertoires range from old French waltzes to lively two-steps and quadrilles. Amid the noisy hubbub of the bar, with the sound of voices and music escalating by the minute, it is hard to believe that a radio program is being produced. Revon himself is tucked away in a dark corner, wearing large headphones, huddled over a table full of paper, his voice audible only to radio listeners far away from Fred's Lounge. The musicians' area is corraled off from the happy, dancing, beer-drinking audience, which consists of Mamou residents, visitors from other parts of Louisiana, and tourists from all over the world. Reed's show is one of the last outposts of old local radio, with its format of live music, funny stories, announcements of forthcoming events, and advertisements for small businesses in the area. An album of the broadcast has been issued by Sonet, but it unfortunately fails to capture the spontaneity of a unique institution.

Revon Reed's credentials do not end with "The Mamou Hour." In 1976 he wrote *Lâche pas la patate*, the first book to describe Cajun Louisiana in a mixture of standard and Cajun French; he has helped launch *Mamou Prairie*, a small journal devoted to the Cajun culture; and he has recorded salty comedy as Nonc Helaire in the controversial Swallow album series "For Koonasses Only." "It's the kind of humor they like in France," he explains, "you don't dare tell them except in French. You translate them into English and they become vulgar immediately. . . ."

In addition to Revon Reed's live program, Cajun music record shows are broadcast from many towns in Acadiana, mostly on weekends. The coverage is better than ever: important disc jockeys include Johnny Janot (KLVI Beaumont), John Lloyd "Tee Bruce" Broussard (KPAC Port Arthur), Jerry Dugas (KJEF Jennings), Dudley Bernard (KLEB Golden Meadow), Leroy Martin (KTIB Thibodaux), Rod Rodrigue (KHOM Houma), Jim Soileau (KVPI Ville Platte), and Camay Doucet and Paul Marx (KSIG Crowley). Cajun music is also featured by WYNK Baton Rouge, KSLO Opelousas, and KLCL Lake Charles.

The most popular Cajun television program is "Passe Partout," hosted by the personable Jim Olivier and broadcast at 5:45 A.M. daily over KLFY-TV, Channel 10, Lafayette. Some Cajuns say the show is the first thing they put on in the morning, even before brewing coffee! But they consider it worthwhile getting up at such an early hour to catch video clips of artists like Clifton Chenier, Freddy Fender, Aldus Roger, and Al Terry. There are also spots for young Cajun bands between news items, farm prices, weather forecasts, and snippets of local information. (Olivier himself records a smooth, country-influenced form of Cajun music for Swallow.)

In March 1980 KADN-TV, Channel 15, Lafayette, announced its arrival by reviving the one-hour all-French music format that had not been televised for over a decade. The new program, called "Laissez Le Bon Temps Rouler," is fronted by none other than Alex Broussard, Happy Fats's partner in the pioneering "Mariné Show."

Cajun clubland comes alive only on weekends. The best-known clubs are La Poussière in Breaux Bridge, the Blue Goose in Eunice, the Belvedere in Judice, the Town and Country in Riceville, the Triangle in Scott, and Snook's in Ville Platte. (Regular club guides are published by *Louisiane,* the CODOFIL-associated bilingual monthly newspaper.) Lower down the scale are the scattered rural roadhouses, often no more than flimsy asbestos or wooden shacks; but these less-than-glamorous institutions are disappearing rapidly in the wake of the oil boom and spiraling land prices.

Until 1982 the closest club to New Orleans was Allen Fontenot's popular Cajun Bandstand, located on Airline Highway in nearby Kenner. Like many of its Acadiana counterparts, the club was housed in an unpretentious brick building containing a large dance floor, raised stage, long tables with chairs, and the inevitable bar, jukebox, and pool table. Allen Fontenot, a squat, chain-smoking fiddler from Ville Platte, led his resident Country Cajuns with professional aplomb through a wide-ranging program of old and new Cajun numbers, genuine hillbilly music, and the occasional swamp-pop tune by standout drummer Darrel Brasseaux of Church Point. Fontenot's band has recorded albums for Antilles and Delta (of Texas). Before the club premises were sold, the cosmopolitan audience at the Cajun Bandstand consisted of young tourists, college students, and Cajun couples of all ages who delighted in showing off the pyrotechnics of the two-step and the waltz. The Cajun Bandstand was the most accessible of all Cajun clubs to the population center of New Orleans, and its demise has left a gaping void.

Festivals have a special place in the traditional Cajun calendar. Celebrations are usually held during the summer months in the bigger towns when the local crops are brought in (Mardi Gras, before Lent, is an obvious exception). At the Crowley Rice Festival a popular event is the prestigious accordion contest in which each musician plays a waltz and two-step; the judges are screened off in order to prevent visual recognition of the entrants. In 1979 Iry LeJune's two sons won awards. Other regular features at the festival are a frog derby and competitions for Creole cooking and rice eating.

Since 1969 the carefree New Orleans Jazz and Heritage Festival, held annually in late spring at the Fair Grounds Race Track, has been a major forum for Louisiana music, crafts, and food. Cajun, zydeco, and blues musicians from South Louisiana contest the grassy infield of the stadium with an army of New Orleans artists, national stars like Bobby Bland and Jerry Lee Lewis, and a hundred others in a unique musical extravaganza. Sadly, swamp-pop is not yet considered "folky" enough to be accepted by the organizers.

The renewed interest in Cajun music has meant an increased demand for musical instruments and records from the music stores of Acadiana. Record men Lee Lavergne and Floyd Soileau—and the Miller family—have their own retail shops. Marc Savoy owns the Savoy Music Center on the outskirts of Eunice. In his early days Marc played with the Rambling Aces, and he has recorded for Crazy Cajun, Swallow, and Arhoolie, among others. He now spends much of his time building accordions in the rear of his store. His exquisite instruments, bearing the "Acadian" trademark, are recognized as the Rolls-Royces of their kind and are used by top Cajun and French-Canadian musicians. The finest models retail at $750 each, a far cry from the $15 or so an accordion cost in Joseph Falcon's day.

All the support offered by CODOFIL, radio, television, clubs, and festivals notwithstanding, the future welfare of Cajun music—and of other South Louisiana sounds—is reliant upon a healthy recording scene to fuel fresh flames and to combat the conglomerate conformity of so much of today's American music. Reassuringly, veteran record men Floyd Soileau, Eddie Shuler, and Lee Lavergne are still active, while Jay Miller's work is being carried on by his son Mark. Their efforts in promoting the Cajun sound are being supplemented by Chris Strachwitz of Arhoolie and Old Timey Records and by Sam Charters of Sonet Records. Between 1979 and 1982 Chris recorded Wallace "Cheese" Read, Marc Savoy, Michael Doucet, and old-timers Octa Clark and Hector Duhon; he also compiled reissue LPs of Amadie Ardoin, Harry Choates, and Leo Soileau. One of Strachwitz's greatest achievements has been to release the five-volume Old Timey "Louisiana Cajun Music" anthology set, which has made available many rare and musically priceless 78s from 1928 through the 1950s. It is the best historical perspective of Cajun recordings ever collated. In 1979, Sam Charters (who originally made his name as author of *The Country Blues*) completed extensive sessions for Sonet, featuring Dewey Balfa, Sady Courville, Don Montoucet and the Wandering Aces, Austin Pitre, Rockin' Dopsie, and Wayne Toups. Thus the tradition of a living music is still being documented for posterity.

Meanwhile, the exemplary Rounder label from Massachusetts has issued albums by the Balfa Brothers, the Louisiana Aces, Rockin' Dopsie, and Joel Sonnier, plus several Cajun and zydeco compilations. In England, Bruce Bastin and Flyright Records continue to release many of the previously unissued Jay Miller tapes, and the company's distribution setup has made South Louisiana music more easily available throughout the world.

In the U.S., Cajun music has not been entirely isolated from the national recording scene. Over the years there have been versions of Cajun tunes by top artists like Asleep At The Wheel, The Band, Waylon Jennings, Ricky Nelson, Buck Owens, even bluesman Clarence "Gatemouth"

Brown—and in 1981 "Jole Blon" by Gary "U.S." Bonds and Bruce Springsteen. In England local stars Shakin' Stevens and Chas & Dave had Top Ten hits in 1982 with singles strongly influenced by Cajun and swamp-pop music. Some observers would call this kind of patronage welcome publicity, others exploitation.

Cajun music, so beautifully simple, has taken two centuries to gain any recognition outside of Louisiana; if international exposure is too hurried it could suffer irreparable damage. However, the language barrier should act in the music's favor as a restraint to excessive commercialization. Ultimately the survival of all forms of South Louisiana music as identifiable, creative forces rests with the people themselves. The Cajuns have injected real character into the region; with their rich heritage to fall back on, the future cannot be without hope. Joe Barry's touching hurricane story says it all:

"Cajun people are very determined people . . . after hurricanes I've seen them wiped out with their homes all down, and they walk up to them in pieces and say, 'Well, the boards, I'd better put more nails in next time . . .' And that was the extent of it, no pleading, no 'God, why did you destroy me?' Simple statement, 'Just gotta rebuild it.' What'cha gonna do, jump in the bayou, you know? That's the way they were."

With any luck, enthusiasts will be able to hear the music of the Cajun bayous—and the prairies—for a long time yet, when they travel "South to Louisiana. . . ."

Bobby Charles, 1956.   *Courtesy Bill Greensmith*

"Later Alligator," 1955.
Bill Greensmith

Bobby Page and the Riff Raffs: V. J. Boulet (piano), Roy Perkins (bass guitar), Bobby Page (vocal), Ulysses Broussard (drums), Jimmy Patin (saxophone), Bessyl Duhon (guitar), 1958. *Courtesy Roy Perkins*

Cookie and the Cupcakes, ca. 1960. *Courtesy Eddie Shuler*

"Mathilda," 1958.
Bill Greensmith

**Eddie Shuler, George
Khoury, Phil Phillips,
1959.**
Courtesy Eddie Shuler

Rod Bernard at KSLO Radio, Opelousas, 1951. *Rod Bernard*

"Rod Bernard Day," Opelousas, with Floyd Soileau (center), 1959. *Courtesy Rod Bernard*

Rod Bernard and the Twisters, 1957. *Courtesy Rod Bernard*

"This Should Go On Forever," 1959.
Bill Greensmith

Walter Mouton and the Scott Playboys with Johnnie Allan
(guitar, right), 1951.   *Courtesy Johnnie Allan*

Johnnie Allan and the Krazy Kats with Al Foreman (guitar), Leroy Castille
(saxophone), Bhuel Hoffpauir (drums), Johnny Redlich (piano), 1958.
Courtesy Johnnie Allan

Clint West and the Boogie Kings, 1964.   *Courtesy Jin Records*

Joe Barry, 1961.
Courtesy Joe Barry

Joe Barry, ca. 1962.
Courtesy Joe Barry

"I'm A Fool To Care" (in French),
1961.   *Bill Greensmith*

Rockin' Sidney, 1969.
          Mike Leadbitter

Tommy McLain, 1966.
Courtesy Jin Records

 "Tee Yeaux Bleu," 1960.
Bill Greensmith

Austin Pitre and the Evangeline Playboys, Ville Platte dry goods store, 1948. *Courtesy Pierre Daigle*

Badeaux and the Louisiana Aces with D. L. Menard (guitar), ca. 1962.
Courtesy Swallow Records

Belton Richard, ca. 1967.
Courtesy Swallow Records

Dewey Balfa (fiddle), Tony Balfa (drums), Nathan Abshire (accordion), 1972. *James La Rocca*

Balfa Brothers, ca. 1977.
Courtesy Swallow Records

Nathan Abshire, 1980.
Charley Nilsson

Warren Storm at a local hop with Merton Thibodeaux (piano), Huey Meaux (MC), Al Foreman (guitar), 1958. *Courtesy Mrs. Boneau*

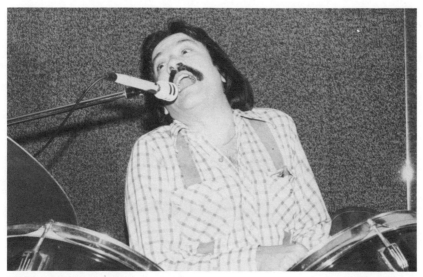

Warren Storm, 1979.   *Paul Harris*

"Mama Mama Mama," 1958.
Bill Greensmith

Joe Carl, 1959.
Courtesy Leroy Martin

"Sugar Bee," 1961.
Bill Greensmith

Jay Stutes, 1961. *Courtesy Eddie Shuler*

**Vorris "Shorty" LeBlanc,
ca. 1963.**
Courtesy Eddie Shuler

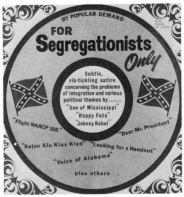

Rebel album. *Bill Greensmith*

Joel Sonnier, 1980. *Courtesy Sonet/Rounder Records*

Dale and Grace, 1963. *Courtesy Montel Records*

Little Bob and the Lollipops with John Hart (saxophone, left), 1964.
Courtesy La Louisianne Records

Lee Lavergne with Gene Autry guitar, ca. 1948. *Courtesy Lee Lavergne*

Shirley Bergeron (steel guitar), Alphee Bergeron (accordion), ca. 1963. *Courtesy Lanor Records*

"Life Problem," 1962.
Bill Greensmith

Main Street, Church Point, 1980.   *John Broven*

Aldus Roger and the Lafayette Playboys with Doc Guidry (fiddle), 1964.
Courtesy La Louisianne Records

"Wild Side Of Life," 1960.
Bill Greensmith

Huey Meaux, ca. 1965.
Courtesy Blues Unlimited

Jay Miller, 1979.
Paul Harris

Eddie Shuler, 1979.
Paul Harris

Floyd Soileau, 1979.
Paul Harris

Mamou, 1972. *Hans Andréasson*

Blue Goose Lounge, Eunice, 1980. *John Broven*

New Orleans Jazz and Heritage Festival. *Courtesy Blues Unlimited*

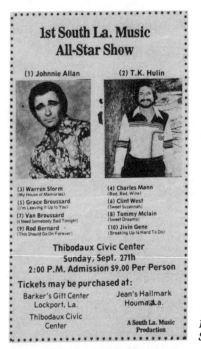

1st South La. Music
All-Star Show

(1) Johnnie Allan   (2) T.K. Hulin

(3) Warren Storm   (4) Charles Mann
(My House of Memories)   (Red, Red, Wine)
(5) Grace Broussard   (6) Clint West
(I'm Leaving It Up to You) (Sweet Suzannah)
(7) Van Broussard   (8) Tommy Mclain
(I Need Somebody Bad Tonight) (Sweet Dreams)
(9) Rod Bernard   (10) Jivin Gene
(This Should Go On Forever) (Breaking Up Is Hard To Do)

Thibodaux Civic Center
Sunday, Sept. 27th
2:00 P.M. Admission $9.00 Per Person

Tickets may be purchased at:
Barker's Gift Center   Jean's Hallmark
Lockport, La.   Houma, La.
Thibodaux Civic
Center   A South La. Music
                          Production

1st South Louisiana Music All-Star Show advertisement, 1981.

1st South Louisiana Music All-Star Show: Charles Mann, Jivin'. Gene, T. K. Hulin, Clint West, Johnnie Allan, Grace Broussard, Van Broussard, Rod Bernard (kneeling), 1981.   *Courtesy Johnnie Allan*

APPENDIXES

Appendix A

South Louisiana Music Time Chart

1755	*Le Grand Dérangement:* the expulsion of the Acadians from their Canadian colony.
late 1700s	Ballads popular with early Acadian settlers in Louisiana.
1800s	Fiddle music becomes more prevalent in Cajun communities.
1870s	Introduction of accordion via Germany.
early 1900s	Cajun accordion and fiddle music, mostly instrumental, popular at *fais-dodos,* house parties, and country picnics. *La musique Creole* is played by "black Cajuns," while brass band and string quartet music is performed for upper-class Acadians.
1920s	First blues and hillbilly recordings and radio broadcasts. Introduction of guitar in Cajun music. End of "old folks" brass bands.
1928	Significant year for Cajun music. First Cajun recording, "Lafayette" by accordionist Joseph Falcon (Columbia), is a regional hit. Leo Soileau and Mayuse Lafleur follow with "Mama Where You At?" (Victor), first Cajun release to feature the fiddle. Amadie Ardoin makes early recording by a Negro-French artist.
1929	Traditional rural Cajun music recorded by Columbia, Victor, Paramount, Brunswick/Vocalion, and OKeh.
1930–33	No Cajun recordings because of Depression, but Cajun music still popular in dance halls.
1934	Decca starts recording Cajun artists, including Joseph Falcon and Amadie Ardoin.
mid-1930s	Cajun sound influenced by western-swing artists, especially Bob Wills, and by cowboy movies. Start of Cajun-country trend by string bands Leo Soileau's Three Aces, Hackberry Ramblers, and Rayne-Bo Ramblers. Appearance of jukebox in beer joints.
1936	Mammoth Bluebird field recording sessions in New Orleans; big Cajun hits "Jole Blonde" by Hackberry Ramblers and "Wondering" by Joe Werner and the Riverside Ramblers. Fiddle starts to oust accordion in Cajun bands.
1937–38	Leo Soileau and Doc Guidry record pop and hillbilly songs in French for Decca.
1939	Happy Fats and the Rayne-Bo Ramblers become first Cajun band to enjoy national radio exposure.
1940–41	Cajun record releases halted. Young Cajuns leave to serve in armed forces and to work in war industries in Texas and California; old Cajuns still playing in Acadiana. Formation of new publishing organization Broadcast Music, Inc., which will help songwriters in the years ahead.

317

1942   Petrillo recording ban. Leo Soileau and band, with Happy Fats and
            Harry Choates, in residence at Silver Star club in Lake Charles.
            Hackberry Ramblers begin playing again.
1946   Start of postwar record boom. Emergence of independent com-
            panies recording blues, hillbilly, and other regional music. "Jole
            Blon" by Harry Choates (Gold Star) an influential Cajun hit. J. D.
            (Jay) Miller of Crowley forms Fais Do Do Records, first South
            Louisiana label; Happy, Doc and the Boys have modest hit with
            "Allons Danse Colinda."
1947   J. D. Miller starts recording hillbilly singers for Feature. Growing
            influence of honky-tonk sound. Electric guitar, steel guitar, string
            bass, and drums are additions to Cajun band instrumentation.
1948   "Love Bridge Waltz" by Iry LeJune (Opera), first release by one of
            the greatest Cajun accordionists, revives the accordion sound in
            Cajun music. Fiddle music starts to wane. Independent labels De
            Luxe and Modern record Cajun music in New Orleans; "Tolan
            Waltz" by Chuck Guillory (Colonial) a local hit. "War Widow
            Waltz" by Lee Sonnier (Feature) another Cajun hit. First "Louisiana
            Hayride" show broadcast over radio KWKH Shreveport.
1949   National independent labels leave Cajun music to local record men.
            Labels set up by Virgil Bozeman (O.T.), George Khoury
            (Khoury's/Lyric), and Eddie Shuler (Folk-Star/Goldband). "Pine
            Grove Blues" by Nathan Abshire (O.T.) is influential Cajun hit. Cajun
            music extremely popular in dance halls and on radio shows.
1950   Zydeco music begins to emerge in present form. "Bon Ton Roula" by
            Clarence Garlow (Macy's) first R&B hit by an artist with zydeco roots.
1951   Khoury's/Lyric most prolific Cajun labels. Lyric has hits with "Reno
            Waltz" and "Evangeline Waltz" by Lawrence Walker, one of the
            most popular accordionists throughout fifties (as was Aldus Roger).
1952   Southeast Louisiana Cajun Vin Bruce has hit with "Dans La
            Louisianne," recorded by Columbia in Nashville. Link Davis popu-
            larizes old Cajun standard "Big Mamou" (OKeh) throughout South.
            Hank Williams records "Jambalaya" (MGM), destined to become
            best-known Cajun-influenced country song. Jay Miller writes "It
            Wasn't God Who Made Honky Tonk Angels," tremendous country
            hit for Kitty Wells on Decca.
1953   Jay Miller makes arrangements for Al Terry and Jimmy Newman to
            record country music for Nashville companies Hickory and Dot. Leo
            Soileau retires from music.
1954   A year of fundamental change. Elvis Presley introduces rockabilly, a
            fusion of white country music and black rhythm and blues, and kicks
            off rock 'n' roll revolution. Gene Rodrigue has Cajun hit with "Jole
            Fille" (Meladee), Boozoo Chavis a zydeco/R&B hit with "Paper In
            My Shoe" (Folk-Star), Lightnin' Slim the first Jay Miller blues hit
            with "Bad Luck" (Feature). Guitar Slim popular in South Louisiana
            through R&B hit "The Things That I Used To Do" (Specialty). Iry
            LeJune killed in car accident.
1955   Cajun and country music stopped in tracks by rock 'n' roll. "You're
            On My Mind" by Roy Perkins (Meladee) and "Later Alligator" by
            Bobby Charles (Chess), first hits by young white South Louisiana

artists, pave way for swamp-pop music. Jay Miller starts leasing blues recordings to Excello in Nashville, also sends Rusty and Doug Kershaw to Nashville to record for Hickory. Miller winds up own Feature label. "Ay-Tete-Fee" by Clifton Chenier (Specialty) is R&B hit. Al Ferrier records rockabilly for Goldband.

1956 Rhythm and blues continues to be strongly featured by local disc jockeys. "Blueberry Hill" by Fats Domino (Imperial) seminal influence on embryo swamp-pop form. "Congo Mombo" by Guitar Gable (Excello) is early R&B hit by South Louisiana artist, as is "Irene" by King Karl (Excello).

1957 Rock 'n' roll is at its peak. "I'm A King Bee" by Slim Harpo (Excello) a regional swamp-blues hit; other Excello recordings in blues idiom by Lightnin' Slim, Lonesome Sundown, and Lazy Lester. "Family Rules" by Guitar Jr. (Goldband) South Louisiana R&B hit. Jimmy Newman has country-pop hit with "A Fallen Star" (Dot).

1958 Floyd Soileau of Ville Platte forms Jin Records concentrating on swamp-pop and Swallow Records for Cajun releases. "Just A Dream" by Jimmy Clanton (Ace) has noticeable influence on swamp-pop. Warren Storm's "Prisoner's Song" (Nasco) is a minor national swamp-pop hit.

1959 Golden year of swamp-pop with national hits "Mathilda" by Cookie and the Cupcakes (Judd), "This Should Go On Forever" by Rod Bernard (Argo), "Sea Of Love" by Phil Phillips (Mercury), and "Breaking Up Is Hard To Do" by Jivin' Gene (Mercury). Huey Meaux begins to exert influence in South Louisiana by negotiating lease of many local hits for national distribution. Appearance of small South Louisiana labels like La Louisianne, Montel, Rocko, Richland, L.K., and Zynn. Discovery of old-style Louisiana bluesman Robert Pete Williams by Harry Oster and Richard Allen at Angola State Penitentiary. Lightnin' Slim's "Rooster Blues" (Excello) a national R&B chart hit.

1960 Local record men step up Cajun recordings, featuring accordion. Comeback by Nathan Abshire on Jay Miller's Kajun label. Lee Lavergne of Church Point forms Lanor Records and has Cajun hit with Shirley and Alphee Bergeron's "J'ai Fait Mon Ede'e." Cajun radio and TV shows enjoy increasing popularity. R&B star Fats Domino records swamp-pop songs by Bobby Charles and Jimmy Donley.

1961 Many swamp-blues recordings at Crowley. Slim Harpo has national hit "Rainin' In My Heart" (Excello); other Baton Rouge bluesmen include Silas Hogan, Jimmy Anderson, and Tabby Thomas. "I'm A Fool To Care" by Joe Barry (Smash) is national Top Thirty swamp-pop success. Floyd Soileau working closely with Huey Meaux and Bill Hall. Cleveland Crochet's "Sugar Bee" first *Billboard Hot 100* entry for Eddie Shuler's Goldband label, biggest Cajun record since Harry Choates's "Jole Blon."

1962 "The Back Door" by Badeaux and Louisiana Aces including D. L. Menard (Swallow) is big local hit and becomes a Cajun standard. Other Cajun hits on Swallow label by Doris Matte, Cajun Trio, and Vin Bruce. Aldus Roger represents Louisiana at Folklore Festival in

Washington, D.C. "You'll Lose A Good Thing" by Barbara Lynn (Jamie) a national Top Ten hit for Huey Meaux, who splits from Floyd Soileau to set up his own organization. Rockin' Sidney has local hit with "No Good Woman" (Jin).

1963   "I'm Leaving It Up To You" by Dale and Grace (Montel) first national No. 1 swamp-pop record (also last hit of classic swamp-pop period). Death of Jimmy Donley. Lightnin' Slim's "Winter Time Blues" (Excello) southern blues hit. End of rock 'n' roll era.

1964   The Beatles usher in new rock epoch; regional music like Cajun, blues, and swamp-pop almost wiped out. Clifton Chenier signs with Arhoolie and is destined to make zydeco a respected form. Soul music takes over from R&B; Lil Bob and the Lollipops are only local soul act of note. Folk musicologist Ralph Rinzler publicly expresses concern for welfare of traditional Cajun music, books Dewey Balfa and other Cajun musicians for Newport Folk Festival; bluesman Robert Pete Williams, now released from Angola, also appears at Newport.

1965   South Louisiana still reeling from effects of Beatles music. Huey Meaux has national hits with Texas artists Sir Douglas Quintet and Roy Head, but records bayou music on his own labels. "Saturday Hop," KLFY-TV show featuring Rod Bernard and Warren Storm of the Shondels, is popular in the Lafayette area. Lightnin' Slim leaves Jay Miller. Joseph Falcon dies.

1966   Slim Harpo's "Baby Scratch My Back" (Excello) is No. 3 national R&B record of the year. Jay Miller forms Rebel Records and enjoys huge sales with discs by the Son of Mississippi and Happy Fats. Tommy McLain has another national hit for Floyd Soileau with "Sweet Dreams" (MSL). George Khoury retires from record business.

1967   Jay Miller loses Slim Harpo, suspends Excello contract, and ceases blues recordings. The Balfa Brothers start recording traditional Cajun music for Swallow, receive acclaim at the Newport Folk Festival. Belton Richard's modern sound makes him most popular Cajun artist. John Fred has international pop hit with "Judy In Disguise" (Paula).

1968   CODOFIL formed. Increasing pride in heritage evident among Cajuns.

1969   Debut of influential New Orleans Jazz and Heritage Festival. West Coast group Creedence Clearwater Revival have international hits with Louisiana swamp-rock sound. Doug Kershaw accepted by rock fans.

1970–71   Root sounds regaining popularity in U.S. Record industry trend toward albums rather than singles continues. Chris Strachwitz starts major LP reissue series "Louisiana Cajun Music" on Old Timey. "Games People Play" by Nathan Abshire (Swallow) is minor Cajun hit. Baton Rouge blues revival sessions by Arhoolie and Excello. Slim Harpo dies.

1972–73   Increased activity at festivals and on record offers further evidence of Cajun revival. Young musicians start to play Cajun music. Revon Reed's live radio show from Mamou and Jim Olivier's "Passe

Partout" on Lafayette TV assist the Cajun music cause. Les Blank makes films on Clifton Chenier and Bois Sec Ardoin. Rufus Jagneaux has Louisiana pop hit with "Opelousas Sostan" (Jin).

1974   Jimmy C. Newman scores surprise Cajun-country success with "Lache Pas La Patate," first hit for La Louisianne; earns gold record in Canada. Johnnie Allan has minor English hit with "The Promised Land" (Jin/Oval). Lightnin' Slim dies.

1975   Clifton Chenier, enjoying great popularity, records his personal best-selling album "Bogalusa Boogie" (Arhoolie). Masterminded by Huey Meaux, Freddy Fender has massive national hits with "Before The Next Teardrop Falls" and "Wasted Days And Wasted Nights" (ABC/Dot) featuring swamp-pop vocals.

1976   Flyright Records in England starts to reissue Jay Miller's master tapes.

1977   Floyd Soileau continues building all-round South Louisiana music catalog.

1978   Extensive Cajun sessions by Sam Charters of Sonet Records.

1979   Jimmy C. Newman making successful introduction of Cajun music to his country-music fans. Zydeco artist Rockin' Dopsie well received during tour of Europe. Rod and Will Balfa killed in car accident.

1980   Joel Sonnier records "Cajun Life" LP, engineered by Mark Miller, for Rounder Records at Crowley. Baton Rouge bluesmen unite to form Blues Possie. Leo Soileau, Alphee Bergeron, and Robert Pete Williams die. Young Cajun group Beausoleil led by Michael Doucet making impression.

1981-82 Cajun artists appearing in festivals throughout U.S., Canada, and Southeast Asia. First zydeco radio show broadcast by KEUN Eunice. Johnnie Allan promotes South Louisiana Music All-Star Show. Record men Floyd Soileau, Eddie Shuler, Mark Miller, and Lee Lavergne still active, as is Chris Strachwitz. Tabby Thomas opens Blues Box club in Baton Rouge featuring local bluesmen. Nathan Abshire and Austin Pitre die.

Appendix B

Oral History

As I have already noted, the principal sources for this book were the interviews I had with the South Louisiana musicians and record men. Other researchers have contributed much material, and this is gratefully acknowledged elsewhere. The major interviews I carried out are listed below. The symbol (T) indicates that the interview was taped and the tape is in my possession; the remaining interviews are represented by field notes, correspondence, or other materials in my files.

Johnnie Allan. Lafayette, 25 April 1979. (T)
Joe Barry. New Orleans, 28 April 1979. (T)
Shirley Bergeron. Church Point, 29 September 1980.
Rod Bernard. Lafayette, 25 April 1979. (T)
Camille "Lil" Bob. Lafayette, 25 April 1979.
Jimmy Dotson. Baton Rouge, 4 May 1982. (T)
Stanley "Buckwheat" Dural Jr. Lafayette, 1 May 1979.
John Fred. New Orleans, 3 May 1979. (T)
Paul Gayten. Los Angeles, 15 June 1975. (T)
Oran "Doc" Guidry. New Orleans, 28 April 1979.
Earl King. New Orleans, 5 May 1979. (T)
Lee Lavergne. Church Point, 1 October 1980. (T)
LeRoy "Happy Fats" LeBlanc. Rayne, 1 May 1979. (T)
Leroy Martin. Thibodaux, 6 October 1980.
Jay Miller. Crowley, 1 May 1979. (T)
Gabriel "Guitar Gable" Perrodin. Lafayette, 30 September 1980. (T)
Mac "Dr. John" Rebennack. London, England, May 1972. (T)
Eddie Shuler. Lake Charles, 30 April 1979. (T)
Harry Simoneaux. Lafayette, 5 October 1981.
Floyd Soileau. Ville Platte, 2 May 1979. (T)
Warren Storm. Lafayette, 26 April 1979. (T)
Al Terry. Lafayette, 28 April 1980.
Charles Thibodeaux. Church Point, 28 September 1980.
Ernest "Tabby" Thomas. New Orleans, 5 May 1979.
Katie Webster. Lake Charles, 30 April 1979. (T)

Appendix C

Song Credits

Extracts from the following songs have been quoted in the text. Acknowledgment is given for permission to reprint material in this book; any inadvertent omission will be corrected in future printings if notification is sent to the publisher. Special thanks must go to Jay Miller, Eddie Shuler, and Floyd Soileau for their kind cooperation. All music publishers are affiliated with BMI unless otherwise stated.

"Ain't Broke Ain't Hungry," S. Kari, Kari Music/Tune-Kel.
"Airport Blues," S. Hogan–J. West, Excellorec.
"Baby Baby," J. West–A. Conroy–K. Webster, Jamil.
"Bad Luck," J. Miller–O. Hicks, Excellorec.
"Big Mamou," L. Davis, Copyright Control.
"Blues Hang-Over," J. Moore–J. West, Excellorec.
"Bon Ton Roula," C. Garlow, Copyright Control.
"Breaking Up Is Hard To Do," G. Bourgeois–H. Meaux, Big Bopper.
"Crawfishin'," L. Rene, Leon Rene, ASCAP.
"Dear Mr. President," L. LeBlanc–J. West, Jamil.
"Fais Do-Do," J. Clement, Big Bopper.
" 'GI' Slim," J. West, Excellorec.
"Goin' Crazy Over T.V.," J. Anderson–J. West, Excellorec.
"Good Deal Lucille," A. Terry–J. Miller–C. Theriot, Acuff-Rose © 1954. (Used by permission of the publisher. All rights reserved.)
"Hey Baby," J. Miller–A. Ferrier, Jamil.
"Hey Mom (Mama Where You At?)," A. Breaux, Jamil.
"Hoodoo Party," T. Thomas–Dee, Excellorec/Jamil.
"I'm A Fool To Care," T. Daffan, Peer Intl.
"I'm A King Bee," J. Moore, Excellorec.
"I'm To Blame," H. Meaux, Crazy Cajun.
"It Wasn't God Who Made Honky Tonk Angels," J. Miller, Southern Music.
"J'ai Fait Mon Ede'e," L. Lavergne–S. Bergeron, Flat Town.
"Jole Blon," A. Breaux, Copyright Control.
"Keep Your Arms Around Me," D. McClinton, East Time.
"Lacassine Special," I. LeJune, Tek.
"Lafayette," J. Falcon, Copyright Control.
"Later Alligator," R. Guidry, Arc.
"Life Problem," K. Karl–J. West, Excellorec.
"Mardi-Gras Song," D. Balfa, Jamil.
"Mathilda," H. Thierry–G. Khoury, Longhorn.
"Mon Coeur T'Appelle," trad. arr. C. Breaux, Copyright Control.
"My Home Is A Prison," J. Miller, Excellorec.

"No Good Woman," S. Simien–F. Soileau, Flat Town.
"Opelousas Sostan," B. Graeff–V. Palmer, Flat Town.
"Pine Grove Blues," N. Abshire, Flat Town.
"Prisoner's Talking Blues," R. P. Williams, Copyright Control.
"Reno Waltz," L. Walker, Copyright Control.
"Route '90'," C. Garlow–L. Rene, Leon Rene ASCAP.
"Sea Of Love," G. Khoury–P. Baptiste, Kamar.
"Small Town Talk," B. Charles–R. Danko, Street People Songs/Canaan.
"South To Louisiana," M. Phillips–D. Redlich–C. Trahan–Sam, Robbins ASCAP.
"Sur Le Courtableau," N. Abshire, Flat Town.
"The Back Door," D. L. Menard, Flat Town.
"The Kangaroo," C. Sheffield, Excellorec.
"This Should Go On Forever," J. Miller–B. Jolivette, Jamil.
"Trouble At Home Blues," S. Hogan–Dee, Excellorec.
"Vain Toi Don A Ma Mort," L. LeBlanc, Copyright Control.
"Whoa Now," J. West, Excellorec/Jamil.
"Winter Time Blues," J. West, Excellorec.
"Wondering," J. Werner, Aberbach.

Appendix D

Biographical Data

Everyone listed was born in Louisiana, except where noted. All available data is quoted.

Nathan Abshire, Gueydan, 27 June 1913–13 May 1981.
Johnnie Allan (Guillot), Rayne, 10 March 1938.
Rockin' Dave Allen (Stich), Houston, Texas, b. 1942.
Alphonse "Bois Sec" Ardoin, Duralde, 16 November 1916.
Dewey Balfa, Mamou, 20 March 1927.
Joe Barry (Barrios), Cut Off, 13 July 1939.
Alphee Bergeron, Point Noir, Church Point, 8 August 1912–28 October 1980.
Shirley Bergeron, Church Point, b. 1933.
Rod Bernard, Opelousas, 12 August 1940.
Boogie Jake (Mathew Jacobs), Marksville, ca. 1929.
Amidie Breaux, Rayne, 7 September 1900–1975.
Van Broussard, Prairieville, 29 March 1937.
Vin Bruce, Cut Off, 25 April 1932.
Buckwheat (Stanley Dural Jr.), Lafayette, 14 November 1947.
Bobby Charles (Robert Guidry), Abbeville, b. 1938.
Wilson "Boozoo" Chavis, Lake Charles, 23 October 1930.
Clifton Chenier, Opelousas, 25 June 1925.
Harry Choates, Rayne, 26 December 1922–17 July 1951.
Cookie (Huey Thierry), Jennings, 16 August 1936.
Lionel Cormier, Eunice, 1913–5 June 1971.
Jimmy Donley, Gulfport, Mississippi, 19 August 1929–20 March 1963.
Michael Doucet, Scott, 14 February 1951.
Joseph Falcon, Rayne, 28 September 1900–29 November 1965.
Freddy Fender (Baldemar Huerta), San Benito, Texas, b. 1936.
Fernest (Arceneaux), Lafayette, 27 August 1940.
Al Ferrier, Montgomery, 19 August 1935.
Allen Fontenot, Evangeline Parish, b. 1932.
John Fred (Gourrier), Baton Rouge, 8 May 1941.
J. B. Fusilier, Oberlin, 17 April 1901–ca. 1980.
Clarence Garlow, Welsh, b. 1911.
Henry Gray, Kenner, 19 January 1925.
Oran "Doc" Guidry, Lafayette, b. 1918.
Guitar Gable (Perrodin), Bellevue, 17 August 1937.
Guitar Jr. (Lee Baker), Dubuisson, 18 December 1933.
Happy Fats (LeRoy LeBlanc), Rayne, 30 January 1915.
Silas Hogan, Westover, 15 September 1911.

Alton James "T. K." Hulin, St. Martinville, 16 August 1943.
Jivin' Gene (Bourgeois), Port Arthur, Texas, 9 February 1940.
Doug Kershaw, Tiel Ridge, 24 January 1936.
Lazy Lester (Leslie Johnson), Torras, 20 June 1933.
Angelais Lejeune, Point Noir, Church Point, 20 May 1900.
Iry LeJune (Ira Lejeune), Point Noir, Church Point, 28 October 1928–8 October 1954.
Lightnin' Slim (Otis Hicks), St. Louis, Missouri, 13 March 1913–27 July 1974.
Lil Bob (Camille Bob), Arnaudville, 7 November 1937.
Lonesome Sundown (Cornelius Green), Donaldsonville, 12 December 1928.
Barbara Lynn (Ozen), Beaumont, Texas, b. 1943.
Dennis McGee, Eunice, 26 January 1893.
Tommy McLain, Jonesville, 15 March 1940.
Lou Millet, Baton Rouge, 5 April 1926.
Raful Neal, Baton Rouge, b. 1936.
Jimmy C. Newman, High Point, 29 August 1927.
Papa Cairo (Julius Lamperez), New Orleans, 27 July 1922.
Roy Perkins (Ernie Suarez), Lafayette, 26 April 1935.
Phil Phillips (Phillip Baptiste), Lake Charles, 14 March 1931.
Austin Pitre, Ville Platte, 23 February 1918–1981.
Polka Dot Slim (Monroe Vincent), Woodville, Mississippi, 9 December 1919–1982.
Rockin' Dopsie (Alton Rubin), Lafayette, 10 February 1932.
Rockin' Sidney (Sidney Simien), Lebeau, 9 April 1938.
Gene (Eugene) Rodrigue, Larose, b. 1926.
Aldus Roger, Carencro, 10 February 1916.
Ashton Savoy, Opelousas, b. 1936.
Schoolboy Cleve (White), Baton Rouge, 10 June 1928.
Slim Harpo (James Moore), Lobdell, 11 January 1924–31 January 1970.
Moses "Whispering" Smith, Union Church, Mississippi, 25 January 1932.
Leo Soileau, Ville Platte, 19 January 1904–2 August 1980.
Joel Sonnier, Rayne, 2 October 1946.
Warren Storm (Schexnider), Vermilion Parish, 1937.
Ambrose Thibodeaux, Eunice, 18 October 1903.
Rufus Thibodeaux, Ridge, 5 January 1934.
Ernest "Tabby" Thomas, Baton Rouge, 5 January 1929.
Lawrence Walker, Scott, 1908–1968.
Katie Webster (Katherine Thorn), Houston, Texas, 9 January 1939.
Clint West (Maurice Guillory), Vidrine, 11 August 1938.
Robert Pete Williams, Zachary, 14 March 1914–31 December 1980.

Appendix E

Important Clubs

These are the most important venues featuring Cajun and swamp-pop (*) music in 1983.

Belvedere Club, Judice (near Duson).
Blue Goose Club, 740 North Second Street, Eunice.
*Cal's, Prairieville
*Carpet Room Lounge, Erath.
Fred's Lounge, 420 Sixth Street, Mamou.
Grant Street Dance Hall, 113 W. Grant Street, Lafayette.
*Lake Shore Club, across bridge from Lake Arthur.
La Poussière, 1212 Grandpoint Avenue, Breaux Bridge.
Pat's Showboat Club, Highway 352, Henderson.
Snook's, Vidrine Road, Ville Platte.
Town and Country, Highway 91, Riceville (between Gueydan and Morse).
Triangle Club, Highway 93, Scott.
*Whiskey River Club, Henderson Station, Breaux Bridge.

Appendix F

Prominent South Louisiana Bands

This compilation gives a breakdown of the personnel of the better-known South Louisiana bands in the year stated. Although vocals were often shared, only the main singer is listed.

Johnnie Allan and the Krazy Kats
1959   Johnnie Allan, vocal and guitar; Leroy Castille, tenor sax; Al Foreman, guitar; U. J. Meaux, piano; Mickey Stutes, bass; Bhuel Hoffpauir, drums.

Jimmy Anderson and the Joy Jumpers
1961   Jimmy Anderson, vocal and harmonica; Eugene Dozier, guitar; Guitar Taylor, bass guitar; Oscar "Jesse" Hogan, drums.

Badeaux and the Louisiana Aces
1962   D. L. Menard, vocal and guitar; Elias Badeaux, accordion; Joseph Lopez, fiddle; Archange Touchet, steel guitar; John Suire, drums.

The Balfa Brothers Orchestra
1978   Dewey Balfa, vocal and fiddle; Rodney Balfa, vocal and guitar; Nathan Menard, accordion; Dick Richard, fiddle; J. W. Pelsia, steel guitar; Tony Balfa, bass guitar; Austin Broussard, drums.

Joe Barry and the Vikings
1961   Joe Barry, vocal and guitar; Don Stevens and Lloyd Toups, tenors; Pat Curole, trumpet; Clifton Fonseca, guitar; Hubert Baudoin or Lenny Boudreaux, piano; Leroy Martin, bass guitar; Sherril Rivet, drums.

Alphee Bergeron and the Veteran Playboys
1972   Alphee Bergeron, accordion; Vinest Lejeune, fiddle; Lewis Semar, steel guitar; Don Guillory, guitar; Leon Lejeune, bass guitar; Lerans Dies, drums.

Rod Bernard and the Twisters
1957   Rod Bernard, vocal and guitar; Charles Boudreaux, trumpet; Marion Presley, guitar; Rick Bernard, bass; Ray Thomasee, drums.

Joe Bonsall and the Orange Playboys
1963   Joe Bonsall, vocal and accordion; Floyd LeBlanc, fiddle; Wilson Lejeune, steel guitar; Bobby Caswell, guitar; Clifton Newman, drums.

Vin Bruce and the Acadians
1980   Vin Bruce, vocal and guitar; Doc Guidry, fiddle; Hartley Dupre, guitar; Leroy Martin, bass guitar; Leonard Ledet, drums. (Regular members during the sixties included Harry Anselmi, guitar and steel guitar; and Johnny Comeaux, steel guitar.)

Buckwheat and his Zydeco Ils Sont Partis Band
1979   Stanley "Buckwheat" Dural Jr., vocal, accordion, piano, and accordion; John Bell, tenor sax; Russell Gordon, guitar; Ted Zerby, bass guitar; Elijah "Put" Cudges, rub board; Jimmy Papillion, drums.

Joe Carl and the Dukes of Rhythm
1960   Joe Carl, vocal; Harry Simoneaux and Raoul Prado, tenor saxes; Clifton Fonseca, guitar; Hubert Baudoin, piano; Bob Tassin, bass guitar; Nolan Adoue, drums.

Bobby Charles and the Cardinals
1955   Bobby Charles, vocal; Harry Simoneaux, Raoul Prado, Carlo Marino, tenor saxes; Larry Guidry, guitar; Ed LeBlanc, piano; Kenneth Theriot, drums.

Clifton Chenier and his Red Hot Louisiana Band
1973   Clifton Chenier, vocal and accordion; Cleveland Chenier, rub board; John Hart, tenor sax; Paul Sinegal, guitar; Joe Brouchet, bass guitar; Robert Peter, drums.

Cookie and the Cupcakes
1960   Huey "Cookie" Thierry, vocal and tenor sax; Shelton Dunaway, vocal and tenor sax; Sidney "Hot Rod" Reynaud, tenor sax; Marshall Laday, guitar; Ernest Jacobs, piano; Joe "Blue" Landry, bass guitar; Ivory Jackson, drums.

Cleveland Crochet and the Sugar Bees
1961   Cleveland Crochet, fiddle; Jay Stutes, vocal and steel guitar; Vorris "Shorty" LeBlanc, vocal and accordion; S. J. Barris, guitar; Mickey Broussard, piano; Bradley Stutes, bass; Clifton Newman, drums.

Joe Falcon and his Silver Bell String Band
1963   Joe Falcon, vocal and accordion; Lionel Leleux, fiddle; Allen Richard, guitar; Theresa Meaux Falcon, drums.

Fernest and the Thunders
1979   Fernest Arceneaux, vocal and accordion; Dalton Arceneaux, rub board; Chester Chevallier, guitar; Peter Helaire, bass guitar; Clarence "Jockey" Etienne, drums.

Chuck Guillory and his Rhythm Boys
1948   Chuck Guillory, vocal and fiddle; Papa Cairo, steel guitar; Jimmy Newman, guitar; Herman Durbin, piano; Pete Duhon, bass; Curzy Roi, drums.

Guitar Gable and his Musical Kings
1956   Guitar Gable, guitar; King Karl, vocal; Freddy Levine, tenor; Clinton "Fats" Perrodin, bass guitar; Clarence "Jockey" Etienne, drums.

The Hackberry Ramblers
1936   Luderin Darbone, vocal and fiddle; Lennis Sonnier, vocal and guitar; Edwin Duhon, guitar; Joe Werner, vocal, harmonica, and guitar; Lonnie Rainwater, guitar; Floyd Rainwater, bass.

Happy Fats and the Rayne-Bo Ramblers
1936   Happy Fats, vocal and guitar; Joe Werner, vocal, harmonica, and guitar; Moise Sonnier or Norris Savoy, fiddle; Roy Romero, dobro; Louis Arceneaux, washboard.

Silas Hogan and the Rhythm Ramblers
1956   Silas Hogan, vocal and guitar; Sylvester Buckley, harmonica; Isaiah Chatman, bass guitar; Jimmy Dotson, drums.

Iry LeJune
1953   Iry LeJune, vocal and accordion; Wilson Granger, fiddle; Alfred "Duckhead" Cormier, guitar; Robert Bertrand, drums.

Lil Bob and the Lollipops
1979   Camille Bob, vocal and drums; Allen "Cat Ray" Broussard, alto sax; Guitar Gable, guitar; Russell Gordon, guitar; J. Clinton "Fats" Perrodin, bass guitar.

Lonesome Sundown
1957   Lonesome Sundown, vocal and guitar; John Hart and Roland Lewis, tenor saxes; John Gradego, harmonica; Albert Lazard, guitar; Milton Lazard, bass; Harry Sew Jr., drums.

Bobby Page and the Riff Raffs
1958   Bobby Page, vocal and trombone; Jimmy Patin, tenor sax; Bessyl Duhon, guitar; V. J. Boulet, piano; Roy Perkins, bass guitar; Ulysses Broussard, drums.

Austin Pitre and the Evangeline Playboys
1948   Austin Pitre, vocal and accordion; Clifton Fontenot, fiddle; Pee Wee Macaulay, electric guitar; Floyd Fontenot, guitar; Clannie Perron, guitar.

The Rambling Aces
1966   Andrew Cormier or Marc Savoy, accordion; Raymond Cormier, steel guitar; Rodney LeJune, guitar; Dallas Roy, drums.

Belton Richard and the Musical Aces
1972   Belton Richard, vocal and accordion; Allen Ardoin and Waldon "Sleepy" Hoffpauir, fiddles; Jesse Credeur, steel guitar; Johnny Credeur, guitar; Andy Johnson, bass guitar; Ray Lavergne, drums.

Rockin' Dopsie and the Twisters
1979   Rockin' Dopsie, vocal and accordion; Chester Zeno, rub board; John Hart, tenor sax; Joseph Major Handy, guitar; Albert Francis, bass guitar; Alton Rubin Jr., drums.

Aldus Roger and the Lafayette Playboys
1965   Aldus Roger, accordion; Doc Guidry, fiddle; Phillip Alleman, vocal and steel guitar; Johnny Credeur, guitar; Tunice Abshire, bass guitar; Fernice "Man" Abshire, vocal and drums.

Slim Harpo
1960   Slim Harpo, vocal and harmonica; Willie "Tomcat" Parker, tenor saxophone; Rudolph Richard and James Johnson, guitars; Geese August, bass guitar; Sammy K. Brown, drums.

Leo Soileau's Three Aces
1935   Leo Soileau, vocal and fiddle; Floyd Shreve, guitar; Bill "Dewey" Landry, guitar; Tony Gonzales, drums.

Warren Storm and Bad Weather
1979   Warren Storm, vocal and drums; Gene Romero, tenor sax; Randy Baras, steel guitar; Grant Clement, guitar; George Betote, bass guitar.

Al Terry and the Southerners
1950   Al Terry, vocal and guitar; Bob Terry, steel guitar; Sexton Trahan, guitar; Danny Boulet, piano; Rufus Alleman, bass; Alton Bernard, drums.

Lawrence Walker and the Wandering Aces
1956   Lawrence Walker, vocal and accordion; U. J. Meaux, fiddle; Al Foreman, guitar; Johnnie Allan, steel guitar; Bhuel Hoffpauir, drums.

Clint West and the Boogie Kings
1964   Clint West, vocal and drums; Johnny Gordano, vocal and organ; Murphy Buford, Mike Pollard, Norris Badeaux, tenor saxes; Dan Silas, baritone sax; Gee Gee Shinn and Ned Theall, trumpets; Jack Hall, guitar; Brian Leger, bass guitar.

Appendix G

Popular Cajun Singles

Charts of best-selling Cajun singles have never been published. This listing can therefore be no more than an approximate guide.

Artist and Record	Label	Year
NATHAN ABSHIRE AND THE PINE GROVE BOYS		
Pine Grove Blues	OT 102	1949
Games People Play	Swallow 10206	1970
AMADIE ARDOIN AND DENNIS McGEE		
Valse De Amities	Bluebird 2189	1936
Oberlin	Bluebird 2190	1936
BADEAUX AND THE LOUISIANA ACES		
Valse De Jolly Rogers	Swallow 121	1961
The Back Door	Swallow 10131	1962
DEWEY BALFA AND HIS MUSICAL BROTHERS		
Drunkard's Sorrow Waltz	Swallow 10172	1967
SHIRLEY BERGERON		
J'ai Fait Mon Ede'e	Lanor 500	1960
French Rocking Boogie	Lanor 510	1963
HOBO BERTRAND		
Starvation Waltz	Goldband 1163	1966
JOE BONSALL AND THE ORANGE PLAYBOYS		
Step It Fast	Swallow 10154	1963
AMIDIE BREAUX		
Hey Mom	Feature 1056	1952
AMIDIE, OPHY, AND CLEOMA BREAUX		
Ma Blonde Est Partie	Columbia 40510	1929
ALEX BROUSSARD		
Le Sud De La Louisianne	La Louisianne 8016	1959
LEROY BROUSSARD		
Lemonade Song	Goldband 1048	1956
SIDNEY BROWN AND THE TRAVELER PLAYBOYS		
Sha Ba Ba	Folk-Star 1132	1955
Pestauche Ah Tante Nana	Goldband 1061	1957

VIN BRUCE

Dans La Louisianne	Columbia 20923	1952
Fille De La Ville	Columbia 20923	1952
Le Delaysay	Swallow 119	1961
Jole Blon	Swallow 129	1962

CAJUN TRIO

Cajun Twist	Swallow 126	1962

BOOZOO CHAVIS

Paper In My Shoe	Folk-Star 1197	1954

CLIFTON CHENIER

Ay-Tete-Fee	Specialty 552	1955
Louisiana Blues	Bayou 701	1965
Oh! Lucille	Crazy Cajun 803	1966

HARRY CHOATES

Jole Blon	Gold Star 1313	1946
Poor Hobo	Gold Star 1336	1947

LINK DAVIS

Big Mamou	OKeh 18001	1952

ELISE DESHOTEL AND HIS
LOUISIANA RHYTHMAIRES

La Valse De Bon Baurche	Khoury's 618	ca. 1951

CAMAY DOUCET

Hold My False Teeth	Swallow 10251	1976
Mom I'm Still Your Little Boy	Swallow 10251	1976

JOSEPH FALCON

Lafayette	Columbia 15275	1928
Fe Fe Ponchaux (with Cleoma Breaux)	Columbia 15301	1929
Ossun One-Step (popularly known as "Osson Two-Step")	Columbia 40506	1929

J. B. FUSILIER

Ma Chere Basett	Bluebird 2052	1936

DOC GUIDRY

Chere Cherie	Decca 28678	1953
The Little Fat Man	Decca 28678	1953

CHUCK GUILLORY AND HIS
RHYTHM BOYS

Tolan Waltz	Colonial 101	1948

THE HACKBERRY RAMBLERS

Jole Blonde	Bluebird 2003	1936
Cajun Pogo	Goldband 1143	1963

HAPPY FATS

Les Veuve A Kita La Coulee	RCA Victor 20-2035	ca. 1941
Colinda (by Happy, Doc and the Boys)	Fais Do Do (?)	1947

FLOYD LEBLANC

Over The Waves	Opera 108	1948

IRY LEJUNE

Love Bridge Waltz	Opera 105	1948
Evangeline Special	Opera 105	1948
Calcasieu Waltz	Folk-Star 100	1949
Teche Special	Folk-Star 101	1950

BILL MATTE		
Parlez-Vous L'Francais	Lanor 503	1961
DORIS MATTE AND THE LAKE		
CHARLES RAMBLERS		
Tracks Of My Buggy	Swallow 128	1962
JIMMY C. NEWMAN		
Lache Pas La Patate	La Louisianne 8139	1974
(see also Appendix H)		
LOUIS NOEL		
La Cravat	Fais Do Do (?)	1947
PAPA CAIRO		
Big Texas	Modern 20-612	1949
AUSTIN PITRE AND THE		
EVANGELINE PLAYBOYS		
Flumes Dans Faires	Swallow 106	1959
Opelousas Waltz	Swallow 106	1959
RAMBLING ACES		
99 Years Waltz	Swallow 111	1960
Musicians Waltz	Crazy Cajun 503	1965
BELTON RICHARD AND HIS		
MUSICAL ACES		
Just En Reve	Chamo 100	1962
Un Autre Soir D'Ennui	Swallow 10187	1967
The Cajun Streak	Swallow 10234	1974
GENE RODRIGUE		
Dans Le Coeur De La Ville	Folk-Star 107	1953
Jolie Fille	Meladee 101	1954
ALDUS ROGER AND THE		
LAFAYETTE PLAYBOYS		
Diga Ding Ding Dong	Goldband 1084	1959
Lafayette Playboy's Waltz	Cajun Classics 106	ca. 1961
Louisiana Waltz	La Louisianne 8076	1966
LEO SOILEAU		
Mama Where You At?	Victor 21769	1928
La Valse De Gueydan	Bluebird 2171	1935
Le Gran' Mamou	Bluebird 2194	1936
La Blues De Port Arthur	Decca 17058	1938
LEE SONNIER AND HIS		
ACADIAN STARS		
War Widow Waltz	Feature 1018	1948
LAWRENCE WALKER AND HIS		
WANDERING ACES		
Evangeline Waltz	Lyric 615	ca. 1951
Reno Waltz	Lyric 623	ca. 1951
JOE WERNER AND THE RIVERSIDE		
RAMBLERS		
Wondering	Bluebird 6926	1936

Appendix H

South Louisiana Singles Chart Entries, 1950–76

This listing of hit singles by artists from—or those having close affiliations with—South Louisiana shows positions on the *Billboard Hot 100*, R&B (*), and C&W (†) charts. Data assembled from Joel Whitburn's *Record Research, Top R&B Records 1949–1971*, and *Top C&W Records 1949–1971*.

Artist and Record	Label	Highest Position	Date of entry
ELTON ANDERSON			
Secret Of Love	Mercury 71542	88	January 1960
JOE BARRY			
I'm A Fool To Care	Smash 1702	24	April 1961
Teardrops In My Heart	Smash 1710	63	August 1961
ROD BERNARD			
This Should Go On Forever	Argo 5327	20	March 1959
One More Chance	Mercury 71507	74	November 1959
BIG BOPPER			
Chantilly Lace	Mercury 71343	6	August 1958
JIMMY CLANTON			
Just A Dream	Ace 546	4	July 1958
COOKIE AND THE CUPCAKES			
Mathilda	Judd 1002	47	January 1959
Got You On My Mind	Chess 1848	94	May 1963
CLEVELAND CROCHET			
Sugar Bee	Goldband 1106	80	January 1961
DALE AND GRACE			
I'm Leaving It Up To You	Montel 921	1	October 1963
Stop And Think It Over	Montel 922	8	January 1964
The Loneliest Night	Montel 928	65	May 1964
FREDDY FENDER			
Before The Next Teardrop Falls	ABC/Dot 17540	1	January 1975
Wasted Days And Wasted Nights	ABC/Dot 17558	8	June 1975
Secret Love	ABC/Dot 17585	20	October 1975
Since I Met You Baby	GRT 031	45	October 1975
You'll Lose A Good Thing	ABC/Dot 17607	32	February 1976
Via Con Dayas	ABC/Dot 17627	59	May 1976
Living It Down	ABC/Dot 17652	72	October 1976

JOHN FRED AND HIS
PLAYBOY BAND

Shirley	Montel 1002	82	March 1959
Judy In Disguise	Paula 282	1	November 1967
Hey, Hey Bunny	Paula 294	57	February 1968

CLARENCE GARLOW

* Bon Ton Roula	Macy's 5001	7	February 1950

T. K. HULIN

I'm Not A Fool Anymore	Smash 1830	92	August 1963

JIVIN' GENE

Breaking Up Is Hard To Do	Mercury 71485	69	September 1959

DOUG KERSHAW (see also
Rusty and Doug)

† Diggy Liggy Lo	Warner Bros. 7329	70	October 1969

LIGHTNIN' SLIM

* Rooster Blues	Excello 2169	23	February 1959

BARBARA LYNN

You'll Lose A Good Thing	Jamie 1220	8	June 1962

TOMMY McLAIN

Sweet Dreams	MSL 197	15	June 1966

JIMMY NEWMAN

† Cry Cry Darling	Dot 1195	9	May 1954
† Daydreamin'	Dot 1237	13	April 1955
† Blue Darlin'	Dot 1260	13	July 1955
A Fallen Star	Dot 1289	42	June 1957
† You're Making A Fool Out Of Me	MGM 12707	7	November 1958
† So Soon	MGM 12749	19	April 1959
† Grin And Bear It	MGM 12812	11	August 1959
† A Lovely Work Of Art	MGM 12894	6	June 1960
† Wanting You With Me Tonight	MGM 12945	11	November 1960
† Everybody's Dyin' For Love	Decca 31217	14	April 1961
† Alligator Man	Decca 31324	22	December 1961
† Bayou Talk	Decca 31440	12	December 1962
† DJ For A Day	Decca 31553	9	December 1963
† Back In Circulation	Decca 31745	13	April 1965
† Artificial Rose	Decca 31841	8	September 1965
† Back Pocket Money	Decca 31916	10	March 1966
† Louisiana Saturday Night	Decca 32130	24	May 1967
† Blue Lonely Winter	Decca 32202	11	October 1967
† Born To Love You	Decca 32366	20	August 1968
† Boo Dan	Decca 32484	31	May 1969

PHIL PHILLIPS

Sea Of Love	Mercury 71465	2	July 1959

JOHNNY PRESTON

Running Bear	Mercury 71474	1	October 1959

RUSTY AND DOUG

† Hey Sheriff	Hickory 1083	22	October 1958
† Louisiana Man	Hickory 1137	10	February 1961
† Diggy Liggy Lo	Hickory 1151	14	August 1961

SLIM HARPO

Rainin' In My Heart	Excello 2194	34	June 1961
Baby Scratch My Back	Excello 2273	16	January 1966
* Tip On In	Excello 2285	37	July 1967
* Te-Ni-Nee-Ni-Nu	Excello 2294	36	March 1968

WARREN STORM

Prisoner's Song	Nasco 6015	81	August 1958

AL TERRY

† Watch Dog	Hickory 1111	28	February 1960

Appendix I

Recommended Albums

This list is a personal choice of the most important South Louisiana albums; many are compilations of singles. European releases are noted in italics.

CAJUN

NATHAN ABSHIRE
"Nathan Abshire And Other Cajun Gems"   Arhoolie 5013
(includes the Khoury's/Lyric/O.T. sides plus Lawrence Walker, Musical Four Plus One, Floyd LeBlanc, Little Yvonne LeBlanc, Harry Choates)
"Nathan Abshire And The Pinegrove Boys"   *Flyright LP 535*
"Pine Grove Blues"   Swallow LP 6014
"The Good Times Are Killing Me"   Swallow LP 6023
AMADIE ARDOIN
"Amadie Ardoin"   Old Timey 124
THE BALFA BROTHERS
"The Balfa Brothers Play Traditional Cajun Music" Swallow LP 6011
BEAUSOLEIL
"Beausoleil"   Swallow LP 6031
SHIRLEY BERGERON WITH ALPHEE BERGERON AND
THE VETERAN PLAYBOYS
"The Sounds Of Cajun Music"   Lanor LP 1000
JOE BONSALL
"Cajun Jamboree"   Swallow LP 6008
VIN BRUCE
"Vin Bruce Sings 'Jole Blon' And Other Cajun Classics" Swallow LP 6002
"Vin Bruce's Greatest Hits"   Swallow LP 6006
HARRY CHOATES
"Jole Blon"   D LP 7000
"The Fiddle King Of Cajun Swing"   Arhoolie LP 5027
CLEVELAND CROCHET
"Cleveland Crochet And All The Sugar Bees" Goldband LP 7749
MICHAEL DOUCET
"Dit Beausoleil"   Arhoolie 5025
JOSEPH FALCON
"Louisiana Cajun Music"   Arhoolie F5005
HACKBERRY RAMBLERS
"Louisiana Cajun Music"   Arhoolie F5003
HAPPY FATS AND ALEX BROUSSARD
"Cajun And Country Songs And Music From Mariné" Swallow LP 6005

IRY LEJUNE
"The Legendary Iry LeJune, Volume One"   Goldband LP 7740
"The Legendary Iry LeJune, Volume Two"   Goldband LP 7741
DENNIS McGEE
"The Early Recordings"   Morning Star 45002
(features Sady Courville and Ernest Fruge)
D. L. MENARD
"D. L. Menard Sings 'The Back Door' And His Other   Swallow LP 6038
Cajun Hits"
JIMMY C. NEWMAN
"Folk Songs Of The Bayou"   Decca 4398, *Brunswick LAT 8587*
"Lache Pas La Patate"   La Louisianne LL-140
"The Happy Cajun"   *Charly CR 30177*
AUSTIN PITRE AND THE EVANGELINE PLAYBOYS
"Austin Pitre And The Evangeline Playboys"   Swallow LP 6041
WALLACE "CHEESE" READ
"Cajun House Party"   Arhoolie 5021
BELTON RICHARD AND THE MUSICAL ACES
"Modern Sounds In Cajun Music"   Swallow LP 6010
ALDUS ROGER
"Aldus Roger Plays The French Music Of South   La Louisianne LL-107
Louisiana"
"King Of The French Accordion Plays His Old Hits"   La Louisianne LL-114
MARC SAVOY
"Oh What A Night"   Arhoolie 5023
LEO SOILEAU
"Leo Soileau"   Old Timey 125
JOEL SONNIER
"Cajun Life"   Rounder 3049, *Sonet SNTF 839*
LAWRENCE WALKER
"A Tribute To The Late Great Lawrence Walker"   La Louisianne LL-126

Anthologies
(Listed alphabetically by record label)

"CAJUN MUSIC THE EARLY 50's"   Arhoolie 5008
(Shuk Richard and his Louisiana Aces, Texas Melody Boys, Floyd LeBlanc,
Nathan Abshire, Lawrence Walker and his Wandering Aces, Elise Deshotel and
his Louisiana Rhythmaires, Amar DeVillier and his Louisiana Jambaleers,
Sandy Austin, Harry Choates)
"FOLKSONGS OF THE LOUISIANA ACADIANS"   Arhoolie 5009
(Chuck Guillory, Wallace "Cheese" Read, Mrs. Odeus Guillory, Mrs. Rodney
Fruge, Isom J. Fontenot, Savy Augustine, Bee Deshotels, Shelby Vidrine)
LOUISIANA CAJUN MUSIC
VOLUME 1: "FIRST RECORDINGS THE 1920s"   Old Timey 108
(Joseph Falcon, Walker Brothers, Soileau and Robin, Segura Brothers,
Columbus Fruge, Cleoma Falcon, Amadie Ardoin, Dennis McGee)
VOLUME 2: "THE EARLY 30's"   Old Timey 109
(Cleoma Breaux Falcon, Amidie Breaux, Lawrence Walker, Guidry Brothers,
Leo Soileau and Mayuse Lafleur, Joseph Falcon, Alleman and Walker)

VOLUME 3: "THE STRING BANDS OF THE 1930s"   Old Timey 110
(Miller's Merrymakers, J. B. Fusilier, Leo Soileau, Hackberry Ramblers,
Cleoma Falcon, Rayne-Bo Ramblers)
VOLUME 4: "FROM THE 30s TO THE 50s"   Old Timey 111
(Joe Werner and the Riverside Ramblers, Hackberry Ramblers, Harry
Choates, Oklahoma Tornadoes, Nathan Abshire, Iry LeJune, Austin Pete,
Lawrence Walker)
VOLUME 5: "THE EARLY YEARS 1928–1938"   Old Timey 114
(Amidie, Ophy, and Cleoma Breaux; Soileau and Robin; Dennis McGee;
Breaux Freres; Blind Uncle Gaspard and Dela Lachney; Angela LeJune;
Dudley and James Favor; Amadie Ardoin; Walter Coquille)
"THE CAJUNS VOLUME 1"   *Sonet SNTF 643*
(Balfa Brothers Orchestra with Nathan Abshire, Ardoin Brothers Orchestra)
"CAJUN CRUISIN' VOLUME 2"   *Sonet SNTF 817*
(Milton Adams, Sheryl Cormier, Blackie Forestier, Joe Bonsall, Wayne Toups,
Pat Savant, Aldus Roger, Cajun Grass Band)
"THE BEST OF THE CAJUN HITS"   Swallow LP 6001
(Aldus Roger, Louis Cormier, Sidney Brown, Lawrence Walker, Austin Pitre,
Adam Hebert, Vin Bruce, Joel Sonnier, Gene Rodrigue)
"CAJUN HITS VOLUME 2"   Swallow LP 6003
(Aldus Roger, Vin Bruce, Austin Pitre, Lawrence Walker, Badeaux and the
Louisiana Aces, Maurice Barzas, Doris Matte, Cajun Trio, Adam Hebert)
"J'ETAIS AU BAL"   Swallow LP 6020
(Agnes Bourque, Balfa Brothers, Carrière Brothers, Octa Clark and the Dixie
Ramblers, Sundown Playboys, Vin Bruce, Lawtell Playboys, Clifton Chenier,
Clint West)

ZYDECO

BUCKWHEAT ILS SONT PARTIS BAND
"One For The Road"   Blues Unlimited 5006
CLIFTON CHENIER
"Bayou Blues"   Specialty SPS 2139, *SNTF 5012*
"Louisiana Blues And Zydeco"   Arhoolie F1024
"King Of The Bayous"   Arhoolie 1052
"Bogalusa Boogie"   Arhoolie 1076
"Boogie & Zydeco"   Maison de Soul LP 1003, *Sonet SNTF 801*
FERNEST AND THE THUNDERS
"Fernest And the Thunders"   Blues Unlimited LP 5005
ROCKIN' DOPSIE AND THE TWISTERS
"Doin' The Zydeco"   *Sonet SNTF 718*

Anthologies

"ZYDECO"   Arhoolie F1009
(Paul McZiel, Sidney Babineaux, Albert Chevalier, Robert Clemon, Willie
Green, Herbert Sam, Amadie Ardoin, Leadbelly, Lightnin' Hopkins, Clifton
Chenier, Clarence Garlow)
"ZYDECO BLUES"   *Flyright LP 539*
(Clifton Chenier, Fernest and the Thunders, Rockin' Dopsie, Marcel Dugas and
the Entertainers)

"ZODICO: LOUISIANA CREOLE MUSIC"   Rounder 6009
(Carrière Brothers, Fremont Fontenot, Inez Catalon, Ardoin Family, Mike and
the Soul Accordion Band, Lawtell Playboys, Sampy and the Bad Habits, Wilfred
Latour and his Travel Aces)

SWAMP-POP, ROCK 'N' ROLL, COUNTRY, AND ROCKABILLY

JOHNNIE ALLAN
"South To Louisiana And Other Hits"   Jin LP 4001
"Johnnie Allan Sings"   Jin LP 9002
ROCKIN' DAVE ALLEN
"Southern Rock 'N' Roll Of The 60's"   Rock-a-Billy Prods. LP-1
ROD BERNARD
"Rod Bernard"   Jin LP 4007
"Boogie In Black And White" (with Clifton Chenier)   Jin LP 9014
VAN BROUSSARD
"Van Broussard"   Bayou Boogie LP 148
BOBBY CHARLES
"Bobby Charles"   Bearsville BR 2104
COOKIE AND THE CUPCAKES
"3 Great Rockers" (with Little Alfred and Shelton Dunaway)   Jin LP 9003
"Cookie And The Cupcakes Volume 2" (includes Carol Fran)   Jin LP 9018
DALE AND GRACE
"I'm Leaving It Up To You"   Michelle LP 100
JIMMY DONLEY
"Born To Be A Loser"   Starflite LP 2002
FREDDY FENDER
"The Best Of Freddy Fender"   ABC ABCL 5221
"Swamp Gold"   ABC AA-1062
AL FERRIER
"The Birth Of Rockabilly"   Goldband LP 7769
JOHNNY JANO
"King Of Louisiana Rockabilly"   *Flyright LP 531*
RUSTY AND DOUG KERSHAW
"Louisiana Man"   *DJM DJB 26080*
"Their First Recordings" (with Wiley Barkdull)   *Flyright LP 571*
TOMMY McLAIN
"The Best Of Tommy McLain"   Jin LP 9016
ROCKIN' SIDNEY AND HIS DUKES
"They Call Me Rockin' "   *Flyright LP 515*
THE SHONDELS
"At The Saturday Hop" (with Rod Bernard,
Warren Storm, Skip Stewart)   La Louisianne LL-109
WARREN STORM
"Family Rules"   Crazy Cajun CCLP 1030
AL TERRY
"This Is Al Terry"   Index LP 5001
KATIE WEBSTER
"Whooee Sweet Daddy"   *Flyright LP 530*
CLINT WEST AND THE FABULOUS BOOGIE KINGS
"Clint West And The Fabulous Boogie Kings"   Jin LP 4003

Anthologies

THE LEGENDARY JAY MILLER SESSIONS
VOLUME 1: "TAG ALONG"   *Flyright LP 516*
(Rocket Morgan, Warren Storm, Joe Mayfield, Wonder Boy Travis, Honey
Boy Allen, Pee Wee Trahan)
VOLUME 2: "BOPPIN' TONIGHT"   *Flyright LP 525*
(Al Ferrier, Warren Storm)
VOLUME 11: "LOUISIANA SWAMP POP"   *Flyright LP 532*
(King Karl, Big Bopper, Billy Tate, Lester Robertson, Henry Clement, Dale
Houston, Jay Nelson, Eddie Hudson, Johnny Sonnier)
VOLUME 15: "ROCKIN' FEVER"   *Flyright LP 540*
(Pee Wee Trahan, Joe Carl, Rocket Morgan, Leroy Castille, Doug Charles,
Slim Harpo, Chuck Martin, Clifton Chenier, Wonder Boy Travis, Al Harris)
VOLUME 17: "BOPPIN' IT!"   *Flyright LP 554*
(Frankie Lowery, Pee Wee Trahan, Tommy Strange, Erwin Babin, Johnny
Bass, Al Ferrier, Arnold Broussard, Johnny Jano)
VOLUME 18: "GIRL IN THE TIGHT BLUE JEANS"   *Flyright LP 555*
(Bert Bradley, Milton Allen, Arnold Broussard, Al Ferrier, Pee Wee Trahan,
Tony Perreau, Terry Clement, Rocket Morgan, Huey and Marge, Merton
Thibodeaux)
VOLUME 19: "BAYOU BOOGIE"   *Flyright LP 557*
(Pee Wee Trahan, Joey Gills, Ronald Bezette, Billy Ray, Benny Fruge, Al
Terry, Mack Hamilton, Smokey Stover, Johnny Bass, Alex Broussard, Pee
Wee Whitewing, Don Ray Coates)
VOLUME 24: "JIMMY NEWMAN AND AL TERRY"   *Flyright LP 573*
"BAYOU ROCK"   Goldband GR-7764
(Larry Hart, Johnny Jano, Count Rockin' Sidney, Al Ferrier)
"A ROCKIN' DATE WITH SOUTH LOUISIANA STARS"   Jin LP 4002
(Rod Bernard, Margo White, Clint West, Johnnie Allan, Rockin' Sidney, Randy
and the Rockets, Jivin' Gene, Bob and the Veltones, Lee Martin, Phil Bo)
"ANOTHER SATURDAY NIGHT"   *Oval OVLP 506*
(Tommy McLain, Belton Richard, Clint West, Vin Bruce, Gary Walker, Johnnie
Allan, Austin Pitre, Rufus Jagneaux, Cookie and the Cupcakes, Margo White)
"THE OTHER SONG OF THE SOUTH   *Philips 6336 256*
(LOUISIANA ROCK 'N' ROLL)"
(Jivin' Gene, Rod Bernard, Elton Anderson, Cookie and the Cupcakes, Guitar
Jr., Roy Byrd, Rollee McGill, Phil Phillips and the Twilights)

BLUES AND R&B

HENRY GRAY
"They Call Me Little Henry"   *Bluebeat S-77332*
GUITAR JR.
"Broke An' Hungry"   Capitol ST-403
SILAS HOGAN
"Trouble"   Excello 8019
LAZY LESTER
"Poor Boy Blues"   *Flyright LP 544*
LIGHTNIN' SLIM
"Rooster Blues"   Excello 8000

"The Early Years"	*Flyright LP 524*
"Trip To Chicago"	*Flyright LP 533*
"The Feature Sides 1954"	*Flyright LP 583*
LITTLE BOB AND THE LOLLIPOPS	
"Nobody But You"	La Louisianne LL-113
LONESOME SUNDOWN	
"Lonesome Sundown"	Excello 8012
"Been Gone Too Long"	Joliet 6002
SLIM HARPO	
"Slim Harpo Sings Rainin' In My Heart"	Excello 8003
"Baby Scratch My Back"	Excello 8005
"He Knew The Blues"	*Blue Horizon 7-63854*
"Blues Hangover"	*Flyright LP 520*
"Got Love If You Want It"	*Flyright LP 558*
TABBY THOMAS	
"25 Years With The Blues"	Blues Unlimited LP 5007
LEROY WASHINGTON	
"Leroy Washington"	*Flyright LP 574*

Anthologies

"ANGOLA PRISONERS' BLUES"   Arhoolie 2011
(Robert Pete Williams, Guitar Welch, Hogman Maxey)
"COUNTRY NEGRO JAM SESSION"   Arhoolie 2018
(including Butch Cage, Willie Thomas, Robert Pete Williams, Clarence
Edwards, Smoky Babe)
"REAL BLUES FROM NEW ORLEANS"   Bandy 70009
(Polka Dot Slim, Boogie Jake, Edgar Blanchard)
"SWAMP BLUES"   *Blue Horizon 7-66263*
(Silas Hogan, Whispering Smith, Clarence Edwards, Arthur "Guitar" Kelley,
Henry Gray)
"THE EXCELLO STORY"   *Blue Horizon 2683 007*
(including Lightnin' Slim, Lonesome Sundown, Blue Charlie, Lazy Lester, Slim
Harpo, Jimmy Anderson, Silas Hogan, Tabby Thomas, Whispering Smith,
Guitar Gable, Warren Storm)
THE LEGENDARY JAY MILLER SESSIONS
VOLUME 2: "GONNA HEAD FOR HOME"   *Flyright LP 517*
(Sylvester Buckley, Boogie Jake, Mr. Calhoun, Henry Gray, Blue Boy Dorsey,
Jimmy Anderson, Joe Johnson, Silas Hogan)
VOLUME 3: "ROOSTER CROWED FOR DAY"   *Flyright LP 518*
(Mr. Calhoun, Silas Hogan, Leroy Washington, Whispering Smith, Jimmy
Dotson, Blue Charlie, Clarence Garlow)
VOLUME 21: "TOO HOT TO HANDLE"   *Flyright LP 570*
(Dukes of Rhythm, Lionel Torrence, Henry Clement, Ken Cameron, Little
Bob, Jay Nelson, Classie Ballou, Joe Carl)
"BLUESVILLE"   Goldband 7774
(Clarence Garlow, Cookie and the Cupcakes, Left Handed Charlie, Boozoo
Chavis, Guitar Jr., Big Walter, Scottie Milford, Tal Miller, Juke Boy Bonner,
Hop Wilson, Big Chenier, Johnny Moses, Rockin' Sidney)

"HOP WILSON BLUES WITH FRIENDS   Goldband 7781
(AT GOLDBAND)"
(Hop Wilson, Guitar Jr., Big Chenier, Ashton Savoy, Tal Miller, Left Handed
Charlie)
"LOUISIANA EXPLOSIVE BLUES"   Maison de Soul LP 1006
(Little Joe Gordon, John Hart with Lil Bob and the Lollipops, Rockin' Dopsie,
Duke Vallery, Margo White, Rockin' Sidney, Donnie Jacobs, Clifton Chenier,
Veltones, Junior Cole, Otis Smith, Boogie Kings)
"LOUISIANA R&B FROM LANOR"   *Red Pepper RP 702*
(Elton Anderson, Duke Stevens, Little Victor, Charles Tyler [Drifting Charles])
"AUTHENTIC R&B"   *Stateside SL 10068*
(Slim Harpo, Lightnin' Slim, Silas Hogan, Lazy Lester, Jimmy Anderson,
Lonesome Sundown, Whispering Smith, Leroy Washington)
BLUESSCENE USA VOL. 2: "THE LOUISIANA BLUES"   *Storyville LP 177*
(Juke Boy Bonner, Ashton Savoy, Big Chenier, Hop Wilson, Jay Stutes)

Most of these albums are available from:
Down Home Music Inc., 10341 San Pablo Avenue, El Cerrito, California 94530
Floyd's Record Shop, P.O. Box 10, Ville Platte, Louisiana 70586

Bibliography

Books

Brasher, Mabel, and others. *Louisiana: A Study of the State.* Richmond: Johnson Publishing Company, 1929.

Broven, John. *Walking to New Orleans: The Story of New Orleans Rhythm & Blues.* Bexhill-on-Sea: Blues Unlimited, 1974.

Browne, Turner. *Louisiana Cajuns: Cajuns de la Louisiane.* Baton Rouge: Louisiana State University Press, 1977.

Calhoun, James, ed. *Louisiana Almanac 1979–80.* Gretna: Pelican Publishing Co., 1979.

Conrad, Glenn R., ed. *The Cajuns: Essays on their History and Culture.* Lafayette: University of Southwestern Louisiana Press, 1978.

Daigle, Pierre V. *Tears, Love, and Laughter.* Church Point: Acadian Publishing, 1972.

Davis, Edwin Adams. *Louisiana—The Pelican State.* Baton Rouge: Louisiana State University Press, 1959.

Dixon, Robert, and Godrich, John. *Recording the Blues.* London: Studio Vista, 1970.

Flippo, Chet. *Your Cheatin' Heart: A Biography of Hank Williams.* New York: Simon and Schuster, 1981.

Gillett, Charlie. *The Sound of the City.* New York: Outerbridge and Dienstfrey, 1970.

Guralnick, Peter. *Feel Like Going Home.* New York: Outerbridge and Dienstfrey, 1971.

Hardy, Phil, and Laing, Dave, ed. *The Encyclopedia of Rock.* London: Hanover Books, 1975.

Harris, Sheldon. *Blues Who's Who.* New York: Arlington House, 1979.

Holmes, Irène Thérèse Whitfield. *Louisiana French Folk Songs.* Baton Rouge: Louisiana State University Press, 1939.

Kershaw, Doug. *Lou'siana Man.* New York: Collier Books, 1971.

Leadbitter, Mike. *Crowley Louisiana Blues.* Bexhill-on-Sea: Blues Unlimited, 1968.
_____ . *French Cajun Music.* Bexhill-on-Sea: Blues Unlimited, 1968.

Leadbitter, Mike, ed. *Nothing but the Blues.* London: Hanover Books, 1971.

Leadbitter, Mike, and Shuler, Eddie. *From the Bayou.* Bexhill-on-Sea: Blues Unlimited, 1969.

Leadbitter, Mike, and Slaven, Neil. *Blues Records 1943–1966.* London: Hanover Books, 1968.

LeBlanc, LeRoy "Happy Fats." *(What Has Made South Louisiana) God's Special Country.* Rayne: LeBlanc, 1973.

Liebling, A. J. *The Earl of Louisiana.* Baton Rouge: Louisiana State University Press, 1970.

Malone, Bill C. *Country Music, U.S.A.* Austin: University of Texas Press, 1968.
_____ . *Southern Music, American Music.* Lexington: University of Kentucky Press, 1979.
Morgan, Elemore, and East, Charles. *The Face of Louisiana.* Baton Rouge: Louisiana State University Press, 1969.
Oliver, Paul. *The Story of the Blues.* London: Barrie and Rockliff, 1969.
Porterfield, Nolan. *The Life and Times of America's Blue Yodeler, Jimmie Rodgers.* Chicago: University of Illinois Press, 1979.
Post, Lauren C. *Cajun Sketches.* Baton Rouge: Louisiana State University Press, 1962.
Reed, Revon. *Lâche pas la patate: Portrait des Acadiens de la Louisiane.* Quebec: Editions Parti Pris, 1976.
Rowe, Mike. *Chicago Breakdown.* London: Eddison Books, 1973.
Rushton, William Faulkner. *The Cajuns: From Acadia to Louisiana.* New York: Farrar Straus & Giroux, 1979.
Russell, Tony. *Blacks, Whites and Blues.* London: Studio Vista, 1970.
Shaw, Arnold. *Honkers and Shouters.* New York: Collier Books, 1978.
Shelton, Robert, and Goldblatt, Burt. *The Country Music Story.* New Jersey: Castle Books, 1966.
Strachwitz, Chris, and Welding, Pete, ed. *The American Folk Music Occasional.* New York: Oak Publications, 1970.
Tassin, Myron. *We Are Acadians: Nous Sommes Acadiens.* Gretna: Pelican Publishing Co., 1976.
Topping, Ray. *New Orleans Rhythm and Blues Label Listings.* Bexhill-on-Sea: Flyright, 1980.
Weill, Gus. *You are my Sunshine: The Jimmie Davis Story.* Waco: Word Inc., 1977.
Whitburn, Joel. *Record Research.* Menomonee Falls, Wis.: Whitburn, 1970.
_____ . *Top C&W Records 1949–1971.* Menomonee Falls, Wis.: Whitburn, 1972.
_____ . *Top R&B Records 1949–1971.* Menomonee Falls, Wis.: Whitburn, 1972.
Wood, Graham. *An A–Z of Rock and Roll.* London: Studio Vista, 1971.
Wootton, Richard. *Honky Tonkin': A Travel Guide to American Music.* London: Travelaid, 1980.

Articles

Ancelet, Barry Jean. "Dewey Balfa: Cajun Music Ambassador." *Louisiana Life,* 1981.

Bastin, Bruce. "Blues from the Bayou." *Crazy Music,* 1977.

_____. "Jay Miller's Blues." *Blues Unlimited,* 1976.

Bromberg, Bruce. "I'm a Mojo Man" (Lonesome Sundown). *Blues Unlimited,* 1971.

Broven, John. "Behind the Sun Again." *Blues Unlimited,* 1973.

Charlesworth, Chris. "How Freddy Fender Hit Lucky." *Melody Maker,* 1975.

Dallas, Karl. "Louisiana Man" (Doug Kershaw). *Melody Maker,* 1974.

_____. "Zydeco a go-go" (Rockin' Dopsie). *Melody Maker,* 1979.

Duplantier, F. R. "Cajun Humor: Is it Funny Only in French?" *La Gazette des Acadiens,* 1976.

Greensmith, Bill. "Bottom of the Top: The Story of Phillip Walker." *Blues Unlimited,* 1974.

Grigg, Andy. "Raful Neal and Sons in Montreal." *Blues Unlimited,* 1981.

Guralnick, Peter. "The Guitarist Who Rocked the World" (Scotty Moore). *Melody Maker,* 1979.

Hawkins, Martin. "Cajun Music and the Big Beat" (Jimmy Newman). *Melody Maker,* 1979.

Keating, Bern. "Cajunland, Louisiana's French Speaking Coast." *National Geographic Magazine,* 1966.

La Rocca, James. "Lost Without Love" (Lonesome Sundown). *Blues Unlimited,* 1971.

_____. "Polka Dot Slim." *Blues Unlimited,* 1970.

LaVere, Steve. "Schoolboy Cleve!" *Blues Unlimited,* 1970.

Leadbitter, Mike. "Cajun Corner" (series). *Blues Unlimited,* 1963–68.

_____. "Harry Choates: Cajun Fiddle Ace." *Old Time Music,* 1972.

_____. "I Know Houston Can't Be Heaven" (series). *Blues Unlimited,* 1967.

_____. "Iry LeJune." *Old Time Music,* 1974.

_____. "Slim '72" (Lightnin' Slim). *Blues Unlimited,* 1972.

_____. "Well I'm Going to Lou'siana" (series). *Blues Unlimited,* 1967–68.

Leadbitter, Mike, and Broven, John. "Behind the Sun" (series). *Blues Unlimited,* 1970.

Macphail, Keith. "Jay Miller: An Interview." *Crazy Music,* 1976.

Millar, Bill. "Hot Rod from the Bayou." (Rod Bernard). *Melody Maker,* 1979.

_____. "Johnnie Allan." *New Kommotion,* 1978.

_____. "Rockin' on the Bayou." *Melody Maker,* 1979.

O'Neal, Jim. "Louisiana Wax Facts: The Blues and Cajun Record Scene 1973." *Living Blues,* 1973.

Pattison, Terry, and Green, Robert S. "I got Roaches in my Kitchen: The Story of Silas Hogan." *Blues Unlimited,* 1970.

Pattison, Terry, and Paterson, Neal. "I Know Y'all Been Lookin' for Me" (Lazy Lester). *Blues Unlimited,* 1970.

Paulsen, Gary. "J. R. Fulbright Interviewed." *Blues Unlimited,* 1968.

Russell, Tony. "Leo Soileau." *Old Time Music,* 1978.

Sacré, Robert. "Kings of the Bayous" (Clifton and Cleveland Chenier). *Blues Unlimited,* 1976 (unpublished).

_____ . "Voyage au pays de 'Jolies Blondes' avec Alphonse 'Bois Sec' Ardoin." *Jazz Hot*, 1979.
Scott, Frank. "Baton Rouge Blues" (Raful Neal). *Blues Unlimited*, 1971.
_____ . "Lloyd Reynaud." *Blues Unlimited*, 1970.
Seidler, Larry. "Robert Pete Williams." *Living Blues*, 1981.
Stelly, Philip. "A Life Full of Blues for Sundown" (Lonesome Sundown). *The* (New Orleans) *States-Item*, 1979.
Topping, Ray. "Freddy Fender Discography." *New Kommotion*, 1976.
_____ . "Link Davis: The Man with the Buzzing Sax." *New Kommotion*, 1979.
Tosches, Nick. "Ted Daffan." *Old Time Music*, 1978.
Turner, Allan. "He's the Cajun Crusader" (Eddie Shuler). *The Atlanta Journal and Constitution*, 1977.
Van Rijn, Guido. "The Guitar Jr./Lonnie Brooks Story." *Blues Unlimited*, 1976.
Watts, Michael. "Hitmaker of the Bayoux" (Huey Meaux). *Melody Maker*, 1974.

Magazines

Billboard, 1 Astor Plaza, 1515 Broadway, New York, New York, 10036.
Blues Research, 65 Grand Avenue, Brooklyn, New York 11205.
Blues Unlimited, 36 Belmont Park, Lewisham, London SE13 5DB, England.
Crazy Music, P.O. Box 1029, Canberra City, ACT 2601, Australia.
Jazz Hot, 14 rue Chaptal, 75009 Paris, France.
Living Blues, 2615 N. Wilton Avenue, Chicago, Illinois 60614.
Louisiane, P.O. Box 3936, Lafayette, Louisiana 70502.
New Kommotion, 3 Bowrons Avenue, Wembley, Middlesex, HAO 4QS, England.
Old Time Music, 22 Upper Tollington Park, London N4 3EL, England.
Sailor's Delight, 19 Brockenhurst Gardens, Mill Hill, London NW7, England.
The Cash Box, 1780 Broadway, New York, New York 10019.
Also consulted were *Jazz & Blues, La Gazette des Acadiens, Let It Rock*, and *R&B Monthly*, which are no longer published.

Other Sources

Angola Prisoners' Blues, booklet by Dr. Harry Oster and Richard B. Allen accompanying Folk-Lyric LP 3/Arhoolie LP 2011.
Cajun Social Music, booklet by Gérard Dole accompanying Folkways LP FA 2621.
Folksongs of the Louisiana Acadians, booklet by Dr. Harry Oster accompanying Folk-Lyric LP 4/Arhoolie LP 5009.
J'Etais au Bal, booklet by Ron and Fay Stanford accompanying Swallow LP 6020.
The Early Recordings of Dennis McGee, booklet by Barry Ancelet accompanying Morning Star LP 45002.
Zodico: Louisiana Creole Music, booklet by Nick Spitzer accompanying Rounder LP 6009.
"A Traveler's Guide to Louisiana," Louisiana Office of Tourism, 1979.
Bobby Charles, an interview by Tad Jones, 1973.

Clarence Garlow, an interview by Norbert Hess, 1980.
"Disc Dating Guide 1940–1949" by Bill Daniels, 1981.
Jimmy C. Newman, an interview by Martin Hawkins, 1979.
Joseph C. Falcon, an interview by Lauren C. Post, 1965.
New Orleans Jazz and Heritage Festival program, 1979.
Roy Perkins, an interview by Ray Topping, 1981.
This Is Cajun Music, a newspaper published by Sonet Records, 1980.
Vin Bruce, a discography by Leroy Martin, 1976.
Album sleeve notes on South Louisiana recordings.

Index of Names

Artists using recognized *noms de disque* are listed alphabetically by their first names. Thus "Lightnin' Slim (*Otis Hicks*)" will be found in the *L* section. The exception to this rule occurs where assumed names are treated through general usage as real names, e.g., Johnnie Allan (under *A*), Bobby Charles (under *C*), and Warren Storm (under *S*).

Index of Song Titles